THE UNKNOWN BRAHMS

AN UNPUBLISHED AND QUITE UNKNOWN PORTRAIT OF BRAHMS

with his arm around the 18-year-old Fräulein Henriette Hemala, in the doorway of the Miller zu Aichholz villa in Gmunden. Snapped, 1894, by Eugen, the young son of the family, whose fingerprints appear to the right of the steps. Silhouetted against a window is the head of his father, who later built the Brahms Museum on this property.

"I find Brahms' expression here incredibly good," writes Frau Ribarz-Hemala. "His glance is so dear, and one seems actually to see the blue of his eyes!"

Courtesy of Herr Eugen von Miller zu Aichholz and Frau Henriette Ribarz-Hemala.

THE
UNKNOWN BRAHMS

His Life, Character and Works; Based on
New Material

by

ROBERT HAVEN SCHAUFFLER

Author of
"The Musical Amateur,"
"Beethoven: the Man Who Freed Music,"
etc.

GREENWOOD PRESS, PUBLISHERS
WESTPORT, CONNECTICUT

The Library of Congress has catalogued this publication as follows:

Library of Congress Cataloging in Publication Data

Schauffler, Robert Haven, 1879-1945.
   The unknown Brahms.

   Bibliography: p.
   1. Brahms, Johannes, 1833-1897. I. Title.
ML410.B8S23 1972   780'.92'4 [B]   70-152602
ISBN 0-8371-6037-5

Originally published in 1933
by Dodd, Mead and Company, New York

Reprinted with the permission
of Dodd, Mead and Company

First Greenwood Reprinting 1972

Library of Congress Catalogue Card Number 70-152602

ISBN 0-8371-6037-5

Printed in the United States of America

To Constance Lily Morris

FOREWORD

Why another life of Brahms?

Because at the approach of this his Centenary year, I found in my hands a large amount of unpublished information and illustrative material which taught me much about this rich personality, this extraordinary amalgam of opposites, unsuspected by those who have written about him or edited his letters. Though many of their books are cited in the following pages, very few are available in English.

Because, moreover, I had made certain discoveries about his music.

It is often true that the biographer who begins by telling a story ends as a "story-teller." I have therefore (except in the brief memoir of Part II) preferred to avoid the conventional structure of biography, in order to escape the marked, though unconscious, falsifying tendencies of the chronological narrative.

It happens that the life and works of Brahms can more appropriately dispense with chronological treatment than those of other musicians; for, relatively, neither his character nor his music changed a great deal from decade to decade. In most essentials he was much the same person in his precocious twenties as in his fresh sixties. And between his first masterpieces, *Liebestreu* and the F minor sonata, and his last, the *Four Serious Songs,* there is less qualitative difference than between the initial and final masterpieces of any other great composer who lived beyond middle life.

When discussing Brahms' artistic growth, critics have here-tofore exaggerated the romanticism of his youth, the class-icism of his age, and the contrast between these. The truth is that, though slightly more romantic at first, and slightly more classical at last, this "central" figure consistently represented a superb fusion of these two tendencies in art which commonly are opposed and mutually exclusive.

Little will be found in the following pages about the history of the period; for Brahms lived not in his own times but *sub specie aeternitatis.* He inhabited a creative eternity of his own, resolutely barricaded against intruders.

Chapter XX represents the first attempt yet made by a biographer to explain, with the help of modern science, Brahms' cryptic love-life. To this day many people resent the suggestion that a man's sexual constitution can vitally affect his character or his creative work. Other reactionaries, without going quite so far as this, would set biography back a century by forbidding it either to associate with psychology, or to make any sort of shocking revelation.

None the less, I believe that thoughtful readers to-day regard psychology as the biographer's indispensable ally in interpreting the significance of soundly established data; and agree with Stefan Zweig that "the mission of science is to teach men to face the facts."

In Brahms' lifetime the biographers delighted to embellish their heroes by suppressing inconvenient evidence and substituting convenient fictions. But such methods did not appeal to the forthright Brahms. Even though a conservative, this half-peasant was all for facing the stark facts. Indeed, he went on record against the emasculation of biography and in agreement with Spinoza that "truth cannot be contrary to the best interests of humanity," when he wrote in 1856 to Clara Schumann:

What would become of all historical research and all biographies if they were always written with consideration for people's feelings? Such a biography as you, for example, would write about your Robert would surely be very beautiful to read, but would it as surely be of historical value?

If the honest man who sent these fearless lines to the woman he loved were living to-day, I think that he would growl amen to James C. Johnston's credo in *The Literature of Personality*:

Since . . . the conception of a biography as a truthful presentation of the essential character and personality of the subject has become dominant, we feel that interpretation has become the first duty of the biographer and that his reconstruction must secure the impression of a life as it was, not as it might have been.

A list of the many kind friends and acquaintances to whom this book is indebted for information, criticism, and other generous help will be found at its close.

R. H. S.

New York City, August, 1933.

CONTENTS

PART I

ADVENTURES IN SEARCH OF THE UNKNOWN BRAHMS

PART II

THE KNOWN BRAHMS

PART III

ASPECTS OF THE UNKNOWN BRAHMS

ILLUSTRATIONS

PART I

ADVENTURES IN SEARCH OF THE UNKNOWN BRAHMS

Chapter I

FREE BUT GLAD

At the outset this unconventionally planned biography waives tradition by inviting the reader to come along on a brief pilgrimage through half a dozen lands in search of The Unknown Brahms.

The origins of the quest go back, in a sense, to the happiest period of Brahms' life. For, owing to the fact that my parents were living in Europe, my first breath was drawn not very far from the spot where the composer was then exuberantly finishing a pair of violin works: the G major sonata and the concerto. And for the next two years I took in very much the same sparkling Austrian air which he breathed while producing the overtures, the first rhapsodies for piano, the B flat concerto, *Nänie,* and the C major trio.

Later on, when I realized these facts, I began to take a special, almost a personal, interest in Brahms; to play and care for his music, to read all the books I could find about him, and to thirst for more information. I longed to question the people who had looked into the great deep-blue eyes, heard the harsh voice, grasped the small pianistic hand, hard and rough as a file, and caromed against the passionately independent nature whose chosen motto, in music and in life, was F–A–F: *Frei aber Froh (Free but Glad)* .

My search for the unknown Brahms began, desultorily enough, in 1902 on my first return to Europe. In Hamburg,

I hastened to the house of his birth in the poor little courtyard called Schlüter's Hof; and in Vienna, to his old home
at Karlsgasse 4. There I came to know the Master's housekeeper, Frau Dr. Celestina Truxa, whose wonderful memory
was destined, decades afterward, to enrich these pages.

That same year, in Berlin University, I took care to choose
Dr. Max Friedländer as professor, a man who had known
Brahms intimately and who told me many things about him
that are not in print.

Five years later, while preparing to write a book about
Germany, I made a study of Hamburg. In one of its suburbs
I became intimate with Gustav Frenssen. The man and his
novels saturated me with the poetic atmosphere of the Dithmarsh—the North Sea country of moor and fen and dune
from which Brahms' forebears came, and from whose
characteristic plant, the yellow-flowering broom, or *Bram*
(*planta genista*), that sturdy family, like the royal Plantagenets of England, took its name.[1]

Ever since then, in the course of fifteen European visits,
I have neglected no opportunity of learning more about the
composer. One trip brought a festival of his works at Heidelberg, under Furtwängler. There, in the informal suppers
after the music, one could talk with Schumann's daughter
Eugenie and many another friend of the Master.

The next year I crossed the Atlantic with the late Dr. Julius
Roentgen, a Dutch composer who had known the great man
well. He was a mine of fresh information, and later I visited
him in Holland and studied his many Brahms documents.
Naturally the travels in search of material for my life of

[1] In French, Johannes Brahms would be—Jean Plantagenet; in English—John Broome.

Brahms' birthplace in Schlüter's Hof, Speckstrasse, 60, Hamburg.
The family is said to have lived up one flight, on the left side.

Beethoven brought to light numerous hidden facts about the successor whose character and career so strikingly echoed Beethoven's own.

In 1929 I suddenly woke to the realization that Brahms had been dead for thirty-two years; that the men and women who had known him were fast dying of old age and post-war privations; that the centenary of his birth was only four years away; and that a Brahms pilgrimage was therefore a matter of now or never. So I embarked, daring greatly to hope for treasure-trove which his biographers, Messrs. Kalbeck, Niemann, and Specht, had missed, and to be able to base my book chiefly on unpublished material. As it has turned out, I have been unexpectedly fortunate in securing new and significant information from more than one hundred and fifty people who once knew Brahms.

The pilgrimage proper commenced with the battle-cry "On to Berlin!" Naturally the first person to consult was my dear old professor, now Geheimrat Max Friedländer, and president of the German Brahms Society.

He helped me to complete my working library. He counselled me look up Herr Gustav Ernest, the excellent biographer of Beethoven, who was then writing on Brahms only a league or two from us. He dwelt sadly on what invaluable help I might have had from Frau Prof. Engelmann, who had been a friend and interpreter of the Master—but alas! she had had a stroke and could see nobody.

He began talking about Brahms and told me a few moderately interesting things, but with an air more and more preoccupied and uncertain. Finally he struck his knee a resounding whack and cried: "I will do it! I will give you that remarkable story. Only, you must come with me out of doors. It is of such a delicate nature that my wife would be shocked were she to overhear." Then, pacing up and down underneath the pines of Grunewald, he unfolded a fascinating and terrible tale about Brahms' attitude towards women.

In a placid old house by an absent-minded canal I found another famous professor of music. Prof. Robert Kahn, a brother of Otto Kahn, the New York financier, is one of the favoured few whom Brahms accepted as pupils. With vivacity he discoursed about his master's bearishness, simplicity, unerring eye for human nature, ready wit, and telegraphic conversational style. When the talk veered to Brahms and sex, he eyed his wife with the same nervousness that Dr. Friedländer had shown. But instead of escaping with me, he simply sent her out of the room. . . .[2]

In Drs. Robert and Richard Fellinger I found the sons of that beloved lady who was privileged to take the most popular of all the photographs of Brahms, the one where he sits in profile musing at the veranda window with his head on his hand. It was with the Fellinger family that he liked to spend his Christmas Eves. The brothers told me that Kalbeck had drawn a good deal of his information from them, but had misunderstood some of it and had got other items quite wrong; and they gave me list of these errors.

One day I learned to my joy that Frau Prof. Engelmann was better and would receive me. I recalled Brahms' description of her as "the laughing Professoress"; and the childless Elisabet von Herzogenberg's wistful letter to him:

[2] See p. 258.

Give my greetings to the charming creature who can do so much; play piano uniquely with her little white pawlets, laugh like a tiny dove, enchant all hearts—and bring babies into the world, ·which after all is the prettiest and most essential act a little woman can perform on earth.

The pallid and ancient ghost of this lady gave me a kind welcome; but such was her charm that in three minutes one actually forgot the bent, palsied body, the feeble voice, the ravaged features, and felt only the irresistible magnetism which had conquered the great companions of her youth.

She brought out a graph which her husband, Dr. Theodor Engelmann, the famous physiologist, had taken of Brahms' pulse in 1873. She allowed me to whistle the opening bars of each movement in Brahms' chamber music, and sang the Master's own tempos for them. She even hobbled to the piano and with her pitifully shaking old hands gave me memorable and technically finished performances of many of her favourite rhapsodies, capriccios, and *intermezzi*. And every now and then, with delicious mimicry, she recalled something new to tell about Brahms' humour or his playing, his kindness to children and servants, his sarcasm, his high spirits, his way with the baton, or his passion for contradiction. As I glance back over my pilgrimage, those five calls on "the laughing Professoress" are five of its high lights.

I need not have hesitated to look up Herr Gustav Ernest, for at once I liked him even more than his valuable books. He came to dine, and we had jovially impassioned disputes about Beethoven and Brahms. He generously warned me against all sorts of inaccuracies he had discovered in Kalbeck, and against various other pitfalls for the unwary. We had the congenial sort of symposium that none but specialists in the same subjects can enjoy—critically discussing the broad seas of biographical literature through which we had voyaged.

He invited me to supper and heaped coals of fire on a rival's head by producing for my delectation no less a find than that Berlin druggist, Herr Ferdinand, the grandson of Robert and Clara Schumann, of whom one started Brahms on his career and the other became his closest lifelong friend.

Cheered that the pilgrimage had already gained momentum, I sought Switzerland. It was important to discover why the town of Thun should have given birth to such music as the last two violin sonatas and the C minor trio.

On a wall near a humble little general shop in the outskirts, I came upon a tablet:

IN THIS HOUSE LIVED
THE MASTER OF GERMAN MUSIC
JOHANNES BRAHMS
IN THE SUMMER MONTHS OF THE YEARS
1886–1888
AND CREATED HERE A NUMBER
OF HIS MOST BEAUTIFUL WORKS
This land, where music once was proud and strong,
Has won a new renown through your great song.[3]

---

[3] *Du hast dies Land, sangfroh in alter Zeit,*
Mit deinem Lied zu neuem Ruhm geweiht.

These lines are from a delightful poem *The Thun Sonata*, by Brahms' friend Widmann, the poet who lived in Berne near by. Since my visit the house has, unfortunately, been demolished.

The shop and house were still in the hands of the same Spring family who had once lodged Brahms. Johann, the present owner, told about sitting on the Master's friendly knee, as a little shaver, and trying in vain to learn his notes.

The freedom of the place was extended to me, and it soon became clear why Brahms was happy there and did such spontaneous work. He had plenty of elbow-room—a whole floor to himself. Near at hand towered a magnificent tree, the Master's favourite Wellingtonia. To the right rose quaint Thun with its picturesquely turreted castle. The vision of lofty peaks above the river Aar, which slid beneath his windows *allegro amabile,* was a thing ideally fitted to stimulate a musical mind and spirit without overexciting them. There was a gorgeous view of the Stockhorn range with the Niesen. And farther on the left gleamed the snows of Eiger, Mönch, and Jungfrau.

Leaning out of those windows at dawn or by moonlight, I could better understand the pure, crisp, exuberant loveliness of the Thun sonatas and trio. The freshness and magic of all Switzerland distil from them.

Father Spring was kind enough to sell me the old account book in which his mother had entered the daily charges against their illustrious lodger. It is a touching commentary on the Spartan frugality toward himself which went with his prodigal generosity to others.

From Thun the way led across the Rubicon to Como and the Villa Carlotta, where Brahms was so often the guest of his admirer, the Duke of Meiningen. Travel in northern Italy reminds one at every turn of the Master and his boyish passion for this land. The way from Genoa to Venice is full of him. In Cremona I searched long before discovering the statue of St. Joachim before which Brahms had remarked how fitting it was that Joachim should be put on a pedestal in this old town sacred to the fiddle. Coming abruptly at night upon a searchlight illumination of the cathedral's campanile, façade, and baptistry, I had much the same shock of pleasure that Brahms himself once felt in turning out of a pitch-dark alley as the full moon burst from a cloud and lit up this dramatic group.

In my Padua hotel I recalled the departing Master's even greater surprise and pleasure when, at a sign from the fat *padrona,* her beautiful young niece advanced upon him, stood tiptoe, flung her arms about his neck, and kissed him full on the mouth—because that was the fitting way to speed such an evidently great man.

Venice brought a reminder of Nottebohm, the crabbèd old musicologist in whom Brahms delighted. I was lying on my couch in the Hotel Bonvecchiati, in vacant and in pensive mood, reconning Kalbeck's massive biography, when I came again upon that curious episode of the wine. It seems that the great-hearted Brahms had invited poor Nottebohm to be his guest on a junket from Vienna to Rome and back. But when the scholar reached Venice he found, in some obscure drinking-place, an old Cyprian wine with which he fell so hopelessly in love that Brahms had to go on without him.

In the circle of journalists at Gause's Bierhalle in Vienna, which both musicians frequented, this incident was afterwards celebrated in choric song:

Bei Gause trank auch Nottebohm,
Der wollte eines Tags nach Rom
Und kam nur bis Venedig;
Ein alter Cyprer macht ihn dort
Der Weiterreise ledig.

(At Gause's, too, drank Nottebohm,
Who started once to get to Rome
But got to Venice merely.
Old wine of Cyprus made the man
Scorn wandering sincerely.)

I read no more in the book that day! Parched with curiosity I bounded forth in quest of a vintage that could so successfully overcome the call of the Eternal City. Following
the gleam without encouragement from Florian's to the Frari
and from the Giardini Pubblici to the Giudecca, I doubled
back and reached my goal near the Piazza in the Caffè Giaco-
muzzi. Outside that magic bottle stood the legend: *Fino
Cypro (Stravecchio)*. Inside the bottle was that which almost exonerated the renegade Nottebohm for the loss of
Brahms' company in the Vatican, the Forum, the Campagna,
and the Castello di Cesare.

It may be that Brahms too, before leaving Venice, appreciated Nottebohm's discovery. For a Viennese lady has told
me how she once beheld him parading in an exalted frame
of mind on the Riva degli Schiavone, and seized his arm just
in time to save him from blissfully sauntering into a canal.
She did this, she explained, to atone for having, in her youth,
tipped him into a snow-bank. Of which more anon.

The way from Venice to Vienna continued to be reminiscent of my hero. Pörtschach on Lake Wörther conjured up mellow memories of the D major symphony and the violin concerto. Mürzzuschlag, with its tangled streams and evergreen forests, told of the E minor symphony; while the Austrian capital, as I approached, seemed to promise a revelation of the entire man.

Chapter II

"THE MUSICIAN'S HOLY CITY"

I NEEDED only to present a few letters of introduction to find myself a cordially accepted part of Brahms' Vienna. Everybody promised to fulfil my wildest dreams and then hastened about obligingly in search of others to promise still more.

One ardent Brahmin (as a Brahms devotee is called) functioned as my private sleuth, and was for ever turning up with fresh lists of aged folk who would tell me things about the Master which had never swum into Kalbeck's ken—patriarchs whom I must see at once. His motto was: "Let us eat, drink, and have interviews, for tomorrow they die." And in all too many instances the sad sequel showed that I had started my pilgrimage not a month too soon. Later pilgrims would fare thinly indeed.

The very first interviews were encouraging. Prof. Julius Winkler, the violinist, threw many a sidelight on Brahms' social relations, and described what a nerve-racking privilege it was to play ensemble music with the ageing Master.

Frau Marie, the witty widow of Ignaz Brüll, the composer and pianist at whose excellent table Brahms loved to dine, amused me with tales of his ingenious brutality to ladies who yearned to play for him. She described his modest fear of influencing the personal readings of his interpreters, which went so far that he refused to play his own pieces to Brüll. Her large collection of unpublished letters was a bonanza.

Past the place in Heiligenstadt where Beethoven had listened to the birds and the brook while composing the *Pastoral* symphony, I made my way to the villa where Kalbeck had written the monumental Life. There his daughter, Frau Dr. Luithlen, showed me many a souvenir of this task, and allowed me to copy unheard-of letters from her collection.

At a musical dinner I met Dr. Hans Gál, composer, pianist, co-editor of the complete edition of Brahms, and author of that brilliant little book, *An Introduction to Score Reading*. Knowing what a task it is for any writer to grow familiar with choral music that is seldom or never heard, he was generous enough to play me from the orchestral score—as few but him can do—such rarely given works as the *Ave Maria*, the *Fest- und Gedenksprüche, Rinaldo*, the motets, etc. And his running commentary pointed out no end of imitations and inversions so recondite that they must necessarily be missed by all but one hearer in ten thousand.

Of course I haunted the energetic professor's home. He would always receive me with the formula: "Well, well, for our pleasure are we not here!" Then he would dash at the piano, prop some enormous volume open on the rack, and proceed to transfer from score to keys The Brahms Who Is Not in the Concerts.

As I naturally wished to be on easy terms with every note of his music, two well known oratorio singers enthusiastically undertook to sing for me, in the course of one winter, the entire two hundred-odd songs, with countless encores. And the lady who, as we shall see later, had once, in a moment of irritation, endeared herself to the Master by telling him that his symphonies were "worthless trash," invited me to specially contrived performances of the vocal duets.

At an autograph dealer's on the Ring, I discovered a large pile of unpublished Brahms letters, and acquired the Master's own cigar case (sealed by the executors!), together with his stub of blue pencil—one of the most important tools in the history of music; for, without its relentless cuttings and revisions, its wielder's fame might never have surpassed even that of Rubinstein.

No one could have been kinder and more enthusiastically resourceful in offering and finding new material than Frau Henriette Ribarz-Hemala, who, as a charming young girl pianist, was a prime favourite with Brahms, as one glance at the merry frontispiece will verify. This lady introduced me to three of the people who have most enriched this volume: Frau Kurzbauer, Herr von Miller zu Aichholz (who took the picture of Brahms hugging Henriette), and Frau Dr. Truxa.

The half-English Frau Else Kurzbauer, though too young to have been more to Brahms than one of his beloved "little ones," contributed to this book by continually unearthing fresh sources of information, by seeking out and copying many unpublished letters, and by helping me in the more difficult interviews, particularly with old peasants whose thorniest dialect and spiniest hostility capitulated to her linguistic ability and her sympathetic persuasiveness. At the very close of my stay in Austria, when I was ill and could not travel to keep an appointment with the most important Brahmin yet uninterviewed, she actually brought the old gentleman in person from his distant town. An excellent violinist, she refreshed my memory of the Brahms trios by

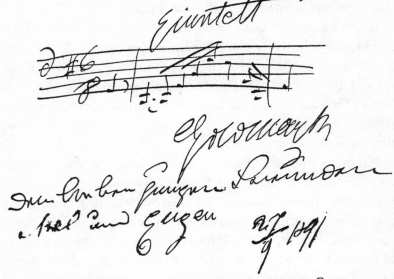

FACSIMILE OF A FRIENDLY SKIRMISH BETWEEN GOLD-
MARK AND BRAHMS, ON TWO OPPOSING PAGES OF

organizing séances where we played them all with Frau
Ribarz-Hemala. After which, with reinforcements, we did
the piano quartets and quintet.

As a youngster Herr Eugen von Miller zu Aichholz took
many of the best snapshots ever made of the Master. He had
unrivalled opportunities, for his father was the wealthy connoisseur who later built the Brahms Museum on his own estate
in Gmunden; and the composer was a frequent family guest
both in the country and in Vienna.

This generous gentleman entered with boyish gusto into
my project. His first act was to lend me the priceless Gmunden guest-book which begins with two pages of badinage between Carl Goldmark, composer of *The Queen of Sheba,* and
Brahms.

THE GUEST-BOOK OF THE MILLER ZU AICHHOLZ CHILDREN, OLGA (NICKNAMED "AXEL") AND EUGEN, AUGUST 9, 1891.

Goldmark led off on the left-hand page with the opening tune of Brahms' G major string quintet,[1] and outrageously signed it "C. Goldmark." Then the other seized the quill and on the right-hand page, with portentous underlinings and other exaggerated expression marks, scrawled, "Leave me room!" (*Platz lassen!*) —and the old copy-book injunction:

> *Ueb' immer Treu' ū. Redlichkeit*
> *bis an—, dein tiefes Grab!;*
> *ū. weiche!! keinen; Fingerbreit:*
> *von—;! Gottes?!:— Regeln ab.*

> (Always be faithful, true and fair
> until—, your burial day!;
> and never swerve!! a single; hair:
> from—;! God's?!:—commands away.)

[1] He got the notes nearly right, but the time signature 6/8 instead of 9/8.

Note the emphatic reference to his opponent's eventual interment. Mark the dig at the Jehovah of the Jewish Goldmark,
the man whom he had once ragged unmercifully for presum-
ing to set some Christian words to music.

It was an eloquent commentary on Brahms' habitually
devious subtlety in verbal expression that nobody could explain the significance of the eight words he had written on
the right of this verse. Neither the owners of the guest-book
nor all the Brahmins and Goldmarkians I found in Europe
could tell what the joke was. And not until I had gained the
perspective of New York did it dawn on me that the eight
words were meant as a satirical heading for the smug copy-
book motto about virtue:

(Karl Goldmark)
"mein Leben
ū. Lieben
im Liede"—
! — !

((Karl Goldmark)
"[An Epitome of] My Life
and Loves
in a Song"—
! — !   )

To finish the page the Master scrawled a large JOHS BRAHMS.

This eccentric guest-book warfare in the jovial villa with
the famous cellar seems to be plainly watermarked—or let
us say wine-marked—with the caption: "After dining well."

Herr Eugen's generosity knew no bounds. He gave me
the last remaining copy of his father's large and sumptuous

Brahms Picture Book, as well as Scharff's bronze medallion of the Master. His mother kindly promised me access to a diary which she had kept during the last seven years of Brahms' life. This, however, was lost; nor could it be found, and sent to me, until after her death, in 1932.

Brahms' old housekeeper, Frau Dr. Truxa, was an entirely different sort of person. She had, of course, quite forgotten our first meeting, more than a quarter of a century before, in Brahms' own rooms. And during my first year in Vienna she always opposed to my advances that hard shell which had so endeared her to her taciturn lodger, the well known hater of effusion.

But on returning from England for the second winter, I found her manner surprisingly mellowed. She had grown used to me, she smilingly explained, and forthwith opened wide a rich treasure-chest of information which she had always resolutely withheld from Kalbeck because, she elucidated, Brahms had not cared much for him, and she had shared this feeling.

She let me, for example, into the secret of his trick rocking-chair. She told curious and homely details about the peasant-like simplicity of his way of living, his kindness and sensitive thoughtfulness, his malice, brutality, and zest in mischief. She cast new light on his health, his relations with women, his system of housekeeping, his secretiveness, his democracy, his reticence, generosity, and courage.

Best of all, apparently, she held out hopes that she might yet lay her hands on the manuscripts of those unpublished songs of his which she had once found dismembered in the waste-basket and had privately pieced together. Alas, when she finally laid her hands on them, the songs proved after all to have been published!

That first and easiest part of my pilgrimage was too perfect to last. For I soon discovered that the kind and trustworthy informants whom I have mentioned by name, and shall mention, were in value far above the average. If one is bent on interviewing the friends of a man who died a third of a century ago, one must expect a rich assortment of handicaps. The inevitable difficulties promptly declared themselves.

The cranks put in an appearance. There were the musical inventors who said they would tell me all about Brahms—but not until after converting me to the new system of notation, or the spiral keyboard, or the plan for introducing literary punctuation into music, as revealed to them by the ghost of Bach.

There were the obscure and disappointed composers who had known Brahms intimately, *jawohl!* and could unfold no end of important and undreamt-of facts about him.

"One moment, however! Before we go into that, let me tell you just a word about myself." And *mein Herr,* ravished to have an audience at last, would pour forth the inevitable tale of having been discovered and publicly embraced by Liszt at the age of seven; of having been acclaimed by the leading critics of the universe as Beethoven's one logical successor; and of the weird chain of unlucky chances which had, up to the present moment, cheated him of his proper recognition.

Deaf to all my diplomatic attempts to give the conversation a Brahmsian twist, he would advance from words to actions louder than words. Throwing his coat off, and himself upon the piano, he would, with the lamentable execution of which composers alone are capable, begin banging his entire 178 opuses. Toward the end of the third hour I would recall a life-and-death engagement and stagger away, sadder but no wiser.

Then there were those good patriots who were outraged that any citizen of such a crude outpost of civilization as America should presume to suppose he could contribute anything new in connexion with a Viennese specialty like music. (Their attitude, of course, was somewhat more advanced than that of the Tyrolese peasants who had once objected that I could be no American because my skin was not copper-coloured and there were no feathers in my hair.)

One of my worst handicaps was an unknown Austrian, a Herr Alfred von Ehrmann, who had for years been writing a life of Brahms. In many an interview I was told that he had been there just before me. And numerous otherwise hopeful sources of information were sealed for fear of what the jealous biographer would say. Gradually I came to look upon him as my evil genius.

Then one day we were brought together at the table of a common acquaintance, an old friend of Kalbeck's who lived in that very Mölker Bastei where Beethoven had written the Fifth symphony. And lo! instead of a venomous and hated rival, I found a delightful person who sparkled in conversation, wrote witty poems, and drew a valiant viola bow as an amateur quartettist. It appeared that I had been an even worse nuisance to him than he had been to me.

After a few meetings we learned anew that acquaintance is the best peace insurance. We formed a compact not to trench on one another's preserves, and became fast friends. Since then what amusing reunions have we not held, trying to trip each other up by whistling obscure Brahms themes for points, while that excellent pianist, the *gnädige Frau* von Ehrmann, officiated as umpire!

Sometimes the Brahmins had to be handled with gloves of sheerest lawn. I found one old lady so prudish as to be shocked at Brahms for writing to Elisabet von Herzogenberg, after a visit in her home, that he had left his nightgown behind— and still more shocked at Elisabet for posting him the indelicate garment.

Soon I came to learn how cautious the seeker after truth must be in this charming and imaginative city. As I was dining in a restaurant opposite the Konzerthaus I noticed an enormous framed photograph of Brahms. "*Jawohl*," admitted the proprietor, "that is the revered table where the great Master was accustomed to eat. Well do I remember him, a little fat man with a hoarse voice. Dr. Billroth used to dine with him there, and Johann Strauss and how many other great ones."

I seated myself reverently beneath the picture, and the food that night seemed peculiarly delicious; but the next day when I told an old Brahmin about my find, he laughed cynically.

"It's funny how little it takes to launch a myth! I was in at the birth of this one. A crowd of us musicians were eating at Wi——'s, and the talk turned on J. B. 'This plain, homely sort of restaurant,' I remarked, 'would have just suited Brahms. What a pity he didn't know about it!'

"The owner was standing near by, and my words gave him

an idea. The next day that big photograph of the Master appeared on the wall, already enveloped in the beginnings of a grand old tradition. And now half Vienna believes that Brahms once had his headquarters at Wi——'s."

Chapter III

HAPPY ENDING

LOOKING back over this pilgrimage, I like to lose sight of the disappointments and other distressful features in recalling by what pleasantly involved and curious routes much of my material arrived.

Some of it was found by penetrating into the most musical part of Vienna—the homes of its chamber musicians. The long chain of events that led me to Frau Ribarz-Hemala began in 1900. I was playing chamber music with David Mannes in a country house at Easthampton, Long Island. Our hostess, a sculptor, introduced me to a composer, from whom the chain led through a psychologist and an editor, then jumped the Atlantic to a Viennese poet, and from her, through a society woman whose glamorous old home overlooked Schönbrunn Park, to a pianist. And the pianist sent me to the invaluable Frau Ribarz-Hemala.

Some of the latter's good deeds have already been mentioned. She accomplished another in taking me and my 'cello to do Brahms' A major piano quartet with Prof. and Frau Alfred Finger. In the middle of our performance I suddenly and overwhelmingly realized that all three of my companions had played music with the composer himself.

Fiddling is not the only sport that has scored points for this book. Ten years ago, on the courts of the T.C.P. (the Tennis Club of Paris), a little adventure befell me that would surely have appealed to the adventurous Brahms. I was at the net preparing to defend my alley, when a scrap of whistled melody sounded behind me:

Jerking my head around I saw that it proceeded from my doubles partner, the dignified president of the club, who was in the rear picking up a ball. Surprised and charmed to have a Brahms quartet contrapuntally entwined with a tennis quartet, I of course instantly whistled back:

The president looked up in amazement at this response from America.

"What! You a tennis-player, and still know that?"

"Well, aren't you another? Besides, I thought you French were supposed to hate Brahms."

In the shower after the game we compared notes. Major Noël Desjoyaux turned out to be a composer who had studied under Brahms for four years. He then and there told me an original, autobiographic version of the bottle-of-Bach story.[1] But it was destined to take ten years of persistent supplication to extract from him his Brahms reminiscences in full.

Tennis in Vienna resulted in more finds: an English merchant who had known Kalbeck intimately; and a Swiss medical student who learned the object of my pilgrimage and,

[1] See p. 192.

after a visit home, handed over, between two fiercely fought sets, an account which his Neuchâtel grandmother had written out for me, of how Brahms had once pushed her from a piano stool.

Billiards was no less fruitful than tennis. At Brahms' old café, the Kremser, on the Ring, I was a *Stammgast,* with all the dignity of a private cue. There I met the portrait painter who told me the Master's brutal remark about the lady and the philosopher's stone. A fellow-guest was a well known singing teacher who spent impassioned hours trying to convince me that Brahms had adored Verdi. The richest yield of that billiard room, however, was Dr. Otto Julius Bauer, the leading wit of town, who told me, between a carom and a miscue, diverting things about his own keen but friendly bouts with the Master.

This informal Vienna lent itself admirably to chance discoveries and pleasant surprises. One day I was browsing around in the shop of Artaria—Beethoven's old publisher. I was buying Brahms etchings for a fellow-fiddler at home when it occurred to me to ask the aged head of the firm if he had personally known my hero. And he was no more than well launched on his reminiscences when a charming lady customer chimed in. She too had matter of moment to communicate. In the end she carried me off in a car to her old palace to tell me stories very much to the point and give me notes of introduction to other Brahmins.

I can never forget the hours spent in the archives of the Friends of Music, going through every volume of Brahms' own library, page by page, in search of marginal notes, and coming upon many an interesting scrawl. How pleasant it was to hold in one's hand his little old *Robinson Crusoe*, by "Daniel von Foë," almost worn out from assiduous reading! How thrilling to find on the cover of the score of Schumann's *"Spring"* symphony this autograph dedication:

To the dear friend
Joh. Brahms
that he may remember
Robert and Clara.

But the thrill turned to a shudder when I remembered what happened to poor mad Robert soon after writing these lines.

It was even more interesting to turn detective in the Municipal Library, under the guidance of Librarian Dr. Alfred Orel, an old colleague of Beethoven research. There I spent breathless mornings comparing the originals of Brahms' letters with the printed volumes, in order to find out what their editor, Kalbeck, had seen fit to suppress. It was worth all the toil, if only to learn how Kalbeck had prettified the composer's relations with the Duke of Meiningen, and to read in Brahms' own scrawl this line which the editor had cut out: "Meiningen is to me a terrible thought." [2]

I bade Vienna a wistful farewell to spend a month in the Salzkammergut at the foot of that Schafberg up which Brahms, in the blindness of his mountaineering fervour, had once urged his father, fondly supposing that he was giving the old man the treat of his life. The latter reached the summit more dead than alive. "What a glorious experience!" ex-

---

[2] *"ein schrecklicher Gedanke."* Omitted from *Correspondence*, Vol. VIII, Letter 124, p. 137.

ulted Johannes. "Yes, yes," panted Johann Jakob. "But, Hannes, look here, promise never to do this to me again!"

Close enough for frequent visits was that town whose name sounds like a gentle sneeze—Ischl, where the Master spent ten of his last summers. There I found a group of his friends, who loaded me down with kindness, unpublished anecdotes, and rare photographs of the great days. The old Gruber house, in which Brahms lived, was full of him, and the Hotel Elisabeth where he ate, and Zauner's where he sipped his coffee, and the shop of Herr Zerbs the barber, who proudly told of trimming the great Brahmsian beard as he condescendingly shaved my own.

Having paid my respects to Wiesbaden as the birthplace of the Third symphony, and Bonn as that of the B flat sextet, and having said farewell to England, where I had talked with that agreeable Brahmin, Sir George Henschel, I embarked, supposing that my quest of the unknown Brahms was now finished. No more material could be hoped for in such a new land as my own.

I was delightfully mistaken! Since reaching home I have met a score of those who once knew the Master. A New York lady, for example, showed me sketches that her painter-husband had made of Brahms in Switzerland. One in California sent me a photograph of the lead soldiers that "Hannes" had played with as a child, which had been given her by his sister Elise. A housewrecker found in a deserted mansion a splendid unpublished portrait of him, which was secured for this book. And Dr. Gerhart Hauptmann, having promised three years before to put his memories of Brahms in order for me, invited me to lunch on the top of the Empire

State Building, and held me fascinated for the better part of two hours while one genius interpreted another.

My adventures in search of The Unknown Brahms have continued all through the writing of this book. I trust that its publication may induce yet undiscovered friends of the Master to turn new light on the alluring subject.

PART II

THE KNOWN BRAHMS

Chapter IV

HAMBURG AND THE OPEN ROAD

(1833–1853)

BEFORE meeting the unknown Brahms portrayed in Part III of this book, let us briefly refresh our memories of the *known* Brahms. His outer life was as poor in dramatic events as his inner life was rich in passion, thought, humour, and all the colourful attributes hinted at or proclaimed by his scores. For this reason, as well as to leave space for a fuller consideration of the many newly discovered facts about this extraordinary personality, and for a revaluation of his music, the chronological story of his career has been condensed into the four chapters of Part II. In this section the reader need not look for many new disclosures.

A poor tenement in the red-light district of the old Hanseatic port of Hamburg became the birthplace of Johannes Brahms on May 7, 1833. It was Number 60 of a gloomy passage known, modestly enough, as Specksgang,[1] or Bacon Alley.

Johann Jakob Brahms, his father, a droll, likable, happy-go-lucky, but stubborn vagabond, was the son of a small inn-and-shopkeeper of Heide in the Dithmarsh, the low country at the mouth of the Elbe. Some untraceable heredi-

---

[1] Now Speckstrasse. The disreputability of this quarter was first clearly described by Alfred von Ehrmann in *Johannes Brahms: Weg, Werk und Welt*, 1933, p. 7.

tary impulse made Johann Jakob early set his heart on becoming a musician. His scandalized parents would not hear
of this; but the boy kept running away from home in pur-
suit of his ideal. Finally the old folks gave in and bound him
over as apprentice to the "town-piper," that sole local reposi-
tory of musical science, picturesquely surviving in the old-
fashioned Dithmarsh countryside as a descendant of the
mediæval musical guilds, or *"Stadt Pfeifereien."*

At twenty Johann Jakob turned from peasant life and,
with his old playmate, Fritz Becker, who was armed with a
horn, set forth, double-bass on back,[2] to make his fortune in
Hamburg, the city of his dreams. At first he was little more
prosperous than a tooting and scraping beggar; then in
course of time he found occasional work as substitute bass-
fiddler in a small pass-round-the-hat string band on the
Alster Basin. The precarious position was afterwards made
regular; but not until a generation later did the poor musician manage to find dignified employment in the orchestra
of the municipal theatre.

After the first four years of desperate struggle for a bare
livelihood, the tall, robust youth had fallen in love with, and
married, Johanna Henrika Christiana Nissen. This woman
must have possessed a rare quality and quantity of charm to
have so successfully offset her too evident shortcomings. She
was small, homely, crippled in one foot, and ailing. She had
a complaining disposition—and was seventeen years older
than Johann Jakob.

On the other hand, she was deeply affectionate and fine-

[2] Florence May was wrong in stating that he took up this instrument only after reaching Hamburg. See Fritz Becker's "Aus Joh. Brahms Jugendzeit," in the *Hamburger
Fremdenblatt.*

feeling, was a skilful needlewoman, and had a remarkable memory. Kalbeck, indeed, asserts that, in her old age, she learned by heart Schiller's complete works.[3] But this seems a large claim when one considers, for example, the staggering length of *The Fall of the United Netherlands*, and *The Thirty Years' War*, and remembers that this plain woman of the people could scarcely have grasped the purport of the *Philosophical Letters* or of the series *Upon the Æsthetic Culture of Man*.

Be that as it may, it was a happily combined pair which produced Johannes as their second child: the sturdy, high-spirited, good-humoured, vital, healthy, though stupid,[4] Dithmarsh sire, and the sensitive mother with her sure instinct for spiritual values. Her affection was intensified by a previous life of emotional starvation and the blessed relief of finally attaining the husband and children of whom the poor little crippled spinster had already begun to despair.

Two other children were born to them: Elise, the eldest, who grew into an unpleasant, querulous woman; and Fritz, the youngest, who managed to become a fashionable piano teacher and whose disposition was not improved by his popular nickname: "The Wrong Brahms."

The small Hannes[5] liked the singing and dancing games which are, to this day, a specialty of Hamburg children. Still better, he loved to sit absorbed in his lead soldiers, combining and marshalling them with the germ of that constructive

---

[3] Max Kalbeck, *Johannes Brahms*, 1904–1914, Vol. I, i, p. 11.
[4] Mr. Gustav Hinrichs who, in his youth, played clarinet in the same orchestra with Johann Jakob, assures me that the latter was known all over Hamburg as "a blockhead," and was "a natural butt for all the boys."
[5] The Low German equivalent of "Johnny."

imagination which was very soon to begin playing with sounds. But he would unhesitatingly abandon even the soldiers in order to hear a musical instrument.

When his father began teaching him his notes on a neighbour's piano he was stupefied to see the five-year-old looking out of the window, yet naming each note correctly. Johann Jakob, whose own ear was none of the most accurate, was overjoyed to discover that little Hannes was endowed with the startling gift of absolute pitch. Furthermore, the young genius had already built himself an infantile but practicable system of notation, without a suspicion that such a thing was already in existence.

At seven he began his formal study of music under Cossel, a local pianist, and made such progress that at ten he appeared in a public concert, playing an étude by Herz, and the piano part of Beethoven's wind quintet. An impresario in the audience was so delighted with the feat that he proposed to make his own fortune, and the prodigy's, by taking him on a concert tour of America; and even offered to pay for the whole family if they wished to come along. This turned the dazzled and delighted parents' heads; and the disastrous exploitation was prevented only by the self-sacrificing efforts of Cossel, who managed to curb Johann Jakob's greed, and to persuade Hamburg's best teacher, the reluctant Eduard Marxsen, to undertake the boy's further education.

Between them these excellent men gave little Hannes an almost ideal preparation for his life-work. They made him an able pianist, harmonist and sight-transposer; gave him a solid grounding in counterpoint and the theory of composi-

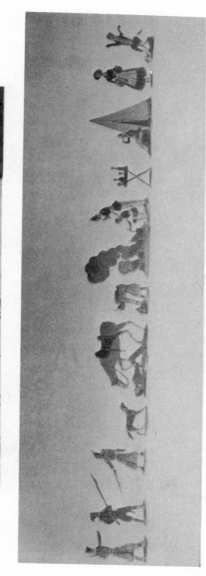

(above) Brahms with his friends, Dr. Richard and Frau Maria Fellinger, and their two sons, Richard and Robert.

(below) Brahms' coloured lead soldiers. Given by his sister to Miss Johanna Sommer of Springfield, Ill. Now owned by Miss Julie Cottet of Alhambra, Cal., with whose kind permission they are here reproduced.

tion; and, helped by the nonexistence of such things as phonograph and radio, they shielded him so jealously from unsettling influences that might have tended to make him a mere hanger-on of this or that modern "school," that he reached twenty before he was familiar with even Schumann's works.

Times were bitterly hard for the Brahmses. They were so poor that Johann Jakob's whole ambition centred on having the family's prodigy contribute to the family's support. For years, from the age of nine on, Hannes often had to play for dances, sometimes all night, in the most infamous dives of the harbour. The remuneration was *"twee Dahler un duhn"* (two thalers and drinks ad libitum). But he was too self-controlled to become a drunkard, and too ambitious to waste his time. It is touching to think of the beautiful blond lad sitting before a decrepit piano, his fingers automatically pounding out rough music for the maudlin sailors and public women, while he bent forward to devour with his near-sighted blue eyes the romantic poetry of his favourite Tieck or Hoffmann or Eichendorff. Fortunately for the progress of this desperately snatched education, the jazz age had not yet come to compel the small player to ogle the dancers, burst into song, and do setting-up exercises.

Naturally this sort of night work was bad for a frail and highly impressionable child. It combined with the poor air and the wretched living conditions of his tenement home to exact its physical toll. Up to the age of fourteen, he was anæmic and suffered almost constantly from nervous head-aches. He was once in serious peril of death; for the absent-minded little fellow was knocked down and run over by a wagon, but escaped lasting injury. The emotional effect of the red-light district was more serious, and will be discussed later.[6]

The poor schools which he attended until he was fifteen gave him not much more than the three R's and the knowledge that schools can treat a sensitive boy more brutally than the roughest of sailors' dance-halls.

Hannes' first taste of the countryside came in 1847, at that psychological moment of adolescence so favourable to the formation of lifelong enthusiasms. A certain Adolph Giesemann, who liked Johann Jakob's playing in the Alster Pavilion, invited the lad to make him a long visit at Winsen, a small town sixty miles from Hamburg across the Luneburg Heath.

Here Hannes first came to know and adore that life of woodland and meadow which was destined to inspire nearly all of his music. He taught Giesemann's little daughter Lisl the piano, conducted a men's chorus, went to town for his weekly lesson with Marxsen, and won the robust health which turned out to be such a shining asset in his career. Mr. Charles Muller of New York tells me that his mother, Mathilde Kock, then a lass of thirteen, used to spend many hours of this vacation playing four-hand duets with Hannes.

That fall he appeared twice before the Hamburg public as pianist, and in 1848 he gave a concert of his own in which he dared affront the popular taste of his period by performing a Bach fugue. He had a rare treat when the already famous Hungarian virtuoso, Joseph Joachim, a lad two years

[6] See pp. 224-27, and 252-85.

his senior, played the Beethoven concerto, which was then a novelty in Hamburg. Hannes heard both the violinist and the composition for the first time; and, in his childish naïveté, took it for granted that the music had been written by Joachim himself.

In 1849, Hannes first played a piece of his own in concert: a *Phantasie on a Favourite Waltz,* which, like so many hundreds of his early compositions, never attained the dignity of print.

The boy had early acquired the rare art—since advocated by Arnold Bennett—of living on twenty-four hours a day. In his later 'teens he made money by numerous expedients: playing in dance-halls; teaching the piano for the record fee of a mark a lesson; as accompanist behind the scenes of the Municipal Theatre; and as slinger-together of easy opera pot-pourris and fantasias on popular melodies. He signed these: "G. W. Marks"; and this fictitious personage had actually published his opus 151 before Johannes Brahms was ready with opus 1. "Karl Würth" was his pen-name for music too good for Marks but too bad for Brahms.

All these occupations, however, were merely incidental to the main business of life: preparing to compose real music, and learning to know literature—especially poetry. In 1852 he wrote the F sharp minor sonata, destined to be his opus 2. And then, the following year, he had the luck to accompany Reményi, the youthful Hungarian violinist, and win his liking. "Come along," suggested Reményi. "Let's knock about Germany a bit, you and I. We'll give concerts here and there; and when we get to Hanover I'll introduce you to my fellow-Hungarian, Joachim."

This plan appealed to the restive young fellow; for it echoed the spirit of that alluring romance of musical vagabondage: *From the Diary of a Good-for-Nothing,* by his favourite Eichendorff. Though he had never ventured farther from his adored mother than Winsen, he accepted at once. Afoot and light-hearted they took to the open road.

The trip did not work out quite so romantically as in the book, but it had its points. At Celle, for instance, Johannes acquired merit by paralleling Beethoven's historic feat at the rehearsal of his first concerto. The fiddler found the piano tuned too low to suit the fiddle. So, in the concert, Johannes transposed his part of the Beethoven C minor sonata from memory, a semitone higher. And Reményi, effective showman that he was, made a speech to the audience, explaining the sensational *tour de force.*

In Hildesheim, home of the Thousand Year Rosebush and of so many other glamorous legends, auditors proved sparse. But the undismayed vagabonds supped well with some newly found friends, then trooped forth to improvise a moonlight serenade under the casements of a certain high-born lady, their chief patroness. Reményi fiddled many a *csárdás* and *toborzó.* The good companions burst into choric song. And Hildesheim, listening in its nightcaps, was so aroused and thrilled that on the next evening the concert hall was packed.

The open road led from there to Joachim in Hanover. When the small blond pianist pulled out of his rucksack and played a manuscript *scherzo* (Op. 4), a violin sonata, a trio, a string quartet, movements of piano sonatas, and songs— the renowned virtuoso saw a great light. Long afterwards he recalled that the *Liebestreu* (Op. 3) had burst upon him as a revelation. The two young men instantly formed the friendship that was to mean much in the development of both and, with but a single interruption, to flourish for nearly half a century.

Chapter V

"NEW PATHS"

(1853–1862)

JOACHIM, who was already one of the foremost violinists of his time, gave Johannes sound advice about publishing, besides a letter to Liszt in Weimar and an invitation to his own home in Göttingen, in case of a break with Reményi.[1] For Joachim, a man extremely jealous by nature, felt sure that the other fiddler was half a charlatan, and no fit comrade for this young god who had descended upon him out of the blue.

In Weimar Brahms was entertained at the Altenburg with such cordiality by Liszt, the great-hearted and hypnotic charmer, that he stayed on for some time, in spite of heartily disliking the celebrity's disciples. The story of the young visitor's lapse in dropping to sleep while the Liszt sonata was being played by its composer, who characteristically forgave the naïve insult, is probably a malicious invention of Reményi's. Liszt read the abashed Johannes' piano pieces brilliantly from the crazily scribbled manuscript, praised them,[2] and tried to win the lad over as an adherent of the modernist school of program music. Failing in this, he finally bade Johannes Godspeed with the gift of an autographed

---

[1] In return, as the great violinist told Mr. Arthur M. Abell, Johannes taught him to smoke.

[2] Klindworth told Mr. Abell that on this occasion Liszt read Brahms' E flat minor *scherzo* at sight; liked it, exclaimed "We must do that again!" and did so.

leather cigarette case, to show that there was no hard feeling. The stifling atmosphere of adulation with which Liszt's hangers-on surrounded their master had been too much for the honest lad from Hamburg. "I saw," he remarked later, "that I did not belong there. I should have had to lie. And that I could not do."

He left Weimar without his companion; for Reményi suddenly put on the airs of a grand seigneur and broke their compact: "I have no more desire to wander as a musical beggar from village to village. You may try your luck alone."

So, in the early autumn of 1853, Johannes, recalling a better violinist's invitation, arrived at Göttingen, where he stayed for two months, deepening his friendship with Joachim, and learning the student-life—an experience which was to be reflected a quarter-century later in the rollicking humour of the *Academic Festival* overture.

The youths became so necessary to each other that Brahms decided to spend the winter in Hanover, where Joachim was concertmaster of the orchestra. But first, like a young Siegfried, he set out alone on a Rhine journey, armed with notes of introduction to various musical families en route. Joachim, their author, had been particularly insistent that, in Düsseldorf, Johannes call on Robert Schumann, whom Joachim had already informed about the new genius. But Schumann, in passing through Hamburg, had once offended Johannes by being too busy to look at some manuscripts which the boy had left at his hotel. And not until young "Siegfried," visiting at a house in Memel during this Rhine journey, learned to know and like the older master's music did he stifle his prejudice and call on the great man.

The pilgrim was well received and was asked at once to play his compositions. Florence May says that he began with the C major sonata. But after a few bars, his host interrupted excitedly: "Clara must hear this!" And when the celebrated piano virtuoso Frau Schumann made her fateful entry into the room, and into the boy's heart, her husband cried: "Now you shall hear such music, my dear Clara, as you have never heard! Young man, begin the piece again!"

In no time Johannes became a beloved guest of the house, and Schumann soon wrote his momentous article, "New Paths," for the *Neue Zeitschrift für Musik,* in which, a modern John the Baptist, he proclaimed that Brahms was "he that should come . . . the Messiah of music." This sudden and extreme claim, by untactfully exalting the novice at the expense of the established composers, naturally raised up against him, even before the publication of opus 1, a horde of bitter enemies. None the less "New Paths" was one of the most powerful bits of publicity ever accorded an unknown genius.

Schumann used his influence with omnipotent publishers in Leipzig, and persuaded them to print his protégé's first few compositions. The most important of these was the F minor sonata for piano (Op. 5). When Johannes went in person to that musical centre, he met Liszt, who again vainly tried to win him for the ranks of the "New Germans," as his clique was called. Berlioz was there and warmly praised the lad. Even the cold Leipzigers were charming to him, and he made a number of new friends, among them Julius Otto Grimm, the young conductor.

In one of the famous soirées of the David Quartet, given

ROBERT AND CLARA SCHUMANN

From a lithograph by Eduard Kaiser

in the Gewandhaus, he played, with fair success, his C major sonata (Op. 1) and E flat minor *scherzo* (Op. 4).

In Hamburg, meanwhile, the humble Brahms family was shocked into a delirium of joy by the arrival of a letter about the absent one, written and signed by the great Schumann himself. Wildly brandishing the sheets, Johann Jakob burst into the room of his old crony, Fritz Becker, seized him by the collar, and shouted in his broad *Platt-Deutsch:* "You, Fritz, now what do you say to this? Schumann declares my Hannes is a great, important artist and he'll be a second Beethoven!" (*Schumann hett seggt, min Hannes is 'nen groten, bedüdenden Künstler, he ward noch mal 'en tweeten Beethoven!*)

The good Fritz was outraged. This sounded to him like blasphemy. "What," he cried, "that foolish, tow-headed old urchin is to be a Beethoven? Have you gone off your head? In all his days your Hannes will turn into no great man. How can you believe such nonsense?" (*Wat? Dien ollen, dämlichen, blonden Bengel sall 'en Beethoven warden? Du büst woll nich klook? Ut dienen Hannes ward sin Lewdag keenen groten Minschen! Wo kannst Du so 'n Unsinn glöben?*) And he went on refuting the proud father's documentary proofs until Johann Jakob, though somewhat dampened, withdrew with the Parthian shot: "But Schumann says so!" (*Schumann hett 't äwer seggt!*)

As for Johannes, he looked forward to the family reunion at Christmas as to the brightest event in his life. And when the young fairy prince appeared after his first sortie into the wide world, and laid his printed music under the tree and saw the joy brimming his parents' eyes, he was not disappointed. "You have no idea," he wrote Joachim, "how very happy this Christmas makes me. Have you ever known such a gay and glorious festival as mine is this year?"

Much refreshed by the days with his beloved family, he returned to Hanover for some quiet creative work. There he put on paper his first piece of chamber music destined to see print, the trio in B (Op. 8), which had come to him during the recent Rhine journey. And there, in January, 1854, he met Schumann for the last time in normal surroundings, shortly before the latter attempted suicide by throwing himself into the Rhine, and had to be locked up as insane.

When he heard the news, Johannes immediately hastened to Düsseldorf to stand by poor Clara and do everything he could in the way of comfort and help. Several times he visited Schumann in the asylum, and gave the unfortunate man great pleasure with his *Variations on a Theme by Robert Schumann* (Op. 9) and the *Ballades* (Op. 10).

In 1855 there was some hope that he might be engaged to succeed Schumann as music director of Düsseldorf. But, fortunately for his creative work, he was disappointed in this, as in so many later expectations of official recognition.

That fall, in Düsseldorf, an incident occurred to Joachim which was to play a rôle of immense importance in Johannes' creative history. An able amateur 'cellist named Von Diest was unpleasantly surprised when the landlord told him that a man in another room, who was busy writing music, had complained of his 'cello playing. Diest controlled his temper and politely promised to spare the scribe as much as possible. Not long after, he had a visit of thanks from the unknown,

who overwhelmed him by turning out to be the famous
Joachim and inviting the gratified amateur to join him and
two other fiddlers in regular evenings of chamber music.

The meetings took place twice a week. Brahms was always
there. When he was not taking part at the piano, he sat in
a corner of the sofa with his hand over his eyes, deeply
moved. It was his first opportunity to hear the classical string
quartet repertory well played. At first he was profoundly
discouraged; then he was stirred to emulation. And, in the
next few years, the impulse given him by those evenings resulted in two sextets, two piano quartets, a 'cello sonata, and
the piano quintet. The enviable Diest naturally felt a thou-
sandfold repaid for his forbearance. It is doubtful if any
other amateur 'cellist has ever been lucky enough to help
inspire such a brilliant page of musical history.

In the autumn of 1855, Clara and Joachim kindly arranged
to replenish Johannes' lean purse by inviting him to be equal
sharer in a concert tour, although the two world-renowned
virtuosi could have made more money without him.

Robert Schumann died July 29, 1856; and Brahms took
on some of the overburdened Clara's pupils, one or two of
whom came from the tiny Court of Detmold. Through her
influence he secured a position there as director of concerts,
chorus leader, and pianist, during the last three months of
the years 1857, 1858, and 1859.[3] In Detmold he gave piano
lessons to Princess Friederike and many of the nobility;
gained valuable experience as a conductor, and orchestral
technic by writing his two Serenades (Op. 11 and 16); ac-

---

[3] Fuller-Maitland is wrong in stating (*Grove's Dictionary*, 3rd ed., Vol. I, p. 455)
that Brahms held this position "for four years (1854–1858)."

quired a permanent distaste for Court etiquette and ceremonial; felt his devastating passion for Clara cool off, and whenever he could, ran over to Göttingen to see his new love, Agathe von Siebold.

The D minor piano concerto (Op. 15) was finally completed in 1859, and performed by the composer at Hanover, Leipzig, and Hamburg. In the first two places, as he whimsically reported, "it enjoyed a brilliant and decided—failure." Indeed, the reactionary Leipzig Gewandhaus, disliking the piece as much as they disliked the performer, hissed him heartily. This was the worst disaster in his whole concert career.

But Johannes, good sportsman that he was, seemed to take the knock-down as a mere fillip to ambition, and picked himself up with the resolve to do better the next time.

I believe [he wrote to Joachim] it is the best thing that could have happened to me: such an occurrence makes one pull one's thoughts properly together, and increases one's courage.

Frankly, the Gewandhaus hardshells had a certain amount of right on their side; for at this time contemporary reports often complained that, in the matter of technical equipment, Brahms was not all a virtuoso should be. His playing was noble, musicianly, often inspired; but far too many notes fell under the piano. We in our day, however, may well rejoice at this deficiency; for if he had done more grinding at scales and finger-exercises he must necessarily have given us fewer quartets and symphonies.

If only to rebuke Leipzig, Johannes' native Hamburg

greeted the D minor concerto almost with cordiality. Its repetition there the following year, however, was received so icily that Brahms rose after the first movement and whispered to the conductor that he wished to stop; so that it needed all the agonized Herr Otten's persuasiveness to induce him to carry on. This shows that the Gewandhaus catastrophe had bitten deeper than was indicated by his brave letter to Joachim.

In May, 1860, at a Hamburg wedding, Brahms heard an excellent choir of ladies, and was so pleased that he asked them to try his *Ave Maria* (Op. 12) and other choruses. These went well, and he formed a regular feminine singing society, for which he wrote many pieces. Such composing and conducting was a valuable and welcome continuation of his work at Detmold. Naturally the girls adored him, and he prudently took good care not to let it be known that he was in love with the only foreigner among them; for his affections had already been transferred from Agathe of Göttingen to Bertha Porubszky, a charming little visitor from Vienna.

Sometimes the whole company went on musical picnics, Johannes the gayest of the lot. And remembering perhaps how in his favourite Good Book—

> Zaccheus, he
> Did climb a tree
> Our Lord to see,

the young conductor would compensate his lack of inches, and of podium, by scrambling up a linden and gaily swinging his baton from a lofty bough.

In 1860 the *Neue Zeitschrift für Musik,* then the official

organ of Liszt and his Weimar coterie, had the impudence to declare that there was in Germany scarcely a musician of importance who did not subscribe to the tenets of the "New Germans." This was more than Brahms and Joachim could silently endure. They foolishly leaped to the assault by drawing up a repudiation of the claim; and were in the process of collecting a large number of important signatures thereto when their guns were spiked by the premature publication of the "manifesto" in the Berlin *Echo,* signed merely by Brahms, Joachim, Grimm, and Scholz, of whom the two latter were barely known. To this day it has never been learned whether the fiasco was due to sharp practice on the part of the "New Germans," or to a mere indiscretion of the *Echo.* At any rate, the quartet of ineffectual protestants was thus made ridiculous, while Weimar rejoiced exceedingly. It is possible that, but for this incident, Wagner would never have libelled Brahms as outrageously as he proceeded to do.

The Rhenish Music Festival of May, 1860, found Johannes in Düsseldorf, where he made new friends. Then he went with some old ones: Joachim, Dietrich, and Stockhausen, the famous singer, to Bonn. In that old town, dear to musicians as the birthplace of Beethoven, he spent most of the summer working on his *"Spring"* sextet for strings (in B flat, Op. 18). The exuberant piece charmed the public as much as the concerto had repelled them, and brought the composer his first taste of popular success. In Bonn he met Fritz Simrock, an impassioned enthusiast for his music, who was destined to be his ideal friend and publisher for life.

For various reasons the decade from 1855 to 1865 was, taken as a whole, the only comparatively barren period in

Brahms' production. The chief trouble may have been the disturbingly late advent, about 1857, of his full physical maturity. (See p. 261.) But in this desert of years there was one highly fertile oasis of untrammelled creativeness, extending from the late summer of 1860 to the fall of 1861. This is known as the Hamm period because Brahms was then living at a village of that name on the bank of the Elbe below Hamburg.[4] There he finished the first two piano quartets (Op. 25 and 26) and the *Handel Variations* (Op. 24), besides working on *A German Requiem*, the *Magelonen Lieder*, and the C minor symphony.

Nor was the summer of 1862 unfruitful, though Brahms made much of what he called his "laziness." After foregathering in June with Grimm and Wüllner at the Rhenish Music Festival in Cologne, he went with Dietrich to Münster am Stein, where Clara had taken a house. There he made such progress with the F minor quintet (Op. 34) that its original setting, for strings only, was finished two months later.

Meanwhile, through the devotion of visiting artists like Clara, Joachim, and Stockhausen, his music was winning its way in Hamburg; and hopes were held out that when Grund, the venerable conductor of the Philharmonic Society, presently retired, Brahms might succeed to the position. It was also intimated that, during this delicate time of waiting, his chances might be bettered if he should win a reputation in some distant musical centre.

Johannes had always longed to know Vienna, which he

---

[4] Fuller-Maitland (in *Grove's Dictionary*, 3rd ed. Vol. I, p. 445) states that, from 1860 'until he finally took up his residence in Vienna in 1862," Brahms made Winterthur, Switzerland, his headquarters. The fact is that he never visited Winterthur until 1865, and then for only a brief stay, which he repeated the year following.

called "the musician's holy city." He wished to breathe the air once breathed by Haydn, Mozart, Beethoven, and Schubert. So, in 1862, without any special practical plan of campaign, he set forth on a journey equalled in momentousness for him only by the Rhine journey which had begun with Joachim to end in the home of the Schumanns.

Chapter VI

IN THE FOOTSTEPS OF BEETHOVEN

(1862–1874)

"FATHER," remarked Johannes with a sly twinkle, as he started for Vienna, "if things ever go badly with you, bear in mind that music is always the best consolation. Just read industriously in my old *Saul,* and there you will find what you need." Johann Jakob did not forget. But when he turned for spiritual comfort to the tattered score of Handel's oratorio, he was electrified to discover it liberally interleaved with banknotes. The incident is typical of the composer's lifelong generous devotion to his own family.

In hospitable Vienna Brahms soon met many of the leading musicians. Goldmark, Nawratil, Cornelius, Tausig, and even the forbidding Nottebohm made him feel at home. Julius Epstein, the celebrated pianist, lived at Schulerstrasse 8, in the very house where Mozart had written *The Marriage of Figaro,* and had prophesied greatness for the adolescent Beethoven. Here Epstein introduced the new arrival to Joseph Hellmesberger, whose string quartet then dominated Viennese chamber music. After the fiddler had finished reading the manuscript of Brahms' G minor piano quartet, he threw his violin upon the bed, hugged and kissed the composer, invited him to play the work at the next concert, and declared to the company: "This is the heir of Beethoven!"

Epstein self-effacingly insisted on the stranger's announcing a piano recital forthwith. And when Johannes proved too shy, the older virtuoso proceeded on his own responsibility to engage the hall. Within a few months Brahms had given two successful recitals, had had both Serenades performed by the leading orchestras, and had won the approbation of the public.

His thoughts, however, kept turning back wistfully to Hamburg and hoping that this foreign success was fortifying his position on the Elbe. Once more, however, true to tradition, a native prophet was to go unhonoured by the people at home. Even had he been a far better musical executant than a great composer ever has the time, strength, or interest to become, the snobbish Hamburgers would never have set up as their musical dictator a person whom they had recently known as a poor urchin clumping about the St. Pauli quarter in wooden clogs. So, in May, 1863, their enlightened choice for the conductorship of the Philharmonic Society fell upon the popular singer, Stockhausen. Of course the rejected candidate was shocked and wounded; while the loyal Joachim indignantly wrote to a Hamburg friend:

I should like to give the committee a moral beating (and a physical one as well!). . . . The history of art will not forget Johannes' mortification.

On the rebound from this slight, Brahms accepted the conductorship of the Singakademie of Vienna, a decrepit choral organization. After a brilliant first concert, the members, with a fickleness characteristically Viennese, revolted against their new leader's German thoroughness and his serious, "Bach-infested" programs. They neglected rehearsals and became their old, happy-go-lucky selves, and at the end of one season Brahms resigned in disgust.

In May, 1863, he had returned home to find his parents at odds with one another, and patched up a truce; but this postponed their final separation for only one year.

He spent the summer of 1864 in Hamburg, Göttingen, and near Clara in Baden-Baden, where he finished the G major sextet for strings (Op. 36), a tribute to Agathe von Siebold, whom he had wildly loved five years before—and brusquely jilted. As partial amends, he wove her name into the score, in the sort of musical anagram at which he was proficient.

News of his mother's death, on February 1, 1865, reached him in Vienna. Soon after the arrival of the telegram, a friend found him alone at the piano, weeping while he played Bach's *Goldberg Variations*. Without interrupting the healing flow of the music, the Master murmured: "That is like oil!" The touching incident recalls Beethoven's use of the music cure in times of special need.

Johannes hastened to the deathbed, then to his father's lodging, and by good words so far overcame Johann Jakob's resentment that the old man appeared at the funeral.

Nine months after the passing of his aged wife, Father Brahms sought to balance the striking disparity of age in his first union by an even more striking disparity in the opposite direction. He suddenly married a widow eighteen years younger than himself. The noble kindness and essential goodness of Johannes is charmingly shown in his letter to Johann Jakob after learning the somewhat startling news, and in his warm-hearted lifelong generosity and amiability to the stepmother Frau Caroline, and her crippled son Fritz Schnack.

The F minor quintet, on which he had worked so long, proved unsuitable for string quartet with an extra 'cello. It was metamorphosed, first into a two-piano sonata, and finally into its present popular form for piano and strings, although to this day it shows souvenir-vestiges of its arduous evolution. As opus 34 it was published in 1865, and dedicated to Princess Anna of Hesse, who showed her appreciation with a truly royal gift—the original manuscript score of Mozart's G minor symphony.

The same year he composed the trio for French horn, violin, and piano (Op. 40). Kalbeck feels that this was a tribute to his mother, because, as a boy, Johannes had played all three of these instruments; because the *finale* recalls a folk-tune which he had learned at his mother's knee; and because there is a dirge-like quality in the *Adagio mesto*.

The E minor 'cello sonata (Op. 38) was finished soon after, and dedicated to Gänsbacher, the Viennese friend who had not only brought about the invitation to conduct the Singakademie, but also secured him a fabulous bargain— the manuscript of Schubert's *Wanderer* for only 32 florins. Originally there were four movements in opus 38; but Brahms cut out the *Adagio* and obstinately refused to let the tantalized Gänsbacher, or anyone else, lay eyes on it. As we shall see, there is reason to believe that this movement was afterwards used in the second 'cello sonata.

Between journeys Brahms spent the winter of 1865–1866 in Hamburg and Karlsruhe, and part of the spring in Winterthur, Switzerland, chiefly at work on *A German Requiem*.

He had already formed an intimacy with the Swiss poet, Josef Viktor Widmann of Berne, who was to be his companion on gay journeys in Italy, and the most delightful of all commentators on his character.[1] And now in Zurich he met another spacious personality in the famous surgeon and musical amateur, Dr. Theodor Billroth, destined to be one of his chief cronies and most creative appreciators.

With Brahms' rising celebrity there began, in the fall of 1866, that long series of concert tours—often with famous colleagues—which was to add largely to his income and gradually to occupy him less as pianist and more as conductor of his own works.

Late in 1866 Brahms returned to Vienna and chose it as his permanent home. This act marked the end of one creative period and the beginning of another. For *A German Requiem* (Op. 45), on which he had been toiling for nine years, was finished, except the fifth number, which he was to write in 1868 as a memorial to his mother. He started this, his most successful choral work as a monument to his benefactor, Schumann.

Its first performance was, in more than one sense, a partial affair. In Vienna, December 1, 1867, the first three movements were brought out by Herbeck, the brilliant but careless conductor who earned the gratitude of music-lovers by bringing Anton Bruckner to Vienna and making public Schubert's *"Unfinished"* symphony, but who consistently acted as Brahms' evil genius. The performance suffered from superficiality and hasty preparation. A far too muscular kettledrummer was allowed to make nonsense of the organ-

[1] See *Johannes Brahms in Erinnerungen*, 1898.

point fugue at the close of Part III. The audience hissed, and the composer's prestige suffered a temporary setback.

On Good Friday, 1868, however, the injustice was partly made good by Bremen with an excellent performance of the six then completed numbers, under Reinthaler in the cathedral, where, at the last moment, Clara surprised and overjoyed Brahms by appearing. The *Requiem's* notable success on this occasion forced its repetition the same month. And its popularity spread so fast that the following year, 1869, it was given no fewer than twenty-one times in Central Europe. But it was forced to wait until 1871 for the rehabilitation of a respectable performance in Vienna.

In a material way, 1869 was an important year for Brahms. The *Requiem* gained a firm place in the choral repertory; foreign countries began to warm towards his chamber music; the *Hungarian Dances* were winning the world; while royalties and concert fees were piling up in the bank to such an extent that the Master showed signs of becoming a small capitalist.

The *Requiem* ushered in a period of vocal writing. This mighty work was followed by a striking foil, the charming, wholly Viennese *Liebeslieder,* waltzes for piano, four hands, and mixed quartet of singers (Op. 52); and by *Rinaldo,* a cantata for tenor solo, men's chorus and orchestra (Op. 50) which, in spite of a few fine passages, is one of Brahms' weakest works.

In refreshing contrast to this came two of his most inspired vocal pieces: the *Rhapsody* for alto, men's chorus and orchestra (Op. 53), which was helped to success by Frau Joachim's ideally suited voice; and the *Schicksalslied* for chorus and orchestra (Op. 54).

Brahms spent the early summer of 1870 with Franz Wüllner in Munich, where he heard much of Wagner's music with deep interest. The outbreak of the Franco-Prussian War stimulated his patriotism to the point where he resolved to enlist as a volunteer as soon as he heard of a decisive German reverse. "Thank God," he afterwards exclaimed, "that things turned out otherwise!"

His actual contribution to the cause was the *Triumphlied* (Op. 55), a noisy and somewhat Handelian anthem, which was enthusiastically seized upon by Germany as a heaven-sent vehicle for celebrating her victory of 1870. It is now definitely dated.

During the hot months of 1871 he worked in Baden-Baden and began his friendship with Hans von Bülow, who was later to abjure the Wagner-Liszt camp and to become his chief propagandist. Johann Jakob Brahms died in 1872 of cancer of the liver—the disease which was, a quarter of a century after, to prove fatal to his son.

From 1872 to 1875 Brahms conducted that Viennese organization, the chorus of the Gesellschaft der Musikfreunde, whose superiority in 1864 had been the undoing of his early venture as leader of the Singakademie. After three years, however, he resigned under the pressure of intrigues conducted by the same Herbeck who had beaten him a decade before, and who now coveted his own former position.

As a newcomer in Vienna, Brahms had, like Beethoven at the corresponding point in his career, been prized more for his playing than for his writing. But now the public changed its tune and proclaimed that Brahms was "a good composer,

an indifferent conductor, and a bad pianist." Though the
audience, orchestra, and light-hearted, hit-or-miss ladies and
gentlemen of the chorus suffered grievously under their me-
ticulous German leader's thoroughness and enthusiasm for
solid works by such Protestant—and therefore alien—masters
as Bach and Handel, Viennese musical standards profited no-
ticeably through their martyrdom.

Early in 1872 Brahms moved into the apartment at Karlsgasse 4 which was to be his home as long as he lived. In 1873,
at Tutzing near Munich, the orchestral *Variations on a
Theme of Joseph Haydn* (Op. 56a) were finished, together
with the first two string quartets (Op. 51). These variations
first showed their composer as a master of the art of orchestration and leaped into sudden popularity. The fact that
the Gewandhaus audience in Leipzig, which in 1859 had
administered the worst rebuff of his career, now began to
warm to his music showed him how far he had come along
the road to recognition.

Chapter VII

THE GOAL

(1874–1897)

In 1874 Brahms finished that old project, the C minor piano quartet (Op. 60) which he had begun in the strenuous Werther-days of 1855, under the stimulus of his mad young passion for Clara. To the detriment of his creative work, a large part of the next few years was consumed by concert tours in Holland, Germany, Switzerland, and Hungary.

Early in 1876, Cambridge University offered him the degree of Doctor of Music on condition that he come in person to receive it. Brahms balked at the journey. In 1892 the offer was renewed, but again the Master declined it. Writing to Henschel, he based his refusal on his "great distaste for concerts and other disturbances." But Mrs. Frederick Partington of New York tells me that he once confessed the real reason to her: he could not overcome his terror of the ocean. He had ventured on it once only, in a skiff, and the experience had been enough to last him all his days. The truth of this confession is confirmed by an incident that happened in Genoa seventeen years later. With three friends he had arranged to sail for Sicily; but on the gangplank he turned back and insisted instead on the long and tiresome railway trip to Reggio, which is in sight of Messina.

The summer of 1876 he spent in Rügen with Henschel. There he finished the C minor symphony, the masterpiece on which he had, at intervals, been toiling for the past twenty-two years. This composition, whose present unfailing popularity and hypnotic quality tempt every débutant conductor, was slow to make its way and, as it eventually did, to crown Brahms as the chief symphonist after Beethoven.

Its initial failure lent added seductiveness to the invitation, received by the composer in the fall of 1876, to become the director of music in Düsseldorf—the city where, a generation before, Robert Schumann, the incumbent of that very position, had launched him on a career, and Clara had kindled his first great passion. In some ways the offer attracted him so much that six months of correspondence and some vigorous intriguing by opponents were required to bring about his eventual refusal.

One of the happiest and most fruitful periods of Brahms' life fell in the three years, 1877–1879, whose summers he spent at Pörtschach on the Wörthersee, the largest and loveliest of south Austrian lakes. There he composed the Second symphony (in D, Op. 73), the violin sonata (in G, Op. 78), and the violin concerto (Op. 77), written with Joachim in mind. All of this music seems saturated with the mellow, smiling charm of that idyllic countryside. As Brahms himself, in a curiously mixed metaphor, phrased it to Hanslick: "The Wörthersee is virgin soil. The air is so full of flying melodies that one must take good care not to tread on them."

The Second symphony, brighter and easier to understand than the First, naturally found a more cordial reception from the start. But the originality of the violin concerto, both in the novel technic required of the solo instrument, and in its unheard-of fusion with the orchestra, for years gave pause, not alone to the listeners, but to the virtuosi as well, who complained that the thing was a concerto "not for, but against, the violin."

When invited, in 1878, to the half-century celebration of the founding of the Hamburg Philharmonic Society, which had twice ignored him in choosing conductors, Brahms refused, bitterly remarking that he felt as if bidden expressly to rejoice over his own reverses. But at the last moment the call of the home town was too strong, and the civic jubilee turned into something very like a jubilee for Hamburg's greatest son.

This spring brought the fulfilment of an old longing. Under the guidance of Billroth, the Master first saw Italy. The land far surpassed even his rosiest dreams. But Billroth's ripe knowledge and authority as a cicerone were somewhat galling to this headstrong man, who had so little of the second violinist in his nature that, like Theodore Roosevelt, he might at a wedding have wished to be the bride, and at a funeral, the corpse. On all future trips with Widmann and other friends, it was Brahms himself who chose the itinerary and set the tempo.

The year 1880 first took him to Ischl in the Salzkammergut, whither he was to return for nine summers; for the lion-hunters had finally succeeded in ruining for him his beloved Pörtschach.

Through the enthusiasm of Bülow, director of music at Meiningen, Brahms established amicable relations in 1881 with the Duke and his court—though the warmth of the Master's cordiality has been exaggerated. In editing for publication Brahms' correspondence with Schubring, Kalbeck, for example, omitted various harsh expressions occurring in the original letters which show that the composer was sometimes far from feeling the affection and admiration for the Duke and his circle attributed to him by the biographers.[1] There is no doubt, however, that, while in the little Duchy Bülow performed an invaluable function as propagandist in showing the world how his friend's music could sound when played by a first-rate orchestra and a first-rate pianist—and that Brahms appreciated this service.

The warm months of 1881 were devoted, in Pressbaum near Vienna, to finishing the second piano concerto (B flat, Op. 83), and setting Schiller's *Nänie* for chorus and orchestra (Op. 82). In this place he surprised his friends by growing the famous beard. The reason he gave was that "with a smooth chin one is taken for either an actor or a priest." But the true reason will be suggested in a later chapter.[2] Here in Pressbaum, when the long-smouldering difficulties between Amalie Joachim and her morbidly jealous husband burst into open warfare and divorce, Johannes took Amalie's part so vigorously as to estrange "Jussuf" for years to come.

Early in 1882 Bülow, who was now the musical dictator of Germany, took Leipzig by storm with the heavy artillery of Brahms' music, and informed the composer that he was ready to lay the keys [3] 𝄢 𝄞 of the reactionary stronghold at his feet.

The harvest of the second Ischl summer, 1882, was the

[1] See p. 27.
[2] See p. 262.
[3] In German, clefs are known as *Schlüssel*, or keys, while musical keys are called *Tonarten*.

Reményi and Brahms, 1853   Brahms and Joachim, 1867

Bülow and Brahms. 1889

Fritz Simrock   Allgeyer, Brahms and Levi
about 1874

BRAHMS AND HIS FRIENDS

Allgeyer stoops to avoid dwarfing the tiny Brahms.

string quintet in F (Op. 88), the C major trio (Op. 87), and a setting of the *Gesang der Parzen* from Goethe's *Iphigenia in Tauris*, for chorus and orchestra (Op. 89).

Happy composers have no history. The outer events of Brahms' life now resolved themselves largely into winter concert tours and creative summer seclusion, with an occasional foray into Italy for recreation. But his inner life grew all the more colourful and dramatically exciting. The Third symphony (in F, Op. 90) was finished, 1883, in Wiesbaden; the Fourth (E minor, Op. 98), in Mürzzuschlag, 1884–1885; and Bülow soon won Europe for them, from the North Sea to the Alps.

During a decade, now, the Master had been a famous and successful man, courted by much of the Western world. He had met with merely enough opposition from enemies like the jealous Wagner and the embittered Wolf to lend piquancy to the struggle. He was constantly refusing offers from publishers and managers which, but for his unyielding artistic rectitude and the unique severity of his self-criticism, would have brought him substantial wealth.

Thun, Switzerland, where he spent the three summers of 1886–1888, inspired one of his most fertile creative periods. "I am entirely happy that I have come here," he wrote on arrival. And soon a flood of music poured out of the Hofstetten house under the huge Wellingtonia tree by the river: the last two violin sonatas (in A, Op. 100, and D minor, Op. 108), the last and perhaps the best of the trios (C minor, Op. 101), the second 'cello sonata (in F, Op. 99), the *Gypsy Songs* (Op. 103), and the Double concerto (Op. 102).

The last-named work was to regain for him the friendship

of Joachim. He began a second double concerto as well, feeling that now he had his hand in and could turn out a better one. But when opus 102 was coolly received and ostentatiously neglected, he dropped the plan, remarking that there was no need for a second as long as nobody wished to play the first.

The year 1887 brought the death of old Fräulein Vogl, his Viennese housekeeper at Karlsgasse 4, and the installation of Frau Dr. Celestina Truxa, to whom Part III of this book owes so much. Until his death she gave him intelligent and devoted care, endearing herself by an apparent coldness and taciturnity in agreeable contrast to the garrulous gush of the female lion-hunters against whom he waged a thirty years' war.

Two outstanding honours came in 1889. The Austrian Emperor awarded him the cross of a Commander of the Leopold Order, a distinction reserved for persons of the most extraordinary achievement and merit. And his native Hamburg tardily conferred upon him the freedom of the city, which had, in recent years, fallen to the lot of only Moltke and Bismarck.

Deeply touched by this attention, Brahms dedicated to the burgomaster of Hamburg an eight-part chorus, the *Fest- und Gedenksprüche* (Op. 109). The music was performed with immense enthusiasm at the festival given by Hamburg in honour of her great son. But surely the latter would neither have joined in the festivities nor dedicated the piece as he did, if he had known that this honour had come to him only through the most determined efforts of Bülow and the burgomaster. For the conventional Hamburgers still remembered the composer as the tow-headed lad who had played in the sailors' resorts of the red-light district, and still echoed the doubts which Fritz Becker had expressed in 1853 to Johann Jakob about Hannes' claims to eminence.

From 1889 until the end, Brahms was true to Ischl in the summer. One of his earliest acts there was to revise the B major trio (Op. 8), that youthful work whose world *première* in New York, on November 27, 1855, won for America the proud distinction of being the first country to hear Brahms' chamber music performed in public.

Simultaneously with this revision, the string quintet in G (Op. 111) was written, to complicate the lives of unfortunate 'cellists with its difficulties, and to recall to fortunate listeners Vienna and its alluring Prater.

Inspired by the playing of a mighty clarinettist, as Mozart and Weber had been before him, he wrote for the virtuoso Richard Mühlfeld of Meiningen the clarinet trio (Op. 114) and sonatas (Op. 120), and the magnificent clarinet quintet (Op. 115) which, with the *Four Serious Songs* (Op. 121) and the last piano pieces (Op. 116–119), constituted his swan-song.

He had quarrelled in 1891 with his growingly difficult old friend Clara Schumann, over the publication of the original version of her husband's D minor symphony, which was a particular favourite of Brahms'; but in the Christmas season of the following year they were reconciled.

The fall of 1895 brought the Master two honours which he thoroughly enjoyed: a three days' festival at Meiningen, where the best living musicians met to play, sing, and delight in "the three B's." There the music of Brahms proved no anticlimax, even after the chef-d'œuvres of Bach and Beethoven. Neither of the latter had, during his lifetime, been so whole-heartedly honoured as Brahms was by his contemporaries at Meiningen. And with a full heart the Master went to another festival in Zurich, where the new concert hall was opened by a performance of the *Triumphlied*. This work shared the program with Beethoven's Ninth symphony; while, from among the portraits of musical immortals on the ceiling, a painted Brahms looked down upon its gratified original.

Clara Schumann died on May 20, 1896. The telegram was long in finding Brahms at Ischl. En route to Frankfort, he missed a train connexion, and read in the papers that the interment was to be in Bonn. There he arrived after an exhausting and irritating journey, barely in time for the ceremony, during which he caught a severe cold.

Before many weeks he was stricken with jaundice, and on April 3, 1897, died of cancer.[4] His funeral was attended by such men as Nikisch, Weingartner, Hellmesberger, Henschel, Mühlfeld, Busoni, Goldmark, and Dvořák. Though he was gloriously buried in the Zentralfriedhof, near the tombs of Mozart, Beethoven, and Schubert, it was long before the world knew the full extent of its loss and saw Johannes Brahms as a master of form co-equal with his mighty neighbours in death.

[4] See p. 292, and Kalbeck IV, ii, 516.

PART III

ASPECTS OF THE UNKNOWN BRAHMS

Chapter VIII

POET AND PEASANT

IN ENJOYING that flower of civilization and culture, the music of Brahms, one is startled to realize the sort of earth from which it grew.

Brahms' paternal ancestors were the rough folk who lived close to the soil of the Dithmarsh, a low region of fen and moor at the mouth of the Elbe. His great-grandfather Peter, the wheelwright of Brunsbüttel, married Sophie Uhl and moved to Heide. To read of them and their son Johann, the country innkeeper of Wöhrden, and of the simple life led by these people, transports one to the atmosphere of the land of Jörn Uhl, Otto Babendieck, and the other memorable characters created by Gustav Frenssen, the Dithmarsh novelist of our day.

Never for a moment was Brahms ashamed of these good people. In 1884, when he had long been an affluent celebrity, he registered with the authorities of Mürzzuschlag as "itinerant musician." This nonsense held in solution as much sense as most of his flippant utterances. It was in the nature of a salute to his stout-hearted sire, Johann Jakob Brahms, and conjured up a vision of that small-town lad setting out from his disapproving birthplace, Heide, double-bass on back, to become a strolling scraper in the dives and narrow courtyards of Hamburg.

Before he was ten, Johannes Jr. suffered many of the hardships of itinerancy. Often he was awakened to pound the piano all night in the lowest sort of sailors' dance-halls. Later in life he reacted against this irregular existence very much as the typical small-town or country person usually reacts against bohemia-with-a-small-b. His unconscious mind harked back of his father's Eichendorffianly adventurous generation, to the stand-patness of his more remote and solid rural ancestors.

This stand-patness is neatly represented in Brahms' anxiety for an official position as conductor or director, long after reaching a point where he had not the slightest need of the salary, and even recognized that such duties must injure his creative work. For a safe, assured position of authority is, to the peasant's type of mind, the loftiest thing in the world; whereas the unattached man, the bohemian, connotes that most contemptible of creatures, the vagabond who is likely to come begging for a cup of his valuable coffee, or even to make off with his chickens. In the country, every unfettered artist is frowned upon as a frivolous ne'er-do-weel.[1]

"Remarkable!" wrote Max Bruch to Brahms, on June 15, 1870. "You long to escape from freedom into restraint, and I, from restraint into freedom." This latter escape, however, was what Brahms also began to long for whenever he felt the prison walls of official duties closing around him. No formal recognition of this truth, though, could permanently stifle the irrational instinct with which he was born.

---

[1] As here used, the word "peasant" is not meant to imply that Brahms or his immediate forebears had actually cultivated the earth, but merely that this son of a very small-town man had inherited certain peasant traits—throw-backs to more remote ancestors who *had* drawn their living from the soil.

When, at the dinner given by the city of Hamburg in his honour, the mature Brahms complained that he was a "vagabond" because his native town had not made him a conductor, and intoned a hymn of hate against those who had balked his possible marriage (meaning those who had offered him no official position), there was in evidence, not the logical brain that had helped create the *Handel Variations* and the E minor symphony, but the deep-seated instinct of one of the most conservative of European stocks. The sober fact is that at any moment, from his twenty-fourth year on, Johannes might have taken a wife with far more financial confidence than had been his father's at marriage. But the rustic feels it immoral to wed when his income is less secure and normal than it might be. Happily for the composer's work and his peace of mind, this instinct joined with others to keep him single; for, as we shall see, the man was not well suited for married life.

Two barely reconcilable characters struggled for ever within him. They are well described in the title of the best known work of Von Suppé, whose proudest distinction it is to have his tomb near that of Brahms—the *Poet and Peasant*. In this duality our hero was consistently loyal to his heritage; for the Dithmarsher is one of the most poetic and musical of all German peasants.[2]

Most of Brahms' music is as healthy, strong, unpretentious, and vitally near the soil as the folk-tunes which inspired so much of it, or as the composer's country ancestors, and their namesake, the broom-plant. And it is no mere coincidence

---

[2] According to Neocorus; quoted in H. Reimann: *Johannes Brahms*, 1900, p. 106, n. 3.

that these should be all open-air products. The Master was passionately fond of the out-of-doors. In his cryptic speech, "to walk" meant "to compose."

His distrust of certain foreign nations had a genuine admixture of rural conservatism. England and the English he disliked as much as Beethoven had loved them. And he never wearied of urging his publisher to bring out the songs without English words. "I am indifferent," he would exclaim, "to everything connected with England!"

Towards America he was no better disposed. I dined once in Vienna, on the terrace of the Kursalon, with an old journalist, Dr. Sigmund Münz, who informed me that he and Brahms used to take their after-dinner coffee just inside that very building. Somebody had scribbled a telephone number on the wall above the table they always used. It was 1492. And Brahms used to make this number a text for sarcastic remarks about the officiousness of Christopher Columbus.

He fancied the French even less. Perhaps he had assimilated with his mother's milk the local hatred caused by their brutal military occupation of Hamburg, before his birth. Reciprocally French music-lovers for a long time disliked his music as heartily as he disliked their nation.

There was so much of the northern farmer in this man that even in his hours of play he could not help being industrious and thorough. Widmann, the poet, his favourite companion on Italian journeys, used to come home exhausted from trying to keep pace with the conscientious Master, who insisted on making the most of each moment. Before setting out, Brahms would concoct elaborate plans for a lazy trip with abundant *dolce far niente*—*"gründlich flüchtig"* (care-lessly thorough) was his characteristic slogan. But the Dithmarsher in him always made the journey strenuous. When Widmann would timidly suggest a slight *ritardando*, the other would cuttingly inquire if he imagined that they were travelling for their pleasure in a land which offered such an infinity of the new and the worthwhile at every step.

In the matter of clothes Brahms was true to the people from whom he sprang. His glass of fashion was sadly chipped and cracked. His hat would have been a windfall for a comedian playing the country cousin. Highly proletarian were his favourite cuffless flannel shirts and the frequent absence of collar and tie, more or less masked by his splendid beard.

Dr. Otto Julius Bauer, the Viennese wit who feared neither composer nor devil, often used to tease him about these eccentricities of dress. After a performance in Vienna of the E minor symphony, he sent Brahms a poem closing with these lines:

> *Vor meiner Seele wuchs das Werk*
> *Zu seiner klassischen Grossheit;*
> *In jedem Satz der Geist von Brahms*
> *Und keine einzige Bosheit!*

> *Ich sende Ihnen dies Gedicht*
> *Mit dankbar ergebenen Grüssen;*
> *Weh mir, dass ich ein Laie bin,*
> *Ich möchte Sie ganz geniessen.*

Freely translated:

> Before my soul the classic grew,
> Large as a royal palace;
> On every page the soul of Brahms,
> And never a touch of malice!
>
> I send this thankful poem to you
> With my devotion—meetly.
> Alas that I'm too sad a dub
> To "get" you quite completely!

This pleased Brahms so well that he called in person on Dr. Bauer and presented him with a photograph which he had caused Frau Maria Fellinger to take of him in gala attire —perhaps for this special purpose.

On the margin he had drawn arrows pointing to his "shot" cuffs, his cravat, and his clean white collar, to ensure visibility for which he had taken care to push his great beard aside. On the reverse of the picture he had scrawled:

> *Best thanks for your jolly greeting! And I express these thanks herewith—so that you may view with satisfaction what you have often missed.*[3]

He did not seem to mind a poet like Bauer's being well dressed; but he drew the line at elegance in his fellow composers. "Moszkowski once came to Ischl," said Dr. Bauer, "and begged me to present him to Brahms, who looked him over, registered strong surprise, and blurted out: 'Ach, I didn't know that you were such a complete dandy!' Without a

---

[3] *I.e.*, cuffs, cravat, and collar.

MARIA FELLINGER

TAKEN AT VIENNA, OCTOBER 6TH, 1895

The arrows were drawn by Brahms himself to direct Dr. Bauer's attention to the exceptionally elegant details of his costume. Never before reproduced with these additions.

Courtesy of Dr. Otto Julius Bauer
© 1932, by Robert Haven Schauffler

word, the furious Moszkowski turned on his heel and strode away."

Herr Emil Hess, Court pianist of the Duke of Cumberland at Gmunden, remembers how the Duke once invited Brahms over from Ischl for a visit. Aggravated by a characteristic love of contradiction, the Master's democratic instincts led him to indulge in the pretext that he could not come because he had no dress coat. Through a lady-in-waiting, the Duke wrote back that it was Brahms they wanted, not his clothes, and to come in whatever he had on.

This was taken *au pied de la lettre,* and the celebrity actually appeared in a flannel shirt without a necktie, and in the faded alpaca coat which is now in the Gmunden Museum. Miss Bugbird, an English lady who was then staying at the castle, has told me how, before Brahms' next visit there, "we were afraid he would come again in that awful collarless shirt. So I hurried into town and bought a wide selection of white collars and a bow tie which I thought suitable for an artist. Sure enough! Brahms turned up in his Jaeger shirt. We finally cajoled him into putting on a turn-down white collar and the tie. But he wasn't very amiable at the Duke's.

"When it was all over, and I was seeing him off at the station, he suddenly longed for a glass of beer. I recall with what boyish gusto he tore the nice white tablecloth from the little restaurant table and cast it on the ground, then ripped off the collar and tie with a huge snort of relief and hurled them after the tablecloth."

There were numerous other occasions when he felt that he must submit to the tyranny of a cravat. And his struggles with the thing were sometimes pitiable to behold. Finally

Frau Maria Fellinger had compassion, and gave him a quantity of made-up ties, in which he came to take a childish pleasure.

An old Viennese lady tells me that she was once in a group with Brahms when the talk turned to handsome stockings. With a mischievous smile, the Master said: "See how elegant mine are." And, raising his trouser leg the fraction of an inch he revealed—his bare ankle.[4]

Brahms' outer garments were informed with his homespun personality. Everyone who inspects those clothes of his in the Gmunden Museum notices their homely, rural quality. His industry and Spartan economy are emphasized by the patches and mends on the right elbow of the alpaca coat, dressed in which he created so much beauty. Here and there it is faded from dark grey almost to light yellow. The shoulders are so small and narrow that Widmann's reference to his "herculean shoulders" must have been poetic exaggeration—or else the Master's very bones must have shrunk extraordinarily during his last illness. But the waistband bears witness that he was what the garment industry so elegantly terms "full-fashioned." The black trousers have an enormous brown patch on the seat and a black patch in front.

His friends had grievous difficulty in getting him ever to order a new suit or, once it was ordered, to have a fitting, or to have the fitting fit. Obstinately he wore the same clothes

---

[4] The same sort of story was once reported to me about another great Poet and Peasant. Old Mrs. Smith of South Orange, N. J., who had kept a small shop in Washington during the Civil War, is speaking. "Abraham Lincoln came in one day asking for socks. I said: 'What colour?' 'Colour? Why, I don't know, I'm sure.' (You see, he didn't bother much 'bout them things.) Finally he stooped down and took hold of the end of his pants. 'Why, I guess this colour is good enough for me.' He pulled it up. I looked for the sock—and saw—his bare skin."

year after year, and could be extremely uncompromising with those who dared criticize his wardrobe. Woe to any who had been rash enough to imitate Beethoven's kind friends and substitute new clothes for old while he slept!

His method of packing for a journey was to pile all his clothes upon a table and then tilt it so that everything spilled helter-skelter into an open trunk—a materialistic variation of Schumann's mystical experiments in table-tipping, highly Brahmsian in its simple originality. This makes it clear why, in his photographs, the coats fit so lamentably and look as though they had never seen an iron.

Like the trousers of a true countryman, his own were always hitched up to ankle height. Mrs. Frederick Partington testifies that, in the summer of 1888, "they were made of gingham, and curled up at the bottom, away from his large feet." When the tailor, secretly egged on by Brahmins, was bold enough to make them the proper length in defiance of orders, Brahms attacked the Gordian pants with his desk shears and simply cut them to ankle length.

Sometimes he sheared and slashed without overmuch regard for the laws of symmetry. Mr. Oscar Ullmann, an American who spent his summers in Ischl as a lad, tells me that "while both Brahmsian pants legs were shy of the ground, one was decidedly shyer than the other. We urchins once mailed him a piece of cloth with directions for piecing out the shorter leg."

Perhaps if these boys had realized how helpless and hopeless their victim was in the matter of clothes, they would have relented. Frau Hermine Schwarz heard him tell of going home and asking his mother: "What's wrong with my suit?

Everyone at the party looked at me so queerly!" "Oh, Johannes," she cried in despair, "why, see, you've gone and put on the coat from which I cut off all the buttons!"

Sir George Henschel recalls that one day Brahms tore from his shirt the button which fastened the collar. "He was sadly embarrassed, so I helped him out. We went to my room. I took my sewing kit and sewed the button on, which awakened memories of his youth: 'Yes, as I first set out from home on my adventures, Mother packed a sewing kit in my bag, and showed me how it should be used. But I still recall quite well that when my pants tore I stuck them together with sealing wax. The only trouble was, they didn't hold very long. . . .' "

His poor tailor never grew rich on this customer! While the D major symphony was assuming shape, Brahms jocosely mentioned his suit in a letter to Simrock: "I am wearing the 58 marks upon my body, which makes me conspicuous for my elegance." Another remark the same year to Reinthaler shows a realization of the rustic quality of his apparel: "I am not so poor and not so dirty as my coat looks. . . . If you like, you may hit me for a loan."

How the man did hate to dress up! Once, in order to appear with great ceremony before the Duke of Meiningen at the Villa Carlotta, he ordered from a little tailor in Cadenabbia a black *Joppe* [5] of a special Brahmsian cut, asserting, with his own singular and autocratic ideas of what fashion should be, that this coat was every whit as elegant as a "smoking."

At the Duke's instance he sent Geheimrat Schnitzler an

[5] A light, short, informal coat.

invitation, pointing out with gusto that his host expressly forbade him to wear a dress coat and a high hat, and added this coda: "As for me, if you should call on me in a dress coat, it would cost you 20 lire."

He once offered as an excuse for not attending a music festival at Düsseldorf, that someone had packed the wrong waistcoat in his bag, and that it was simpler to cancel the journey than to buy another en route. During a cold snap he showed a friend his hands, which were chapped, cracked, and painful, remarking that he had mislaid his gloves and could not make up his mind to get another pair.

On one historic occasion his trousers temporarily overcame their notorious ground-shyness. Joachim was introducing Brahms' new violin concerto to the crabbèd audience of Leipzig, with the composer wielding the baton. Brahms unfortunately had not had time to finish his toilet. He emerged in grey street trousers. And all too soon it became evident that he had forgotten to fasten the braces, so that more and more shirt was continually revealed between upper and nether garments. The audience shuddered to think what might have happened if the concerto had been one movement longer. As it was, the piece made but an indifferent impression upon the Leipzigers. Their attention had wandered elsewhere.

On the occasion of Brahms' first appearance in the tiny Court of Detmold, the wife of the Minister, who was doing the honours, discovered to her consternation that the young musician's clothes would not pass muster. Finally Concertmaster Bargheer saved the situation by lending him a proper suit, and completed the hasty toilet by tying "a masterly white bow." It was not long, however, before the newcomer fell from grace by appearing at Court one evening without any necktie at all.

A third of a century later, when the Emperor of Austria decorated him with the Order of Leopold, he had learned little more about Court dress than he knew at Detmold. Kalbeck describes what pains it cost the Prince of Reuss to convince him that a ceremonial visit of thanks was inescapable. Early that morning, fearing that he might be held up during the day by visitors, Brahms dressed in evening clothes. He wanted to hang the decoration in his buttonhole, to spare the extravagant new coat, and would allow his housekeeper to sew it on according to prescribed regulations—only after she had rushed into town and brought back irrefragable documentary proof of the necessity for thread. Even so, he stipulated that, after the audience, he must be able to tear the thing off easily.

He proposed to proceed to the palace barehanded, insisting that the Kaiser would not look at his hands. But at length he compromised on an old pair of concert gloves, long past their virgin whiteness, and put on the left one. He would have gone on foot. But when it was pointed out that he really should not enter the audience chamber with muddy boots, he resigned himself to the sort of one-horse shay which the Viennese call a *"Komfortabel."*

Just what protection he would have proposed if it had rained or snowed on this gala day is worth a moment's speculation; for, during stormy weather, in both town and country, he often wore a large old greyish-brown plaid shawl, fastened in front by a gigantic safety-pin—an eye-filling phenomenon for the astonished passer-by.

His serene unconsciousness of the figure he cut was little short of sublime. Once, in leaving a distinguished assembly of musicians and writers, he absent-mindedly took a too lengthy overcoat belonging to Ludwig Schneegans, who then reluctantly added to the gaiety of Vienna by departing in Brahms' far too short and shabby one.

There was a touch of peasant uncouthness about Brahms' squat torso, about his vigorous and somewhat ungainly walk —the way he slightly toed in with his right foot—and about the startling texture of his hands which, as the late Frau Gottinger-Wilt assured me, "were always very rough—hard and rough as files"—owing perhaps to economy in gloves. Mrs. Frederick Partington found something countrified, as well, in the way he usually crouched at the piano and shrugged his shoulders on leaving it. "When I met him in 1888," she recalled, "he had a pleasant, ruddy, outdoor complexion. He was so burly and florid that he looked more like a farmer than like a man who had spent his days in writing music."

If one concentrated, however, on the admirable features: the superb brow, the great blue eyes, the aristocratic modelling of the nose, the sensitive yet virile mouth—one almost saw a kind of noble radiance about him. There the poet began—the tone-poet of genius.

The Italians, who as a race are highly sensitive to visual impressions, often recognized at sight the human superiority of this queerly dressed little figure. Widmann tells how, more than once, when the Master had fallen asleep in a corner of the railway carriage, he overheard his fellow travellers confiding to one another in whispers that yonder must be *"un uomo di genio,"* a man of genius.

After such evidence one is not surprised to learn that his head was reproduced to represent "the typical Caucasian" in Baenitz's *Lehrbuch der Geographie.* Brahms felt highly flattered. But there was no need! Studying a good portrait of him, one feels how grossly this claim of typicality flatters, not the composer but—the so-called "Caucasian race."

In his boyhood, he had to put up with uncomfortable and primitive housing conditions. A member of the Viennese Philharmonic Orchestra who once made a pilgrimage to the Master's birth-house asked how on earth the elder Brahms had managed to squeeze his double-bass up those exclusive stairs; for such was their narrowness that even coffins had to be lowered from the windows.

With the years Johannes' demands increased a little. In 1854 he wrote to Clara Schumann from Hamburg: "I can no longer live with three others in two small rooms." His last Vienna apartment meant comparative luxury to him; for he had moved there from a room which could not be heated at all. Even in Karlsgasse 4, however, the standard of comfort was curiously low. It had no bathroom and was hard to heat. The living quarters could be reached only through the bed-chamber. The furniture was ugly and uncomfortable; but he resolutely frustrated the housekeeper's efforts to replace it with anything better.

That this was the sort of simplicity of which the rustic in him heartily approved is shown by his letter to Clara about Menzel, the painter. "It gives me special pleasure that he is the only one of our famous men who lives in the most modest and frugal way. His rooms are not half so large and lofty as yours, and you've never seen so ultra-simple a studio."

Frau Gottinger-Wilt assured me that Brahms took small pride in his environment, and that his visitors had a hard time discovering a place to sit down, because all the chairs were usually full of books and music. Photographs of his library show volumes piled on volumes in apparent disorder. But, according to his housekeeper, "he knew by heart the position of every single book; and, on his travels, would write me to send him, for example, the fifth from the left on the second shelf from the top."

Many of his habits, too, told of his humble ancestry and early surroundings. The gross sounds of moaning, sighing, grunting, puffing, snorting, groaning, etc., that issued from him at the keyboard were somewhat reminiscent of noises made by robust peasants in sleeping, or eating, or during violent exertion.

He was less a slave of the clock than most dwellers in cities. "In order to know when it is time to sleep," he often declared, "I *never* look at my watch. I do that *only* mornings, to find out when it is time to get up." That time was early enough to dismay the city-bred. Like any ploughboy, he was always up at dawn.

Brahms was as offhand in his correspondence as in his costume. After having long repelled invitations to visit the Herzogenbergs in Leipzig, he accepted, at last, with this original formula: "Disaster, take thine own way over all our heads!" And when the father of his hostess died, he sent her five lines of condolence on a common postcard.

Another postal bore his thanks for the doctor's degree

conferred on him by the University of Breslau. It was actually addressed to a third party, asking him to pass the message on to the university authorities. As much cajoling was needed to induce him to acknowledge the distinction properly with a composition and a visit as his housekeeper expended in order to get him dressed for his audience with the Austrian Emperor.

Once he had become a doctor, however, he took an inordinate, almost peasant-like, pride in the title. He hated to be called *Meister* (Master) or *Tonkünstler,* for, he contended, "you might as well call me 'Cobblermaster' or 'Maker of Clay Stoves,' and have done with it!" [6]

If he had cared to, Brahms might have associated on honoured terms with the wealth and aristocracy of all Europe. But his tastes were too homespun for this. Eleven years before his death he remarked to Professor Robert Kahn: "I live in Vienna as if I were in the country"—meaning that he had little to do with any but simple folk. His love for children was deep and tender, but was largely concentrated on those with poor parents.

In a homely, personal way he used to interest himself in his own food supply. Frau Prof. Engelmann has told me how, when he was her guest in Holland, he liked to go marketing with her. He gloated especially over the contents of those fish-halls for which Holland is famous. And he loudly demanded whitebait, which had been the favourite food of poor families like the Brahmses when he was a slum boy in Hamburg.

---

[6] In Austria "Master" is often used for the artisan. As *"Ton"* means both "tone" and "clay," *Tonkünstler* might be stretched to denote both "tone-artist" and "claywright."

In Vienna he had a particular weakness for the delicacies purveyed by the Kalbecks, whose daughter writes me: "In my mind's eye I see a well stocked table full of variegated glasses and bottles. Father walks about and keeps on filling the guests' glasses. My brother and I see all this through the open door. There at the head of the table sits the uncle with the long, white-flowing beard. The laughter with which he signs receipts for jokes roars its way out to us. Yes, Uncle Brahms can drink and eat! Mother would have a big herring salad made for him and he would spoon the whole dish empty, because he loved it so. Indeed, we once went with our nurse to his home in the Karlsgasse to carry him a gigantic portion of this same salad."

He was especially attached to that coarse proletarian dish, *Rindspilaw* (beef-pilaf). One summer at the Hotel Post in Ischl, when certain too elegant visitors had deprived him of this for days, he ordered three portions of it, and dispatched them one after the other, thus vindicating his native Hamburg's reputation as the mother of doughty trenchermen.

According to his housekeeper, the Brahmsian supper consisted of that selection of cold meat called a *kalter Aufschnitt*, and a box of French sardines. This provender he bought in person and carried home in his coat-tail pocket.

The *Delikatessen* shop he regularly patronized was Kühne's in the Operngasse facing the Opera House. It is still there, almost unchanged. Frau Raschke, the proprietress, smiled all over her ample face when I mentioned Brahms. "Yes, yes! I remember the *Herr Doktor* very well. He often came in here with Billroth. His clothes? Ha, ha, they were queer! I would not exactly say they looked sloppy. He just dressed like a genius. (*Er war genial angezogen.*) Ah, he was a nice person, the *Herr Doktor,* a merry soul (*ein fideles Haus*)!"

His manner of eating and drinking sometimes smacked of the farm. Liza Lehmann recalls that when the sardines were opened he would drink the oil directly out of the can "at a draught"—a truly rural touch. And that his way with other beverages was not always wholly Chesterfieldian is shown by the cognac incident told me by Dr. Bauer.

"During the Master's last summer in Ischl, when his complexion was already dark-brown from jaundice, I was once his guest and lived through a terrible moment. He gave me a glass to hold, poured cognac into it, and intentionally made it overflow. Then he seized my dripping hand and licked it off. I was stupefied with surprise, and asked him why he did that. 'Oh,' was the answer, 'the doctors forbid me to drink; but they say not a word about licking.' "

Striking as were such habits, however, Brahms could be impressed by still more striking habits in others. He always roared in recalling an incident in the Alt-Aussee home of the notoriously parsimonious Countess S. He was dining there with Goldmark when a bottle of red wine was overturned and the precious liquid ran all over the table. The Countess sprang up, made for her bedroom, reappeared with a funnel and a sponge, and, to everyone's astonishment, proceeded to sop up the wine and squeeze it back into the bottle. Noticing the expressions of her guests, she murmured: "Never mind; this is, of course, my face-sponge."

In society and in public the Master's gestures and bearing never pretended to be other than homespun, although his method of acknowledging applause improved somewhat after an early occasion described by Joachim to Clara Schumann. The twenty-five-year-old Brahms had just played his own piano concerto in D minor to the music lovers of Hanover. "They honoured the concerto by calling out the composer and performer, who looked, when bowing, as though he had dived into the water and were trying to shake the drops out of his hair."

When it came to financial matters, Brahms was atavistically disinclined to invest his money. If let alone he would doubtless have buried his savings in the traditional peasant's stocking.

In nearly everything that had to do with expenditure on himself he was as close-fisted as a countryman. Once he refused three manuscript cantatas by his patron saint, J. S. Bach, which an intimate friend had taken pains to secure for him at a tremendous bargain, and which he dearly coveted. On the railway he habitually travelled third class. And he viewed with apprehension the least sums spent on him by friends. In 1881, famous and well off, he wrote Clara:

My best thanks for your friendly idea of buying me a travelling bag. What I have in that line really ought to do me. Truly I am a person so far from spoiled and sophisticated that such a gift would be sheer waste.

It is touching to read the modest, frugal, monotonous entries in the little account book, now in my possession, which the Spring family kept of their expenditures for Brahms in 1887, the second summer he passed under their roof in Thun, Switzerland. It reveals that his one personal extravagance there was nothing more high-flown than shoe-leather.

When it came to spending money on others, however, all peasantry ceased. Frugality went to the winds, and, as we shall learn in another chapter, he became the most generous of men. That is—with two exceptions. We all have our pet stinginesses. Both of his were homespun: a reluctance to put enough stamps on his letters, and to pay duty on what he smoked.

He was always asking his foreign friends, when they visited Austria, to smuggle tobacco across the frontier. Once he himself turned contrabandist, but with disastrous results. Kalbeck tells how Brahms hid a large quantity of his favourite Turkish mixture in his bag, with, as he fondly supposed, an imaginative cunning calculated to deceive the ablest of customs sleuths. But at the frontier, to his unspeakable dismay, the revenue officers unerringly and promptly drew forth an object that looked like an amputated leg. The Master had stuffed a stocking full, not of savings, but of tobacco, under the naïve impression that no official would bother with such a thing. This whimsy cost the composer loud cries of rage and anguish, the amputated leg, and a fine of seventy gulden.

TWO SILHOUETTES OF BRAHMS BY OTTO BÖHLER. NOTE THE MASTER'S "GROUND-SHY" TROUSERS, QUAINT HAT AND CHARACTERISTIC POSTURE.

RAFFIA CIGAR-CASE CARRIED BY BRAHMS

Chapter IX

GREATHEART

IN SPITE of Brahms' bearishness, his malice, his temper, and his niggardliness in spending money on himself, he was one of the kindest, most essentially generous artists who ever lived. I know of no other creative musician except Liszt whose greatness of heart measured up to his.

Richard von Perger, who knew him well, bore witness that, behind their backs, he "could defend to the last ditch those whom he had insulted, and then go secretly to do them a good turn. . . . In serious and difficult circumstances he was helpful and self-forgetful." In other words, he was the ideal foul-weather friend.

When he was twenty-one, it is true, Joachim described him in a letter to Gisela von Arnim as "the most inveterate egotist imaginable." But some of the accompanying details temper this accusation for those who understand the mind of the great violinist. Joachim went on to tell how easily and "ruthlessly" Brahms shook off "all the worries of earth. His way of keeping at a distance all the unhealthy feelings and imaginary pains of others is truly masterly." To one who, like the unhappy Joachim, habitually fills his own mind with the rank poisons of suspicion and jealousy, such an instinctive system of mental hygiene always seems inveterate egotism. Those who enjoy emotional bad health, as a rule take umbrage at those who refuse to do likewise, and they find

relief in calling them bad names. Through their defence-
mechanisms they persuade themselves that their vice is a virtue
and that anyone who does not give way to it is necessarily vicious. In Joachim's generous praise of Brahms' mental
hygiene one may read the jealous disapproval of a man who
erected into a virtue the non-possession of this saving technic.

There is, however, in the possession of Kalbeck's daughter
a slightly earlier letter of Joachim's, which sings a different
tune. It is addressed to Fräulein Hedwig Salomon, and introduces Brahms as "a great talent—but far more yet, a noble,
lovable man." The present chapter will show how right were
these last words.

Surely it was no "inveterate egotist" but an utterly self-
forgetful altruist who turned fireman at Mürzzuschlag in
the summer of 1885. In the block where he lived, fire broke
out in the workroom of a small carpenter. Brahms rushed in
shirt-sleeves from his desk, toiled ardently in the bucket brigade, and incited the lazy and fashionable bystanders to lend
a hand. When warned that the fire was threatening his rooms
and the manuscript of the almost completed E minor symphony, the news gave him a moment's pause. Then he calmly
went on with the work. And Dr. Fellinger had difficulty in
extorting the key from him in order to carry the priceless
manuscript to safety. When taken to task for such behaviour,
he simply remarked: "Oh, the poor people needed help
worse than I did!" In the end, the burned-out carpenter
found Brahms so generous that he actually profited through
the fire.

How charmingly he befriended another humble resident
of this village, Frau Anna Brauneis has told me. As young

Annie Wenzel, the daughter of a small innkeeper, she once attended a wedding at a farmer's house.

"Coming away, I met three men who begged me to sing and yodel a Styrian folk song. I was ashamed, and said no. But soon in the dark I met some young friends, and as I had had a good deal of wine at the wedding, I began to sing. Presently we met the trio again, this time under a light, and they turned out to be Brahms with two other celebrities. Brahms said: 'Well, my dear, in spite of your refusal, we've heard you!'

"The next day I was told the great man had declared my voice was splendid and that I must study singing. This I refused to believe without hearing it from his own lips. But when I went to call on him he was very amiable and said the same again and gave me a letter to Prof. Gänsbacher in Vienna.

"Climbing the stairs to his studio I met a baroness who asked what I held in my hand. I said: 'A letter from Herr Brahms.' You see I was so green that I didn't even know enough to call him 'Master'! Prof. Gänsbacher found I had three full octaves and declared I must be a Wagner singer and must study seven years.

"I took this report to Brahms at Karlsgasse 4. There on the sofa was Hanslick, the music critic. Brahms said I must sing for Hanslick *Du bist die Ruh*. He sat down at the piano and began playing a tremolo. I was indignant, for this was wrong. I struck his fingers from the keys and told him he must play the accompaniment properly. ('*Aber naa, so geht's ja net!*')

" 'Well, how then?'

" 'It must go this way.' And I sang:

ti   ti   ti'

'ta   ta   ta

"Hanslick shook himself with tremendous laughter, and
Brahms shook too. But this time he played it correctly:

ti   ti   ti'

'ta   ta   ta

and I sang.

"When the two heard that about my singing Wagner, they
looked very grave and decided that Prof. Gänsbacher must
not teach me after all, for he would force my voice. So
Brahms sent me to Frau Professorin Wilczek at the Conservatory, who taught me for nothing.

"Whenever I called on Master Brahms he was most
friendly, and would even accompany me in my Concone and
Aprile exercises! But he did not like it at all when, after a year
of study, I went on the light opera stage."

Brahms was no less kind to another young girl of talent,
the fifteen-year-old violinist Marie Soldat.[1] Frau Bertha Gasteiger, an eyewitness, has told me how Marie arrived almost
penniless at Pörtschach and how Frau Svoboda diplomatically persuaded the almost unapproachable Brahms to hear
her. After she had played him the Mendelssohn concerto, the
Master, looking very serious, left the room without a word.
All feared the worst. But when Frau Svoboda held him up
on the stairs for his opinion, he replied: "That is an extraordinary talent. I'm going at once to beg Frau Dustmann [the
celebrated operatic prima donna] to sing in Marie's concert."
He said nothing whatever of his kind intention to accompany the singer in person.

---

[1] After her marriage, Frau Röger-Soldat.

"The concert was an enormous success. Little Soldat (The Little Soldier), as she was familiarly called, also played the piano brilliantly. And afterwards Brahms said: 'Now that you've played violin and piano so beautifully, why don't you *sing* for us too?'

"The next day when Marie called to thank him, he had already drawn up her complete life-program: 'In a fortnight you must come to Salzburg and play for Joachim—I'll be there too—and he will then accept you for the Berlin Hochschule.'

"This worked out so perfectly that in a year and a half Joachim declared she had outgrown the Hochschule and should now be his private pupil. Marie was destined to be the first woman to play the Brahms violin concerto in public. This was 1886, in Vienna.

"Before the rehearsal the Master was visibly excited and anxious, because the concerto was generally thought to be too difficult for any woman. But afterwards he beamed with happiness, and when the ordeal was over he brought her the edition de luxe of the concerto and two lovely fans, one of which he had autographed. He could not do enough for her in his joy and unspoken gratitude."

The despised and rejected often found in this great-hearted man a ready ally. Widmann tells how, one night under the arcades of Bologna, Brahms enthusiastically admired a deaf-and-dumb sidewalk artist who had drawn on the flags a portrait of Cavour. "A plate stood near by, into which one could throw the soldo which one might feel like offering to such art of the highways. But there was a new surprise when the coin, ringing on the hard stone, showed that the plate was not a real one but a well and truly drawn imitation. Brahms could not find words enough to praise this fine idea of the poor artist. And his offering showed how deeply he was moved by learning that in this gifted race, even the street beggar knew how to cover his nakedness with a corner of the hem of Art's sumptuous robe."

Brahms' kind-heartedness and essential politeness knew no class distinctions. In writing to friends he as often as not sent his good wishes by name to the servant-girl or governess. During the first private performance of his *Gypsy Songs* at the Brülls', he suddenly stormed into the nursery, dragged out Fräulein Witzl, the modest little "Hungarian" governess, and seated her in the place of honour, as the "instigator" of the new work. For he thought she had found the texts and roughly translated them from the Hungarian, so that Hugo Conrat could give them a metrical dress in German. Unfortunately the Master had his facts wrong; for Fräulein Witzl was a newcomer who knew not a word of Hungarian; while her predecessor, Fräulein Marie Szalay, had actually done all the "instigating." But his heart was, none the less, in the right place.

Brahms stood so high in the good graces of the young woman who kept the postoffice in Pörtschach that she even made up his packages and rolls of music for him. "Did you notice," he wrote Simrock, "the pretty roll made by the pretty postmistress?" And on this same postcard appeared, in a feminine hand, the following eloquent endorsement: "For such an amiable gentleman, everything is done with the greatest pleasure.

"POSTMISTRESS."

Not to be outdone in courtesy, Brahms made his friends invite the obliging Fräulein to dinner with him.

In many ways he was truly a gentleman. It is well known that, even when travelling in a smoking compartment, he would scrupulously ask the ladies' permission to light a cigarette; and on entering a Catholic church, he would pretend, with his Protestant hand, to take holy water. In hotels he would place his only pair of shoes in the corridor in the early evening, and go about stocking-footed on the cold stone floor, "so as not to shorten the sleep of some poor servant."

It is not so well known, however, that when he came back to his native Hamburg, famous and fêted, he had his modest old stepmother, a plain woman of the people, live at his own hotel and share his triumphs with him.

His delicacy in sparing the feelings of his interpreters was often extraordinary. Mr. Percy Such remembers that, in 1896, Brahms conducted the orchestra of Joachim's Berlin Hochschule. Fearing that he might discredit Joachim's tempi, he made the players a charming little speech: "Ladies and gentlemen, let me confess that I grasp this baton with great diffidence. Now if we were to do a Beethoven symphony, I might conduct it well; but it is so long since I have conducted this Third of mine that I feel very shaky about it—even to the tempi."

A similar instance comes from Mr. Paolo Gallico: "While rehearsing the *Andante* of his F minor quintet, at the place in the middle which is usually taken too fast, Brahms made an elaborate business of putting on his *pince-nez* and examining the piano part. 'Hm, hm,' he grunted, 'I see I've marked that wrong!' and, getting out his pencil, he wrote in a *meno mosso*. This indirect criticism was given half delicately, half humorously. Most composers, of course, would have bluntly said: 'Gentlemen, don't hurry!' The *meno mosso* never found its way into print."

As his housekeeper has told me, his sensitive regard for the rights of others went so far that, though the banging of his neighbour, Frau Ronchetti, disturbed him agonizingly, he himself was considerate enough to cover his own piano with thick fabrics. He even had a special mute made for it. This was the exact opposite of Beethoven's procedure who—very excusably—ordered an amplifier for his own. "He did not play a great deal," said Frau Dr. Truxa—"merely stippled at the keys [*nur so getippt*]. It was only during his last illness that he played much, and that was mostly evenings in the twilight.

"What a good, kind, thoughtful person he was! Once when I had to make a trip to Graz he went out and bought me all sorts of extravagant presents to make the journey agreeable: two plaid shawls, fur shoes, travelling bags of real leather, a trunk, and so on. In order to take them all along I should have had to have an express van! So I secretly locked them up and made as though I were using them."

"I shall never forget," Frau Prof. Engelmann told me, "what a dear, kind, thoughtful friend, what an ideal guest Brahms was in our home in Utrecht. He was pleased with everything and gave no trouble. His praise was enough to warm the heart of any hostess: 'Such beefsteaks!' he would exclaim. 'I'd like to eat them every day until I die!'

"The first time we played piano duets for four hands he

insisted on taking the second part, and quietly observed: 'Well, I know you're not fond of playing bass notes, so I'll sit myself down here.' It was a glorious experience! Without his saying a word, one understood exactly what he wanted."

His kindness often revealed a finely imaginative quality. During his concert tour in Hungary with Joachim, the audience one evening consisted of a solitary man. The violinist was all for giving him back his money and closing before the start. "No," said Brahms, "our unique partisan does not deserve such disrespect. Let us get on with the program." So they began, and soon were enthusiastically playing whatever their fortunate solo audience suggested.

Never was a famous composer kinder than Brahms to his young colleagues—where he found genuine talent. With might and main he urged Simrock to publish the works of Knorr, Roentgen, Fuchs, and Novak. He rescued Dvořák from the direst poverty, made Simrock bring out the *Slavonic Dances,* and helped them to their wide success. Twice he begged Dvořák, with all his heart, to consider the Brahmsian fortune as his own. And when he learned that the Bohemian was a most incompetent proof-reader, he himself actually assumed the drudgery of correcting all his friend's proofs.

When it came to sparing the professional pride of the humblest musician, even so stern an artistic conscience as his own would sometimes deign to wink an eye. "The songs of X," he wrote Simrock, "when I take his young wife into consideration, please me very much. You see, I am really more human being than musician."

Of this assertion he once gave engaging proof while playing the Schumann piano concerto. In the opening movement, where first the oboe and then the piano state the principal theme, the oboist had a temporary lapse, and played, as the grace-note before D, F sharp instead of E. When it came Brahms' turn he deliberately made the same error "in order," as he afterwards put it, "not to show up the unlucky oboist."

Prof. Otto Dorn remembers that when Brahms drilled Wiesbaden's modest Kur orchestra in the Third symphony he closed each rehearsal with this benignant assurance: "The gentlemen have done their utmost."

The kindness he showed Marxsen, his early Hamburg teacher, is thrown into all the higher relief by the mistaken remark which he once made, in a contrary mood, that he had learned as good as nothing from the old man. In spite of this, no less a work than the B flat piano concerto was dedicated to him. And for his half-century jubilee the pupil not only made Simrock publish Marxsen's *100 Variations,* at his (Brahms') expense, but forced the publisher to pretend that he had included this work in his catalogue on account of its own intrinsic worth.

Robert Keller had long arranged the piano versions of Brahms' larger compositions, but the composer did not much relish them and once asked Simrock to let Kirchner make them instead. But when he learned how deeply this would hurt Keller's feelings, he hastily withdrew the request.

Of course you must consider [he wrote Simrock] that I have said nothing about arrangements. . . . (It is true that the Philistine peeps a little out of his [Keller's] two-hand versions. But just that may be very good in a business way.)

The clarinet quintet was first played in Vienna by the Rosé Quartet with an obscure clarinettist named Steiner, and shortly after by the Joachims and Mühlfeld. At the ensuing gala dinner, to the despair of all the beautiful ladies, Brahms settled himself between his two clarinettists. Steiner being a stranger, the Master treated him with special distinction, to prevent his feeling embarrassed in the presence of the famous Mühlfeld.

The humbler the musician, the kinder was Brahms. In an unpublished letter sent with a manuscript sonata to Kupfer, his 'cello-playing copyist, he wrote: "I'll be glad to let you copy out the 'cello part for your own pleasure, but of course you must let nobody see any of the manuscript." Such geniality is a stark contrast to the brutal way in which Beethoven treated his own quill-driving slaves; but Brahms' affability to obscure little orchestras was truly Beethovenian. Frau Ribarz-Hemala tells me that when, at his villa in Gmunden, Miller zu Aichholz engaged the local Kur orchestra to play some of the *Hungarian Dances* in the next room, Brahms was charming and insisted on shaking hands with each of the men.

During a house party there this same informant was once kept from table by a heavy cold, and Brahms asked to have some champagne warmed and sent to her room with a friendly message. "The act was so characteristic of his kindness and thoughtfulness!" When Brüll, his companion on regular strolls in Ischl, was laid up with an injured foot, the restless Brahms, who hated all forms of ill health, "sat walking (*sass spazieren*)" with his friend for an hour or two daily, "in order to continue the custom."

Nor was he less kind to animals. His housekeeper tells me that he always used to feed the birds on the window-sill with crumbs from his breakfast. When Carmen von Lührsen was fourteen and was visiting the Dumbas', where Brahms was dining, her pug dog Flockie, sensing a congenial friend, jumped upon his shoulder and ate confidently from his fork, to the Master's huge delight.

Widmann's small dog Argos had been given up for lost on the Grindelwald Glacier and won heroic fame by turning up at home in Berne four days later. When he was heard, at six in the morning, scratching at the door, everybody tumbled out of bed to welcome him.

Relatively speaking [wrote Widmann], the most fully dressed was Brahms, the early riser, and I can still see him bending down to Argos and without hesitation abandoning his hands and face to the caresses of the joy-crazed animal. "So that's what it is!" he cried. "This is no mere hunter's yarn (*Jägerlatein*)." . . . And in his first letter from Vienna he asked: "How is Argos getting on? Wouldn't he take it as a tender greeting from me if, for a change, instead of dog-biscuit, you gave him a nice piece of meat?"—(which was naturally done according to his wish.)

His sympathies were warm for the human under-dog, as well. When the news came from America that the Sioux Indians had massacred General Custer and his three hundred soldiers, the Master was enraptured and cried to Henschel: "You wouldn't believe what joy that gives me! Of course I know it will not help the poor fellows; but still it was granted them to take one good bath in the blood of their persecutors!"

His delicate thoughtfulness and tenderness were perhaps most touching in his relations with his intimate friends and family. In her old age Clara Schumann set about publishing some of her cadenzas to piano concertos, but found to her dismay that she had taken certain passages from Brahms and then forgotten the circumstance, so that she was on the point of "decking herself with borrowed plumes." She asked his permission to acknowledge these loans on the title-page. But Johannes generously pooh-poohed her scruples:

Even the smallest J.B. would look strange. . . . Then too, by rights, I would have to inscribe my best melodies: "Really by Cl. Sch."!—For if I think of myself, nothing worth while or beautiful can occur to me! I owe you more melodies than all the passages and such-like you can borrow from me!!

When these old friends had a misunderstanding about the publication of Schumann's D minor symphony in the original version, Clara wrote Johannes a letter which has never been printed, but whose scathing tenor may easily be inferred from his reply:

In your letter you treat Wüllner and me, not like two honourable men and artists, who are in your opinion perhaps mistaken, yet who, according to their lights, are working for a dear and holy cause earnestly and with love. Far from that, you treat us as the exact opposite of all this. What is between the lines of your letter, what it really breathes out, is something into which I prefer not to go.

A few days later he sadly wrote her:

It is hard, after forty years of faithful service (or whatever you wish to call my relationship to you), to be nothing else than "one more bad experience." Well, that must be borne. I am used to being lonely; and if it must be, I can become resigned to the thought of this great emptiness. But today you must allow me to repeat again to you that you and your husband represent the most beautiful experience of my life, that you stand for its greatest wealth and noblest meaning.

As Elisabet von Herzogenberg expressed herself about a certain page of his music: "None but a very good man could have written that!" Clara's heart was touched by the letter, and they were reconciled, to remain close friends until her death.

As we have seen, Brahms was as open-handed to others as he was close-fisted toward himself. More than once he forced large sums upon the hard-pressed Clara, acting as if by her acceptance she were doing him the kindest possible favour.

He supported the sister of the dead Keller, whose piano arrangements had been a trial to him. He educated the daughter of Lieschen Giesemann, a friend of his childhood. He sent periodical sums to the broken-down composer Kirchner. More than once during Daniel Spitzer's last illness he tried to make the old wit accept large amounts and use him as a banker. "I didn't need the money so much as Brahms supposed," said the dying satirist, "but his offers made me happy. And *this* is the man whom I had taken for a colossal egotist!"

When Brahms heard that Nottebohm was ill in Graz, he left everything, hurried there, and insisted that the old Beethoven scholar spend the winter in Italy at his expense. But when, instead, he went on a longer journey, Brahms closed the eyes of his fellow-bachelor, settled the funeral ex-

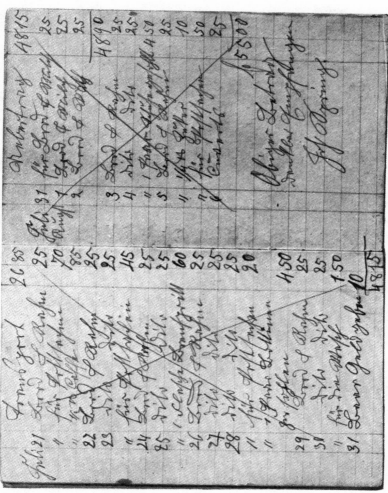

TWO PAGES FROM THE SMALL LEDGER KEPT BY FRAU SPRING IN ACCOUNT WITH BRAHMS, her lodger at Thun, Switzerland, in the summer of 1887. Besides the first item, for piano-moving, the most extravagant charges are for shoe-leather.

penses, and with enormous zeal brought about the posthumous publication of his best books.

His treatment of legacies was characteristic of his honest kindness. One unhappily married Viennese lady bequeathed him a locked chest of music. Among the scores she had hidden a large sum in securities, with a note saying that they were for him. These he at once turned over to the husband, explaining that they had been left in the chest by mistake.

An English lover of his music gave him deep pleasure by willing him £1,000. When Joachim sent the news Brahms replied:

One can experience nothing more beautiful, nothing that does one more good, than what you have just told me.

That a perfect stranger, who has, as far as I know, never even written me, should remember me thus, touches me most deeply and intimately. Once before I have had the inestimable joy of experiencing the like. All exterior honours are nothing in comparison.

As I do not need to "invest" the money, I am enjoying it in the most agreeable manner, by taking pleasure in its distribution. . . .

He had a charming way of sharing his fortune with his family:

DEAREST FATHER, very pleased, most happy, I am sending you this heavy letter and beg you to forward 100 thaler to Elise through Aunty, and to use the other 100 thaler for your own pleasure. And how it would delight me if you employed it for nothing but quite useless, jolly things!

This to his stepmother is characteristic:

I beg you always to remember that I have more money than I need and that it gives me the greatest joy if you make use of it for yourself and yours.

With Simrock also, this notorious bear was capable of the most tender and delicate thoughtfulness. The publisher, who handled Brahms' money, once made a mistake of a thousand marks in his own favour. Discovering this, he wrote his client, who answered:

Naturally I noticed the error, but didn't want to make a fuss over a paltry thousand.

When a wildcat speculation into which Simrock had plunged against his friend's judgment lost the latter twenty thousand marks, he answered the publisher's offer of restitution:

Don't make any silly hullaballoo about the famous "bankruptcy." That would be laughable, especially if you should want to make it good. You know that for the present I still have enough to live on in spite of the "bankruptcy." It goes without saying that—except while writing you—I haven't given the matter an instant's thought.

When in 1888 Simrock bought up from other publishers as many old compositions of his friend's as he could, Brahms, deeply touched by this mark of confidence, first rated him soundly for what he branded as foolishness, then made him a proposition which is, as far as I know, unparalleled in the annals of music-publishing, namely: that from then on, for all his future compositions, he would accept no payments. Naturally the noble-hearted Simrock would not hear of any such quixotism.

It was characteristic of Brahms to reverse, occasionally, the usual order by which a little charity is made to cover a multitude of sins, and make fictitious sins cover a multitude of charities. He once begged Simrock to send him two or three thousand marks:

My beautiful concert-winnings are as good as gone—flown out of the window—and it is just as well that I need not render an account of how they went!

Whereupon Kalbeck comments, aside:

The shamedfaced benefactor humorously masquerades as the frivolous man-about-town.

Ischl is, to this day, filled with memories of Brahms' generosity. The owner of the Hotel Elisabeth, where Brahms regularly ate, told me about her sister, Julie Koch, who was sixteen at the time: "We used to have our family table next to the Master's. Julie adored riding, and often begged Father to buy her a horse. But Father was so close-fisted, he hated to spend a kreutzer on luxuries, and always refused. But one day Brahms mixed into the argument with: 'Look here, Julie must have her horse! And as it will be so expensive to maintain, I myself will pay for its feed.' He would have done it, too! But for all that, Julie never had her horse."

From an old peasant woman I learned how Brahms' gold watch was stolen one day from his rooms, which he never locked. When the police came and urged him to take the matter up officially, he simply said: "Leave me in peace! The watch was probably carried away by some poor devil who needs it more than I do."

Chapter X

THE BARREL OF GUNPOWDER

"Sitting next to Brahms is like sitting next to a barrel of gunpowder!" A Viennese lady tells me she once heard Joachim say this, under some great provocation. It was the sort of complaint which Beethoven's friends might well have uttered. And indeed, the third of the Three B's must have had a temper fully as explosive as that of the second.

In Pörtschach one summer a friend came by appointment to fetch Brahms for dinner. Happening to notice a ladder upright near the composer's window, and thinking no harm, the young man blithely ran up and peeped in with a smile, which was suddenly wiped out when he saw the Master striding up and down like one possessed, evidently engaged in a struggle with his work. The visitor immediately ducked, but not before he had been noticed. With a yell of rage Brahms leaped to the window and made as if to hurl the ladder into the street, along with the unpardonable intruder who, as he thought, was trying to violate his inner sanctuary. Of course, when one considers that this incident may have rudely interrupted the D major symphony or the violin concerto, one's sympathies are not wholly with the young man.

The physician who took care of Brahms in Karlsbad a few months before his death informs me that: "In those days he was a man wholly without self-control. A friend came and begged me to get Brahms and two of my royal patients to give their autographs. I told him I could easily manage their Royal Highnesses, but the musician was a far more difficult proposition.

"A few days after this Brahms was in a very benign mood and said: 'You have been so good to me, dear Herr Doktor. Now what can I do in return? I am yours to command. There is only one thing you can not have from me: an autograph.'

"Whereupon I threw up my hands: 'But, dear Herr Doktor, that is unfortunately the very thing I was going to beg of you!'

"Instantly he gave way to a real access of fury. He jumped to his feet and shouted all manner of insults. He called me such things as 'old maid,' and 'village gossip' (*Klatschbase*). My waiting room was full, and I fear the patients heard him yell out that he now perceived I was no serious doctor, and nevermore would he have anything to do with such a ridiculous creature. Words of abuse by the hundred literally seemed to pour out of that white beard.

"I made an effort and kept my head, and thought: 'Here is a sick man and a great genius. I know my Brahms. He will soon get over this!' And sure enough, in three or four days he turned up again as though nothing had happened, and never referred in the slightest way to our little trouble.

"Well, at the end of the third week, he paid me a farewell call and thanked me for having treated him with my heart as well as with my head. Then he produced an envelope full of money and silently handed it over. When I saw some writing on it I began to smile. At once he fired up and shouted: 'What are you laughing at? You don't know what's inside.'

" 'I don't care in the least what's inside,' I answered. 'But

I have my autograph!'

"His mood changed in a flash. Playfully he shook his fist
at me and went away muttering half aloud: 'Cursed fellow!'

"On the envelope stood:

" '*To his dear friend Doktor Grünberger, the grateful*
Johannes Brahms.' "

Just before her recent death Frau Gottinger-Wilt, the
daughter of Marie Wilt, the famous Brahms singer, explained
to me how she had once given the Master somewhat better
justification for an explosion of rage.

"Raoul Walter and Pepi Hellmesberger and I, young devils
all about sixteen years old, cooked up a plot against the Master, because he had been rude to us. We went to a skating-
rink, the Eislaufplatz, and persuaded Mother to bring Brahms
along. The latter did not skate, so we coaxed him into a chair
on runners, and whirled the poor little man round the rink
at a breath-taking speed. As a *finale* we tipped him over, chair
and all, into a deep snow-bank. When he climbed out, shaking
himself, he looked more than ever like Santa Claus. But how
he did scold and curse!"

This lady, however, assured me that he usually liked
people to stand up to him courageously and assert their own
rights against the force of his dominant personality. If they
meekly knuckled down, he never respected them.

"He was an intimate family friend and dropped in every
day or so. I remember one afternoon when I was fifteen, sitting and ripping a dress apart, when he appeared and started
to help me. But he was so awkward that at once he cut into
the material, and I told him to go and play me something
on the piano instead. He liked my impudence, and obeyed

at once."

Herr Emil Hess told me that, as a youth, he set his heart on studying with Brahms. He found him at home and began: "Master, I am only a poor musician——" But at the words, Brahms seemed to swell with anger. Locking his arms behind his back, he shouted furiously: "How dare you approach me?" "I saw," said Herr Hess, "that I was on the wrong tack, and hastily added: '——who has come to beg you to accept me as a pupil in counterpoint.' Presto, change! The arms came out from behind the back. Instantly he was all courtesy and consideration, offering me cigarettes and drinks. Very politely he explained that his frequent concert tours prevented his doing any teaching. 'Then,' said I, 'I suppose I shall have to go to the Conservatory.' 'Where you will not learn a thing!' cried the Master. 'Here, I will give you a card to Nottebohm.'"

A Viennese lady, whose name I am not allowed to give, recalls that in the home of Brahms' dear friends the Chrobaks, as a girl of fifteen, she overheard him issuing directions to her violin teacher, Prof. Julius Winkler, about the interpretation of a piece of his own. Brusquely he warned the violinist to play a certain passage with increasing speed. She knew that this was unnecessary, because the place was marked *accelerando,* and was annoyed. "Brahms," she said, "was often in bad temper early in the evening, and worked off his irritation on those nearest at hand. A little later he found the piano stool too low and asked me to fetch him a book to make it higher. I brought a thick volume, which he gravely refused, saying that he was not worthy to sit on the symphonies of Beethoven. But I was still angry over the insult to my teacher.

I flounced away, brought him a volume of his own symphonies, and said: 'Here's some worthless trash for you to sit on!'

"He laughed immoderately at my pertness and was apparently so pleased at my defence of my teacher that he made me sit beside him the whole evening. And before going home he tried to patch up a peace by remarking: 'Your master played very well to-night.' "

Brahms liked the few whose tongues were brave and mordant enough to cope with his own in rapier-play. He was delighted with a riposte by the Jewish Max Bruch. "Good-day, Baruch," said Brahms. "How are you, Abrahams?" was the quick response.

Widmann described a lively theological dispute he had with the Master, which ended by cementing their friendship further! "My rather heated opposition did not seem to make my company displeasing to Brahms. All his life he was an eager disputant who preferred having a clash of opinions enliven a conversation to having folks, out of respect for his ability and success, agree servilely with everything he said."

Dr. Otto Julius Bauer once proposed the famous toast to Brahms as "the greatest *Schimpfoniker* [1] of all time." He told me of a silver wedding party at Concert Manager Kugel's in Ischl, "where Brahms got rather tipsy and made a harsh speech directed against his future biographer Kalbeck, who was there with his wife. After scolding the good man for this and that, he ridiculed the long program books the latter wrote, alleging that their sole reason for existence was in

---

[1] *Schimpfoniker* is a portmanteau word of Bauer's coining, compounded of *Symphoniker* (symphonist) and *Schimpf* (insult).

Max Kalbeck, the Brahms biographer, and Dr. Otto Julius Bauer, Brahms' witty Viennese friend, have exchanged hats. Kalbeck the poet bestrides a wooden Pegasus. Taken in Ischl, 1892.

Courtesy of Dr. Bauer

order that the music critics might be given some idea of what was going on.

"All this made me boil. 'Aha!' I said silently to Brahms. 'I'll get you now!' When he had done I got up and went for him as vigorously as he had gone for Kalbeck. I called him 'Master in *Unfugen*.' [2] I denounced him for being so outrageous to this good disciple of his, who would go through fire for him. 'Ingratitude,' I cried, 'is the cheapest form of vice; therefore he practises it'; and added as many more brutalities as I could think of.

"Even in his tipsy state, Brahms was far from taking offence. Indeed, he seemed thoroughly pleased with me for having had the nerve to outface him. But on the morrow, at another party in Gmunden, he had so far forgotten these wine-blurred events as to tell Miller zu Aichholz about the wonderful speech I had made in his honour!"

Prof. Alfred Finger furnishes another instance of his respect for those who outfaced him. "Brahms had misunderstood our previous agreement about dressing for a musical gathering, and appeared in his ordinary clothes. Though costume meant little to him, he was very punctilious about agreements, and expected others to be, as well. When he saw my dress coat he came for me like a mad bull, heaped me with reproaches, and insultingly accused me of having broken my word. I only answered, 'You are mistaken.'

"But at seven the next morning I called at his house and firmly gave him to understand that I would not submit to any such treatment. This seemed to please him very much.

[2] *Unfugen* sounds to American ears as though it should be the opposite of *Fugen* (fugues), but in reality it means "disorderly conduct."

He apologized in touching terms, made me sit down to breakfast with him, and kept me the whole morning. We had a delightful time together."

Sometimes, however, the Master merely exercised his very
considerable histrionic talent and played at being angry. Prof.
Julius Winkler, the violinist who figured in the incident
which led to the Master's sitting on his own "worthless" symphonies, remembers a story about the Tonkünstlerverein.
"About 1887 they asked me, as a younger member, to do
more playing in our concerts. I said I would be glad to, only
I had no time to run around and look up music. 'I'll send you
some,' said Brahms, who was our honorary president.

"Not long afterward a package came from him. I was dis-
agreeably surprised to find nothing in it but chamber music
by Kiel. I tried it with my colleagues, but we found the stuff
so deadly dull that we could not last to the end, and vowed
we would not play a note of it in any concert. The next day
we were dining at the club table when Brahms came and sat
opposite. Julius Epstein whispered in his ear, and I knew he
was reporting the news of our revolt. Whereupon the Master
struck the table a terrific whack with his fist and put on a
look of formidable anger. But he had been dining well, and
his eye kept a good-tempered twinkle.

"In a few minutes he offered me one of his cigarettes. I
smoked and acknowledged its goodness by a gesture. On
which he beckoned me over to him and pretending to whisper confidentially, spoke so that all could hear: 'Yes, dear
Winkler, Kiel, you know, is one of those immortals of whom
nobody wants to hear anything more.'"

Chapter XI

"UNCLE BAHMS"

THE favourite flower of St. Anthony, that lover of children, was the blossom of the broom plant from which the Brahms family took its name. In Italy, it is known as *"il fior' di Sant' Antonio."* How appropriate, then, that children should have been a ruling passion with Brahms!

Always and everywhere he was on the lookout for them, peering about eagerly with his short-sighted eyes. To a tactless acquaintance who once inquired if he did not need glasses while wielding the baton, he wittily replied: "When, in such a score as Schumann's *Faust* I meet with the stage direction, 'Here women pass by,' I quickly clap on my *pince-nez*." But in order to see the little ones he required no such artificial aids. Nor did they need to have their "Uncle Bahms" pointed out.

When he sighted them, the Master would put on an expression of mock severity, far from convincing. He would pace along slowly, hands clasped behind, pretending to be deep in thought and particularly dead to the juvenile world. But his small friends were seldom taken in. Trooping along in the rear, they watched developments closely. For most of them knew they could count on candy escaping now and then from those austerely clasped hands. Or sometimes a dribble of kreutzers would descend upon the sidewalk, to be scrabbled for and pounced upon with shrill cries. Then, the pretence of sternness punctured, he would find himself on a wayside bench with tots swarming over his ample knees.

An old peasant woman, the eldest daughter of the house in Ischl where Brahms spent many of his last summers, testifies that "though Master Brahms hated many kinds of sound, the children never bothered him, no matter how much noise they made. Once he bought a lot of toys for them from a strolling gypsy-woman. Then he pretended to be very much excited, and told Mother the gypsy had forgotten the toys and to make the children run after her and give them back. But Mother had happened to see Master Brahms pay for them, so she did not fall into *that* snare."

You ought to see me here [he wrote to Clara Schumann from this same Ischl], in the rôle of the children's friend! There are no more lovable and agreeable folks and little folks anywhere than in this neighbourhood. I cannot go for a walk without my heart laughing; and when I caress a couple of these adorable children, I feel as though I'd taken a cooling drink.

As sometimes in his music and in his witty conversation, he liked to prepare artistic climaxes by means of unpromising starts. Into a sceptical and apprehensive little mouth he would shove an object cunningly contrived to look like a miniature cobblestone. Then he would batten upon the consequent gamut of facial expression, swiftly ranging from consternation, through astonishment, surmise, and realization to delight when the stone turned out to be not bread but a delicious bon-bon. In this proceeding one recognizes salient Brahmsian traits: circuitousness, contrariety, love of practical joking, and fondness for children—all characteristically fused.

A friend once sent him a superior substitute for his imitation cobblestones—candy in paper wrappers giving the illusion of an assortment of mineral specimens.

Your mineral collection [he wrote in reply], is something too superb for words. It's a thing I've long known. I used to notice it with pleasure every day in the Stephans Platz on the way to the Hedgehog.[1] But I never dreamed that such magnificence could be anything for me and "my little ones." So many thanks for all the fun it will bring me and others!

Frau Dr. Truxa, his housekeeper, was called from town for some days on urgent business, and had to leave her two little boys at home in charge of the servant. On returning she was surprised and touched to hear that the Master had gone in every noon to see if the children had the right food, and every night to see if they were properly covered.

But she was shocked at the dirty and neglected state of his rooms. She scolded the maid, who only laughed: "Yes, but the Herr Doktor wouldn't let me clean up for him while you were gone. All he'd allow me was to make the bed and empty the slops. Nothing else whatever. He told me: 'A neglected apartment is easily fixed up. But if one of those children should fall from a chair and break his little leg, that couldn't be so quickly mended!'" "You may well imagine my gratitude," said Frau Truxa; "but the old Brahms crept back into his snail-shell, and I didn't dare say even a word for all his kindness!"

What Brahms seemed most of all to miss in his bachelor life was babies of his own.

---

[1] *Der Rote Igel*, a tavern where he habitually dined with his friends.

I wish you a right merry Christmas [he wrote wistfully to Simrock]. What with the laughing faces of children and the bright tree, it makes good wishing. That's enough to turn a publisher into a human being who can feel that he has a heart which laughs along with the others.

During the decade that Frau Dr. Truxa was, as Brahms politely called her, his "house-hostess," a Christmas tree was trimmed every year in his rooms and smothered in gifts for the young Truxas.

"The last Christmas he was alive," said their mother, "he was so ill I didn't have the heart to bother him with all that. But on the 22nd he stopped me and growled abruptly: 'How's this? I find no Christmas tree in my room.'

" 'Oh, there has been so much to do,' I assured him; 'but it will come.'

"Of course I rushed out, bought a tree, set it up as usual in there, and trimmed it. That Christmas Eve one hardly noticed the terrible effort he made to cover up his pain and exhaustion. Not for anything would he have cast a gloom over the children's party. So good and thoughtful was the Herr Doktor!"

Many a man and woman of today remembers with affectionate gratitude how kind this great man was to him long ago. When Mr. Ernest Schelling, the pianist and composer, was a spindling lad of ten he played for Brahms, who picked him up, kissed him and remarked: "This little boy needs more oatmeal and cream and fewer scales."

The present owner of the house in Thun, Switzerland, where Brahms lived for three summers, bears witness that when he was a shaver the Master used to take him on his knee and try to teach him the rudiments of his art. "Too bad that there was no music in me! Otherwise I'd have had lessons from our lodger. Lessons from Brahms; that would have been something to boast of! As a matter of fact he *did* start me on the piano. But I was so stupid that he groaned: 'Yes, my dear Hans, music lessons for you would be wasted malt and hops!'" Which was the homely Brahmsian way of indicating a waste of good material.

With children of more talent he dearly liked to make music. He would play piano duets with four-year-old Agnes Pyllemann, improvising wrong basses to enjoy her indignant cry: "But, Uncle, what is this? You are playing quite false!"

Mr. Oscar Ullmann tells me of a certain young boy named Theodor, who could read music so well that, when it came to tryouts of new compositions, the Master liked to see the old prophecy fulfilled: "a little child shall lead them." Often when he spied Theodor in Gmunden, he would pull a freshly written manuscript song from his right-hand coat pocket, lead him to the piano, and make him sing it at sight.

When he played in public he liked to have little ones in the audience. Frau von Miller zu Aichholz's journal records that once as he was seating himself at the piano he spied her son and daughter in the front row and exclaimed with a smile of welcome, *"Ah, die Kinder!"* (Ah, the children!)

Children soon learned to call him *"Onkel* Bahms," and he gloried in this form of salutation. Indeed, in closing a letter to Simrock, he himself once carried it to a higher power of affectionate diminutiveness:

Best greetings, also to the little ones, from *Onkel*
BÄHMSCHEN.

To feel his own creative fires gloriously crackling and roaring within often gave him no deeper satisfaction than to kindle a small flame of surprise and joy in the eyes of some ragged child whom he might chance upon, flattening its nose wistfully against a bakeshop window, and for whom he would dive into his capacious coat-tails and produce a bit of his own recent dessert, laid by in·shrewd prevision of some such emergency. Indeed, there was a close relation between these two sorts of fire.

Nobody well acquainted with the character of that Mr. Gruffenuf, the everyday Brahms, however, would for a moment imagine that his association with those whom he so touchingly called "my little ones" was invariably a cloudless idyll. One day a regrettable incident happened in Vienna's great park, the Prater. He had all the children about him as usual, playing boyishly with them and giving them presents, when one precocious urchin, thinking to ingratiate himself still more, began to whistle (in quite the wrong key) a Brahms tune. This intrusion of "shop" spoiled the atmosphere. Presto, change! Without a word the irate Master jerked to his feet and vanished.

Something similar took place on the Ringstrasse, but without any musical cause. A charming lady confesses that when she was a girl of fifteen she saw Brahms near the Opera, looking at concert notices on a kiosk. "I sidled up and gazed adoringly at him. With his great deep blue eyes, he returned my glance most expressively. We walked along like this, keeping parallel, until we came to where the Goethe monument now stands. Here, no longer able to contain myself, I blurted out: 'Good-day, Herr Doktor!' That broke the spell. He gave out two queer, gruff, staccato sounds, more like the yap of an outraged dog than anything else, and turned abruptly away."

Children's tears sometimes stirred him to laughter instead of commiseration. Baroness Rinaldini recalls how he came into the nursery when she was eight. Having heard that he was a distinguished person, and eager to show him due respect, she called him "Mr. Master," a form of address commonly reserved for tinkers, cobblers, and other small artisans. From his facial expression she gathered that she had committed a *faux pas,* and immediately began to howl bitterly. But "Mr. Master" was vastly amused and rushed away to tell everyone about his new title.

According to his "house-hostess," the children of the rich found less favour with him than the others because to his taste they were spoiled. And they had few presents from him. Kalbeck's daughter has told me: "As children my brother and I used to come downstairs for dessert. Brahms, who was a frequent guest, would ironically call me 'the Princess,' and my brother, 'the Mister Doctor,' because we were rich people's children, and quite spoiled. We always used to fear him, because his hands were so hard. His love-pats used to hurt."

This report was confirmed by her father.

Brahms [wrote Kalbeck] certainly loved children above all—in contrast to the grown-ups—for their holy simplicity, innocence, and honour. . . . His teasings were awkward expressions of tenderness, or more often well meant attempts at education, if he thought the little ones were being made too soft or were spoiled by their parents. My small daughter, who loved to climb upon dear *Onkel* Bahms' knee, once had from him a caressing tap on the cheek that drove tears to her eyes. But he liked it when she bravely overcame her weakness and kept on loving him all the more. . . . One Christmas while my wife and I were away from home, he came to the house with his pockets full. But when he saw the many luxurious presents with which, sorely against our wills, the children had been surfeited by friends, he gave each of them a slap, and went away grumbling.

Brahms used to tease the Scholz children unmercifully.

He would take a little one on his knee with apparent friendliness [their mother reported]. But scarcely was he seated there before Brahms would threaten to snip off his nose with a cigar-cutter. When he was reassured, and asked perhaps for a drink of water, the Master would pour it down the back of his neck inside his little dress. The small girls, on the other hand, always had their apron strings untied, turn and twist as they might. Then, when they were all worked up with apprehension and fear, Brahms went away well pleased.

No doubt he looked upon the slaps and the teasings as valuable character-builders.

For poor children, though—with only one exception—I have never heard that Brahms' hands or his bearish playfulness were too hard. This may have been because the poor ones were of tougher fibre; but more probably because he liked them better and felt they needed no more discipline than a childhood like his own had given them.

The exception was told me by his "house-hostess," and the incident scared the composer quite as much as it did his victims. "Just before Christmas, the first year I was at Karlsgasse 4, Brahms found my two little boys playing together. He pulled a grievously long face and said: 'Oh, children, I have some sad news for you. The Christ Child has influenza and can't bring you anything this Christmas!'

"Being quite young, the boys took him literally and burst into the most hideous howls of grief and despair. The Master had not meant his little joke to have such a powerful effect, and was greatly embarrassed. He rushed to his rooms for candy. But even that was no good. Then he came helplessly to me and confessed: 'Look here, Frau Truxa, now I don't know any more which way to turn! Can you not pacify the children? Assure them that the Christ Child has already recovered!' Which I did with great success."

YULE FIRE IN A SLUM

Between a refuse pile and a pedlar's tray,
I saw pale children circling, hand in hand,
Round a green branch—their gutter fairy-land.
Deep in the slush they frolicked, lost in play,
For this was all the Christmas tree they had:
A scrap of wilted pine. They had made it glad
With paper ribbons full of curious holes—
The spoil of broken player-piano rolls:
Festoons of silent music, draped among
The twigs where toys and candy should have hung.

"Let's make it burn!" The tiny blaze leaped higher.
Their Christmas tree was now their Christmas fire.
And, in the sudden glare, I could plainly see,
Printed upon a burning paper's end:
"Johannes Brahms . . . G minor Rhapsody."

I thought how it would please that children's friend
If he could watch his flaming tones achieve
Such radiance for a gutter Christmas Eve;
Though rhapsodies must, phoenix-like, progress
Into another form of loveliness.
How that Pied Piper's coat-tails would grow fat
With sugar toys; how every bright-eyed brat
Would encore "Uncle Bahms" with crow and shout!
.   .   .   .
Children, is there a candy-shop about?

BRAHMS WITH THE BAG OF CANDY

By Dorrit Schwarz, a Viennese lady, five years old, whose blood is half American. Dorrit was much interested in the author's researches and of her own accord made this picture as an illustration for his book.

Chapter XII

THE HEART OF A CHILD

As long as the world still possesses people who, like Brahms, have the heart of a child and the character of a hero — I do not fear for humanity.

DR. RICHARD FELLINGER, SR.

ONE reason why the little ones were so attached to Brahms is that he was a child among children. Instinctively they felt his essential youthfulness. And whether he was with them or not, this person with the big beard and the gruff voice carried about in him the heart of a child.

Even as a man he still loved to play with the toy soldiers which had entranced him as an urchin. They actually brought him musical ideas. And in one of his earlier letters to Frau Schumann there is a passage of touching naïveté in which he innocently promises that mature mother of seven living children a treat in helping him manœuvre his beloved leaden regiments.

No more did he outgrow the favourite books of his youth. Late in life he showed a friend his battered *Robinson Crusoe* and *Paul und Virginie,* confessing that they still captivated and thrilled him.

At twenty-three this great boy, in answering Joachim, who had praised his music, admitted: "I had to rush outdoors because I couldn't very well jump about for joy in the room."

Corresponding with certain friends the grown man often gleefully used a sort of picture-writing which one would ordinarily associate with a lad of eight. These illustrations were sometimes dragged into the text with surprising awkwardness.

He began a letter to Clara with a sketch of a house-fly:

Flies are a nuisance, even when they are pretty, and so the above indicates that I am about to be a nuisance to you.

To this serious matron he dispatched many such illustrations. Urging her to expedite the manuscript of the *German Folk-Songs:*

I would beg you most humbly, as the figure shows [a kneeling grasshopper], not to hold up the parcel.

He began a note about his coming visit to play her the new clarinet sonatas, on notepaper decorated with a picture of a cockchafer:

DEAR CLARA,
    In anticipation of the coming days I am as pleased as a cockchafer, i.e. quite incredibly, for I have no notion how such a creature is pleased.

To send the same friend another insect, he took paper decorated with a lady-bird and artfully used it upside down in order to close:

> With hearty greetings
> Your [picture of a lady-bird]
> JOHANNES.

These juvenilia are the more astonishing when one finds that they were all perpetrated after the ageing Master had nearly finished his life-work.

Another letter to Clara ends:

> And so, with the heartiest greetings . . . I take most polite leave and walk out [here he pasted in a small snapshot of himself in the act of sauntering off the page] as
> Your
>
> JOHANNES.

And when she had decided not to visit Vienna, he began another letter:

rit.

Such a large sigh is forwarded in advance.

In a letter about a projected trip to Bayreuth with his publisher-friend Simrock, the latter discovered an absurd imitation of an Austrian gulden note: "Enclosed find some money, in case you haven't enough for the pilgrimage."

Brahms doubtless showed this boyish side to Clara more easily than to others, because he had transferred to her a part of his mother-adoration.[1] At twenty-one, soon after falling

---

[1] See p. 254 f. For a discussion of the delayed puberty which may have accentuated his boyishness, see p. 261.

in love with her, he went to visit his friend Grimm in Hanover. From there, with all the eager innocence of a child of six, he wrote her about his latest toy—then turned around and analysed its performance with the sophistication of a ripe musician.

My arrival here was droll. . . . I got out of the train and looked about long and vainly for Grimm. At last I pulled from my pocket a trumpet which I had bought, and tooted it. Then Grimm recognized me and came running.

The trumpet sounds lovely: E flat and G are out of tune and sound sharp. A hollow low C flat growls along, also a trace of contra F!

Sometimes his love of child's play and his sensitive ear disported themselves outrageously with vowels instead of tin trumpets. Once, having scribbled three lines of a note to a friend, he found he had used the long *i* sound four times. So he perversely decided to go all out for the exploitation of this shattering vowel effect and in the ensuing four lines of nonsense managed to work in long *i* no fewer than twenty-seven times.

At home in his own country, this prophet seemed to have had his boyish exuberance somewhat damped by an inferiority consciousness bred of his own slum origin and the knowledge that his fellow Hamburgers knew how many years he had been compelled to play the piano in low dives. Sometimes he shook off this incubus and became unself-conscious, as when he scandalized the stolid burghers by conducting his girls' choir from the branches of a tree.

Laughing, light-hearted Austria, however, was a very different matter from the stiff, gloomy Hamburg of his early years. Among the young and exuberant Viennese, Brahms' natural youthfulness [2] was congenially at home. Anybody can understand this who has admired the debonair way in which these people have carried off their dreadful troubles since the Great War. One has only to take part in a *Heurigen* in Grinzing or the Concordia Ball in the Konzerthaus. One has only to watch, on the Rote Berg in Hietzing, some windy autumn afternoon, the dozens of grown men happily flying their kites.

Brahms spent thirty-five years, a little more than half of his life, among such people, who must have helped to keep him young. It is hard to imagine Johann Sebastian Bach joining in the party that took place at Rudolph von der Leyen's house in Krefeld, where the town orchestra serenaded Brahms. This cheered the dinner guests to such a point that everybody seized some trophy and did a triumphal march through the rooms. Brahms led the procession, brandishing a music stand.

When they had said good-night [wrote Von der Leyen] and were putting on their coats in the hall below, Brahms asked me: "Shall I call them all back once more?" With the doors wide open he sat down and played Viennese waltzes as only he knew how. And whenever one of the friends softly stole in, he nodded gaily to me, until at last he had lured the whole party upstairs.

What could be more boyish than the way in which, aged forty-three, he played with frogs on the island of Rügen? Sir George Henschel relates: "We lay in the grass . . . and caught tiny frogs and let them jump from a stone down into

[2] According to Levi, Brahms at thirty-two was denied admission to the Baden-Baden Casino on the ground that he had not yet reached the legal age of eighteen!

the water. This pleased him enormously, in particular when the sprightly little creatures, glad to be again in their element, hastily swam away and moved their hind leglets in accordance with all the laws of the swimmer's art. Then when the little frog thought it had escaped, Brahms caught it gently again and, letting it go, laughed with all his soul."

· He disliked cards, preferring more active amusements.[3]

During the Rügen vacation he met Xaver Scharwenka and at once characteristically invited him to go flounder-fishing the next morning at three. When Scharwenka did not appear in time, Brahms drove him from bed by smashing a window of his room with a long iron rod.

At Aarau in Switzerland, during supper after a concert which he had given with Joachim, the thirty-three-year-old Brahms proposed that they "divvy the swag" like true bandits. No sooner said than done! In the presence of their wildly cheering fellow-guests, the two celebrities alternately drew a "doubloon" from the hoard until one indivisible twenty-franc piece remained. Over this the friends staged a pirates' brawl with such blood-curdling realism that one spectator rushed out in alarm and hastily returned with—change. At which the reconciled cut-throats fell with bathetic gratitude upon the neck of their preserver.

Brahms had a healthy urchin's delight in conflagrations, intensified perhaps by boyhood memories of the great Hamburg fire of 1842 which levelled five thousand buildings.

Not for a long time [he wrote Simrock with gusto] have I had such a beautiful treat at a fire as in Schwerin. Standing

---

[3] Dr. Bauer assures me that Böhler's well known silhouette of him playing skat with Richter and Johann Strauss is wholly fictitious.

near a hose, on the flat roof of the house adjoining, I looked right down upon it. It was extraordinary! If a house *must* burn, at least one enjoys watching it.

An eyewitness tells me she thinks it was the promise of fireworks which made Brahms break his custom of not spending nights at friends' houses, and attend Hanslick's seventieth birthday party at the Miller zu Aichholzes' in Gmunden. "Customarily he excused himself from such hospitality on the specious ground that he did not possess a suitable coat. But this time he had been promised fireworks, which he adored. I watched him leaning over the balustrade; and as each rocket went up he gave a great 'Oh!' in which his whole stocky frame took part. He almost yodelled with joy at the spectacle."

According to the same informant, the Master was fond of bowling, a game to which he brought more enthusiasm than skill: "He was a sight! He stood awkwardly with his legs wide apart, the right foot foremost and the balance all wrong, rolling the balls with enormous zeal. But he could not hit anything."

With a rock—the poor boy's missile—in his hand he was more effective. Von der Leyen has told how, during a picnic at Lake Loppio, empty champagne bottles were corked and cast into the water. "Then began the championship stone-throwing contest to hit and smash the swimming bottles. Brahms took part in the game with enthusiasm and skill, and when a shot of his succeeded he was as tickled as a small boy." The same friend has told how whole-heartedly the Master used to romp with the rather wild dogs on the lawn, and engage in snowball fights with the Krefeld schoolgirls.

Sometimes he could be as hare-brained as a fifteen-year-old lad. At sixty, in climbing down from the Saracen village of Mola, behind Taormina in Sicily, he as usual outdistanced his companions, lost the way, reached the edge of a quarry, scorned to turn back, started to clamber down the sheer rock-face, and was rescued from probable death by a day-labourer who happened to notice the escapade, and put him on the right path.

Kalbeck writes of another feat of strength, this time in more formal surroundings, which has brought the Master un-deserved athletic laurels. He represents Brahms, at fifty-eight, after a performance of his G major quintet by the Joachims in Berlin, jumping from the audience directly upon the stage. But Dr. Richard Fellinger has furnished a correc-tion: "Kalbeck's story of Brahms' leap to the stage of the Singakademie, for which he quotes me as authority, is incor-rect in this form. Kalbeck wholly misunderstood me. Natu-rally Brahms did not jump from the floor of the hall directly upon the high stage, but after he had acknowledged the ap-plause from the smaller stage where the players were, he swung himself across with a leap to the step-wise orchestral stage in order to reach the greenroom behind it. When I took into account his corpulence and near-sightedness, the feat gave me a strong impression of agility and freshness."

The Master, however, was not always so sure-footed in Berlin. Frau Dr. Gerhart Hauptmann has told me that, when she studied violin with Joachim, she once saw Brahms and d'Albert make a unique entrance. The former was to con-duct a concerto, the latter to play the solo part. Brahms missed the top step and nearly fell to the stage, while d'Albert

BRAHMS AMONG HIS FRIENDS

Brüll   Door   Gänsbacher   Epstein   Hausmann   Mandyczewski
Gustav Walter   Hanslick   Brahms   Mühlfeld

Hausmann is jocosely pretending to "play Brahms."

Courtesy of Herr Eugen von Miller zu Aichholz, who took this picture in his
own town house

came tumbling after and nearly landed on top of him.

Brahms often amused himself boyishly in taking off amusing characters; and he was no mean actor. Opposite p. 368 he is shown making an exit from the Miller zu Aichholz villa, in the character of an affected old maid, "in order to feel"—as the son of the house who snapped this picture, assures me—"if it is still raining."

These youthful high jinks of the Master's were infectious. The picture shows Hausmann, the 'cellist of the Joachim Quartet, standing behind Brahms and using the latter's venerable head as the bridge of an imaginary 'cello. The reader will notice that only three of the group seem to be aware of the by-play. Mandyczewski and Walter are smiling in sympathy, while Gänsbacher, the amateur 'cellist, is averting shocked eyes from the impious spectacle.

After the Yuletide celebration in his own rooms for the young Truxa boys, the ageing Brahms always adjourned to the house of his friends the Fellingers on Christmas Eve, but he made the condition that no real presents were to be given him. Frau Maria Fellinger herself was infinitely resourceful in the sort of roguery dear to his adolescent heart. One year he was dismayed to find at his place a formidable music manuscript with the forbidding inscription: *"The Seasons, dedicated to the honoured master Johannes Brahms by Maria Fellinger."* As presentation copies from amateur composers were his bane, he was vastly relieved to find beneath this title page only a calendar and writing pad.

Another Christmas at the same house he was led up to a lady's charmingly decorated toilet table, complete with flowered curtains and mirror. Assuming there must be some mistake he turned away, only to be assured that his secret passion for feminine adornment and such-like fripperies had been discovered. That made him smell a rat! Investigation revealed that the rouge pot and powder boxes were filled with tarts, and the perfume bottles with his favourite liqueurs. The mirror turned out to be only the highly polished metal of a coffee-tray. And a score of other ostensible adjuncts of a luxurious feminine toilet became, in the turn of a hand, homely articles useful in a plain bachelor establishment.

The *chef d'œuvre* was the waste-basket, that receptacle destined for importunate letters and music condemned to death. It was adorned with a staff made of pencils, a gingerbread violin clef, and sugar notes which sang, in allusion to opus 3: *"O versenk', O versenk' dein Leid"* (Oh sink, Oh sink thy grief). This sort of fooling was highly popular with the Master.

Like Beethoven, he had a keen relish for hoaxes and practical jokes, a taste probably acquired by both from a rough and uncultivated early environment, though the later composer was uniquely sportsmanlike enough to enjoy those rare occasions when he himself was cast for the victim's rôle.

We hear of Johannes as an urchin going with his pal, Chris Miller, to knock at the doors of houses where Hamburg's great men had once lived. With serious politeness they would inquire for Herr Johann Heinrich Voss or Herr Georg Friedrich Händel. When the excellent people declared they knew nothing of these gentlemen, the lads would register astonishment while quivering with inner laughter over the good faith of the inmates.

When later on he visited Cologne, Johannes used to stop

some worthy citizen and ask the whereabouts of the celebrated cathedral. And when it was proudly shown him, loom-
ing overhead, he would cry in great disappointment: "Is that
so? Really? Is *that* the famous Cologne cathedral? Why, I
had thought it was lots larger!"

At the Court of Detmold, when he and Bargheer had to
play Mozart violin sonatas by request of the Prince, he liked
to start without warning in the wrong key, making the poor
fiddler transpose for his life.

Eating once in a Mürzzuschlag restaurant at the same table
with those somewhat less than immortal musicians, Gänsbacher, Door, and Epstein, he secretly paid their checks. And
he fed with glee upon the bewildered expressions of the trio
when the well coached proprietor reverently drew near and
assured them that he could not think of taking a kreutzer
from such celebrities, because it was already impossible sufficiently to appreciate the honour they had shown his humble
establishment.

At twenty-one Johannes confessed to Clara that, as a composer, he enjoyed hoaxing people with false names. He often
gave his own things out as the work of Kullak. "Mendelssohn's name I never use before bad people, and only when I
am especially proud of a piece."

This habit clung to him, and he particularly liked to trick
importunate and irksome lion-hunters. Widmann tells that

when the schoolmasterish music director of a very small
Swiss town graciously assured Brahms that he was familiar
with every one of his compositions, the Master motioned him
with his hand to be still and listen attentively, as the festival
orchestra was just then playing something of his own. It was,

however, a military march by Gungl. I can still see the good man before me, how with open mouth and reverently contorted eyes he listened to the rather commonplace fanfares, which he now really held to be a Brahms composition, while Brahms, in outrageous glee over his successful trick, whispered to the rest of us: "Just look at the Basilio!" [4]

It requires a brave composer to play such tricks on the moulders of public opinion. But if a promising hoax was in question, Brahms was not the man to shrink from even this step. When a newspaper reporter approached him on the Wiesbaden promenade, the Master politely explained: "You must be looking for my brother the composer. Just you hasten along this rough path through the forest and up yonder mountain, and you will probably overtake him."

At Göttingen in his middle twenties he perpetrated another adolescent prank. He was in love with Agathe von Siebold, who was then studying composition with Grimm (nicknamed Ise). The latter once scolded her for handing in bad exercises. Michelmann relates how she told her troubles to Johannes, who rubbed his hands and cried: "All right for Ise. Now we'll astonish him!" and fell to writing notes. Agathe copied the new Brahms composition and bore it proudly to her teacher. But when Ise looked it through he raised his eyebrows, wrinkled his forehead, and shouted in great indignation: "Where did this swinish mess come from? Never will you amount to anything—never!"

Torn out of her fool's paradise, poor Agathe stammered: "But what if Johannes wrote it?" "Then," came the withering reply, "it would be still worse!" Not until that point did

[4] Basilio, the hypocritical dupe in Rossini's opera, *The Barber of Seville.*

it dawn on the pair that their young friend had been fooling them both.

Carl Goldmark told a friend of mine of another purely musical impersonation. He went with Brahms to call on the Chrobaks at Grundelsee, and they reached the music-room without encountering a soul. Czerny's *School of Velocity* lay open on the piano. Brahms began to play from it, stumbling over the notes like an eight-year-old.

Suddenly a monitory voice issued from the next room: "False! There you are again playing C for C sharp!" Brahms shook with silent laughter and played on, miserably, pitiably, going steadily from bad to worse.

"But, Hans," came the voice, "what on earth are you doing? Only last evening you played *much* better than that!"

The two housebreakers had a desperate time to keep their mirth from betraying them. Meanwhile Brahms played on "badly enough to make a stone tender." There came a short cry of displeasure and a rustling of skirts. The door was violently flung open and the lady of the house burst in. "Miserable boy!——" she cried, then stopped in stupefaction.

Brahms leaned back and held his sides.

"Oh, my God, Master, is it you?"

"Yes," chuckled the pianist; "naturally I can't play as well as Hans!"

Brahms once took the most elaborate pains to hoax Gustav Nottebohm. The poverty-stricken scholar often strolled with him in the Prater, and habitually bought his cold supper there from a certain cheese-and-sausage peddler. Kalbeck amusingly reports how "one evening he received his victuals wrapped in old music-paper covered with crabbed notes, apparently in Beethoven's handwriting. Fighting down his excitement, he marched to the next lamp-post, unfolded the paper, examined it carefully through his spectacles, smoothed it, and, without a word, shoved it into his pocket. The cheese he kept in his hand and ate as he walked, assuring the others that he was unusually hungry to-day. And never did he drop a syllable about his find—to the huge disappointment of the company, who had been let by Brahms into the secret. For the mysterious sheet contained a variation of the latest popular song-hit. That rascal Brahms had fabricated it in masterly imitation of Beethoven's hen-scratches, and enjoined the peddler to wrap it around the professor's cheese."

Herr Emil Hess, who witnessed this comedy, has described to me how Nottebohm started when he caught sight of the paper; how he held it farther and ever farther from his far-sighted eyes, which grew progressively rounder and seemed about to pop from his head; and how desperate the hoaxers were over his canny silence.

This was one of the notable occasions on which the Beethoven specialist blushed. Brahms once wrote Simrock: "Has your wife noticed how charmingly Nottebohm—in spite of everything—can blush?" And Kalbeck, in editing this correspondence, explained in a note: "The then fifty-three-year Nottebohm was not blessed with beauty. Malicious tongues asserted that his blushing was merely a reflection from his nose."

This same Kalbeck told how the Master played on him a manuscript trick of a far nobler nature than the one he had tried on Nottebohm. Soon after publishing an essay on Beethoven's quartets, he had a call from Brahms, who handed

BRAHMS' WORK-ROOM

The trick rocker is to the left of the table. Above it hangs Ingres' portrait of Cherubini. Brahms disliked the sentimental muse of music who hovers over the composer; so he hid her behind a cardboard curtain. Between the Sistine Madonna and Beethoven is a relief of Bismarck which Brahms decorated with a laurel wreath from one of his own concert-tours.

him a roll of music. This proved to be a cheap salon-piece by X, and the critic angrily bade him keep the rubbish for himself.

BRAHMS: But look here, the composition is not so bad as to justify your insulting me right off like that. I give you my word that this X has quite a decent idea every now and then.

KALBECK (ungraciously casting the roll upon the piano): Well, seeing it's from you I'll keep it.

BRAHMS: But why not at least look it over?

Kalbeck, struck by a sudden wild surmise, tears open the roll, and finds within that banal wrapping—original manuscript sketches by Beethoven for the C sharp minor quartet!

BRAHMS (laughing in his beard): Well, what did I tell you? That's not such a sorry idea, is it?

A visit to the Master's home was not without risk, especially for the pompous, the prim, or the easily embarrassed. For he had a trick rocking-chair. (See opp. p. 140.) His housekeeper assures me that "he often amused himself by making his visitors take this chair—especially handsome women. If the fair arrival perched gingerly on the front edge, she either fell on her knees or ignominiously plumped down upon the floor. If on the other hand, she boldly sat well back, her feet flew up to an alarming height. In either case, Brahms would turn away and laugh heartily to himself."

Sometimes his idea of fun was yet more crudely identical with that of Max and Moritz, those deathless creations of his favourite Wilhelm Busch. Widmann recalls how he liked to cower back of a fire-screen and, at the psychological moment, burst forth with dæmonic laughter like a mischievous hobgoblin.

But his friends sometimes paid him back in like coin. In her *Reminiscences,* Schumann's daughter Eugenie recalls how, at their home in Baden-Baden, Levi once heard Brahms approaching and hastily concealed himself, like Falstaff, in a clothes-hamper. "Is Levi here?" asked Brahms. "No!" chorused the little girls in high glee.

The Master turned to go, when, to his amazement the hamper emitted the opening baritone solo from Beethoven's Ninth symphony—

O *Freunde, nicht diese Töne!*
(O friends, not tones like these!)

followed by the apparition of Jack-in-the-Box Levi.

Herr Emil Hess has told me that once, in a circle of friends, Brahms spoke slightingly about the oratorio of a certain young Dutch composer. Kalbeck objected: "But he's the very man you recommended to us."

Brahms bristled at once, barking roughly and angrily: "I recommend nobody!"

"Except yourself," retorted Kalbeck.

General consternation! Here was Kalbeck, the humble Brahms-slave who ate out of the hand, suddenly turning and insulting to his face this super-modest genius who never lifted a finger in his own interest, and spoke of his own music only to run it down!

Brahms grew purple with fury and scowled menacingly at his disciple, who added: "When you leave a room you say, '*Ich empfehle mich*' (I recommend myself)." That broke the fearful tension and everybody roared. For once the worm had turned—a phrase as witty as it was audacious.

Dr. Sigmund Münz assures me that Brahms often stopped with him before the Schubert memorial in the Vienna Stadt Park and praised it as the ideal artist's monument (which is, by the way, a commentary on the Master's immature taste in the arts of design).

At this spot the noted wit Bela Haas once obtained from him a record "rise." "In a hundred years' time, Herr Doktor," he began heavily, "over there on the other side of the park, they will be admiring your monument——"

"Oh, cut that out!" Brahms broke in roughly, for he could not abide fulsome praise.

"But please let me finish. You don't know what I was going to say."

"Well, what?" cried the angry composer.

"I had in mind to observe that people will stand before your statue and look it all over and say to one another: 'Johannes Brahms—now who on earth was that?' "

Chapter XIII

QUITE CONTRARY

JOHANNES BRAHMS was anything but that amiably inverte-
brate assenter to all propositions, vulgarly known as the Yes-
man. Almost any positive statement was likely to touch off
his combativeness. He was a born denier, a standing member
of the Opposition.

This independence of opinion was inherited from his Dithmarsh ancestors. Those sturdy individualists, the marshmen
and moormen who inhabit the bracing coasts of the North
Sea, are people not easily led about by the nose. Whether it
is apocryphal or not, that well worn story which one finds
in all the books, about Johannes' father and his instrument,
admirably illustrates the temper of the stock from which he
sprang. When the conductor of the little Hamburg orchestra
begged the muscular Johann Jakob Brahms to restrain his
ardour, the latter spoke up strong and clear: "Mr. Conductor, this here is my double-bass and I can play on it just as loud
as I want!"

His famous son was a chip of the old double-bass. Robert
Schumann's daughter Eugenie declares that Brahms lived

in a perpetual state of self-defence against supposed infringe-
ments on his personality and independence. If anyone ever
assumed that he held any particular opinion or judgment, he
would always assert the contrary.[1]

[1] *Erinnerungen*, 1925, p. 250.

He used to justify this sort of automatic reaction by quoting Beethoven's sceptical slogan: "The contrary is probably just as true."

Such truculent self-assertion usually implies unbearable conceit. But Brahms, strange to say, was one of the most essentially modest and self-depreciative of men. His habit of contradiction was an unconsciously defensive self-assertion against the sense of inferiority produced by his lowly social origin, his small stature, his high-pitched voice, and other physical and psychical handicaps—from all of which he must have suffered terribly at the start of his professional career.

When it comes to Brahms, wrote Hanslick, "one must always be ready for surprises." And he kept on surprising people until they learned that in matters of Brahmsian opinion the unexpected usually happened. Two months before his death he complained of the often married d'Albert, finding it monotonous that the fellow still had the same wife as on his previous visit. And Dr. Gerhart Hauptmann in the late eighties heard Brahms deploring the fact that the public no longer hissed his music!

When he used Joachim as a critic he was naturally expected to profit by the hints of that skilled technician about bowing, fingering, and technical practicability, and to ignore the more fundamental musical counsel of that second-rate composer. Whereupon, of course, he proceeded with gusto to do the exact opposite.

His automatic spirit of contradiction is neatly shown in the incident of the G major string quintet, which he began with a solo for the lower strings of the 'cello.

I had prescribed a simple *forte* for the four upper voices [he wrote Joachim]. In my opinion folks around here are far too much accustomed to accompany every solo *p*. At once the 'cellist Hummer [then a member of the Rosé Quartet] was also of the opinion that he should have a *p* over him. I didn't give in, but I must admit that the right effect has not yet been worked out.

Feeling the reasonableness of Hummer's reluctance to be drowned in a raging sea of accompaniment, Joachim begged for mitigation of the fatal *f* to *mf*—arguing that otherwise a Gargantuan super-'cello would be needed. For the moment Brahms acquiesced and was delighted with the improved result. But in the end his contrary spirit proved too Antæan. Crushed to earth, it rose seven times stronger. And when the printed score appeared, those fatal *f*s were back again under each part. In his dislike of convention he decreed the impossible: the soloist must be predominantly audible, though the four accompanying fiddles play just as loud as he!

Ever since, when the G major quintet is given, one of two things happens. Either the Master's directions are swept aside, or the agonized 'cellist saws so desperately that one hears considerably more resin, sheepgut, copper wire, horse-tail, and bow-wood than Brahms. And there are some who feel that this serves the composer right for wanting to have his dynamic cake and eat it too.

This passion for reconciling the irreconcilable stimulated his talent for coining paradoxical phrases. Once while he was conducting an orchestral rehearsal, Emma Engelmann heard him implore: "Gentlemen, a right powerful *piano!*" Another of his inventions was "carelessly thorough" (*gründlich flüchtig*).

Toward himself he was quite as contrary as toward others. His own pleasure and capacity were tempting victims for his spirit of denial. "Whenever," he once declared, "a work of mine has made an immediate success with the public, I've always reflected: 'You must have written better things than this!' "

His contrariety, however, once made an invaluable contribution to the musical repertory. Toward the end of his life Brahms confided to a friend: "Recently I started various things, symphonies and so on, but nothing would work out well. Then I thought: I'm already too old, and resolved energetically to write no more. I considered that I had all my life been sufficiently industrious and had achieved enough; here I had before me a care-free old age and could enjoy it in peace. And that made me so happy, so contented, so delighted— that all at once the writing began to go." For the words "that made me so, etc.," the psychologist would perhaps substitute: "my spirit of contradiction stimulated me so powerfully."

This spirit contributed more to the repertory, however, than the clarinet chamber music, the last piano pieces, and the *Four Serious Songs*. To it we are indebted for one of the gayest, most sparkling overtures in the orchestral library. The doctor's diploma conferred on Brahms by Breslau University, which described him as *"princeps musicae severioris"* prompted him to make the rollicking *Academic Festival* overture anything but severely in keeping with the pedantic solemnities of academic convention. It made him long to show the pompous dignitaries how material even so *infra dig.*

as a handful of students' drinking songs could be elevated and fused into a work of art. Whereas, on the other hand, we may be fairly certain that if the doctor's diploma had come off its high horse and set forth the Master's blithe and genial humanity as a composer, he would have brought those frivolous men of learning up with a round turn by sending them the austere *Tragic* overture instead.

When, with his characteristic ability in understatement he informed the scandalized Kalbeck that he had sent as his doctor's thesis "a very jolly *pot-pourri* of student songs *à la Suppé*," the latter ironically inquired if the *Fuchslied* had also been included. "Yes, indeed," was the gleeful response. And when, with hands wrung to heaven, Kalbeck groaned that he was unable to imagine how Brahms could have committed such a shocking act, the latter dryly returned: "Fortunately, however, it is quite unnecessary that you should!"

This instinct for championing such under-dogs of art as student songs against the established conventions of the dignitaries was responsible for many another full-flavoured page. In the spirit of "He hath cast down the mighty from their seats and exalted them that are of low degree," Brahms once defended a passage in the rondo of Beethoven's *"Emperor"* concerto against a friend who complained that it reminded him of a music-box.

Automatically he took up the cudgels: "Well, why not? Music-boxes are also not to be sneezed at, if there is something in or behind them." The friend did not realize that here Brahms was in reality defending the 22nd of his *Handel Variations* and the 5th variation in the *Andante* of his B flat sextet. How like the democratic master to have been a pioneer [2] in dignifying the music-box, that humble toy of a bygone proletariat! One is reminded of the warm interest he once took in another low-born instrument, the banjo, as played in Leipzig by a young American miss; and how chivalrously he defended against Widmann's superciliousness the brass bands and singing societies of the Swiss workingmen, despite their lamentable effect on sensitive ears. There never was a nobler "man of the people" in music.

It gave him an impish joy to indulge his instinct for balking the expectations of the formalists and of the "regular fellows." To this instinct, in part, we owe the rich resourcefulness of that rhythmical variety which—to mention only one instance—makes the pulse of such a piece as the opening movement of the D major symphony [3] so delightfully tricky and unpredictable.

He even disliked to have his true thoughts and emotions inferred from his demeanour. Frau Bertha Gasteiger tells me that when he first heard young Marie Soldat play he frightened her by looking very serious. "Later on I met him at a really bad concert, and asked him why, after such miserable music, he was looking so happy and vivacious. 'Oh,' he answered, 'that's the way I am built. If a piece or a performer impresses me I am serious; but if I seem vivacious and sympathetic, then the music has certainly not appealed to me.' "

It is amusing to note how often his contrary spirit forced him thus to abandon every pretence of consistency. In searching the Bible for choral texts, the more "heathenish" and

[2] For the Beethoven passage is no more than a faint allusion, and both the Brahms passages in question were written long before the music-box variation of the Tschaikowsky trio.

[3] See p. 314.

"godless" the passage, the better he was pleased. Although a non-church-going Protestant, he used to reproach the Roman Catholic servant girl who cleaned his rooms, for not attending church on Sunday, gravely admonishing her that members of each communion should live up to their duties.

Kalbeck relates an instance of the same sort. As he and Brahms were waiting in the cemetery for the funeral procession of their beloved friend Dr. Billroth, Brahms pointed out approvingly that among the thousands of mourners there was not a cigarette to be seen. And all the while he himself was puffing forth clouds of smoke.

This criss-cross instinct was so strong that if he suspected anybody of a tendency to run after him, his idea was to make off, still faster, or else grimly to await the indiscreet wooer with some form of violence.

His housekeeper, Frau Dr. Truxa, admitted to me that, before their first meeting, she had been cautioned not to betray the slightest eagerness to serve him, nor to seem in any way impressed by his fame. "Don't let him notice that you want him as a lodger, or he'll run away!" Taking the hint, she feigned independence and harsh indifference so well that she succeeded brilliantly where all other candidates before her had lamentably failed.

At their first interview she made her manner so aloof and forbidding that the eager Brahms soon came all the way to the Schwarzspanierstrasse to urge that they lease the apartment at Karlsgasse 4, together.

Although this man would automatically attack with violence almost any statement advanced by friend or foe, his sportsmanlike partiality for opposition by others made him fond of dialectic. Far from being the overbearing autocrat of opinion that Beethoven had been, during a good part of his life he enjoyed a spirited argument so much that he found it conducive to digestion. "It is advantageous," he wrote Widmann, "to skirmish with you. One experiences something and learns something, and eats a happy dinner!"

When in 1863 he assumed the direction of the Singakademie, he looked over the light, somewhat superficial programs of his predecessors and, naturally, found them all wrong. These frivolous, careless, delightful, pleasure-loving Viennese should thenceforth, he decided, be made to sharpen their wisdom teeth on sterner fare.

As an earnest for the future, he opened the season's pleasure (it was destined to be his sole season there!) with Bach's lengthy cantata *Ich hatte viel Bekümmerniss* (I Had Much Grief). How straight from the heart, with what a poignant note of autobiographic conviction did the startled and contradicted and sternly drilled ladies and gentlemen of the happy-go-lucky Singakademie echo these words before the close of that inauspicious season! And with the sound of what a deep amen might all the Master's friends and acquaintances, whenever they recalled his spirit of contradiction, have re-echoed: "I had much grief!"

Kalbeck bears witness that in his last days Brahms "developed such a sensitive, touch-me-not belief in the infallibility of his own personal judgment" that if any friend ventured to sustain another opinion against him, he would show a surprisingly ruthless brutality in breaking off relations with the presumptuous heretic. After such a scene he would confess: "I could have been rough just now if I hadn't long ago cured myself of the habit." [4]

The Master's intolerance, however, was of longer standing than his last illness. A generation before, in the middle seventies, this quality lost him his warm friend and zealous propagandist, the conductor Hermann Levi. Brahms was visiting Levi in Munich when, in the course of a musical conversation, Levi mentioned the names of Gluck and Wagner in the same connexion. Whereupon the Master shouted angrily: "One doesn't pronounce these two names like that, one after the other!" He rushed from the room, and left town the following day.

This put an end to the friendship. Levi, up to then Brahms' St. Paul, was changed in a flash to Saul, and before long was saying incredible things, such as that the Master had composed nothing pre-eminent for a quarter of a century, and everything that he now wrote was a repetition of his earlier work. Which goes to show how the sound critical judgment of even extraordinary men (like Levi) can be wrecked by personal bias; and how much harm, in many an influential quarter, Brahms' unmannerly manners and imperious spirit of contradiction must have done to the cause of his music.

And yet, so little was the Master conscious of his own bearish intolerance that he could write to Simrock in 1886:

One couldn't associate with anybody at all if he demanded from everyone without exception full sympathy and identical opinions on those things which one takes more or less to heart.

Closely allied to this contrary spirit was the fierce love of independence, which almost never allowed his broad musical

[4] IV, II, 499–500.

judgment and catholic tastes to be narrowed by the pettiness of cliques, coteries, and "schools." This passion for liberty was also one of his mainsprings of action and thought as a man.

It was partly for the sake of liberty that he renounced marriage with his beloved Agathe von Siebold, and wounded her by declaring that he could not be "fettered."

"I could not love thee, dear, so much," he seemed to say, "loved I not freedom more."

Brahms loathed having kind attentions forced on him and feeling that he was expected to be grateful. He regarded these things as handicaps to his inner freedom. And, far from returning polite thanks, he would often answer kindness with insults of which he afterwards sincerely repented. For the only way in which he was content to offer himself was as an unasked and spontaneous gift.

In fact—as could be inferred from the way in which he came to terms with his housekeeper, Frau Dr. Truxa—he was what American slang inelegantly but expressively calls a "chaser." If there was any pursuing to be done, he wanted to be the hunter, not the quarry. If any initiative was to be taken, he wanted to be the initiator. Despite his profound modesty, it went sore against his grain to play second fiddle. We have already seen that when the experienced Dr. Billroth acted as his cicerone in Italy, Brahms felt his supply of the fresh air of freedom cut off, and had all he could do not to reverse the rôles at once, and take Billroth instead under his own masterful direction.

As a loyal son of the proud Free City of Hamburg, the Master was such a good democrat that at times he would "scorn to change his state with kings." Sometimes he even went out of the way to register his disdain of court etiquette. Once, at Gmunden, during a visit to the Duke of Cumberland, not knowing that guests were expected, without being urged, to help themselves to smoking materials as soon as the Duke had lit up, Brahms took offence at his royal host for not offering him a cigar. This overcast the cordiality of their relations. Some time after, young Fräulein Hemala was riding in a carriage with Brahms when the Duke's party hove in sight. As it passed, the composer ignored it, leaning ostentatiously out of the other side in order to wave to some poor country children. This incident is a neat pendant to the meeting of Beethoven and Goethe with the Imperial Court, when the bearish musician rammed his hat down on his head, put his hands behind him, and ignored the polite greetings of the Empress and her suite.

Brahms' passion for independence made him dislike asking for anything. To obviate the necessity for this at home he developed a curious code. According to Frau Dr. Truxa, whenever he found a hole in a garment he would leave the glove-finger, sock-toe, or other defective part protruding from a crack in his bureau drawer. The discreet widow would then find, mend, and restore it to the same position. This, Brahms once explained, "did away with useless chatter."

Frau Dr. Truxa went on to illustrate how annoyed he could be when his unexpressed wishes were not swiftly divined. "One day the maid burst into tears and complained: 'Herr Brahms is so unfriendly! For some days now he has not greeted me. I have no idea why.'

"So I went into his place and spied around. At length I happened to notice that the lid of the waste-paper basket was shut. I thought I would try leaving it open every day.

"Before long the girl came beaming to me and exclaimed: 'Herr Brahms greets again!' That had been the whole trouble. He wanted that lid always up, but could not bring himself to say so. He never found out that opening the basket was my idea."

As a matter of fact, Brahms' waste-paper basket was— symbolically speaking—never closed. It was his most important article of furniture; for to its rapacious maw we owe the strikingly high average quality of his work. No wonder he was disturbed when the lid went down.

Chapter XIV

WHAT HE HID BETWEEN THE LINES

BRAHMS was a curious amalgam of opposites. The peasant in him fought the poet and the gentleman of culture. A fiery, aggressive temper and a malicious fondness for mischief off-set a kindness tenderly thoughtful. His noble and delicate generosity was held within reasonable bounds by an imperious instinct for contradiction and an intolerance of every sort of constraint. His coarse brutal directness warred with a deep-seated instinct for secretiveness and a subtle obliqueness of tongue and pen. His was a truly schizoid personality.

Privacy was with him a ruling passion. The tall desk on which he wrote his music had a hinged top. Whenever his sensitive ears heard a caller coming, he hastily tore open the lid and concealed his manuscript inside. Anybody whom he had caught indiscreetly trying to overhear him composing at the piano would have forfeited his goodwill for ever. We have seen how he might have killed a friend who, in fun, climbed a ladder and looked into his window.[1]

About his own creative work Brahms was more reticent than a prude is about sex. It went against his grain to drop even the most devious hint about music which he had in hand, until it was wholly completed, and even then his com-munications usually came out in the guise of vague jests or faint and desperately guarded allusions or burschikos whop-

[1] See p. 108.

pers. Sometimes these adumbrations remind one of Scripture: "Without a parable spake He not unto them."

"In truth," he confessed to Clara toward the close of his life, "I always write only half-sentences, and the reader himself must supply the other half." This is true of his music as well, and is one source of its fascination for the creative listener.

When, in October, 1876, the First symphony had been all but finished on the island of Rügen, he wrote Simrock— the man who, next to himself, had most at stake in the work —suggesting that a lovely symphony had remained hanging to the treetops and chalk cliffs of Stubnitz, and that his companion Henschel had happened upon it and turned it into a song, E flat major, ¼ time. This passed completely over the head of the guileless publisher, who had not yet come to realize the significance of his star composer's frothiest utterances. He had no idea that the fantastic rigmarole was intended to announce the birth of the C minor symphony. And not until the second message came, three weeks later, did Simrock taste the joy of a wild surmise.

Too bad that you are not a music-director. Otherwise you could have a symphony. It will be performed on the 4th in Karlsruhe. I expect from you and other friendly publishers a present of honour (*Ehrengeschenk*) in recognition of my not importuning them with such things.

This, of course, was understood. Needless to say, the "importuning" was all on the part of the eager publisher.

And here are the dark sayings from which, in 1884, the now highly sophisticated Simrock deduced the existence of the songs and choruses opus 91–97, and guessed that the Fourth symphony was under way: "My copyist is industrious . . . but it seems to me that I shall take better paper with more systems." In other words: the sort of music paper on which orchestral scores are written. To Bülow he described the Fourth as "a couple of entr'actes."

Before releasing the Second symphony, Brahms (to use one of his own favourite expressions) enjoyed himself "like a snow-king" in misleading his friends as to its real character. He wrote Elisabet von Herzogenberg that it was not at all necessary for him to play her the new symphony:

All you need to do is sit yourself down at the piano, depress the two pedals alternately with your little feet, and strike the F minor chord a good while, now above, now below, *ff* and *pp* —then bit by bit you'll obtain the clearest picture of my "latest."

The same day he wrote Simrock in a like farcical strain:

The new symphony is so melancholy that you will not be able to put up with it. Never before have I penned anything so sorrowful, so minor-y. The score must be published with a black border. Don't say I haven't sufficiently warned you. Do you really consider investing in such a thing?

And then, when the Second burst upon the world, blithe, dimpled, and radiating the happiness of its exuberant vitality, the mischievously contorted visage of the "snow-king" smoothed itself out and broke into as rollicking a roar of enjoyment as if Santa Claus, whom with his great beard he so closely resembled, had suddenly torn away the not too convincing mask of Old Nick and appeared before all the children *in propria persona,* his pack overflowing with presents.

The Master loved privacy and secrecy about many things besides his own work. Until late in life he almost consistently refused to be photographed, painted, or modelled, and led the artists who wistfully shadowed him a dog's life. Once when Clara Schumann stopped over to see him in Mürzzuschlag, he had the entire railway restaurant cleared so that he could dine with her undisturbed. When a fund was being raised by subscription for this same friend he contributed heavily, but with strict injunctions not to let his name be known. "In that sort of thing," he remarked, "the name of the donor should never appear. Otherwise it's not nice."

His courage and secretiveness never ceased to walk hand in hand. A week before the end of his life he wrote his stepmother:

For a change I have lain down a little and so cannot write very comfortably. But don't worry; nothing has altered, and as usual all I need is patience.

This master of indirection was eminently resourceful in keeping woman in her place. And that place was—not on his piano-stool. When fifteen-year-old Henriette Hemala was sent by her teacher Epstein to play him the *Handel Variations,* he politely excused himself on the preposterous ground that his piano was out of tune. "Imagine Brahms if you can," she recently exclaimed to me, "tolerating in his rooms an out-of-tune piano!"

Of his deviousness in social intercourse I have heard a curious instance from Frau von Kaiserfeld, the grandniece of Beethoven's dear friend Baroness Dorothea von Ertmann: "The year when I was bringing out my daughter and staying late at many dances, I once saw Brahms, who complained that we never met any more at dinners. I told him I had no time just then for that sort of thing, on account of specializing in balls.

"Soon after, I was induced to dine at the Franzes'. When I appeared, my hostess laughed and told me Brahms had confided to her that I had complained because she never invited me to dinner with him!"

In conversation Brahms sometimes resorted to a sort of labour-saving code-language which impressed his own private meaning on phrases utterly misleading to the uninitiated— a meaning often the exact opposite of their face value.

A Viennese doctor once brought him for appraisal some compositions by a friend. "Tell the gentleman they're all wonderfully beautiful," said Brahms, returning them. Kalbeck, who was present, and understood the Brahmsian code, saw that the doctor was taken aback by such warm praise from a critic usually so cold-blooded. "That means," he interpreted, "the stuff isn't worth wasting a syllable on." The Master twinkled, then bleated in a serio-comic voice: "Now did I say that? My God, my God! What sinners men are!"

This code helped to simplify and enliven the weary task of finding summer lodgings quiet enough for a composer who wished to hear himself think.

BRAHMS: I have rather an ear for music and like to hear plenty of it going on around me. I hope there is someone in this house who practises an instrument.

LANDLADY: Oh yes, indeed! Let the gentleman only make himself no worries on that score. The maiden lady below keeps her piano going all day. My daughter studies for the

operetta stage; the neighbour's hired man often blows the
cornet; and hand-organs visit our garden in great numbers
—perhaps even more than the gentleman would always like
to hear.

BRAHMS (preparing for flight): Splendid! Perfect! To-
morrow I shall return in order to take these charming rooms.

His aversion to the obvious seldom allowed him to write
out his meaning fully and baldly. He preferred to rely on
the mental agility, resourcefulness, and sympathetic intuition of his friends. Consequently, in reading his letters one
must be constantly on the alert for what he himself once defined as "a Delphic sentence."

Both in words and notes, his writings are often like good
poetry in that there is even more between the lines than in
them. What Spitta wrote to him about his *Intermezzi,* opus
117, applies also to many a page of his letters:

Intermezzi are things that by their nature necessarily have
antecedents and consequents which, in this case, every player
and hearer must formulate for himself.

One of the things which often make his letters almost as
fascinating as his music is common to both: the force of understatement, the fine subtlety of economy whereby he conjures the most meaning out of the fewest pen-scratches. He
never scratches idly. Each stroke counts—often far more
than, at first or second sight, one realizes. His utterances in
either medium seem to "look before and after," which is one
reason for their extraordinary wearing qualities.

For example, an hour's tirade against artistic laziness and
lack of musicianship lurks behind the apparently off-hand

pleasantry of these lines to the singer, Hermine Spies:

The other night I dreamed that you skipped half a measure's rest and sang a quarter instead of an eighth note—incredible fantasy!

Most of his significant understatements resemble this one, in wearing a smile. He sent the original manuscript of the G major violin sonata to Miller zu Aichholz through his wife, explaining that he understood she wished

stronger paper in which to pack birthday presents for your husband. Should the shape or anything else about this paper not be agreeable to you, I shall be glad to exchange it for other kinds—also from other manufacturers.

The happy recipient was moved to tears.

His shorthand—and offhand—designations for his own works are enough to scandalize any serious-minded Brahmin. For example, he always called the *Four Serious Songs, "die Schnadahüpferln,"* a word meaning a light and jolly kind of lay improvised by the Austrian mountain peasantry with dance accompaniment.

His modest and oblique mind hated direct references to himself, and he often used instead the name of a composer-friend which began with the same letters. Writing of an English trip by a certain pianist he mentioned "how she charmed the islanders through the enchantments which she shed particularly over Bach and Brüll."

His veiled style and his hatred of personal questions were poorly calculated to slake the curiosity of the indiscreet. When Franz Wüllner wanted to know his summer plans he parried: "Where am I going? There is much water in the wide world!"

His utterances were often too "Delphic" to be appreciated. "O my cursed economy!" he wrote Rieter the publisher. "Always too few letters [of the alphabet] in my letters!"

This "cursed economy" once lost for Emma Engelmann, the piano virtuoso, a signal honour. Through a friend her husband received this message from Brahms: "Offer him the B minor piece for his Emma." This was taken as a hint that the Capriccio, Op. 76, No. 2, was well suited to Emma's pianistic style. When the composer, having had no answer, published the piece without dedication, the little pianist was finally made to realize that she had both lost the honour and annoyed her friend. He never forgot her unresponsiveness, and years later ironically intimated that he would dedicate to her ladyship a fictitious piano concerto in A flat, "instead of thumped-to-death capriccios and rhapsodies."

Sometimes his letters reveal curt phrases that are consummate little masterpieces of reticent economy combined with sweeping suggestion. His sister Elise was an unpleasant character, a sharp thorn in the side of the brother who loyally and lovingly stood by her while she lived. In 1863 he wrote Dietrich: "My sister, with whose sharp steel pen I torture myself, sends her best regards." This is all we read of the woman, the sharp steel nibs of whose nature had tortured him not a little. Here he said nothing, while—consciously or unconsciously—suggesting much.

Brahms liked to cue into his scores little greetings to the past masters of music. Many know of his allusions to Wag-

ner, not in words alone, but also in the first movement of the
F major symphony, in the B flat concerto,[2] and in the opening notes of the A major (*"Prize Song"*) violin sonata.

But few realize that *Vergebliches Ständchen* waves not a
hand but a whole arm at Mozart;[3] that the oboe, at *espressivo* in the C minor symphony's Introduction, with its constantly broadening strides, evokes the gigantic pacings of the
'cellos in the *Eroica;*[4] and that the piano part of *Der Gang
zum Liebchen* (Op. 48, No. 1) smiles fraternally at Chopin's
C sharp minor *Waltz.*

In Part IV we shall find many more such allusions, and see
Brahms' fondness for the musical anagram. A good example
of the latter occurs in one cadenza to Beethoven's G major
concerto, into which he insinuated the name of the father of
music. He even took care to write the letters B–A–C–H[5]
over the notes—a rare act for one who was usually delighted
if his anagrams passed over the heads of the public.

The Master had a remarkably eloquent way of making a
few notes of music, scratched down perhaps on a postcard,
speak volumes. When his friend Anton Door, the pianist,
married Ernestine Groag, they received from him this original communication—

---

[2] In the symphony, the Venusberg music is echoed just before the second subject;
and in the concerto, the F sharp major clarinet solo, near the close of the *Andante,*
transports the hearer for a moment back to Venus' notorious mountain resort. Brahms
was remarkably inconsistent in his various utterances about the genius who had pur-
sued him with such bitter enmity. Here his Puckish instinct, which often disported
itself none too delicately, may have been tempted by chances for discreetly veiled allusions to the looser side of Wagner's character.

[3] See *The Marriage of Figaro,* Act III, Scene v, at the words *"Höre, Geliebte."*

[4] Opening *Allegro,* bar 338.

[5] H is the German for B natural, while B means B flat.

with best wishes for the musical union!

JOHANNES BRAHMS

Ex. 1

A little study shows that the four notes represented the four violin strings and at the same time the initials of the contracting parties; while the artful slurs insinuated perhaps that E.G. was capable of "getting around" A.D.

Brahms liked to mail his friends scraps of song-melody, leaving the unwritten words to speak for themselves to the initiated. A postcard to Frau von Miller zu Aichholz began with the tune to Schubert's *"Guten Morgen, schöne Mi(ü)l-lerin!"* (Good-morning, lovely Milleress!) He ended a long estrangement from one of his devoted friends by leaving at the rooms of Hans von Bülow a card with eight notes which in *The Magic Flute* accompany the words

Soll ich Dich, Teurer, nicht mehr seh'n?
(Shall I, dear friend, see you no more?)

I recall with what pleasure I discovered, among Frau Ignaz Brüll's mementos, a postcard bearing, in F major, simply the eight notes E E E E E F C C followed by the words:

Least of all
Your devoted
J. BR.

The tune was familiar as part of the minuet in Mozart's *Don Juan;* but, to my shame, I could not offhand supply the words. Rushing to the score, I found that these were in answer to Leporello's invitation: *"Zum Ball und Hoch-zeitschmause entbittet Sie mein Herr"* (To ball and wedding banquet my master bids you come). Whereupon Ottavio answers, to the tune on the postcard:

Wer kann da wi-der-ste-hen!
(Who could decline this charming bid?)

Not long after, however, my discoverer's pride was suddenly damped by finding that the Master had written the same tune, two months later, to Maria Fellinger, in response to an invitation to eat *Metzelsuppe*. And afterwards, in the Gmunden Brahms Museum, I found the quotation a third time, with Ottavio's words joined to the notes.

Much as he demanded of his friends in the way of subtlety and instant comprehension of trebly masked persiflage and the joke of the seven veils, he asked no more than he was prepared to give. The delicate allusions and darkly dominoed hints of the most oblique humorist found him lightning on the uptake—particularly if they dealt with music.

How many readers, bearing in mind that the first three Brahms symphonies were in C (minor), D, and F—will instantly appreciate the following jest? On the appearance of the Fourth symphony, in E (minor), young Robert Kahn remarked to the Master: "Your next three must all be in A." Without a moment's consideration, Brahms gave a great laugh and shouted: "Mozart!" He had realized that the fugue *finale* of Mozart's *"Jupiter"* symphony begins with the notes C D F E A A A.

Chapter XV

THE FLAUBERT OF MUSIC

I. BRAHMS AS A SELF-CRITIC

. . . Brahms was so far from thinking himself infallible that he consented to the publication of nothing to which he had not devoted more severe criticism, long after the work was finished, than could be collected from all the sensible remarks that have ever been made on his works since they appeared.

DR. DONALD F. TOVEY.[1]

"It is not hard to compose," Brahms once remarked to a disciple, "but it is wonderfully hard to let the superfluous notes fall under the table." He went on to confess that, before giving the world his "first" string quartet (Op. 51), he had already written and let fall under the table more than twenty of its predecessors. "A good many hundred songs" had fared no better, as compared with the 125 published before opus 51. And the slaughter of symphonies and other compositions had been terrific.

To this gift for resolute ruthlessness, almost as much as to any other quality, Brahms owes his high place among the immortals. He joined Bach and Beethoven to form the "Three B's" only by virtue of a self-criticism even more severe than theirs. Indeed he was harder on himself than any other composer of the first rank has ever been, or than any great author except Gustave Flaubert. And only the extraordinary vitality

---

[1] In *Cobbett's Cyclopedic Survey of Chamber Music*, Vol. I, p. 182.

of his inspiration saved him from the tragic impotence of those wretched creatures, the Amiels, in whom a strong creative urge is paralyzed by a stronger critical sense.

As it is, we shall never know the untold treasures sacrificed by Brahms' self-savagery. For after falling under the table, his notes were relentlessly fed into the furnace. Only a very few of the fallen have ever, by some miraculous chance, been saved like brands from the burning.

For example, the original opening bars of the E minor symphony were registered in the mind of my friend Dr. Julius Roentgen, the man whose phonographic memory was among the wonders of the musical world, and written down by him for this book. When he played with Brahms the composer's own two-piano arrangement, the symphony began as follows:

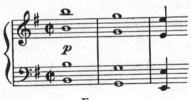

Ex. 2

which is very different from the version given by Kalbeck.[2] It is such an improvement over the present abrupt start as to nourish wistful speculations as to how much we may have been defrauded by the overzealous stoking of Brahms' furnace.

But on the whole we should not complain of his self-criticism, to the point of looking a gift-Pegasus in the mouth. For *the average quality of his works as compared with that*

[2] III, II, 461.

of his natural creative ability was thereby raised higher than that of any other composer. Brahms is the Flaubert of music.

Please do not misunderstand. It is not claimed that Brahms was as great a genius as Bach, Beethoven, Mozart, or Schubert, but merely that his severe standards made him give far more consistently and exclusively of his best than those masters did of theirs. If he had not had the iron will to let the superfluous notes fall under the table, he would still have cut a respectable figure in the history of music; but he might not have risen above that Cherubinesque level of ultimate fame which he somewhat ruefully predicted for himself—any more than a prolific and easily satisfied Flaubert might have outsoared the Paul Bourgets and the Theodore Dreisers.

The effectiveness of his talent for self-criticism was enhanced by a remarkable gift for intensive concentration on the matter in hand. This must have magnified his musical shortcomings, in his own view, to more than life size. Mr. Arthur M. Abell bears witness that "if he was talking to someone, and another broke in, Brahms would not know that the interrupter was there. He'd either give you all he had, or ignore you."

Another secret of his consistently high average of quality was his contempt for mere contrapuntal ability, for cleverness in itself. "I send you the same lot of canons again," he wrote to Joachim, the crony with whom he had agreed to exchange weekly counterpoint exercises and criticisms, any delinquency to be fined one thaler. "Apart from the scientific side, is it good music? Does the ingenuity lend it more beauty and value?"

"Is it good music?" All his life long he insisted with grow-

ing tenacity upon an honest answer to this query. And at
the first suspicion of a negative, open flew the furnace door!

Thirty-seven years after its publication, his B major trio
failed to return him a satisfactory reply to this question.
So, as it could not be burned, it had to be rewritten. Brahms
held so indomitably true to his lofty standard that page after
page of brilliant contrapuntal cleverness, as well as much
dryness, reminiscence, and rhythmical infelicity, fell under
the table, to the marked advantage of the work.

You wouldn't guess [he wrote Clara in September 1889],
on what a piece of childishness I have squandered beautiful
summer days. I have written my B major trio once more, and
can call it Op. 108 [3] instead of Op. 8. It will not be so muddled
up as it was—but will it be better?

The second version was finished during one of Brahms' re-
current periods of self-distrust. He confessed to Simrock:

About the renewed trio I must expressly state that while
the old one is bad, I do not assert that the new is good!

And he went on about the "ugliness" of the original version
and its "many unnecessary difficulties."

To Clara, who begged him to perform the rewritten work
in Frankfort, he confessed:

How gladly would I play my trio there! For that would be
a sign that I was more or less pleased with it. But unfortunately I am not, not in the least. And as I cannot have this
pleasure, I must renounce that.

His fears were unfounded. Even though he necessarily sac-

---

[3] In the end the trio revision was given no separate number, and the D minor violin
sonata became Op. 108.

rificed a certain amount of youthful freshness, the mature version improved the trio immeasurably. With that dissatisfaction of his he found himself in an overwhelming minority. The musical world was delighted, and has continued to be.

For a facile and prolix young composer there is perhaps no advice that will be more valuable—and more resented—than the advice to compare the two versions of opus 8 and find out for himself what led Brahms to make the second shorter than the first by 499 measures.

After hearing what had been done to this trio, some wag remarked that he only wished Brahms would do the same for the complete works of David Popper. Dr. Hans Gál, my informant, thinks the remark may have been made by the witty Hungarian 'cellist-composer himself.[4]

Up to the very end, Brahms was viciously hard on his own works. The 'cellist Sulzer once came late to a piano recital and, having no program, asked Brahms, whom he found at the back of the hall: "What can that thing be he is playing? It sounds somewhat familiar." "Yes," said the Master, with a faint smile, "it sounds so Mendelssohnian that it might have been written by Reinecke. But it's an *intermezzo* of my own!"

His self-criticism was staunchly seconded by his sterling North-German thoroughness. If ever an artist lent plausibility to that lopsided adage about genius being an infinite capacity for taking pains, it was Brahms.

"My themes," he told Mr. Arthur M. Abell, "come to me

[4] At any rate, a recent *bon mot* by Miss Marion Bauer lent it additional cogency. After a performance of the *Elfentanz* she sighed: "This Popper begins to sound like Grand-Popper!"

in a flash. They are intuitive. Long after their arrival I take them up and work very hard over them."

To do one's level best is never in vain [he wrote Kalbeck]. The benefits of this need not necessarily show in the place you intended.

During his Italian journeys he was never done admiring and praising the conscientious and loving toil bestowed by long-forgotten sculptors on obscure details that only one visitor in ten thousand would ever notice, such as are hidden away among the three-thousand-odd statues on the roof of Milan cathedral. His tireless patience over minutiæ which might never be appreciated made him a kindred spirit of those old sculptors. No pains were too great that seemed to promise the slightest improvement in his music.

Half-measures were anathema. When a publisher sent him, for a few finishing touches, Schneider's piano version of the Schubert Mass in E flat, Brahms ended by making a brand-new arrangement of it, and confessed:

While I very lovingly revised the piano score, I felt my ability to improve it increasing daily, little by little. So that in the end it was necessary to write a wholly new arrangement in which not a single measure of the former one remained.

Such qualities as his capacity for fearless and searching self-criticism and his infinite thoroughness were only detailed manifestations of his utter uprightness of character. Those who realize this would thrill if they should discover, as I recently did, a certain note which he pencilled in one of his own books. On a margin of the *Diaries* of Varnhagen von Ense he had noted: "In reading Goethe it occurred to me that uprightness is the foundation of genius." And this reminded me of what his old friend Prof. Robert Kahn had remarked to me a few days before: "Goethe's saying was very applicable to Brahms: 'The first and last thing that is demanded of genius is love of truth.'"

II. WHAT BRAHMS THOUGHT OF HIMSELF

To his close friends, not to mention strangers, Brahms could scarcely ever manage a reference to his more intimate concerns or to his work. He could almost say with Lionel Johnson

> I have not spoken of these things
> Save to one man, and unto God.

And even when he managed to overcome this almost morbid reticence, the revelation usually took the form of more or less awkward self-ridicule.

Perhaps it was in answer to one of her frequent complaints about his never revealing his deeper self to her that he wrote to Frau Schumann in 1858:

Do not wonder, dear Clara, that I write you nothing about my work. I do not want to do it and cannot do it.—I have . . . so little disposition and desire to lament to others about my lack of genius and skill. . . .

And in 1880, Clara said to Kalbeck:

Would you believe that, despite our long and intimate friendship, Johannes has never spoken to me of what moved his spirit? To-day he is just as great a puzzle—I might almost say, just as much of a stranger—as he was to me a quarter of a century ago.[5]

That he was poignantly conscious of this inexorable reserve and of how it hampered friendship and social intercourse is shown by his frequent half-derisive references to himself as "the Outsider" (*der Abseiter*)—an allusion to the wretched Goethean recluse of his alto *Rhapsody*, opus 53. This composition he loved well enough to keep under his pillow when he slept. Yet a year after its publication a revulsion of feeling made him write: "I always wonder how people can abide the piece."

Apart from purely ironic or witty references, Brahms' remarks about his own works have the value of extreme rarity. In 1862 he wrote Schubring:

Yesterday I sent Härtels some *Variations and a Fugue on a theme by Handel*. Look out for them when they come to the light of day. Compared with my other music I consider this

piece ~~highly~~ *very* special, and am fond of it.

Notice how, for a moment, he broke through his habitual moderation and wrote "highly"; then substituted for it the milder "very"; and then, with characteristic self-discipline, crossed out both adverbs.

In 1879, after having rather severely criticized two songs of Dessoff's—both in A flat—he wrote:

You mustn't take my strictures too hard or let them deprive the public of the sweetest songs in A flat major! Look at me! I too print the worst sort of "*Wonnevoll*," and then people sing it by preference!

[5] I, II, 298, n.

By *"Wonnevoll"* he actually meant *Wie bist du, meine Königin*—a masterpiece which, to this day, has rightly held its own among the world's prime favourites. Perhaps his scorn was merely the product of a passing mood. Most likely the popularity of this *Lied* aroused his ever alert spirit of contradiction.

A slur on the cantata *Rinaldo* was better justified. "It seems to me," he wrote Reinecke, "that it is a right useless piece." A rare flash of insight; for, as a rule, he was jealous on behalf of this crippled child of his.

And here is a highly original introduction to the D major symphony. In 1877 he informed Schubring that he was to bring out a new symphony the following January:

But a quite innocent, gay little one. Expect nothing, and for a month before, drum nothing but Berlioz, Liszt, and Wagner; then its tender amiability will do you a lot of good.

In a small circle of friends, after the finale of his G major violin sonata, he once remarked to Dr. Julius Roentgen: "Here even one listener is too many." "This," Dr. Roentgen told me, "was the Brahmsian way of suggesting the intimate character of that glorious piece."

Once in a purple moon Brahms would come within hailing distance of artistic self-satisfaction. An instance is recalled by Sir George Henschel, with whom he spent a summer on the island of Rügen. Sir George, an excellent whistler, was performing for himself the eminently whistle-able *Andante* from the C minor quartet. This caught the ear of its composer. "It appeared to please him well; for at a certain point he made rocking movements with his hands, and his face beamed. Finally he began: 'Yes, I am not ashamed to confess that it is a great joy to me if I have apparently succeeded in a song or an *Andante* or something. How must those gods Mozart, Beethoven, and the others who had such success as their daily bread—how must they have felt in putting the final stroke to *The Marriage of Figaro* and *Fidelio*, only to turn around and begin the next day on *Don Juan* and the Ninth symphony!—What beats me is how chaps like us can be vain. As high as we humans who walk upright on the earth's crust are above the creatures that crawl under it, so high are our gods above us. If it were not ridiculous it would disgust me to hear my colleagues praise me so fulsomely to my face.'

"That was the way he talked. It was more than a feeling of modesty, it was almost humility; and I was careful not to break the spell by so much as a word."

Mr. Arthur M. Abell, an American violinist, was one of the few who could make the Master talk intimately about his own work: "A year before Brahms died," said Mr. Abell, "he asked me whether I played the banjo. 'No,' I replied. 'Why?' 'Because at Klengel's I met an American girl who played for me, on that curious instrument, a sort of music which she called Ragtime. Do you know this?'—And he hummed the well known tune which goes to the words:

> If you refuse me,
> Honey, you lose me.

'Well,' the Master continued, with a far-away look in his eyes, 'I thought I would use, not the stupid tunes, but the interesting rhythms of this Ragtime. But I do not know whether

I shall ever get around to it. My ideas no longer flow as easily as they used to.'

"This remark gave me an opening for certain questions that I had longed to ask him ever since I had first met him five years before—questions concerning his mental processes while composing. Joachim had told me that Brahms was exceedingly difficult to draw out on the subject of his inspirations, but the illustrious composer's mood was right, the setting was ideal, so I ventured and won.

" 'Apropos of your flow of ideas,' I asked, 'do you ever have, when composing, sensations such as those described by Mozart in a letter to a friend? He wrote: "The process with me is like a vivid dream." '

" 'Yes, I do,' replied Brahms. 'Mozart is right. When at my best it is a dreamlike state, and in that condition the ideas flow much more easily.'

" 'Are you conscious when in this state?'

" 'Certainly, fully conscious, otherwise I would not be able to write the ideas down as they come. It is important to get them on paper immediately.'

" 'Do you ever lose consciousness while in this mental condition?'

" 'Yes, sometimes I become so drowsy that I fall asleep, and then I lose the ideas.'

" 'Can you do anything to induce this dreamlike state?'

" 'Yes, I early discovered that to obtain good results certain conditions had to be met. First of all, I have to be absolutely alone and undisturbed. Without these two requisites I cannot even think of trying to compose.'

" 'Do you mean that you always have to be locked up in

your room?'

" 'By no means; if I am alone and free from intrusion, I often get themes when out walking, especially when I am in the country. But I always have to jot them down immediately, otherwise they quickly fade.'

" 'Do you work these ideas out on paper as soon as you return home?'

" 'Not always. I let them germinate, sometimes for years, but I occasionally look at them again. This habit is important, for it engenders the same state of mind that gave birth to them, and in this way the original thoughts grow and expand.'

" 'Are there any other requirements for entering this mysterious realm, aside from isolation and freedom from disturbance?'

" 'Yes, concentration to the point of complete absorption seems to be the key that unlocks the door to the soul realm, once I have the other requisites.'

" 'Then you do not believe that composing is purely an intellectual process?'

" 'It is an intellectual process as far as the mechanics of composition are concerned. It requires patience and much hard work to acquire technical skill, but that has nothing to do with inspiration, which is a spiritual process.'

" 'Then you would not endorse Carlyle's famous definition of genius?'

" 'Certainly not. I consider it a very faulty definition. If taking great pains were all there is to genius, any patient plodder could become a Mozart or a Beethoven. I never could understand how so keen an observer as Carlyle could fall into such an error.'

" 'Who, in your opinion, was a perfect type of the creative genius?'

" 'Beethoven. He had lofty inspirations, and at the same time he was an indefatigable worker. We all have to work hard.'

" 'Have you ever been disturbed when in this dreamlike state of which you speak?'

" 'Yes, often, especially in the early years of my work, and then the ideas took wings and flew away. They deserted me completely and they never came back. Those experiences forced me to the conclusion that the Muse is a jealous patroness, like Jehovah in the second commandment.' "

As a rule Brahms mentioned his music only when protected by the brazen shield of irony. In September, 1885, Kalbeck called, and could not hide his curiosity as to what the summer had brought forth. "You evidently want to know," said the Master, "if I've been careless about composition. . . . Once more I've only chucked together one of those sets of waltzes and polkas. If you're absolutely set on hearing it, I'll play you the thing."

I went [wrote Kalbeck] to open the piano. "No," he parried, "don't do that. The business is not quite so simple. Nazy must help." He meant Ignaz Brüll and a second piano. Now I grasped the fact that he was speaking of a large piece for orchestra, probably a symphony, but was careful not to inquire further, for I seemed to notice that he already regretted having come out with so much.

This "set of waltzes and polkas" turned out to be the E minor symphony! The same year Brahms made another statement, considerably less fantastic, about a part of this mighty work. A journalist named Grosser had published a surmise that Brahms had been inspired to write the *passacaglia finale* by Thorwaldsen's frieze of Alexander's procession in the Villa Carlotta on Lake Como. Now Brahms, as a wise man and a true musician, had no cordial liking for the hybrid called program music.

For heaven's sake [he wrote to Simrock], Grosser's Procession of Alexander hasn't mounted to your head and Klinger's, has it? That would be an atrocious piece of stupidity; and to register my horror thereat, I now content myself by loudly crying "Ha!"—

He once attended a rehearsal of his clarinet quintet by the Soldat-Röger Quartet, and was so touched that tears came to his eyes. To cover his emotion he marched across the room, closed the first violin part, and growled: "Stop the terrible music!" (*Hörts auf mit der schrecklichen Musik!*)

Unlike the second of the three great B's, who sponsored the metronome, the third B had but a low opinion of Maelzel's invention. When Henschel was preparing a performance of the *German Requiem* in London, he wrote the composer to know if the metronome marking should be accurately followed. And this was the significant reply:

Yes—as accurately as in the case of all other music.—I think that also in the case of all other music the metronome is of no value. So far at least as my experience goes, everyone has later repented of the figures he has given out. Those metronome marks which one finds on my compositions, I was cozened by good friends into putting there; for I myself have never believed that my blood and a machine could get on so well together.

The Master's ideas of the proper tempo varied violently from day to day, according to his mood. Sometimes these ideas were highly eccentric. Dr. Ernest Walker told my friend, Mr. Philip Barr, that Brahms originally wanted his A major piano quartet to start so slowly that Joachim had to overrule him. And many old friends of Brahms have told me similar things. As a rule his tempi slowed down with advancing years—particularly when he himself was performing. As he dropped out of practice he more and more resembled the notorious

> . . . young lady of Rio
> Who played in a Beethoven trio;
> But her technic was scanty,
> So she played it *Andante*
> Instead of *Allegro con brio.*

Brahms set very little store by the gift of absolute pitch. Herr Emil Hess recalls that when Miller zu Aichholz was once rhapsodizing about this gift, the Master demurred: "I have known two people who understood something of music. One of them plagued himself in vain for a lifetime to learn absolute pitch. The other took no pains because he knew he could never acquire it. One of them was called Julius Stockhausen; the other—Richard Wagner. Still, you know, in spite of their lack, both had *some* idea of music!"

From the entire eighteen volumes of Brahms' correspondence one gleans but a few scattered hints of what went on in his jealously guarded "studio." To Simrock, who was besieging him for new compositions, he wrote:

Stop hounding your composer! It might be as dangerous as it usually is useless. One cannot compose as one spins or sews. Certain honoured colleagues (Bach, Mozart, Schubert) have badly spoiled the world. But if we cannot imitate them in beauty of writing, we must guard against endeavouring to rival them in speed of writing.

Of his inclination to lighten the lot of the performer and swell the money-bags of Simrock, he wrote the latter:

I am for ever committing follies. At the last moment I always want to make a thing easier than it really is, or can be.

This was in connexion with his song *Beim Abschied*.

For one person, at least, he never succeeded in making his penwork easy—and that was himself. Of the *Wechsellied zum Tanze* and other songs he wrote Clara in 1860:

Even if the things are small, they are all the harder to make, as, unfortunately, everything is still difficult for me.

Another case of hard writing making easy hearing.

III. WHAT BRAHMS THOUGHT OF CERTAIN CONTEMPORARIES

Though a pre-eminent self-critic, Brahms was but an indifferent judge of other composers. Indeed, the great creative musicians seldom are anything more; for, if they possessed a broad, catholic appreciation of all schools of music, none of them could immerse himself with the needful passionate intensity in his own particular one. As a rule, the creator has a far too highly specialized view of his field to see art steadily and see it whole.

A really great artist [wrote Oscar Wilde] can never judge of other people's work at all. . . . That very concentration of vision that makes a man an artist limits by its sheer intensity his faculty of fine appreciation. . . . The gods are hidden from each other. They can recognize their worshippers. That is all.

Space remains for little more than a few of Brahms' hitherto unrecorded opinions about other composers of his day. The only one of these men whom he heartily admired was his own "find"—Dvořák. Of him the Master once remarked to Eusebius Mandyczewski: [6] "That fellow has more ideas than any of us!" The Bohemian's strong national flavour and his interest in folk-music helped to endear him to Brahms; and similar qualities in Grieg lent the Norwegian a mild interest for the Master.

Tschaikowsky he could not endure, and the feeling was mutual. Massenet [7] he so heartily despised that when his intimate, Dr. Billroth, showed the visiting Frenchman some attention, Brahms grew violent, and the old friends had a serious quarrel which was never quite made up.

The Master liked Liszt's music no better, and once wrote of the latter's *Christus* as "so incredibly boring, foolish and senseless that I can't understand how the humbug . . . can

---

[6] Who told Prof. Michalek, the painter, who passed it on to me.

[7] Major Desjoyaux writes me as follows:

"Brahms avoua une fois qu'il ne comprenait pas la musique italienne, et ne goutait guère Massenet parceque trop différente de sa conception musicale. Et comme je citais le dicton: 'l'Art n'a pas de Patrie,' 'cela est vrai,' dit-il, 'pour ceux qui écoutent, mais pas pour ceux qui écrivent. Ainsi, tu es "echt Latiner" et moi "echt Deutsch."' A ce sujet, il me montra tout ce que le Folklore avait indirectement inspiré à Beethoven, Schubert, Schumann, etc., et il disait: 'le musicien ne peut se libérer de l'ambiance dans laquelle il vit: il respire le Folklore avec l'air natal et s'en nourrit, s'en imprègne sans le savoir.' Rien n'est plus vrai, mais jamais je n'avais vu cette vérité illustrée par autant d'exemples que Brahms m'en donna ce soir là."

be put across." The quality that chiefly struck him about Bruch was his fecundity.

Brahms' consistently contemptuous unfairness toward that peasant of genius, his rival symphonist Bruckner, will be touched on in the following chapter.

Towards Bayreuth his attitude was never consistent, except in his highly sportsmanlike refusal to answer any of Wagner's scurrilous printed attacks.[8] Now he writes to Clara of *Die Meistersinger*: "I am not enthusiastic about this work, or about Wagner in general." Now he assures Specht:[9] "I consider a few bars of this work of more value than all the operas that have since been composed." Mr. Harold Bauer tells me that Carl Friedberg once went for a walk with Brahms, after they had heard a performance of the *Siegfried Idyll*. For two hours the Master never said a word. Then, at parting, he blurted out: "But one can't hear such music *all* the time!"

The truth is that Brahms was continually torn by an inner struggle. His old Adam directed him to despise and ridicule the persecutor who had been so despicably cruel to him. His better self, however, almost always had the upper hand. Filled with a sense of his rival's greatness, he held aloof from the hostilities of the anti-Wagner–pro-Brahms clique, a group which had grown up without his connivance.

Of course, if Brahms had been a demi-god he might possibly have made his partisans behave with his own correctness, and silently turn the other cheek also. In default of such perfection, he acted like the generous, highly human

[8] Such as may be found in Wagner's *Bayreuther Blätter*, 1879, VII; in the *Open Letter to Friedrich Schön*, in *Über das Dirigieren*, p. 261, and other writings.
[9] Am. ed., p. 262.

being that he was.

A striking instance of his sportsmanship in this connexion has been told me by Dr. Heinrich Schenker: "Once when a project was on foot for a monument in Vienna to the Brahms-apostle and apostate Wagnerian Hans von Bülow, Brahms informed me that he was not in favour of it, adding: 'Why, we haven't a Wagner monument yet!' Now from a man who had been treated as Wagner had treated Brahms, I consider this downright handsome!"

For all his sportsmanship, however, he drew the line at any Wagnerization of his pupils. Major Desjoyaux relates: "At the time when Brahms was good enough to give me those admirable counsels to which I owe my clearest knowledge, I was very young. En route to Austria I stopped at Bayreuth in order to hear the *Tetralogy* and *Parsifal*. On reaching Ischl I told Madame Schumann about the experience, and she reported my enthusiasm to Brahms, who seemed very angry, and for several days was at outs with me.

"Restored finally to grace, I timidly asked him why he had been so annoyed over my stay at Bayreuth. In the crusty way which he so often assumed, and with his original manner of expressing himself, he answered: '*Wenn man Gift trinken will und nicht sterben, so muss man das Gegengift im Sacke haben; und Du hast 's noch nicht!*' (If one would drink poison without dying, one must have the antidote in his pocket; and you haven't it yet!)

"Apropos of this sally, it has often been said that Brahms detested Wagner because he was jealous of him. Nothing is further from the truth. The character of Brahms was too lofty to permit him to envy anyone. Besides, he held a position in the world of music so commanding as to preclude his being jealous of anybody.

"But he hated the æsthetics of Wagner who, as he asserted with reason, put music at the beck and call of literature and of dramatic action by the constant and quasi-obligatory use of the leit-motif.

" 'Wagner has turned the queen into a servant,' Brahms said to me, giving various reasons which he believed he had for cursing this 'destroyer of the cathedral,' this vandal let loose amid the architecture of music.

"Certain superpositions of themes, as for example in the *finale* of *Die Meistersinger*, made him bound from his seat and cry out that, so far as counterpoint was concerned, these pages were not worthy of a student. 'Literary necessities,' he added, 'never palliate such looseness in writing!' "

These quotations constitute a sufficient refutation of Specht's extreme statement about the Master: "He never uttered a disrespectful word against Wagner." [10] But Brahms' admirable attitude toward his persecutor was acknowledged after his death in a letter to Hans Richter, by a Wagnerite no less impassioned than Cosima herself:

It has not remained unknown to me how fine his [Brahms'] disposition and attitude was toward our (sic!) art, and that his intelligence was too lofty to misunderstand what was perhaps alien to him, and his character too noble to let hostilities spring up.

"It is deeply to be regretted," writes Herr Ernest, in quoting these words, "that this could not be said of Wagner!" [11]

[10] Am. ed., p. 258.
[11] *Johannes Brahms,* 1930, p. 149.

According to Frau Bertha Gasteiger, Brahms was conducting a choral rehearsal when a note was handed up to him announcing the death of Wagner in Venice. Brahms read it, and laid down his baton. "To-day," he announced simply, "we sing no more. A master has died."

Chapter XVI

BRAHMS: WIT AND HUMORIST

READERS have already caught so many glimpses of Brahms' laughing side that they will not be unduly surprised to learn how sure-fire his wit could be. That it was occasionally caustic should not blind us to the fact that he was often genial, and usually meant to be amiable and fair-minded. But this intention promptly deserted him when it was a question of the one living symphonist who could be called his rival. He was never tired of poking fun at Anton Bruckner's fecundity which, though he wrote more symphonies than his rival, was all in all no greater than Brahms' own.

In the possession of Frau Marie, the widow of Ignaz Brüll, I came upon a piquant example of the Master's anti-Bruckner bias. Alluding to Brahms' horror of autograph-hunters, and playing on the fantastic lengths to which these gentry would often go to obtain his signature, as well as on his fondness for being invited to the home of the Brülls—these two friends concocted and mailed him the following parody of a fake epistle, signed with their composite name:

My husband and I have found here in a merchant's shop sketches of the Tenth symphony [of Beethoven]. You alone are worthy to receive it. But we do not wish to entrust this treasure to the post. Please come and get the sketches in person.

MARIGNAZ BRÜLL

Entering into the spirit of the jest, Brahms replied:

It begins with a cruel cartoon by Robert Lienau, successor to Beethoven's publisher, Haslinger. Anton Bruckner is represented as leaving the latter's office: *"Die XII Sinfonie ist angebracht!! Erleichtert beginnt er das zweite Dutzend!"* (The twelfth symphony has been worked off!! Relieved, he starts the second dozen.) Signed by the committee:

J. Brahms	R. Lienau
J. M. Grün	Carl Goldmark
Julius Epstein	Ignaz Brüll
	Tini ū Tony (Frau and Herr Anton Door)

Courtesy of Herr Eugen von Miller zu Aichholz

DEAR FRAU BRÜLL,—

Your Ignaz and your merchant have taken you in! The Tenth has long been in existence; and the fact that you are not aware of this somewhat saddens

Your most devoted
ANTON BR.

Naturally the "Br." means Bruckner, who had at that time finished only seven symphonies. "The Tenth" may be a composite allusion to that composer's industry, and to Bülow's nickname for Brahms' own C minor symphony.

His frequent jibes at Bruckner's fecundity were sometimes varied by indirect irony. After the performance of a new orchestral work he liked to hail the old peasant with: "Ah, Bruckner, so you also compose symphonies?"

Nobody was proof against the Master's barbed shafts. When Henschel once spoke disparagingly of the music of a certain royal personage, the Master interrupted: "Look here, one can't be too careful in criticizing the compositions of a prince. One never knows who wrote them."

The long and close parallel between Brahms and Beethoven breaks down entirely at one point—that of good sportsmanship in taking a joke. Beethoven's wit was a one-way street, admitting of no come-back upon himself. Brahms, on the other hand, enjoyed a joke none the less when he himself was the victim. Indeed, he often went in zestfully for ingrowing witticisms. Hearing that a certain producer intended to bring out a new oratorio, *The Sinner,* he chuckled and wrote to Clara: "A lovely choice he has, from Cain to Brahms!"

In coining jokes on himself he showed an astonishingly fertile resource. Wahliss, a Viennese porcelain manufacturer (the sort of person whom he liked punningly to call *"Tonsetzer"*), looked every inch a musician, resembling the Master in height and bearing. "The other evening," Brahms recounted, "I went to the Burgtheater. There near the orchestra stood Wahliss in his satin coat. Behind me sat two pretty girls, and I heard one of them ask the other: 'Listen, who is that man of genius over there?'

" 'Don't you know him? That's Brahms!'

" 'Brahms? Who on earth is that?'

" 'Well, of all things! I call that rich! Why, haven't you ever heard of Brahm's *Natural History*? [1] ' "

When it came to joking depreciation of his own compositions, the Master showed some of the same inventiveness that had gone to their making. He mailed the new F major symphony to a friend and bade him keep it in the wine-cellar beside the choicest vintage. "Wrap it daily in a cloth moistened with the best Rhine-wine—and do whatever else one does for such dry products."

He admonished Simrock about the E minor symphony, which was to be published a few months after its first public performance: "It is a scandal: the work will be printed when its immortality is already finished."

Sending the same friend his 51 *Technical Studies for Pianoforte,* he played amusingly upon their bleak unmelodious austerity, the aches and pains they were bound to cause in pianistic fingers, and his publisher's weakness for tasteless and unsuitable cover designs:

---

[1] Brehm's many-volumed *Natural History,* the standard work of its kind.

Here I am actually sending those highly melodious exercises which have become almost a myth and are at least twenty-five years old. Not that you will buy and print them, but merely that your connoisseur's eye may linger on them a moment. Apart from the melodies the only things capable of attracting you are their bulk (?!) and the title-page, which must be very beautiful and loud in colour. I have in mind that all possible instruments of torture should be represented, from the thumbscrews to the Iron Maiden; perhaps some anatomical designs as well, and all in lovely blood-red and fiery gold.

To the same friend, who had a clever employee named Keller, he wrote in 1879, at the zenith of his powers:

The proof-correction of the songs is admirable, like everything that Keller does. Can't you make him do the composing too, so that I can for once in a way enjoy that as well?

To the same:

The parts of the G major quintet may go to Pest uncorrected by me without holding up the history of the world.

Sometimes he made merry over the looks of his friends, as when he remarked that a portrait of Mühlfeld the clarinettist was "most flatteringly unlike him." But he was no less hard on his own appearance. He once gave a friend the Brasch photograph which stresses his facial lines and wrinkles, and penned on the margin some notes of music followed by a fat exclamation point. These notes turned out to be the beginning of his song "O *liebliche Wangen, ihr macht mir Verlangen*," which in the official translation is lamentably Englished as: "O fair cheeks of roses, where young love reposes"!

He was diplomatically induced to sit for his portrait to the etcher Michalek. Brahms insisted that Tilgner, the sculptor, should model him at the same time. "If it really must be," was his unflattering metaphor, "then in God's name, two flies at a single blow!" "Our sitter," said Prof. Michalek, "was so bored, he promptly went to sleep. The next time, Miller zu Aichholz, who had kindly arranged the sittings,[2] brought him very black coffee and thus managed to keep him awake."

Brahms reported this affair to Simrock as follows:

I was well befooled by Tilgner. I thought I would very craftily get rid of him and the etcher Michalek by saying I couldn't sit twice. Now I must pose for both simultaneously. One depicts me from in front, the other from the rear where, moreover, the most brilliant views are to be found.

Major Desjoyaux informs me that Brahms, "without being a *gourmand,* was a *gourmet,* and knew the best places for good cheer. One evening when we were dining in a little Viennese restaurant (which I have never been able to find again), he wished to entertain his guests particularly well, and said to the *sommelier:* 'Waiter, give us a good bottle of wine—but it must be your best.'

"In a few moments the man reappeared with a bottle cradled in its basket, a venerable affair covered with dust and spiderwebs.

" 'What sort is that?' demanded our host. The waiter inclined himself obsequiously: 'It is a bottle of Brahms.' But at once the Master, tapping it and pushing it away, cried: 'Well, then, give us a bottle of Bach!' "

---

[2] Brahms consented with the words: "Oh, well, if it's only that! I thought you wanted to hit me for a loan."

This is a new form of a hoary anecdote which has often been related, each time with a different setting. When Brahms got hold of a witty idea he liked to use it as frequently as Beethoven liked to revive his own good workable themes. It would, for example, be interesting to know how often a wistful composer who had played his own piece and palpitatingly awaited Brahms' verdict was regaled with something to this effect: "Look here, where did you buy this splendid music-paper?" Or: "How well you *do* play the piano!" The ingenuity with which these clichés were varied according to the time, the place, and the victim all together, was masterly. It showed Brahms' genius for variations emerging even in the field of wit.

But he was not above occasionally converting the bright sayings of others to his own ends. In conducting the choral concerts of the Friends of Music he was much criticized by the gay, indolent, and somewhat superficial Viennese singers for his untiring thoroughness and the sombreness of his programs. After one sepulchral performance which consisted of Bach's cantata, *Dearest Lord, When Shall I Die,* and Cherubini's *Requiem* in C minor, Hanslick intimated that the Viennese objected to being buried twice—once as a Protestant and once as a Catholic—in the same evening. And the poet Mosenthal observed: "When Brahms is feeling particularly genial and jolly, he sets to music, '*Halli, hallo,* the tomb is my joy!' "

Frau Gottinger-Wilt told me that she passed on to Brahms this latter remark and the aspersions of the Society. And at the next rehearsal he addressed them: "Ladies and Gentlemen, I hear that you have been criticizing the sad tone of the programs. I have therefore prepared for you an agreeable surprise. Our next concert will begin with: *Death is my delight.* Of course everyone laughed tremendously, and Brahms was given a new lease of public confidence."

In the domain of wit—though of wit only—the Master was not above borrowing from Rossini. The old story will be recalled of how Meyerbeer's nephew brought Rossini a funeral march he himself had composed on the death of his uncle, and was bluntly told: "I would have liked the music better if Meyerbeer had written it for *your* funeral."

This formula was after Brahms' own heart. One summer in Ischl, Frau Flegmann lent him a one-act play by Hoffmannsthal, *The Death of Titian,* which he returned in three days. She expressed surprise at his speed.

BRAHMS: What! Do you take me for one of those wretches who never return books?

FRAU FLEGMANN: Not at all. But I hoped you would bring it back in a few months with an opera score.

BRAHMS: Oh, it would have interested me more to compose this play if Titian had written it about the death of Hoffmannsthal!

The Brahmsian wit was never more zestful and spontaneous than when ragging Simrock, his publisher, man of affairs, and favourite butt. The fact that Simrock was one of his dearest friends did not save the latter from merciless teasing about all manner of things such as his passion for making *infra dig.* arrangements of respectable music, for unnecessarily printing out repeats, for the exorbitant prices of his wares, and even for the peculiarities of his epistolary style.

He ironically advised the poor publisher to have the *Academic Festival* overture arranged for brass band, and to print an edition of the *Cradle Song* in a minor key "for naughty or ailing children."

In his jests at Simrock's high prices there was often a drop of gall, as when he recommended that a note be printed on the *Sapphic Ode* to the effect that as this song was usually encored, the repetition was also printed out, which would bring the cost up to 3.50 marks. And, in subtle allusion to the modest rates of a rival firm, he added: "God bless Peters!"

Once in a while Brahms playfully contended that this most quixotic and generous of publishers was cheating him: "I'd be a donkey if I ever let you have a symphony or such. From another publisher I could get cash, while you would make out—that I still owed you something!!"

Offering him the F major quintet, the C major trio, and the *Parzenlied*, he pretended that Simrock was a Shylock, eager for any low advantage, and that his own affluent self was cowering in the shadow of the poorhouse:

Tell me if the rubbish is worth 1,000 thalers apiece to you. Trio, quintet, *Parzenlied*. Speak right out! I shall certainly not complain that you have taken unfair advantage of my temporarily destitute condition. Truly you could have the whole bag of tricks for 1,000 marks if you sent them immediately. I don't know what I shall have to live on in another week, to say nothing of rent and tailor.

Of course the quintet has only three movements—you could cut down the price on that account—but in the trio there are variations, and in that line folks have an idea that I amount to something. . . . In short, mull this over fine. I'm a person you can bargain with.

After setting his *Song from Fingal* for mixed choir and orchestra, he wrote the same friend in a similar strain, dishing up a Beethoven-like pun:

Might I ask 100 thalers as hono-rare-ium? I'd be satisfied with even 10.[3]

The high prices that Simrock charged the public, and the expensive format in which he clothed his publications were a never-ending source of real irritation to the democratic Brahms, whose wit on this theme usually developed a sting:

Notes already on page 6! A song like *Liebestreu* merely 6 pages long instead of the former 2! Here I don't need to inquire what price you charge.

And when Simrock took over from Breitkopf & Härtel the original edition of the B major trio:

You can get along a good while with the copies of the trio which you have on hand—if every six months you raise the price 2 marks.

Less downright and obvious is his pseudo-sympathetic note of condolence after Simrock had tried in vain to buy *A German Requiem* from its fortunate publisher in Leipzig. Brahms assumes that his friend has been ejected at the boot's point, and hopes that his ignominious descent was not too painful: "How were the stairs in Leipzig? Swathed in soft carpets? Fitted with comfortable banisters?" Here one distinctly catches a hoarse and hearty chuckle of malicious glee.

Brahms had a knack for coining epithets. His young

---

[3] This pun appears in the original as *Hono-rarstes,* which might go into English as "honor-rarest."

friend, the pianist Fräulein Henriette Hemala, he liked to call "*Himmela*," which might be taken to signify "Heavenly One." Incidentally, this lady tells me that Goldmark called her "*Sakuntala*," after his own familiar overture. A very different sort of pianist, Frau Ronchetti who, as we have seen, lived just below him at Karlsgasse 4 and at times made his life hideous, he christened "the female piano-beast."

With the highly Bohemian name of his friend Dvořák he liked to play fast and loose, amusing himself by barricading it between a double hedge of fanciful, self-invented accents and expression marks, thus:

$$D \underset{,}{y} \underset{C}{o} \underset{,}{\check{r}} \underset{a}{\check{a}} \underset{\smile}{\check{k}}$$

"On producing my first lyrical work, *Gyptis*, at the Théâtre de la Monnaie in Brussels," Major Desjoyaux tells me, "knowing the ideas of my old master, I took good care not to let him learn of the event. Common friends in Vienna, however, reported it. . . . And lo, I received a word from Brahms with his cordial felicitations. But on the envelope, following my name, he had added: '*Opern Fabrikant*' (Manufacturer of Operas), which incidentally showed how little stock he took in the musical theatre."

There is a characteristic slap at celebrity's tormentors in a postcard to the publisher Fritsch, dated May 15, 1895:

To friends and well-wishers, publishers and editors, the devoted announcement that I am opening for the summer, in Ischl, the popular branch-office for the criticism of manuscripts and the hearing of lady pianists!

Heartily greeting,
J. BRAHMS.

The Master could seldom resist a tender gibe at the short-comings of the tardy and inaccurate though lovable Viennese. Walking with a friend near his home, he came to a house where, as he suddenly realized, a pupil expected him. "Just wait ten minutes," he exclaimed, in a broad parody of the local dialect. "Here I must quickly give an hour's lesson!" And once in discussing with Sigismund Stojowski Vienna's lack of musical enterprise, he remarked: "Every year the momentous question comes up: What novelty shall we perform, *The Creation* or *The Seasons?*"

Irony, sarcasm, that untranslatable thing called *Schadenfreude,* and Puckish zest in exposing human frailty were second—if not first—nature with Brahms. "I malicious?" he wrote to Simrock. "Nobody has ever yet called me that!" Unless these words were set down in mock hypocrisy, they merely show how his friends feared to risk his devastating temper by telling him the truth.

Frau Prof. Max Friedländer is speaking: "When I first met Brahms I was embarrassed. Scarcely realizing what I was saying, I remarked on the discrepancy between my husband's long acquaintance with him and my own short one. 'I only wish,' barked Brahms at us, 'that it had been the other way 'round!' Even in paying compliments he could not help his sarcastic, mischievous, biting tone."

His wit was unusually quick on the trigger. A conceited young Viennese composer was once presented to the Master, who inquired: "Well, have you been composing anything new?" "No," said the conceited one, visibly preening himself, "I only write off and on" (*Ich schreibe nur ab und zu*). "*Sooo?*" cried Brahms, registering infinite astonishment, "do you also write *on?*" As *abschreiben* means to plagiarize, the implication was of course, that the young composer only "wrote off" the works of others.

Robert Fuchs, another reminiscent composer, was present one day when a highly Brahmsian composition of his was played to Brahms, and nearly fainted with embarrassment when the Master, assuming innocent bewilderment, asked him: "But what piece of mine *is* that?"

Praise from Puck was all the more eagerly coveted because so fabulously rare. His mischievous soul enjoyed raising hopes and then, by a dextrous final turn, dashing them. To a musician who rashly angled for compliments he spoke in the deep chest-tones of full conviction: "Yes, you have talent." Then, suddenly changing the vocal register to falsetto, he added with roguish regret—"But very little!"

Truly, his friends would have done well to adopt as their motto: *Caveat piscator!* Let the angler beware! We shall see what gruesome things befell the poor fiddlers in the rehearsal of the C minor trio.[4] And all the world knows that when Bachrich, the viola of the Rosé Quartet, once asked Brahms if he was satisfied with the tempo of a certain movement, the sting-in-the-tail reply snapped back: "Yes—especially with the viola's."

Such craftily prearranged anticlimaxes were dear to his heart. At a banquet where Hiller was present, the foremost contemporary music-makers had been toasted when Brahms rose and said: "And now, having drunk to so many living composers, let us drink to a dead one! I lift my glass to Ferdinand Hiller." With somewhat rueful sportsmanship

[4] See p. 234.

Dr. Roentgen confessed: "He remarked of a certain too reminiscent violin piece of mine: 'That sounds like a promenade through a beautiful landscape—sometimes, also, a familiar landscape.' To another musician he observed, in handing back his manuscript: 'Here is a thing which you must compose.' You see," the good Doctor added, "sarcasms came as natural to him as melodies."

A group of famous composers were discussing Henschel, when one of them exclaimed: "Happy man! He can sing as well as compose, while we can merely compose." "And not even that," put in Brahms, with assumed naïveté.

There was another neat ironical formula upon which the Master at various times set his hand and seal. Marie Soldat-Röger, who, as we have seen, was the first woman to play Brahms' violin concerto in public, once sat at dinner between him and Goldmark. The latter complimented her on her girlish exploit, and remarked: "I too have written a violin concerto." "But mine," put in Brahms, "is better, isn't it?" "I can't tell. I haven't heard Herr Goldmark's." "You lucky one!" (*Sie Glückliche!*) cried Brahms. To which Goldmark plaintively retorted: "Oh, but it's not so bad as all that!" Brahms is known to have got off this same *jeu d'esprit* on a number of other occasions.

Dr. Roentgen confessed a hit against himself: "Brahms once enthusiastically recommended to me the library of the Gesellschaft der Musikfreunde in Vienna: 'We have there all sorts of the rarest works which nobody knows anything about; for example the *Serenade for Wind Instruments* by Julius Roentgen.' "

His dispraise, however, could often be much more frankly

brutal. At a celebration in honour of the seventieth birthday of Eduard Hanslick, a famous music critic of none too impeccable taste,[5] Brahms remarked that the friend about whom they had gathered loved Bach best in his composite form—as Offenbach.

To the self-critical Brahms who, after mature deliberation, slowly produced his works—more often for the furnace than for the concert hall—any sign of superficial facility, diffuseness, and overproduction in others was anathema. When told: "Yesterday I listened to Ferdinand Hiller's most recent composition," he retorted: "Careful there! One can never be sure of that with Hiller!"

The never-ending matrimonial difficulties of his young friend and interpreter Eugen d'Albert provided him a welcome target, as well as a solace for bachelorhood. Late one evening at the Sign of the Red Hedgehog, he rose to his feet with: *"Freunde, es muss geschieden sein—sagt d'Albert."* [6]

At the close of a long midday dinner in Kalbeck's home, Brahms was told that d'Albert and his recently acquired third wife were presently coming to the Red Hedgehog to greet him. But the Master was sleepy and preferred to sup at home. "Dear me!" he remarked, "d'Albert is bound to marry several times more. I'll just skip the third wife." His prophecy was fulfilled.

In a large gathering Dr. von Hornbostel once spilled black

---

[5] Wagner used Hanslick as his model for *Beckmesser* in *Die Meistersinger*. In the first draft this character was called *Hans Lich*.

[6] As *geschieden* means both "parted" and "divorced," the quip might be inadequately translated: "Friends, we must part—says d'Albert." There is a curiously Brahmsian flavour in another divorce joke made by a Chicago music critic about one of d'Albert's ex-wives: "Yesterday, for the first time in America, at the second of these concerts, Madame Carreño played the third concerto of her fourth husband."

coffee on a charming young lady's white dress. "Come to my laboratory," offered Hofrat Oser, "and I'll get those spots out for you." "Don't you believe him!" countered Frau von Hornbostel. "He once promised me the same thing, and ruined my gown." Then Brahms took part in the conversation: "Impossible! Hofrat Oser removes spots only for *young* women."

Whenever he met with hypocrisy, he quickly uncorked the vials of his most acid sarcasm. Iwan Knorr tells of a double-faced patron of music in Frankfort who adored Brahms, but who, when Cosima Wagner came to call, had carefully put out of sight all pictures and music that could suggest Brahms and Schumann. Shortly after this, Knorr was invited to his house with Barth, the violinist, and Brahms.

I must say [confessed Knorr] that I have seldom lived through a more painful evening. Towards us Brahms was exquisitely polite, but of his host and hostess he took slight notice. In their presence he nudged me, pointed to his photograph and his songs lying on the piano, and observed, as loud as possible: "See here, Brahms everywhere you look! But you mustn't for an instant suppose that this is always the case! Here one modulates in various keys. Well, Frau X, how about singing a bit of Peter Cornelius?" The hostess swore that she owned nothing by that ardent Wagnerite. But, with enormous zeal, Brahms turned the music cupboard inside out and finally convinced her by producing in triumph the songs of Cornelius.

Insisting on their performance, he accompanied the singer with a prodigious outlay of expression and feeling. In the weakest passages he always cried: "Bit different chap from Brahms, eh, what?" Finally Frau X burst into tears. The Master had agreed to do a violin sonata with Barth. "We really wanted to play Mozart," he explained to the host, "but as you're not worthy of it we shall, for your punishment, play Brahms A major."

He was an adept at mimicry. The Miller zu Aichholz journal recounts, for example, how convulsively he took off the pianist Pirani's mannerisms in playing and turning pages.

The wit of Brahms often had so much point, cutting-edge, and malice as to suggest that he could never justly be called by the sympathetic name of humorist. Then, the next moment the true Brahmsian humour would beam out as mellow and kindly as any lover of his art could wish.

Of this there are almost countless instances. When the Elberfeld choir sang his motet, O Heiland, reiss die Himmel auf, he exclaimed: "I didn't *compose* it as beautiful as that!"

At the first meeting with that charmer, Hermine Spies, he was in the same sunny mood. She sang *Vergebliches Ständchen*, the witty song where the lover wheedles in vain for admission to the scornful lady's lattice. "In the end," declared the composer, "I'm sure she'll let him in."

The following incident baffles translation; but even those ignorant of German will notice how deftly the syllables are interchanged between the two pairs of German words. At an evening party a beautiful countess in a dress with an extremely *décolleté* back was singing for Brahms some of his songs. "How do you like her?" inquired the Count. "Does she not sing with *berückenden Zauber* [fascinating magic]?" "No," said Brahms, "but with *bezaubernden Rücken* [a bewitching back]."

On those rare occasions when he permitted himself to talk

about music, the Master often showed almost as much originality as in writing it. "More civil-marriage between bass and soprano," he recommended to a composer friend. Before the première of his *Requiem,* commenting on the heavy-footedness of North German choirs, he warned Reinthaler: "In Bremen one ascends to high A more warily than in Vienna."

While corresponding with the same friend about the forthcoming *début* of the *Triumphlied,* his high spirits were in boyish effervescence.

If we are up against it let us do a bit of faking in the *Triumphlied.* We'll let the chorus sing whatever it likes. You will accompany them on the organ as loud as Bismarck alone deserves, and I will beat time for the whole business to the melody:

Hoch soll er le - ben, hoch soll er le - ben, drei - mal hoch!
High shall he flour-ish, high shall he flour-ish, three times high!

Ex. 3

Whenever he could honestly admire some musical performance, it was a pleasure for him to convert the sword-thrust of wit into the love-pat of humour. Klengel the 'cello virtuoso once played him a home-made arrangement of Paganini's *Perpetuum Mobile* which closed with a staggeringly difficult passage in chromatic octaves. "The octave business at the end," Brahms told him, "is a pure swindle [*der reine Schwindel*]—I mean one gets dizzy [*es schwindelt einem*] just hearing it." This double meaning of *Schwindel*

recalls Hans Richter's unintentional pun, when he was conducting in England before having mastered the language.
Asked how his wife was, he shook his head gloomily: "She iss
vairy bad; she lies und swindles!"

We have already seen with what malicious wit Brahms
could rag his publisher, Simrock. When this same wit had its
sting painlessly extracted it was no less amusing.

Only one thing is sure [he wrote this gratified man of business in a characteristically veiled announcement that the F
major symphony was as good as finished]: soon I'll not have a
groschen of money left! Now, I am counting on the appreciation and gratitude of you and all your fellow publishers. You
will pass around the hat and send me an eminent reward—
because I leave you so nicely in peace and you need not run
any risks for me. . . .
God shall requite you, and if I should some day happen again
to find sheets of music manuscript dating from my youth, I'll
send them along.

Into this so Brahmsily oblique disclosure Kalbeck, that in-
curable concocter of poetic programs, actually read "a secret
hint as to the spiritual content and romantic character" of
the Third symphony! He would have us believe that this
music circumstantially delineates the journey from the land
of youth to the empire of manhood, the stream from source
to mouth. As a matter of fact, Brahms meant nothing of
the sort by his extravaganza, but was merely having his bit
of fun with the eager Simrock.

Two years later he gave Simrock a somewhat similar hint
of the approaching completion of the Fourth symphony,
writing of "the next one or two works which I perhaps may

still find in an old drawer. For you surely can not believe that a man so comfortably situated as I am will keep on working?"

Custom could not stale his infinite variety in running down his own music. When the *Triumphlied* came out, he nicknamed it to Simrock "the imperial *Schnadahüpferl*." Then he went on about the two string quartets, opus 51, which had just been finished:

I take the greatest pains [with my quartets] and always hope that a large and terribly difficult one will occur to me— and they always turn out small and pitiable!

I wonder if any other composer has ever bubbled over with such care-free fun in discussing money matters with a publisher as he did with Simrock.

I barely keep myself alive by hitting friends for loans [*von Pump*], so that people talk very disrespectfully of you!

Here is a parody of a begging letter to the same address:

The so often praised goodness and charity of your Wellbornship give me the courage to approach with a great petition. My situation is terrible, a horrifying future stares me in the face; the abyss appears yawning for me, I fall therein—unless your rescuing hand draws me back. With the last 100-mark note must I now proceed at once to the Eagle restaurant—but with what feelings shall I eat, and indeed drink! Too imminent I see before me the noon hour when there will be no more of the latter. In this disconsolate situation, might I most devotedly beg your Highwellbornship for the loan of 100 thalers? By the middle of September I solemnly promise to pay the money back! Moreover, a hostile fate compels me to-

COURTYARD VIEW OF THE HOUSE IN MÜRZZUSCHLAG WHERE THE
FOURTH SYMPHONY WAS COMPOSED

Taken for this book

day or to-morrow to embark on a pleasure trip, the great heat forces me to drink always more and more—help, save me!

Your thousand [he writes this friend] was of the worst, least reliable sort. It shrank immediately to half its size.

And of another remittance:

I said it right away: drops on a hot stone!—Went straight up in steam! Won't you please let fall another similar drop?! . . .

Clamouring from out the profoundest destitution, Your

J. B.

To scare and tease Simrock, he submitted a burlesque bill amounting to 5,000 reichsthaler ($3,750) for the string quartet in B flat.[7]

Therefrom, out of inborn baseness, you will deduct 1,000 reichsthaler; for being kept waiting 500; for further waiting for the four-hand arrangement, 500; for a signature of only two flats, 250 rtlr.; for cigars, tobacco, eau de Cologne, etc. 750 rtlr.; an additional thousand will be lost through false figures and reckoning, and you have lent me 200 rtlr. There remains a balance of 800 reichsthaler. Then there's a bill for 24 shirts and 48 handkerchiefs. Still less remains. . . . But the balance is to be paid me punctually in quarterly installments of at least 10 reichsthaler. . . . Outside of that I have further to demand: because merely the *Adagio* is short, 15 rtlr.; because I send you the original manuscript, per movement 2½ silbergroschen—10; for models for the tender movement, each 2 florins = = ?

As it turned out, the chief joke in the above burlesque was really on its author. For if he were living today he would find that original manuscript alone fetching, instead of 10

[7] See pp. 260 and 400 f.

silbergroschen, more than the $3,750 which then seemed to him such a farcical overvaluation of copyright and manuscript together.

He had a weakness for concocting such accounts. Having coerced Simrock into publishing a Nocturne for a girl friend, Mademoiselle Anne de D., he presented his bill for repairs executed:

A fresh modulation, per key	3	pfennigs
(i.e., from C to E flat, through F to B flat)	12	pf.
A new bass for the melody	1½	silbergroschen
Sentimental ending of 4 measures	5	sgr.
A middle portion patched	3½	sgr.
Entire new middle portion manufactured	15	sgr.

In inventing excuses for being a poor correspondent he was well nigh as resourceful as in slandering his compositions. Having dedicated the famous *Wiegenlied* to Bertha Faber without one previous word of preparation, he finally wrote her:

You will not take [the dedication] amiss? I always wanted to ask your permission, but my pen was of late so busy with boring revisions that it quite unlearned the well mannered amble of correspondence.

He hailed the invention of the postcard as a marvellous boon to suffering humanity, and used it thereafter for a large part of his messages by mail. One to Maria Fellinger contained but two lines, beginning: "The 16 pages follow at once"—pages which naturally never materialized.

To Simrock this card went as a receipt for certain delicacies:

Ever higher mounts the sacrificial smoke of gratitude to you. To accompany it one can only sing psalms; writing is impossible—nor in my reading can I discover that the Israelites would have written in similar circumstances.

In a sprightly moment he invented the original epistolary dodge of dividing his phrases between two postcards, like this pair addressed to the Fellinger boys:

Magnificent Glorious Best to father and everything possi- from one who heartily	San Marino, 12, 5, 88 weather! journey! greetings! and mother ble and impossible remembers you all J.B.

An excuse he sent Simrock from Vienna in 1873 might have been penned by an Irishman:

Now I'd have liked to furnish you with a lovely description of the World's Fair, but I have no time—besides, I haven't yet been there.

Such surprise endings as this were dear to his heart. Begging the same correspondent for another shipment of his favourite smoked eels, he explained:

You see, the local eels are pretty thin, not so fat by far as the composers—like to eat!

Few publishers have ever had from their writers any such assurance about sales possibilities as Simrock received about the new C minor trio, and the F major 'cello and A major violin sonatas:

All in all, the things can be very easily and nicely—given away.

One more surprise ending:

I have seen the parents [he wrote to Prof. Engelmann from Amsterdam]. I have seen the little one. It has been sold for 10,000 florins. I mean the hippopotamus.

The Master's compendious knowledge of Scripture was shown, not only by the excellent texts he compiled for the choral works, but also by certain parodies of Biblical style to be found in his letters. He appreciated the tempting table set by Widmann. And, in allusion to the tale of Benjamin in Genesis 43, he wrote his late host:

And he took and sent messes unto them from before him. But that of B[rahms] was fivefold so much as any of theirs. And they drank and were merry with him— So was their custom and so will it be in Joseph's palace to the rejoicing of B.

Widmann's name was Josef, and B. stood equally well for Benjamin and for that stout trencherman, Brahms. Moreover, the latter being not averse to slight illumination at that convivial board, the parallel between ancient Egypt and modern Switzerland was complete.

No less Biblical was his letter to Joachim's wife asking her to sing under his own direction at a Gesellschafts concert in Vienna. This time I Chronicles 14 was invoked, with Frau

Amalie assuming the rôle of King David. Incidentally it is worth noting that, even in those pre-war days, the musical audience of Vienna was unhesitatingly assigned the rôle of the Philistines:

And David inquired of God, saying, Shall I go up against the Philistines? and wilt thou deliver them into mine hand? And the Lord spake unto him, Go up; for I will deliver them into thine hand. And so you can find counsel further in the Books of the Chronicles and you will find that the Lord, like Nottebohm, is always in favour of such a venture. I, however, want very much to know whether this time David is keen about it and thinks of surely coming. . . .
But furthermore it is known to you that David always thoroughly plundered the land of the Philistines! What do you think of doing about this? In the language of a music director, what's your price?

One aspect of his humour is exactly what one would expect of any Brahmsian product: its imaginative quality. He wrote Simrock from Rügen, an island full of Stone Age relics:

I peep about eagerly in the cairns and barrows to find you something, perhaps an amber cigar mouthpiece.

Even in his last illness his laughter deserted him no more than Beethoven's had when "The Great One" lay dying. He conceived his alarming loss of weight as a transition from Romanesque to Gothic, and excused himself for not sitting to Unger the etcher, "because my round-arch style has passed over into that of the pointed arch."

At times his fun resembled his best music in its terse simplicity combined with mellowness and surprise. Coming to visit friends, and finding the garden full of family wash on the line, he inquired: "Have you beflagged the place in our honour?"

Brahms and Deiters, with the latter's mother and mother-in-law, once had supper together, after which the two men played four-handed duets. The music was finished, the hour late, and one old lady observed: "I believe, Frau Deiters, it is time for us to go." Brahms looked up wonderingly. "Overwhelming success!" he cried.

In closing, here is Uncle Brahms in the gaily tender *Allegretto grazioso* mood of the D major symphony. A young pianist confided to him that she was studying the violin in order to be a more intelligent chamber musician. "I must hear you!" cried the Master. And when the girl, greatly abashed, replied that she fiddled far too badly: "But if I compose something for you, won't you play it?"

"Alas!" she lisped, "I have only got as far as the second violin."

He laughed. "Well then, I'll write a piece for second violin alone. It's something I've never tried."

Chapter XVII

HIS GIFT FOR WORDS

MANY who have merely been amused at Brahms for calling the D major symphony "a set of waltzes," and the *Four Serious Songs,* "the *Schnadahüpferln,*" have read with conviction his eloquent diatribes against his own letters, mingled with his howls of impatience and exasperation over the necessity for writing them—and have been frightened away from the letters themselves. If these people had only read on, they would have seen that the Master had been unfair to his own gift for verbal expression. Even while belittling this gift, he often wrote charmingly.

Please never scold me for my correspondence [he begged Clara Schumann, whose husband had recently become insane]! How many times have I told you that I very seldom succeed in putting my thoughts on paper direct from the heart. . . . So I often sit before the letter-paper longing to send you right comforting, right beautiful words—but I've never been able to.

The idea that he was a cold, unimaginative, and sterile letter-writer could have gained currency only through a literal acceptance of the abuse and ridicule which this most modest of artists habitually poured upon himself. As a rule, he spoke of his productions in a way which, if it had been generally accepted *au pied de la lettre,* would have assigned him a place in the history of music somewhat below that of

Ganne or Gungl, and ranked him as a correspondent beside Sam Weller. But the truth is that this man of the people, whose formal education had consisted chiefly of music lessons, possessed a flair for words.[1]

Following the example of Schütz, the predecessor of Bach, and mining the texts for his choral works directly out of the Bible, Brahms showed editorial ability of no mean order. The words of the *Requiem*, the *Fest- und Gedenksprüche*, the *Four Serious Songs*, etc., show his intimate knowledge of Scripture, his almost unerring instinct for the right material, and his powers of effective combination.

The writer, however, outshines the editor. In the eighteen volumes of the correspondence, one may savour his whole rare personality. They are filled with humour, wit, irony, memorable aphorisms. They bubble over with the man's superb vitality and inextinguishable zest in life. Sometimes in their suggestiveness, their high organization and depth of meaning, his words, like his notes, are contrapuntally conceived, with the important unwritten playing against the obvious written.

To my taste Brahms was one of the most satisfying correspondents who ever wielded a professional music-pen. He could scarcely scratch four lines on a postcard without stumbling, despite himself, on some whimsical, comely, sardonic, wise, or wittily original turn of phrase.

When Simrock greedily wrote to inquire whether opus 77 was done, the highly Brahmsian retort came:

[1] It is too bad that the quality of this gift cannot be more adequately conveyed in translation!

Done! What is done? The violin concerto? No. You or I?
No. And if you should want to say yes, I'd be sorry for you
and for it. . . .

I think of spending Christmas in Frankfurt. One knows
nothing definite; even the most credulous doesn't. . . . And
I am credulous. Indeed, I believe in immortality—; I believe
that when an immortal dies, people will keep on for 50,000
years and more, talking stupidly and badly about him—
therefore I believe in immortality, without which beautiful
and agreeable attribute I have the honour to be

Your
J. Br.

Note how the same instinct for organic unity which made
him the greatest master of form since Bach, and gave us such
highly unified works as the F major symphony and the piano
and clarinet quintets, impelled him to weave his letter-
endings skilfully into the woof of the preceding text.

My friend the Dutch composer, who so generously enriched these pages, contributed a felicitous card of introduction with which the Master once armed him for a trip to
Switzerland:

I recommend most heartily to Mr. Widmann, Mr. Julius
Roentgen, conductor in Amsterdam—for the first half-hour
—for the further hours he himself will recommend himself
far better than can

Your heartily greeting
J. Br.

And in this unique wise did he answer Elisabet von
Herzogenberg's dun for an acknowledgment of her photograph, a gift destined to stand for years on his desk:

Certainly I received your picture. Oh *ich undankbarer* (I the thankless)

J. Br.

In his letters, almost as frequently as in his scores, one finds such passages as this to Clara about the *Choral* symphony:

The Ninth went atrociously. How often is Beethoven still crucified, even after death!

Here is an unexpected turn of phrase to Joachim:

I can be happy only if others think better of it [my music] than I do—and marvel that with such slight encouragement *on my own part*, I can always continue to compete with myself.

Every now and again one comes upon small nuggets of wisdom, worded so as to be characteristic of the man:

Art is a republic.

Without industry, no genius.

As a rule, the artist who is set on making money belongs wholly to the devil.   •

[Of owning the works of Beethoven and Shakespeare]— For this pair no youth should have to wait long; but, once he owns them, he need not run rapidly after any others. In these two he has the whole world.

This claim, however, was made without prejudice to the father of music. Dr. Roentgen told me that once after Brahms had played his own arrangement of Bach's F major organ *Toccata* to a small group of Dutch friends, Verhulst, the conductor, exclaimed: "How far that man Bach was in advance of his own time!" "Of his own time?" parried Brahms. "No, of all times!"

For a musician of his imaginative power, no drama on any actual stage could furnish entertainment comparable to that which Brahms could at any moment enjoy in the *théâtre intime* of his own mind. Thanking Simrock for the score of *Fidelio*, he added:

Immediately on receipt of it I enjoyed the very best performance—quietly here in the room, at my desk.

In declining an invitation to the Villa Carlotta on Lake Como, he showed how slight a distinction existed for him between action and imagination:

My greetings to the azaleas, the glowworms, the nightingales—really there is not so much difference between actually being in that place, and thinking of it!

His opinions on almost every subject were definite, and expressed clearly and forcefully. When asked to bestir himself on behalf of an infant prodigy he answered:

Wonder-children interest me only in so far as their performances can amuse me! Only too often have I seen the most miraculous things in this line—and the nothing in which they later lose themselves. What a lousy (*lausiger*) young person must he be about whom everyone, including himself, does not have the sure feeling that some day he may become anything at all!

Major Desjoyaux tells me that "one day Brahms remarked to a small circle: 'In France and Italy they lay too much stress on classes in harmony. Indeed, what *is* harmony?' And, when no one found a good definition: 'Don't bother your heads! Harmony is a collection of baptismal cognomens, brought together so that one may, in calling them by name, politely salute the chords: that is to say, the groups of more or less consonant notes which counterpoint has united."

About Nottebohm's valuable researches he wrote to Schubring:

When they appeared you perhaps bored yourself to tears over his articles about Beethoven's studies, but most likely you took the fact into account that a serious investigation of a serious matter does not immediately look amusing.

At twenty-three Herr Franz Marschner, who wished to write music, sought Brahms' advice, and was told: "One cannot live from serious composition alone. You see, a composer is poetic only from his twentieth to his thirtieth year."

Two years before his death, however, the Master somewhat modified this startling exaggeration by informing Clara that "one is productive only until fifty." And this was the man who, since his half-century mark, had produced the E minor symphony, the C minor trio, the last two violin sonatas, the G major and clarinet quintets, and the last piano pieces!

When a critic named Van Bruyck described Brahms as the summit of the finished cathedral of music, the young Master wrote Clara:

Who can ever say that something has reached its end, which never has an end? Little people have always wished to write down a period after every genius.

It is interesting to know, however, that toward the end of his days, he fell into Van Bruyck's selfsame error, only to be set right by an artist inferior to himself. One afternoon, while walking with Gustav Mahler, he was in a bad mood and exclaimed: "Music is done for! From now on, nothing new can be created!" Soon after, in crossing a bridge, Mahler stopped, gazed into the water, and quietly observed: "Doctor, I have just seen the *last* ripple." Indeed, the Master's very existence was a cogent commentary on the futility of pessimism about art; for no sooner had Wagner declared that absolute music was played out—than Brahms appeared.

Curiously enough, Brahms was a better prophet about national affairs than about his art. Thirty-five years before the German-Austrian débâcle of 1918, he wrote Simrock from Vienna, about Austria:

In a land where everything—not goes, but—falls down hill, you must not expect music to fare better. Truly it is a pity and a mournful shame—not alone for the music—but for the whole lovely land and the beautiful, splendid people. In my opinion catastrophe is coming.

His harsh virility, his very impatience to be done with what he cursed as "this scribbling," lend to Brahms' letters some of the same compactness, simplicity, clarity, and economy of material which are so noteworthy in his scores.

"I write as if I were telegraphing," he once remarked. But here again, as usual, the Master exaggerated, to his own discredit. Far from resulting in the barren style of a newspaper dispatch, his economy often secured admirable æsthetic effects.

The only approach to the truly telegraphic which I am able to find in his writings is the message which, for a joke, he

sent from Karlsbad to friends gathered in Gmunden to celebrate Hanslick's birthday, and which he mailed as an ordinary
letter. The joke lay in his enjoying the informalities of a
telegram while paying the lower rate of mail matter, and
protesting that correspondence was *"kurwidrig"* (*contrary
to Cure regulations*). The clipped quality, however, which he
unjustly denounced in his own writing, was often to be heard
in his conversation. "He never spoke whole sentences," Professor Robert Kahn tells me, "but talked more in the style
of a telegram."

When his fancy found vent in words, the result was what
one might expect from the brain which produced the *Intermezzo* of the G minor piano quartet, *Vergebliches Ständchen,* the *Allegretto graziozo* of the D major symphony, the
Academic Festival overture, and the *scherzo* of the C minor
trio.

He dated a letter to Clara:

> Düsseldorf on the Rhine
> In the year of grace [*des Heils*]—— —— 1855
> (In the year of calamity [*des Unheils*] of the birth
> of Friedrich Wilhelm IV—— —— 61.)
> . . . The streets along the Rhine are . . . under water.
> . . . They cannot hold performances in the theatre because
> the pit, etc., is flooded. Now if the singers would only do their
> singing, kissing, and murdering in punts and gondolas, and
> the spectators glide about the pit in boats, I'd attend.
> In that case, the guest of stone would have to arrive in a
> skiff, and instead of drawing Don Juan to the lower regions,
> would have to chuck him into the water.

After lamenting to Elisabet the huge number of invitations that he was obliged to refuse by writing variations on the theme "I hate to give concerts," he modulated to the major in this unexpected fashion: "Now quick, let me make a friendly face here on the paper."

The simplicity with which he mentioned the passing of those for whom he cared was none the less touching for its terseness:

Nottebohm had no strength to wrestle with Death, who barely beckoned and he fell asleep.

He mourned the decease of old Gottfried Keller as an untimely thing, and wistfully observed:

One sees a beautiful sunset with so much pleasure.

He condoled with a friend because another friend was moving away:

Why can't a man keep sitting, like a beetle on a green bush, where he is comfortable? But who knows, at that, whether the beetles are in this respect any better off than we are? Perhaps, even among them, ambition has crept in.

A jocose scribble on a calling-card acknowledged the honorarium for the *Schicksalslied*:

Here is the receipt for my heart's blood, also my thanks for the purchase price of the poor little piece of soul.

Brahms, the stark but expressive economist of words, had a natural talent for titles. One of his best was the designation of his last piano pieces as *"Wiegenlieder meiner Schmerzen"* (Cradlesongs of My Sufferings). Thus, as early as 1890, he anticipated that movement for the use of music and poetry in neutralizing certain adverse emotions and moods, which was to gather momentum in America a generation later.

The most workaday business discussions with publishers were enlivened by the play of his fancy.

Where [he asked Simrock] am I to get time? Here it is pulled out from under one's feet, so that one does not notice its whereabouts.

Again, in requesting a remittance:

Take me under the arms with a little thousand [marks]—but don't tickle! A pleasant sense of duty well performed will then beautify your holidays.

And he surprisingly ended a parley about terms for the first two string quartets:

> Your devoted
> Somebody
> J. BRAHMS.

Walking with Widmann, in high good-humour, he once burst out with: "We please me! [*Wir gefallen mir!*] Well, may not one perhaps put it thus, you German stylist, you? Maybe you've never heard such a phrase. But only think it over; it's quite correct." And zestfully he echoed the terse novelty: "We please me!"

Considering that the Master grew up in wretched poverty, and associated with poor, easy-going, and uncultivated folk until his twentieth year, it is hard to understand how he could so often have attained a felicity with words which many a successful writer might covet.

Chapter XVIII

THE LION AS BEAR

THE bearish side of Brahms, like that of Beethoven, came from a neglected childhood among rough poor people and surroundings; from much spoiling on the part of adorers; from the instinctive concealment of his extreme shyness, and soft-heartedness; and from the exasperating effect of long years in charming but slow, lax, irresponsible, and happy-go-lucky Vienna upon an accurate, conscientious, and energetic northern temperament. His exaggerated social uncouthness was a self-defence against a consciousness of inferiority resulting from his humble origin, scanty schooling, lack of social training, and physical handicaps. This self-defence helped to make his manners far worse than they need otherwise have been.

Sometimes, however, his words and deeds grew so outrageous, gave such gratuitous pain to the innocent, as to merit the harsh word cruel, and make the staunchest Brahmin wonder if the Master may not occasionally have been actuated by some obscurely sadistic impulse.

Toward my friends [Brahms wrote once to Clara Schumann] I am aware of having but one fault: clumsiness in association with them.

To call his bearish side "clumsiness" is almost as choice a euphemism as Beethoven coined in terming one of his own spasms of violent and abusive language "a hearty free word."

The following incident was told to me by Geheimrat Max Friedländer: "In the eighties, I dined with Brahms on his birthday at the house of one of his most intimate Viennese friends, a man whose charming wife and two half-grown children made up the party. Unfortunately, French champagne was served before table. Now Brahms was usually a temperate person. He never drank in his own home. At the Sign of the Red Hedgehog where he ate, his ration was one glass of wine and charged water. But in society he would drink with enthusiasm. Well, this champagne tasted so good that three bottles were served to the six of us. And at dinner we had some rather strong red wine.

"Brahms grew more and more silent, but nobody noticed anything curious about him. The talk turned on a beautiful and beloved woman whom we all knew. Still the Master was silent—until some one pressed him for his opinion. That was a moment which I shall never forget! Abruptly his harsh voice broke into a horrible, coarse tirade against this lady, broadening out to include women in general, and actually ended by applying to them all an incredible, unspeakable epithet—a word so vile that I have never been able to repeat it, even to my wife."

The old professor flushed purple. He tried to tell me the word, but could not get it across his tongue, and let it go at that.[1]

"Then Brahms fell back into his drunken silence. Of course the tirade had burst among us like a gas-bomb. Our embarrassment was appalling. I remember that the host began a

---

[1] I never found out what was in the dear old professor's mind. Perhaps it was only some expression common in Holy Writ.

constrained conversation with me about the theatre, to which I replied wholly at random. As soon as we rose from table I went up to the hostess and blurted out that I would now go. But she looked frightened, and begged me: 'For God's sake, don't leave us alone with him!' So I stayed.

"Brahms drank some very black coffee, which began to clear his head. We left together. On the street I said good-bye. But he held on to me and inquired: 'Have you any work you must do now?'

"With those great, deep-blue, honest eyes looking at one it was simply impossible to tell a lie. I said 'No.' 'Then come with me to the Prater, will you?' I agreed.

"The fresh air of the park revived him still more. We trudged a long stretch in silence. At last, without turning toward me he muttered: 'Was it, after all, so very bad?' And I had to tell him: 'Yes, very bad.'

" 'Look here,' he demanded abruptly, 'how were you brought up?' So I told him of my childhood in the rather poor Silesian home with the six brothers and sisters of us; how devotedly my parents were attached to one another, how tenderly we were guarded from everything ugly and painful, and so on.

"Suddenly Brahms burst with violence into my reminiscences, making a furiously angry scene in the middle of the Prater. His eyes grew bloodshot. The veins in his forehead stood out. His hair and beard seemed to bristle.

" 'And you,' he cried menacingly, 'you who have been reared in cotton wool; you who have been protected from everything coarse—you tell me I should have the same respect, the same exalted homage for women that you have!'

(I had not, of course, put this into words, but his sensitive soul had caught my unuttered reproaches.) 'You expect that of a man cursed with a childhood like mine!'

"Then, with bitter passion he recounted his poverty-stricken youth in the wretched slums of Hamburg; how as a shaver of nine, he was already a fairly competent pianist; and how his father would drag him from bed to play for dancing and accompany obscene songs in the most depraved dives of the St. Pauli quarter.

" 'Do you know those places?' he asked. 'Only from the outside.' 'Then you can't have the least idea of what they are really like. And in those days they were still worse. They were filled with the lowest sort of public women—the so-called "Singing Girls." When the sailing ships made port after months of continuous voyaging, the sailors would rush out of them like beasts of prey, looking for women. And these half-clad girls, to make the men still wilder, used to take me on their laps between dances, kiss and caress and excite me. That was my first impression of the love of women. And you expect *me* to honour them as you do!' It was long before his anger simmered down and we left the park.

"The following year, our hostess of that day told me that some time after the disastrous birthday dinner, Brahms appeared at her house as though nothing had happened, except that he brought her a bouquet. This was doubly surprising because, of course, she had not invited him; and he never gave flowers—not even to Clara Schumann, who used to complain of the neglect. In his gruff way he inquired about the possibility of meeting in the country that summer.

" 'But,' she answered, 'don't you realize that it's already

been settled that we're all going to X together, and that we've even engaged your room for you?'

" 'Hm, well then, that's all right,' muttered the Master in high contentment. The flowers and the inquiry were the nearest that his reticent nature could come to an apology. That was a thing he simply could not manage."

All his life Brahms was kind and charming to the unfortunate women of the class that first woke his boyish passions. But he was very different with the society woman, and often dealt her the roughest language and the rudest shocks of her life. Once when a coy, piscatorial dinner partner asked him if he did not find that she resembled Frau N., a famous beauty, he growled: "I simply can't tell you two apart. When I sit beside one of you I invariably wish it were the other!"

Frau Prof. Brüll recalls that Brahms used to complain of so many women plaguing him to let them play for him: "Now if they'd only invert it and ask *me* to play for *them*, that would be something different."

"A noted woman pianist," says this informant, "was at our house for dinner, after having teased us to invite Brahms. Two other ladies were there, both of them from Vienna. Except when actually eating, the Master spent the entire evening on the piano stool for fear the Parisian would play. At dinner he got up and drank a toast to us three Viennese women. How could he more obviously have given the French lady a black eye?"

Sometimes, even when the women succeeded in carrying the keyboard by storm, they found they had gone farther only to fare worse. The aggressiveness of Gisela von Ehrenstein was stronger than her sense of rhythm. By persistent efforts she finally got herself invited to dinner with Brahms. It took much pleading to induce the Master to play his clarinet quintet with her as a four-hand duet. But, after a few wobbly measures, he abruptly cut short the music and the amenities by assaulting the keys with both fists.

Mr. Artur Bodanzky tells me that when a woman composer asked Brahms to come to the Brülls' and hear one of her compositions, he flippantly answered: "No. If I want to hear good music I write some of my own."

Unlike copybook charity, his diplomacy did not begin at home. Underneath his Viennese apartment at Karlsgasse 4 lived a certain Frau Ronchetti. This lady considered herself extremely musical, and having placed her concert grand immediately below Brahms' study, she very often gave him the treat of hearing his own music.

"Who is the person," he asked his housekeeper, Frau Dr. Truxa, "that makes such an infernal noise under me?"

"Frau Ronchetti."

"She brings me to desperation! She plays always my things —and how badly!"

Frau Dr. Truxa has told me that she offered to reason with the lady, but her lodger said No, he would do that himself.

"At once I noticed an alarming increase in the volume and duration of the sounds. And then I learned what an ominous thing had happened. Brahms had, in his best diplomatic manner, asked the Frau to perform his music no more because she played it atrociously. This made her so furious that she hired a conservatory pupil to come every day and bang Brahms *fortissimo*.

"The Master soon came to me and groaned: 'Nothing is

any good! Life here has now grown unendurable!'

"So I thought of a plan. I went down to Frau Ronchetti and told her she had so much musical talent it was a shame for her to confine her gifts to a single instrument. Being very stupid, she swallowed the bait at once and asked me to suggest how she should branch out.

" 'Try the zither. I play it myself, and will teach you for nothing.'

"Soon I had her enthusiastic, and lent her my own zither and went down frequently to give her lessons. But I took care to choose a room not under Brahms, and to complain that the piano-playing of the conservatory pupil interfered with our progress. So she sent the girl away and became absorbed in the zither. As for my lodger, he could not hear the weak tones of the new instrument, and took heart again."

Most people can form no idea what suffering the Master's hypersensitive ears caused him. Once, when asked why he had seemed so exasperated at dinner, he burst out: "How could I be in good humour when the lady on my right talked in E major, and the one on my left, in E minor?"

When Brahms disliked people, no regard for worldly expediency or fear of possible reprisals could muffle his devastating frankness. He was heard loudly and bluntly to define Frau Gutmann, the wife of his rich and powerful concert manager, as "an emetic."

Mr. Samuel Thewman tells of a huge dinner in honour of Brahms at the Conrats' in Vienna. Dr. Sigmund Münz, the journalist, rose and began entertaining the company. "He talked at length and vociferously, attacking Bismarck, ridiculing him, pointing out where he had made mistakes. I saw that Brahms was growing more and more silent. He was pale, and he actually seemed to shrink in stature, as a lion shrinks when he contracts his muscles, preparatory to a great spring.

"Finally, when Münz was building up one of his best climaxes, Brahms jumped from his place, smote his fist full on the table, so that the glasses clattered, and shouted: 'Stop! that's quite enough of your filthy newspaper talk!' And in the complete, dumbfounded silence that followed, Brahms left his seat, made punctiliously formal adieus to his hostess, and left the party."

Such evidences of the Master's spiny exterior remind one that Bram, the original form of his name, is represented in the English word "bramble."

Prof. Robert Kahn has told me of the Master's sudden pounce upon a middle-aged belle who was kittenishly trying to make herself seem young. With a particularly sharp look he rapped out: "Exactly how old *are* you, madame?"

A famous Viennese painter, who does not wish his name involved, was dining with Brahms and Dr. Billroth at the house of Hanslick, the critic who did more for the composer's fame than any other. "Our host and the great surgeon were discussing the philosopher's stone [*der Stein der Weisen*]. This expression was new to me, and I asked Brahms what it meant. He put on a look of profound solemnity: 'It's what Frau Hanslick will be stoned to death with when Hanslick is no more.'"

Collectively the ladies fared little better with him, and it is small wonder that he was not overpopular with those of the choirs he conducted. In Vienna he was once rehearsing *The Creation* of Haydn who, be it noted, had passed away in

1809. The performers were probably the same snowy-haired Gesellschafts chorus in whose presence some wit once aptly quoted Napoleon's address before the Pyramids: "Comrades, forty centuries are looking down upon you . . ." The sopranos in the first row were especially mature, and could not be induced to keep up to tempo. Finally Brahms lost all patience, rapped for attention, and barked: "But, my dear ladies, why do you drag so? Surely you took this much faster under Haydn!"

Admirers often sent the Master flowers. They might have ingratiated themselves better by sending him brickbats. When, wrapped in their lace-paper, the bouquets arrived, Brahms cursed in his great beard and either hurled them through the open window, or gave them to his friends the children to stick in their hats. During his last illness he received a choice bunch from Frau Johann Strauss, a woman whom he cordially disliked. Instantly he gave them away, and growled roughly to his housekeeper: "One doesn't send flowers to a person who is seriously ill. Time enough for that, later"—a remark peculiarly touching in its stark simplicity.

Once in a long while he clumsily tried to make himself agreeable to ladies, even though pianists, particularly if they were young and charming. But such attempts sometimes lent themselves to misinterpretation.

"In the eighties," an old Swiss lady recalls, "when I was fourteen or so, I visited a girl singer three years older than myself at Bad Faulensee on Lake Thun. One morning I was accompanying her on the hotel piano in the empty diningroom. We had been doing Brahms songs for about ten minutes when the door opened, and an elderly fat man with a long grizzled beard came shuffling in, with both hands deep in his trousers pockets. Just back of us, he stopped. We looked him over and were rather annoyed at the intrusion, but kept on.

"Suddenly the man came to my side, shoved me bodily from the piano stool, and muttered: 'Just give me room, there. I'll show you how that must go.'

"Naturally we were petrified at such rudeness. But he began to play, and there was something compelling in the sound. So that my friend managed to sing the song through. When it was finished he got to his feet and went as he had come, without saying another word.

"In high indignation we hurried to the hall porter and asked who the shameless old man was. 'Why, don't you know? That is Herr Brahms!'

"Of course we were overcome and rushed to look for a hiding-place, and never saw Brahms again."

Women were by no means the only victims of this bear. Many a man ruefully remembers to this day how rough his paws were. Prince Heinrich XXIV of Reuss was one of his most adoring worshippers. But the Master who, far from being a respecter of high personages, disliked everything aristocratic, "treated him like the least of the least," according to an American 'cellist who once overheard him tell the Joachim Quartet: "Attention there! Keep an eye out for the cigars in your pockets. Here comes Reuss!"

No character, even one of unimaginable perfection, could have been absolutely guaranteed against the outbursts of his bearish irascibility. Frau Olga von Miller zu Aichholz was kindness and sweetness personified. Yet one day at her table, when she was apologizing for the simplicity of the meal, Brahms, who liked good food, suddenly hit the table a mighty blow with his fist and rapped out: "*Aber warum denn?*" (But why?) Kalbeck tells[2] how he was at Ischl with Brahms when the lady's husband appeared in the doorway. This most ardent of all Brahms enthusiasts had, as they afterwards learned, come over especially to invite them to Gmunden. They urged him repeatedly to enter, but the sensitive man held back for fear of intruding. All at once the Brahmsian back was turned, the Brahmsian fist buffeted the table, and the Brahmsian voice bellowed: "Well then, *don't!*" The terrified Miller vanished.

Later when the Master had cooled down he observed: "Miller would be an absolutely tip-top fellow if he weren't always begging one's pardon for being alive. A bit ago I had to pull myself together like hell to keep from being rough with him." And Kalbeck adds: "Such singular conceptions had the impatient Brahms, at times, of politeness and roughness."

One is glad that Elisabet von Herzogenberg had the backbone to rally him about his manners, in the following ironical lines:

I work untiringly for the good of your reputation, and tell everybody that you are the politest, most affable, most urbane of men; that you have taken lessons in bowing of Frappart [the solo dancer of the Vienna Opera]; and that it simply betokens the crudest want of understanding not to appreciate your graceful compliments as they deserve.

Possibly owing to the protracted tortures he suffered in his home at the hands of Frau Ronchetti and her conservatory

2 IV, I, 169–170.

pupil, he could be a most uncomfortable associate for those whom he caught maltreating his music. At the first Viennese rehearsal of the C minor trio, Brahms stormed through the piano part with such ruthless *rubato* that the fiddlers Heckmann and Bellmann could hardly call their solos their own. After the first movement Heckmann was incautious enough to ask the irritated composer if he was satisfied, and the resulting sarcastic "Yes, very" was like a slap across the cheek.

In the *scherzo* Brahms developed a mad pace. Of course Heckmann and Bellmann came to grief and shame at the catastrophic spot where innumerable fiddlers have, ever since, followed their example. I mean the F minor passage in the Trio where first the 'cello, and hard after him the violin, falls upstairs, stubbing—so to speak—his pizzica-toes, that is, unless he knows the passage very well indeed and the pianist is indulgent. Here the composer, no doubt with a bit of his characteristic malice, speeded up even more relentlessly (an interesting fact in view of the sedentary pace at which this movement is generally taken).[3] When the unfortunate wretches had fallen upstairs several times quite hopelessly, and broken their crowns, the Master flashed to his feet with an angry growl: "So comes one not to rehearsal!" And he burst from the house as the concertmaster burst into tears.

Even with his most intimate friends, and in play, his love-pats were more frequently claw than velvet. "Your good reputation—" he wrote to his beloved publisher Simrock, "what one doesn't possess one cannot lose!"

---

[3] But Miss Fanny Davies heard Brahms play this *scherzo* later with Joachim and Hausmann. She testifies about the printed time-direction *Presto non assai:* "What one usually hears is '*presto.*' What one heard from Brahms was '*non assai.*' . . . I marked my copy 'not the least idea of *presto.*'" (In Cobbett, Vol. I, p. 183.) See p. 388.

Another playful sally left scars. In society the Master was once introduced by a certain orchestral conductor to his fiancée. "Why, this is a splendid thing!" cried Brahms with great earnestness. "You are bringing a musical element into the family."

"That was meant wittily, I am sure," my informant added. "But he made such angry faces as he said these things that you really couldn't tell, at the moment, how he meant them. Personally I believe it was usually half jest and half malice. It simply wasn't in him to behave conventionally. So he tried to persuade himself that the amenities did not matter. I can tell you, my mother was awfully anxious whenever he was to come to our house!"

He did not always succeed, however, in fully rationalizing his bearishness. In 1877, having painfully offended Max Bruch about some piece by the latter, he wrote to Simrock: "Bruch is terribly angry at me—but how can I help my brutal nature, and my abhorrence of *Adagios?*"

Before an orchestral concert the widow of Wilhelm Gericke, the conductor, was once in the artists' room of the Musikverein in Vienna. It was full of famous men. One of them, d'Albert, was to play. And a piece by another (Hugo Wolf, she thinks) was on the program. Brahms was there and in his best form. Before leaving he turned to d'Albert (whom he had nicknamed "The Concert-Baby") and said: "Amuse us!" But to the composer: "Amuse yourself!" Mrs. Gericke remembers that her husband was quite dumbfounded by this piece of rudeness.

Whenever the Master came to realize, however, that he had hurt somebody's feelings, no one could be more contrite.

Then, in his own peculiar style, he would try to set things straight. Prof. Julius Winkler has told me a characteristic instance. "In a concert of the Viennese Tonkünstler Verein, the Master once turned pages for Zellner, who was playing the piano part of his own trio. When it was finished and the modest composer waited wistfully for some word of praise from the Master, Brahms stood up in evident embarrassment and exclaimed: 'How that man *does* play the piano!' It was a very bad moment for us all.

"Not long after, I dropped into see the Zellners and found his wife radiant. 'Who do you suppose was here just now? Brahms!'

"Realizing what pain he had given, the Master had gone in his really kind, noble way, to make it good."

Chapter XIX

HIS MODESTY

If I were a *creative* artist like my honoured new friend Brahms, I should not only be entitled—I should be bound—to be an egoist—to run others down in order to affirm my great self—an idea made flesh.

HANS VON BÜLOW.[1]

WHEN it came to self-appraisal, the Master was far more truly representative of the modest plant which provided his surname than were those namesakes of his, the royal Plantagenets.[2] Not only for a genius but even for an ordinary man, Johannes Brahms was extraordinarily modest. No other artist of the first magnitude ever so consistently ran down his own work. This was done sometimes in jest but very often in deadly earnest.

His subtle fooling is frequently hard to distinguish from genuine self-depreciation. The light touch sometimes connotes a quiet self-approval. When he asked Simrock: "Would you mind if Peters were to print my bad violin concerto?" one may be sure that he was ragging his ardent admirer and jealously watchful publisher. And this is also true of his reply to Mr. Arthur M. Abell, who asked him if he would not write another violin concerto: "In no circumstances! 'Sufficient unto the day is the evil thereof.' " One is more doubtful when

---

[1] *Hans von Bülow in Leben und Wort*, by Marie von Bülow, 1925, p. 241.

[2] "She had perhaps said more, having some touch of the temper of that house, which, deriving their name and cognizance from the lowly broom (*Planta genista*), assumed as an emblem of humility, were perhaps one of the proudest families that ever ruled in England." Sir Walter Scott: *The Talisman*, Chap. XXVI.

he called his masterly revision of opus 8 "the worsened trio" (*das verböserte Trio*). But one is certain of his sad sincerity in writing Joachim about the next opus, the *Variations on a Theme of Robert Schumann:*

The Variations are too small, and trifling, aren't they? One really does not need such bits of childishness any more.

In response, Joachim needed all his best superlatives to reassure young Johannes.

This man, who was alarmed at the "trials" to which his Leipzig friends were subjected in hearing *A German Requiem* twice in one month, and who wrote to Clara: "I never believe that a new work of mine can please anybody," once sent Simrock a sheaf of songs with the annotation, "If the songlets are too vulgar for your taste, return them to me!" And several weeks later, about the same batch, to the same friend:

Yes, here they are at last, the songs which have been awaited, and whose advent has been advertised, for months! I have been ashamed; not that anyone can write this sort of thing—what nonsense can a man not devise, the livelong day?—but that anyone prints such stuff and sells it for dear money! Is there, then, no government examination for publishers, so that one can be satisfied that they are able to distinguish garbage from salad and vegetables?

Incredible though it may seem, this collection of so-called "songlets" and "stuff" actually included *Nachtwandler*, *Todessehnen*, and *In Waldeinsamkeit*, such distinguished masterpieces as *Therese* and *Vergebliches Ständchen*, and that supreme song *Feldeinsamkeit* which, as hummed by Nietzsche, plays such a dramatic part in Anne Douglas Sedgwick's novel,

The Encounter.

Surely the proudest moment in the career of Josef Gäns-bacher was when he received the dedication of opus 38. But Brahms announced the honour to him in these modest words, which are copied from a manuscript letter: "Do not be alarmed or annoyed if I put your name on the violoncello sonata that I'm about to send you."

In the days when political feeling ran high in music, the most rabid partisans of Wagner, Wolf, and Bruckner were scarcely more unjust to the works of Brahms than their creator himself could be. Once in submitting a large number of manuscript songs from Op. 69–72 to Clara, he prescribed formulas to facilitate and shorten the labour of criticism. From their drift one may gather the intensity of his proud self-confidence!

Write me, if possible, *one short word* with each. You may note merely the opus or the number:

<blockquote>
Op. x. 5. bad
6. shameful
7. ridiculous, etc.
</blockquote>

When he had finished the Fourth symphony, he looked it over with even more than his customary mistrust, and wrote to Elisabet von Herzogenberg:

In general my pieces are unfortunately more agreeable than I myself am, and have less in them to correct. But around here the cherries are not sweet and eatable—if the thing doesn't please you, don't make any bones about it. I am not at all eager to write a bad No. 4.

About the same noble work he sent Simrock this message:

Taking it all in all I haven't the ghost of an idea whether I shall let the thing be printed.

And he added roundly:

You would be insane to invest a groschen in it!

Once he consented to play his own G major sonata with Joachim in Gmunden, provided the violinist would first do Bach's sonata in the same key. But when Joachim had finished, Brahms hurled his own music to the floor, and cried: "After that, how could anyone play such stuff as this?"

Almost as meek and lowly was his large utterance to Joachim, accompanying the manuscript of the superb G major quintet.

Well, I heartily wish that the piece may please you a little, but you mustn't mind telling me the contrary. In that case I will comfort myself with the first quintet [F major], and for both—with the quintets of Mozart.[3]

Surely none but a person of the largest calibre could thus compensate himself for his own fancied shortcomings by comparing them with the *chef-d'œuvres* of an acknowledged master!

But Brahms had begun early with such sportsmanlike tactics. Immediately after the most disastrous and humiliating reverse of his career, when in 1859 the reactionary Leipzig Gewandhaus had hissed him and his D minor concerto, he wrote Joachim:

My ensuing bit of bad and dreary mood vanished on hearing Haydn's C major symphony and *The Ruins of Athens*.

[3] Herr Emil Hess reports him as tapping the score of *The Marriage of Figaro*, and crying: "That *one* man could have written this all alone, is to me absolutely incredible!"

For his own publications he was always uncannily sparing of good words down to the end of his career and the appearance of the *German Folk-songs,* to which he had merely supplied accompaniments.

It is perhaps the first time [he wrote Clara] that I look forward with pleasure to correcting the proofs, and to the publication, of a work of mine.

And mentioning these songs to Simrock, he inquired:

How much more do I get for them than for my own? (But so much money does not exist at all, at all.)

In Krefeld, where he had come to direct his *Gesang der Parzen* and play his B flat concerto, he entered the building as the *Leonore No. 3* overture was being rehearsed. Listening a while in the vestibule he exclaimed: "My bad luck will have it that everywhere I go to conduct my works, *this* piece is on the program! But really, you know, side by side with this, nothing else can stand up."

Humility of this sort he carried to astonishing lengths. Adolph Exner once told him how much he had recently enjoyed hearing the Winkler Quartet play some quite unknown chamber music of Haydn's. Brahms laughingly remarked what a scandal it was that such works as these, and Viotti's A minor violin concerto, should be unknown to the public, and exclaimed: "Ah yes, that's how folks like us make our living!" This was a characteristically Brahmsian way of asserting that modern composers were encouraged merely because people were so ignorant of the works of their elders and betters. The monstrous and shocking comparison between Viotti and himself was drawn in earnest good faith. It stands out in stark

contrast to the sound common sense which he so often showed
—and to the usual blind egotism of genius. But how this curious touch of unjustified servility in a great man flatters the
vanity of ordinary people!

The mere thought of Schubert was enough to fill Brahms
with a sense of his own insignificance. "Once in my life," he
exclaimed to Frau Brüll, "I wish I might come to know the
feeling of happiness that Schubert must have enjoyed when
one of his melodies occurred to him!" He showed Barth the
first three volumes of the compete edition of that master, and
cried enthusiastically: "Look, three volumes, and we haven't
even got to *Erlkönig* yet, which is opus 1! The amount the
man wrote in the year 1815—it's enough to drive one crazy!"

His respect for Mendelssohn, too, was prodigious. Frau Prof.
Engelmann told me that he once said to her: "Mendelssohn is
a great master before whom we should all take off our hats!"
And she repeated that other cry of his, which stands at the
head of the Brahms-Engelmann *Correspondence*: "I'd give all
my compositions if I could have written such a piece as the
Hebrides overture!"

It is a mistake, however, to take as serious gospel every
Brahmsian remark about any composer whomsoever: for example, his famous endorsement on Frau Johann Strauss' autograph fan, where he wrote, beneath a fragment of the *Beautiful Blue Danube* waltz: "Unfortunately not by Johannes
Brahms." This *jeu d'esprit* is, I am inclined to believe, in somewhat the same class with those sportive sallies in which he
designated his own most serious and sublime works as "polkas," "entr'actes," and "*Schnadahüpfln.*" Remember that he
once jestingly called his D major symphony "a set of waltzes,"

because it contained two movements in ¾ time! The fan inscription reads to me like a product of his wit, plus his spirit of contradiction, plus his sincere liking for Strauss' masterly tunes, plus his democracy, with just a dash of modesty for flavour. To take it quite *au pied de la lettre* and then use it as a weapon against him is unfair.

Concerning his undeniable superiors, however, he was never equivocal in word or action. Unlike Beethoven, who truly declared that he never wanted to hear any music but his own, Brahms preferred the product of better makers. From the palace of the Duke of Meiningen he wrote to Clara: "My first morning in Meiningen I treated myself to a rehearsal, and indeed I was the sole listener. When my noble hosts are here, the cry is Brahms and again Brahms. But I had the musicians play me a concerto for four wind instruments by Mozart and one by Bach for three violins, three violas, and three 'cellos!"

Publisher Simrock was always sending his star composer luxuriously bound copies of his scores, and the latter was always rating him soundly for such attentions. Of the *Gesang der Parzen* in gala attire he wrote:

I am not vain enough to enjoy my things in so brilliant a uniform. . . . But one can't be rough when somebody tries to give one pleasure?

He informed the sympathetic Widmann that he usually slept badly after a performance of his own music. He was too excited—not, however, from pleasure in hearing the stuff, but from a strong feeling of how far the finished product had lagged behind his intention. On another occasion he humbly confessed that he should have married, in order possibly—like Mozart's father—to have a son of genius to whom he might bequeath all his musical knowledge, so that the lad could really become that which he himself had never been.

Composers are usually autocratic about the interpretation of their own works. Not so Brahms. Mr. Stephen Townsend tells me that Max Heinrich once did *Ständchen* for the Master, and added: "Perhaps I don't sing that as you intended it."

"That's all right," was the perfectly sincere reply. "Maybe a good interpreter knows better how to perform music than the composer himself."

And when Franz Kneisel, after playing Brahms, asked the Master whether the tempos were right, his answer was: "Just play beautifully!" [*Nur schön spielen!*]

When Simrock wanted to buy Brahms' earlier compositions from other firms so as to make a uniform edition, the frugal composer was instantly up in arms to combat his publisher-friend's lavishness and fight against his own interests:

What can I do to prevent it if you quite hopelessly overestimate me? Most certainly neither in action nor in word have I encouraged you in this. But I can't exactly try the opposite, and peel off my whole lovely skin so that you may see what's underneath!?

I am to feel "sympathetically"! Good God, yes; your sympathy touches me. But I find it extremely silly of you to buy things from Härtels—I can't imagine how dear— . . . which will very shortly not be worth the powder to blow them up.

Sometimes he thought so poorly of his own abilities that a

little praise from a source that he thoroughly respected filled a genuine need.

I wouldn't exactly say [he confessed to Billroth after the C minor symphony was finished] that my bit of composing was nothing but vain exertion and toil, just a perpetual anger because nothing better will materialize—but you wouldn't believe how beautiful and warming one finds sympathy like yours. When it comes, one has the feeling that here is the best feature of composing and everything connected with composing.

That most charming person, Elisabet von Herzogenberg, was another whose delightful letters of praise had this effect on him. But he sometimes warned her not to be mealy-mouthed, and asserted that she "often saw sky-blue where he saw merely grey."

In the first place, I don't feel as though I had written much of anything worth while [he was then composing the Fourth symphony, and had already done the great bulk of his life-work!]; then, I do not overestimate a provisional judgment; and finally, tastes differ.

But often the encomiums of even those he most respected were too much for him. "The praises that Hans von Bülow lavishes upon me," he once remarked, "bite like salt in the eyes, so that tears flow out of mine."

His self-disparagement was infinitely resourceful in expression. When Bülow announced his engagement, Brahms wrote, in rueful reference to his own celibacy and unexpectedly swift and facile rise to fortune: "It is sad that one cannot find out and believe, early in life, how fruitful the two-spots are!" By this he meant that if only he had known how quickly and easily the untalented can make money, he might have arranged his own life differently.

"Such a person! . . ." exclaimed the twenty-three-year-old creator of the piano sonatas, the B major trio, *Liebestreu*, and the *Edward* ballade: "It distresses me still that I am not yet a real musician." And one year before, the lad had actually confessed to Clara: "As I have written myself out, yes, I am already too old, the composing doesn't go."

All his life he was subject to periodic attacks of this same dire conviction that he was "too old." At forty-nine, for example, he felt that the game was up, and solemnly assured Simrock that he probably would print nothing more. It was just at this moment that the F major symphony began stirring within his brain, to bring new confidence and zest in life.

From this time on, however, the consciousness of inferiority grew stronger. He kept protesting that creative artists have no more poetry in them after fifty, and should retire! He had more adverse criticism to contend with, and it depressed him more. For he did not realize that this attitude on the part of his friends came from the natural conservatism of ageing people who incline to disapprove whatever differs from that which they loved when all the world was young.

He did what he could to prevent Simrock from printing a thematic catalogue of his complete works. With might and main he combated All-Brahms programs. And, so far as I know, he is the only composer who more frequently discouraged than encouraged the performance of even single works, often urging program-makers to reduce the number of his "tricks" (*Gaukeleien*) as he liked to call his compositions.

In his own consciousness he never played the great man. A friend of mine once introduced him to a lady without pronouncing his name, assuming as a matter of course that a personage so famous needed no label. But afterwards he took her to task for what he branded a breach of etiquette.

On another occasion, after her brother-in-law, Ignaz Brüll, had played for the Tonkünstlerverein Brahms' brand-new *Intermezzi* (Op. 118), everybody else had crowded up to congratulate the composer. But my friend had held back, knowing from dire experience that he usually answered compliments with bad jokes. At supper, however, he turned to her and remarked in a low voice: "You might also have deigned to tell me a word about the new pieces."

Nothing lay further from his shy, direct, and simple nature than any hint of pomp and circumstance in connexion with his work. "My studio!" he wrote to Clara seven years before his death and long after he had become a world figure: "Good God, I've never pretended to belong among those enviable beings who possess a 'studio'!"

One may well imagine him visiting colleagues less homespun than himself, and entering one of those studios which his irony enclosed in quotation marks. On such occasions his bearing and discourse did not always make for peace on earth or good will toward attitudinizing composers. Widmann tells of the Master's first call on Hermann Goetz in Winterthur. Brahms noticed upon a standing desk an unfinished chamber-music manuscript. "Ah," he observed lightly, strolling up to examine it, "you sometimes amuse yourself with the likes of this, eh?"

Goetz lost control of himself. With a solemn gesture he spread both hands before his creation and, with a sort of adolescent pomp, exclaimed: "It is my Holiest of Holies!" Whereupon the exasperated Brahms turned his back—and the conversation—and soon vanished. Which simply goes to show how awkward his shyness could be in seeking light-worded detours around the grand manner. Goetz, much to his credit, was made of such loyal stuff that this incident never shook his allegiance to the other's music.

As may be gathered from what has already been told, Brahms did not lack a touch of that naïve and petty vanity which is apt to accompany modest greatness. When Hanslick sent him to Dr. Grünberger at Karlsbad (as that aged doctor assures me), he wrote him a line: "Don't forget the Doctor title, of which Brahms is very proud!"

Another small weakness was a dislike of figuring in second place on concert programs. Before starting a tour with Joachim he informed his old friend that their names should be printed in alphabetical order. To which the king of fiddlers responded that Brahms-Joachim had already occurred to him as the one fitting formula, although a good argument might be put up for the arrangement:

Joachim - Brahms

Ex. 4

Such small frailties, however, only served to bring out in bolder relief the Master's essentially modest habit of mind, which reached its extreme nadir when he speculated on his future fame. "I know very well," he remarked, three years before his death, "the place I shall one day have in the history of music: the place that Cherubini once had and has today. That is my lot—my fate."

In view of the fact that, a generation before, Cherubini had almost ceased to be a living force in music, this pronouncement is calculated to offend music-lovers almost as much as the outrageous comparison which, in conversation with Exner, Brahms drew between himself and Viotti [4]—but not quite so much as those ribald remarks he let fall on the subject of his own immortality.

After the initial rehearsal of the E minor symphony he wrote to Bülow:

> I am not greatly interested in a first performance; but more in a performance after ten or twenty years—which is immortality for a person like me.

When Clara tried to extort from him some information for a would-be biographer, he fobbed her off cavalierly:

> The *Children's Songs* are much older than you think. About other data—and especially about dates, I haven't the faintest notion. Bad for the next volume of universal history!

And in response to a lady who had sent him a farcical announcement of the death of her pet fox, ending with an assurance that the skin should go to the taxidermist, he wrote:

—"But he will be stuffed!" [5]
Ah, perhaps when I am gone, some tender friend will say:—
But he will be bound! And then, like your fox's skin, my music

---

[4] See p. 241.
[5] Quoted from the lady's letter.

will enter upon its immortality, which will endure—just as long as the binding, the material, holds out!

In the entire history of art there has probably never been a more wretchedly poor self-propagandist and advance agent than Brahms. What a pitiable publicity man he was is amusingly revealed by his highly negative remarks about the autobiographical blank which he was once besought to fill out.

"Happily impossible, I would have to paint nothing but zeros and dashes in these columns. I have had no experiences that I could communicate. I have attended no high schools or institutions for musical culture. I have embarked on no travels for purposes of study. I have received no instruction from eminent masters. I am the incumbent of no public offices. Well then, what am I to write here?" It was banteringly suggested that, as these truth-seekers were so hungry for information, he might at least do them the favour of setting down in the last column a list of his orders and other distinctions. *"Nee!"* cried the Master in consternation, *"that* would go least of all! *That* would plunge me into the most hideous embarrassment!"

Brahms had a horror of the self-worship so common among artists of every kind. He held up as a horrible example a certain well known composer who dined at a hotel with himself and others after a performance of that gentleman's symphony. In talking over the work the composer wrought himself up to such a pitch of enthusiasm that he sprang to his feet, rushed to the small upright piano, and was not content until he had played the complete symphony through once again.

Brahms was more likely to take the opposite course. One day at the Fellingers' when the Joachim Quartet was performing a piece of his own, the composer was listening from an alcove. Abruptly he arose, growled: "That's too boring for my taste!" and hurried from the house.

About his playing he was equally modest. The Miller zu Aichholz journal records that once, after performing "most wonderfully" some of the later piano pieces, he consented to an encore with the words: "As far as I am concerned; but understand, I am not to be held responsible for this cruelty to animals!"

He was always ready to discount encomiums on himself. "I have always," he wrote to Mandyczewski in 1891, "thought it an exaggeration to believe the half of what people say." When laurel-wreaths, or flowers tied with ribbons flatteringly inscribed in gilt, were presented to him on the concert stage, they lured no self-satisfied smirks to the Brahmsian visage; nor were they received in the gracious, suavely blithe way consecrated by custom. The Master usually bundled them under the piano or motioned the usher to make off with them. For, when it came to his art, Brahms might, as truly as any musician that ever lived, have echoed the poet who sang:

> I love thee freely, as men strive for Right;
> I love thee purely, as they turn from Praise.

Chapter XX

THE SINGING GIRLS

You must know a man's weakness before you truly know his strength. It is often in the "weaknesses" . . . that the source of the hero's strength lies . . . ; but if you refuse to note them you are false to any intelligible conception of a biographer's function, and you have produced a lie which is as immoral as every untrue picture of life necessarily is. . . . It corrupts the tree of life at the core to deny such associations. . . . Nothing shall induce you to admit that your Achilles had a vulnerable heel?—And yet, if you rightly consider the matter, without that heel Achilles would have been no hero at all.

HAVELOCK ELLIS.

Opera and marriage were two questions about which Brahms was never able to make up his mind. His relation toward Wagner was as contradictory as his attitude toward . . . the fair sex, by whom he was inwardly attracted and outwardly repelled. These psychological problems— some of them belong to psychopathology—merit further investigation.

GUIDO ADLER (1933).

Comprendre c'est pardonner.

MADAME DE STAËL.

IT IS the duty of the modern biographer to tell, so far as he sees it, the whole truth about his subject. This is, at times, an unpleasant and thankless task. Particularly in lands with a Puritan tradition, those who have fallen under the spell of some genius are often offended and angered by a faithful portrait of him, and demand instead a bowdlerized and prettified picture.

None the less, however much we may dislike even a hint of imperfection in a man who has given us so many exalted hours, if we are to comprehend Johannes Brahms in his subtle complexity we must face the truth about his sex-life.

When biography deals with sex, the present-day reader naturally expects to learn how far the hero's early experiences at home affected the love-life of his maturity. Among these experiences the main point of interest is his relation to the people he loves best—especially to his mother. Meagre information on this vital subject seriously embarrasses the biographer of Brahms. One needs to know more about his affectionateness, his desires, his responsiveness, and his more or less fully expressed fantasies about the persons nearest to him.

Here, unfortunately, the earlier biographers, and Brahms' passion for burning family letters, have left us in the lurch. With the scanty material already published, it is hard to form a clear picture of the character of either parent. We can only try to enlarge our knowledge in the hope of reaching valuable, though perhaps tentative, conclusions on important points.

Johannes' mother was crippled in one foot and limped badly. In addition she was undersized and frail-looking and was described by her contemporaries as homely. Seventeen years older than her easy-going, good-natured, and stupid husband, she was fiercely jealous and prodigal of affection. Kalbeck [1] reports that she was a clever needlewoman with some creative ability in inventing her own designs, had a lively imagination, loved poetry, possessed a remarkable memory, and outranked her husband in character and intelligence quite as much as she did in age and experience.

[1] I, I, 10–11.

We should expect that people like Frau Brahms, afflicted with marked physical defects which constantly expose them to pity or scorn, and struggling with dire poverty, would develop traits tending toward unamiability, tartness, and a refusal to compromise. This would result in a personality inclined to aggressiveness and social friction.

From what we can learn, Johannes' mother was such a person. Kalbeck [2] declares that when she was a feeble crone of seventy-five she was still wildly jealous of her fifty-eight-year-old husband, and with her daughter's backing wielded such authority in the house that she forced poor Johann Jakob to practise the double-bass, at the risk of his health, in the draughty and unheated attic.

It might seem far-fetched to draw a conclusion from a single circumstance. But this is a very striking one. The twenty-four-year-old father married a woman of forty-one. The domineering quality of her character arose not alone from her seniority, but probably from her basic physical defect as well. This fact suggests that the young father was the weaker parent. Now it is no wonder that the unusual combination of a strong mother and a weak father should have serious consequences in the character development and sex-life of the children.[3]

On the basis of these known facts, it is a fair assumption that, in the family's early days, Johannes' mother, as the stronger element, may have injured the lad without realizing it, by lavishing on him too much affection. All the evidence we have goes to indicate that the young boy developed a very

[2] II, I, 62–63, 143–44.
[3] Note that Fritz, like his brother Johannes, remained a bachelor; and that their sister Elise married, like her mother, as an old maid.

JOHANNES BRAHMS' FATHER AND MOTHER

powerful attachment to her. If we had enough information about his early years, the existence of a mother-complex unsuspected by himself might perhaps be deduced. True, the Viennese psychoanalyst Dr. Eduard Hitschmann categorically states that Brahms suffered from a mother-complex.[4] But the facts which he brings forward do not seem quite sufficient to warrant such a positive assertion.

We are sure, however, that Brahms adored his mother with a most ardent tenderness. Louisa Japha, his boyhood's playmate, bears witness that "it went to one's heart when he spoke of his old mother, he was so utterly devoted to her." In Herr Ernest's words: "His letters to her breathe such a gratitude and reverence as if she had made his childhood a paradise." At the age of twenty-nine he wrote to Clara from Vienna: "I am as fervently attached to my father-town [Hamburg] as if it were my mother." And the following year he wrote from the same city to Joachim: "I shall be a fool, and shall leave the Prater and the mountains in the loveliest season, and go to Mother. In this matter I am very old-fashioned."

Two years later, over that good woman's fresh grave, he is reported to have said words indicating that his strong maternal attachment had hitherto prevented his marriage, or made it unnecessary. It is well known that in cases of fixation on a mother, her death is often the signal for marriage experiments by the son. "I no longer have a mother," cried Brahms. "I must marry!" And he once assured Prof. Robert Kahn that "the most beautiful thing in the world is to possess

<hr>

[4] See his essay *Brahms und die Frauen* in *Psychoanalytische Bewegung*, April, 1933, pp. 118 and 121.

a mother"—a declaration which might well serve as motto for that fifth part of *A German Requiem* into which he infused so touching an intensity of filial tenderness.

Freud has shown that, paradoxical though it may seem, an ardent, unbroken attachment to a mother often strangely results in preventing the natural and necessary fusion of those two fundamental manifestations of love in a boy's life: idealistic tenderness, and passion. In certain unfortunates, this excess of fondness for the mother builds a permanent and fatal dike between the original stream of tenderness and the later-formed stream of sensuousness, so that these—so to speak—sacred and profane loves flow parallel and never merge into one. Now in Johannes' case, the outward unattractiveness of crippled old Frau Brahms, together with her rich spirituality and goodness and her glowing affection, encouraged the forming of such a fatal dike.

It is an established fact that men who have formed an exaggerated attachment to their mothers are often mysteriously unable to respond passionately to respectable women of the sort who evoke their tenderness and aspirations toward marriage. Except possibly for those who directly remind them of the adored mother, the only women who fully arouse them physically are those of, or near, the prostitute class. As Freud puts it: "Where they love they feel no passion, and where they feel passion they cannot love." [5] "In such cases," writes Dr. Hitschmann, "sex is degraded to the rôle of a humble physical function."

It is recognized that many men, at one time in their lives,

[5] Sigmund Freud, *Contributions to the Psychology of Love*, in *Collected Papers*, 1925, Vol. IV, pp. 192–216.

develop a temporary prostitute habit. But this forms a mere episode, after which most of them succeed in establishing sound love relations with respectable women, and in founding happy homes. Later, they prefer to look back upon the episode as a strange period—not really belonging to themselves. And some even deny its existence.

Occasionally, however, as it did with Brahms, the prostitute habit obstinately persists. It is impossible to comprehend this great man fully without realizing to how large an extent his peculiar whims, his moodiness, his bearishness, his modesty and aggressiveness and certain aspects of his attitude towards respectable women were the products of this bias. Readers of Kalbeck and Specht have long known that the outstanding features of Brahms' sex-life were a lack of sound and happy love relationships, and a continuing preference for prostitutes. But these biographers, though they lived in Vienna, the birthplace of the new psychology, apparently had no inkling of the reason for this state of affairs, or of its effect on Brahms' projects for matrimony and on his creative work.

"*Comprendre, c'est pardonner.* To understand is to forgive." In view of his early history I firmly believe that Brahms should not be held responsible for his unsavoury habits. As we shall see, moreover, because they made for more complete sublimation, these dung-like things seem to have helped his art to a richer flowering. And I trust that readers who have hitherto been repelled by what they know of the Master's sex-life, may finish this chapter with a more sympathetic understanding of the man and with a more adequate appreciation of his essentially noble and lofty character.

From his birth the environment of Johannes seems to have inclined him towards public women. For he actually grew up in the red-light district of Hamburg, popularly known as Adulterers' Walk (Ehebrechergang.) He lived next door to prostitutes, rubbed elbows with them at all hours on narrow tenement stairways and in dark halls, and often until dawn made music for their orgies in the lowest dives of the harbour. In a former chapter [6] his own words have told how, between dances, the notorious Singing Girls of the St. Pauli quarter used to sing their obscene songs to his accompaniment and then, half-clad, take the nine-year-old pianist on their laps, and show a wanton pleasure in rousing his first erotic impulses.

Small wonder, then, that this species of premature introduction to the mysteries of sex helped to give little Johannes an infantile bias in favour of prostitutes from which he never recovered.[7] As a rule, he was never to know sex relations with any but the simple daughters of the people.[8] "I never knew of his having an affair with a lady," his pupil, Prof. Robert Kahn, assured me, "but he very often went with prostitutes." And a large number of his old friends have told me the same thing.

Before he had lived long in Vienna, Brahms knew most

[6] See p. 224 ff.

[7] "Such impressions, such seductions must be considered momentous in their consequences. Here, perhaps, we have to do with a brusque, early initiation into the dark secrets of life, which at first alarms and repels the lad, but for ever draws the man back into its net." (Hitschmann, *op. cit.*, p. 114.)

"Let no one imagine," wrote Goethe, "that he can overcome the first impressions of his youth." And Brahms himself confessed to Kufferath: "Whatever I took to my heart when I was young stayed there firmly embedded. Thereafter, all my life, it was impossible for me to consider it and judge it differently." (Kalbeck IV, II, 413.)

[8] See Hitschmann, *op. cit.*, p. 106: "The objects of his sexuality were only girls of the people, mostly paid prostitutes."

of the daughters of joy by name, and when he walked up the Kärnthnerstrasse they would greet him with affectionate enthusiasm as "Herr Doktor!" If hard pressed, they would seek him out in some café, and he would always cheerfully give them two gulden, or more if they needed it.

A now celebrated musician has told me that in his youth Brahms recommended a certain public woman to him; and when he looked her up, she could not find words enough in praise of the Herr Doktor, who had, she bore witness, treated her with the indulgent tenderness of a father.[9]

He would not have been the intensely human creature he was if he had not rationalized the effects of his habit and made a virtue of his inclinations. He was proud of never having broken up households or seduced girls of good family, though these frequently offered themselves to him. "After a concert," Frau Prof. Brüll tells me, "our party set out for a café. Brahms gave me his arm and we met some streetwalkers, who hailed him with enthusiasm, embarrassing him very much. Finally, with his face a study in scarlet, he muttered: 'I want you to know that I have never made a married woman or a *Fräulein* unhappy.'" Such a boast is very characteristic. The psychologists would say that it betrays the boaster's basic fear of respectable women. The painful anecdote which begins the chapter called "The Lion as Bear" shows how alcohol could convert this fear into—or possibly reveal it as—disdain.

---

[9] Brahms' deep shyness no doubt helped in the formation of his prostitute habit. "For the shy man, that is to say, the man who doesn't know how to deal with real situations and people, b——s are the only possible lovers, because they're the only women who are prepared to come to meet him, the only ones who'll make the advances he doesn't know how to make." Aldous Huxley, *Brief Candles* (Tauchnitz), pp. 18–19.

Brahms' physical preference for women of easy virtue had other glints of silver lining: it ensured freedom of action, and saved valuable hours for work. "I have always had plenty of time," he used to declare, "because I have never frittered it away on cards and women"—another echo of the peasant in him, the worker whose time is seriously precious.

When he went so far, however, as to joke about his habits in connexion with his music, it made many a staunch Brahmin wince. We have seen that he once submitted to Simrock a burlesque itemized bill for the B flat string quartet, which ended in these terms:

"For models for the tender movement, each 2 florins = = ?"

By "the tender movement" he evidently meant the *Agitato,* as more in keeping with the spirit of his sex adventures than the almost religious atmosphere of the *Andante.* The number of "models" required, he left discreetly vague.

Viennese *laissez faire* well suited his limitations. In 1877, after declining an official position in Düsseldorf, he informed Dr. Billroth that "in Vienna one may remain single without any ado, but in a small town an old bachelor is a caricature. I no longer wish to marry and—have certain reasons to fear the fair sex." [10]

The faster Brahms' fame grew, the greater the scandal which his habits caused. After inviting him to fill Bach's one-time position of cantor in Leipzig, the burgomaster of that correct town was seized with misgivings about what he called the composer's "dissolute way of life." On such occasions, Brahms would unconvincingly defend himself, explain-

[10] Kalbeck, III, 1, 121–122.

BRAHMS AT TWENTY

Silver-point by the French artist, J. J. B. Laurens, made at Robert Schumann's request.
Note Johannes' adolescent appearance

ing that notions like this had got abroad through a mere bit of tomfoolery on his own part. "For years now, when I have left the tavern before the others, it has been my custom to remark: 'I must visit Schwender or Sperl.' [11] As a matter of fact, I go there only about once a year, but always with old Lachner or Nottebohm along." He once informed Frau Flegmann that it was a very good thing for a youth to visit such places of amusement as he had early frequented in Hamburg, because "in his manhood similar dives disgust him." The truth is, however, that all through his life he often patronized houses of ill-fame.

Certain physical peculiarities doubtless served to strengthen his exclusive preference. He was very short. His beard was alarmingly late in growing. The worst handicap of all in impressing the other sex was vocal. When he was twenty, Hedwig Salomon confided to her diary: "Brahms has a thin, boyish little voice that has not yet changed, and a child's countenance that any girl might kiss without blushing." Up to the age of twenty-four, his voice remained piping and girlish. These symptoms would indicate that in Brahms' case the normal changes of adolescence were deferred for something like a decade.

Thus handicapped, he naturally found trouble in getting respectable girls to take his young virility seriously; whereas the daughters of joy, besides possessing a deep knowledge of masculine psychology and being blasé to sex appeal, would take any man as seriously as they could take his pocketbook.

Talking with Richard Heuberger, Brahms once attributed the rough, hoarse voice of his manhood to his having sung

[11] Houses of recreation then flourishing.

overmuch during the mutation period. But Julius Schmidt, who knew him at Detmold, remembers that the composer, at twenty-four, was so ashamed of his girlish tones that he forced his voice down the bass clef by means of vocal gymnastics. Dr. Alfred Grünberger, a physician who attended him later, has assured me that these exercises must have made him hoarse.

This doctor believes that the exaggeratedly hirsute and virile appearance of his long-bearded middle age was encouraged by Brahms as a psychic compensation for the humiliation he had suffered on account of the smooth cheeks of his early twenties, and the insult of those unblushing kisses described by Hedwig Salomon.

His boyishly short stature was, alas, beyond remedy. One reads his sensitiveness to it between the lines of those letters, in writing which he drew an unconscious solace from underlining the even lesser inches of tiny friends like Frau Prof. Engelmann. "It built him right up," as a Maine woodsman might phrase it, to find any adult shorter than himself.

In the years before the vocal gymnastics, however, he had found one lady who took him seriously as a male being and for whom he could, as a temporary exception, feel both tenderness and passion. Clara Schumann, moved at the outset by her deep appreciation of the twenty-year-old lad's genius, and by his worship-at-first-sight of herself, was soon led not only to discount his physical deficiencies but to love him, first as a mother, then as a sweetheart.

Now Clara, born in 1819, was almost old enough to have brought a boy of Johannes' age into the world. He met her during his first absence from his parents, and soon we find him writing to her as *"meine liebe Frau Mama"* (my dear Madame Mother). The mysterious nature of the attraction troubled the lad, and he sometimes rebelled against the invincible enigma. "What have you done to me?" he wrote her. "Can you not release me from this magic?"

Clara brought out all Johannes' boyishness because, except at the height of his passion, he always felt towards her even more as a son than as a lover. As we have already seen,[12] he filled his letters with childish pictures, and actually expected the matron to take a sympathetic delight in that infantile infatuation for lead soldiers which continued well into his manhood.

In the light of such a study as Dr. Hitschmann's, it is hard to avoid the conclusion that the tiny blond stripling was first attracted to the great lady of music in large part as a result of that adoration for his own mother, which seems to have acted as a ground-bass to the melody of his life.

In Clara he found a second mother who not only guided and loved him and ministered to his everyday wants, but also did what Frau Brahms could never do. For she understood and ministered to that musical part of his nature which sometimes seemed greater than the whole.

At first the adopted son fought a determined battle with the lover.

I believe [he confided to Grimm] that I esteem and revere her [Clara] really no more than I love her. . . . I believe I can never love a girl again; at any rate, I've quite forgotten them all. They merely promise us the heaven which Clara opens.

[12] See p. 127 ff.

The beginnings of his recently published letters to her reveal the gradual progress of the affair: "Respected Madam," they started, early in 1854. After eight months, "Dearest Madam"; in another fortnight, "Dearest Friend." Very soon, "Fervently loved Friend." Three months later the crescendo had reached:

MY MOST BELOVED CLARA, no letter came from you this morning; with what yearning I await each post! Every day is now an eternity to me; I can begin nothing. . . . I can neither play nor think.

On June 23rd, 1855, four months after this confession, he wrote: "Every day I greet and kiss you a thousand times." Two days more, and he first allowed himself to address her with the intimate *Du* (thou); and from then on for some time, his letters glowed with fervid embraces and kisses.

On July 17th, accompanied by her maid, she met him at St. Goar and, together for five blissful days at the height of this passionate episode, they made a knapsack tour up the Rhine to Mannheim and thence to Heidelberg, a distance of a hundred-odd miles.[13] Such was their infatuation that the following year Clara could doubtless have married Johannes at will. But the mother of seven living children was wise, and refrained.

Whatever they may in private believe, certain biographers publicly profess outrage at any suggestion that the relations of this pair were ever anything more than Platonic; and they savagely vilify those who honestly differ. But one of these writers has orally admitted to me in private his literary

[13] See Kalbeck, I, 1, 250.

hypocrisy, and agreed with the many old friends of Brahms who consider it probable that a liaison took place, and that it cooled inside of two years, leaving Clara and Johannes dear and lifelong friends.

It should be borne in mind, however, that Brahms later confessed to Deiters that this affair had made of him "a man for whom nothing is left, and who wishes to make away with himself"—which would hardly seem to connote a successful liaison. In my own opinion, all that we know about Brahms' relations with other women lessens the probability of his having been Clara's lover; but, in the absence of definite proof, the question must remain open.

It is likely that the eventual awakening and rebound from love's first dream helped to aggravate the boy's distorted love-life and his instinctive fear of marriage. But powerful counter-forces were active, urging him to wed. The conservative, homespun side of him—that peasant throwback [14] which played such a leading part in forming his character— kept insisting that a free, unmarried existence was far from respectable, and that a bachelor was nothing but a "vagabond."

Then, too, the single are inclined to exaggerate the delights and advantages of the unknown wedded state, no less than those overestimate what they have missed who have never been to college—or Carcassonne. Brahms often complained that in going without wife and children he was "missing really the best things in existence." [15]

These conscious motives for marriage, then, fought against

[14] Described on p. 71 ff.
[15] His longing for children—unlike his wish for a wife—was genuine, both consciously and unconsciously.

unconscious impulses and fears which issued vague warnings that marriage was not for him, and were strengthened by a conscious dread of losing his artistic freedom through financial pressure. According to the psychologists, such fears as the latter are often little more than rationalizations—excuses which people offer themselves for yielding to their own unrealized inhibitions.

It will be necessary to give here a brief account of Brahms' love relations with other respectable women, in order to show their significant similarity.

One is struck by the stereotyped monotony of his reactions to the idea of marriage. Dr. Helene Deutsch of Vienna rightly calls such an inveterate inclination a "fate-neurosis," [16] by which she means a compulsion always to react in the same way to experience on account of unsolved and unsolvable inner conflicts. This is the usual order of events. First, Brahms' tenderness is aroused by some girl. But presently he begins to realize that something essential is lacking in the relationship. Finally he causes more or less wear and tear to the lady's heart, and his own, by brusquely drawing back.

In 1858 Johannes fell in love with Agathe von Siebold, the plain but charming daughter of a Göttingen professor, and she with him. He wrote songs for her, and she sang them delightfully from the manuscript. Clara visited Göttingen and did not like what she saw. "Now," Johannes would whisper to Agathe, "I must walk with her for a bit. Otherwise she'll be jealous." But one evening the great lady discovered his

16 *Psychoanalyse der Neurosen*, 1930, p. 90.

arm about the young girl's waist. At once she packed her trunks and left town in high dudgeon, thus stepping out of her mother-rôle in a truly feminine way. Later we find her using her powerful influence with Johannes to keep him from marrying Agathe.

Early in 1859 he again visited Göttingen and, before he left, the two young people had exchanged kisses and rings,[17] and regarded themselves as half engaged. But when Agathe, in her equivocal position, had waited long and vainly for the decisive word to come from her sweetheart, their common friend Julius Otto Grimm wrote Johannes an energetic admonition. As long, he said, as they were openly understood to be in love with each other, Johannes really must not return to Göttingen before having declared, yes or no, whether he had decided to bind himself to Agathe for life.

Grimm's undiplomatic words had the effect which any attempt at coercion always exerted on the wildly independent Brahms. Agathe later confessed that, when the reply came which she "had awaited with hopes and prayers and tears," she read her sentence in these words:

I love you! I must see you again! But fetters I can not wear! Write me whether I may come back to fold you in my arms, to kiss you, to tell you that I love you! [18]

As Agathe, years later, impersonally confessed—

the girl fought a hard battle, the hardest of her life. Love would have held him at any price, come what would. Duty

---

[17] Emil Michelmann, in *Agathe von Siebold*, 1930, was the first to publish the photograph of Brahms with the engagement ring.

[18] See Michelmann, *op. cit.*, p. 171. Specht was mistaken in stating (*Johannes Brahms*, 1928, p. 83) that Brahms never told Agathe he loved her.

and honour counselled renunciation; and duty and honour won. The girl wrote her parting letter and wept, wept for years over her dead happiness.

She never again saw Johannes.

After having helped to wreck this marriage, Clara Schumann actually reproached Johannes in a letter of 1860:

> I had some bad days in Cassel. The poor Agathe, and much besides, would not leave my mind. In spirit I kept seeing the poor abandoned girl, and lived all her suffering over with her. Ah, dear Johannes, you should not have let things go so far! I saw her also in person at my concert. I marvelled at her strength in coming; for it is impossible that she could have enjoyed herself there!

Johannes was remorseful, and exclaimed bitterly to a friend: "I have played the scoundrel towards Agathe!" But, in 1864, he found the relief and escape of self-expression by finishing the G major sextet. Tapping the manuscript, he told Gänsbacher: "Here I have emancipated myself from my last love." In his inner circle, this piece was always known as the *"Agathe"* sextet on account of the musical anagrams which dedicated the work to her in the subtlety of notes rather than in the obviousness of words.[19]

In weighing the self-accusation just quoted, we should remember that Brahms was always at his most severe when he judged himself and his own work. We should also bear in mind that, in view of his evident failure to foresee the inevitable collapse of each successive matrimonial project, it is highly probable that he was not aware of the unrelaxing grip of his inhibition Finally, he was speaking less from a

[19] See p. 414.

direct conviction of personal guilt than with the conventional voice of the Dithmarsh countryside from which his family came. Sounding through him one hears the voice of the north shore peasant—that traditional bigot who on principle disapproves of everything connected with the unfettered life of a bachelor and an artist.

When she reached the perspective of middle age, Agathe achieved such a sane and courageous view of the tragedy as to fill one with admiration for her supreme sportsmanship. In the reminiscences which have already been drawn upon [20] she spoke of herself in these third-personal terms: "The memory of her great love for the youth, of the young days transfigured by poetry and loveliness, has never been quenched in her. . . . His immortal works have often and often been the joy of her life. He himself went forward on the path of his fame, growing greater and greater. And as he belonged, like every genius, to humanity, she also learned little by little to understand that he was in the right to burst the bonds which bade fair to fetter him;—that she, with her great love, would never have been able completely to fill his life." [21]

This last phrase suggests that Agathe may, indeed, have had some inkling of the true nature of her lover's conflicts. She may also have thought him fickle for falling so promptly in love with her successors, and may have realized that married happiness would probably have been unable to make headway in such circumstances.

When, in 1864, the Master remarked that by writing the

[20] Michelmann, *op. cit.*, pp. 209–210.
[21] Brahms seems to have been fortunate in nearly always caring for ladies who loved him more than themselves.

G major sextet he had emancipated himself from Agathe, his "last love," he strangely enough forgot three other inter-vening passions. In Hamburg, a few months after his break with Agathe, he had met a young Viennese singer named Bertha Porubszky. Her Austrian charm and beauty, her un-affected naturalness set her off in piquant contrast to the primly starched and inexpressive girls of the North, enchant-ing the susceptible young man with his first taste of the quality of that glamorous land where he was destined to live and die. He wrote to Joachim that, through Bertha, "Vienna, which is after all the musician's holy city, has taken on for me a double magic."

Prof. Jakob Fischer, an old friend of his, has told me how Brahms flamed up at the first sight of Bertha, and actually fell on his knees to Frau Grädener, begging for an invitation to meet the girl. Their love was mutual, but in the end it succumbed to the old invincible obstacles in the way of wed-lock.

Johannes' relief, when he moved to Vienna in 1862, on finding that Bertha had not taken the affair to heart with the tragic intensity of an Agathe, may be felt in his note to Joachim:

B. P. is engaged to a rich young man. When first I saw her here she was pallid and ailing; and my conscience felt much more healthy when I presently received the announcement in question, with a few words.

She married a Herr Faber; and on the birth of their sec-ond child, Brahms dedicated and sent to her, "for joyful use on every occasion," a piece destined to be the most celebrated of cradle-songs. The melody of *"Guten Abend, gut' Nacht"* is a freely invented counterpoint to an old Austrian dialect *Ländler* which Bertha had often sung to him in the Hamburg days:

Du moanst wohl, Du glabst wohl
Die Lieb lasst si zwinga?

(You think perhaps, you dream perhaps
That love will ever yield to force?)

The accompaniment gives this folk-melody almost note for note. It would be hard to find a message of combined reminiscence and congratulation to an old sweetheart more tenderly and charmingly conveyed than in this little song.

The second love that he had forgotten when he said those words about the *"Agathe"* sextet flared up in 1863 for Luise Dustmann, the famous singer whose impersonation of Leonora in *Fidelio* at the Vienna Opera was the sensation of the moment.[22] But before long this emotion too went the way of the others.

The third came very soon. That same year the Master accepted as pupil one of the most fascinating persons ever connected with musical history, the blonde and lovely sixteen-year-old Baroness Elisabet von Stockhausen. Her former teacher, Julius Epstein, laid it down as a law of nature that no man could possibly keep from falling in love with this brilliant, sympathetic, kind, and magnetic young creature.[23]

How slightly he exaggerated may be gathered from her

---

[22] She had married five years before, but was now "free," according to Alfred von Ehrmann, *Johannes Brahms: Weg, Werk und Welt*, 1933, p. 138.

[23] See *Correspondence*, I, x.

letters to Brahms, which disengage a more captivating magic and a fresher, more delicious humour than any other musical letters, not excepting those which passed between Wagner and Mathilde Wesendonck. It was not long before Brahms abruptly broke off the lessons, alleging that he was unwilling to take her away from Epstein. The truth is, he was afraid. Elisabet disturbed his peace of mind. And he feared that his love-history might repeat itself.

But, though she married the composer Heinrich von Herzogenberg, their friendship continued. How profoundly Brahms was affected by her beauty and charm, her marvellous musical intuition, her almost unfailing critical taste, and her fabulous memory—she could reproduce a new symphony on the piano after two hearings—may be read between the many lines they exchanged.

On his part, however, the feeling was more than friendship. He had given this pupil up too late, though these are the warmest words in his letters:

You must know and believe this, that you belong among the few people whom one loves so much that—as your husband is always there to read and hear—one can not tell you.

For years Brahms loved the bewitching Elisabet, and hers was long the only photograph of a woman to stand on his desk. Kalbeck states [24] that it remained there to the end of his life. But Frau Dr. Truxa, the Master's old housekeeper, assures me that this is not so. "The picture stood there for some years," she says. "Then suddenly something troubled the relations of those two. One day it disappeared from the desk,

[24] *Correspondence*, II, p. 171, n.

Agathe von Siebold

Julie Schumann

Alice Barbi and Brahms

Elisabet von Herzogenberg

Hermine Spies

LADIES WHOM BRAHMS LOVED

and Brahms casually gave me the frame. 'You can put your husband's portrait in this,' he said gruffly. I have that frame yet."

After Elisabet's untimely death, Brahms' love for her re-awakened. He refused at first to give up her letters for publication; and in the following lines to Herzogenberg one may feel his jealousy. He wrote of cherishing in these letters, above all, "one of the most precious memories of my life, also a rich treasure of temperament and spirit, which belongs naturally to me alone." Fortunately for the world, he was persuaded to alter this resolve.

In 1869 he came deeply under the spell of Julie, Clara Schumann's third daughter, in whom he had for seven years been interested. Her resemblance to Clara suggests that his mother-love may have found a new stimulus in the next generation of Schumanns. His intimate friend Levi told Clara that Johannes "was deeply in love with Julie" (*dass Johannes Julie ganz schwärmerisch lieb habe*).[25]

Suddenly he had news of her engagement to a Count Marmorito, which hurled him into the Slough of Despond. "Now," he exclaimed bitterly, "it merely remains for me to compose a bridal song!" And to Simrock he wrote: "Here I have written a bridal song for the Schumann Countess—but I do this sort of thing with concealed wrath—with rage!" These words recall his exclamation on the death of Frau Brahms: "I no longer have a mother: I must marry!" Here is an example of his fatal inability to cope adequately with life. We see the Master helplessly turning to compensatory substitutes for his lost objects of desire. No sooner does his

[25] *Cf.* Litzmann, *Clara Schumann*, III, 230.

mother die, than he thinks of marriage. Hearing that the girl he loves has been taken by someone else, he reverts with the more passionate intensity to his music paper.

The "bridal song" turned out to be nothing less than the *Rhapsody* (Op. 53), for alto solo, men's chorus, and orchestra. One may read the disappointed lover's mood in those words of Goethe which he there so expressively set: "Ah, shall any heal his anguish whose balsam has turned to poison —who has drunk hatred for men from the plenitude of love?"

Soon after reaching the age of fifty,[26] Brahms is generally understood to have lost his heart to Hermine Spies, a celebrated young singer and interpreter of his music. He called her by such pet names as "my songstress," "the Rhine-maiden," "Herma," "Herminche," and, in Shakesperean mood, "Hermione without an o." But, though he wrote her one of his most tenderly passionate songs, *Komm' bald,* his "fate neurosis," and perhaps Hermine's too plainly shown infatuation,[27] helped the wide discrepancy in their ages to frustrate the romance.

An old friend of the Master's, however, gathered from something he said that he was not very serious with Hermine. He once told Frau Prof. Brüll that, "after middle age," the only woman he ever *really* wanted to marry was Alice Barbi, the celebrated Italian singer whom he met in 1892. "I understood from what he said that he actually proposed; and she refused him because he was old, and she wanted children."

[26] At that critical period Brahms told Kalbeck (III, II, 541): "I have now arrived at the age when a man easily commits a folly, and must be doubly on my guard."

[27] Brahms liked to do all the wooing. Any initiative on the lady's part roused his contrary spirit and put him off.

But who knows what meaning he attached to that elastic expression, "middle age"?

It is worthy of note that of these eight women whom Brahms loved, Agathe, Bertha, Luise, Hermine, and Alice were, first and foremost, singers. Elisabet sang in public; while the Schumanns, mother and daughter, could "sing" on the piano. Indeed, at twenty-one Johannes sent Clara his second collection of songs inscribed "To the best song-stress." [28] Surely it was no mere coincidence that he, who had been first appealed to in early boyhood by the notorious Singing Girls of Hamburg's red-light district, should, at intervals all his life long, have been attracted by vocalists of a far more respectable kind. And it seems most probable that an even stronger factor than casual fickleness or love of free-dom, in frustrating his successive projects of marriage with the latter kind of singing girls, was the persistent influence of the former kind. To the former—and to them almost alone—could his passion respond. It is very probable that the excessive mother-love of his early youth helped to keep the stream of his sensuousness from merging, but by rare exception, with the stream of his tenderness.

Very likely he himself was at the most but dimly conscious of the determining rôle played all through his love life by the dance halls of Hamburg. And he actually maintained that the chief part in defeating his marriage projects had been taken by finance. Often he savagely blamed those who had kept him single by refusing him official appointments and not understanding his early music. "I've missed it!" he con-

[28] "Brahms could seldom withstand the magic of a beautiful voice; and it is worth noting that all his more intimate friends had sympathetic voices." Kalbeck, I, II, 475.

fided to Widmann in his middle fifties. "At the time when I would have best liked to marry, my things were hissed off the concert-stage, or at least accepted with icy coldness. I myself could endure this sort of treatment well enough. . . . But if, in such moments, I had had to go to my wife and see her questioning eyes anxiously fastened on mine, and been obliged to confess: 'Another fiasco!'—I couldn't have borne that! But," he added suddenly, "the way it has turned out has also been good!"

Naturally he would not have cared to risk such poverty as his own childhood had known. But as we have already seen [29] from his twenty-fourth year on, he might have wedded with far more financial security than had been his father's at marriage. And from his middle thirties no fear of material pressure injuring his work need have kept him a bachelor. The fact that this sort of reasoning on his part was largely rationalization, an unconscious self-excuse, did not escape the astute intuition of Clara Schumann, who once wrote him: "You blame upon others that which—at least in part—you should seek within yourself!" In his above-quoted words to Widmann, as Dr. Hitschmann acutely observes, we see Brahms, in the grip of an inferiority complex caused by his lowly origin and his sexual limitation, recoiling in fear from the respectable woman. "Here the exposure of his failure as a musician stands for the exposure of the failure of his masculinity, and is therefore a real obstacle to marriage." [30]

This sense of inferiority explains Brahms' extraordinary modesty and the severity of his self-criticism. And the nat-

[29] See p. 73.
[30] Op. cit., p. 111.

ural, unconscious reaction of self-defence against this painful and paralyzing complex explains his aggressiveness, malice, and love of mischief, his explosive temper, his contrariness, his caustic irony, his brutality in criticizing certain contemporaries, notably Bruckner and Liszt, and the bearishness which made matters so difficult for his friends.

To compensate his failures in the matter of the respectable singing girls, and the bewildered struggles, entailed by each affair, against an uncomprehended hindrance—Brahms found what solace he could in his venal loves of the moment. In general it may be safely asserted that servants, provided they were simple enough daughters of simple enough people, were the prostitutes' only rivals for his sexual interest.

Mr. Oscar Ullmann of New York, who in his youth used to know Brahms in Ischl, tells me that a very pretty girl working for concert manager Kugel was a favourite with the Master. She told my informant what a passionate but awkward lover Brahms was. The unexpected testimony is important; for in reading of Brahms' belated adolescence the reader may have inferred too great an impairment of his masculinity. This information, however, indicates that it was a psychological and not only a physical disturbance that so bewilderingly interfered with his plans for marriage.

Some realization of the composer's true condition may have been a factor in the impression he produced upon Nietzsche who, in an angry moment of wounded vanity, rushed into print with a tirade in which he accused Brahms of suffering from "the melancholy of impotence," and of being "the musician of the unsatisfied."

This was far from completely exact. It was of course true

that Brahms, a man of immense affection for his own rela-
tives and for children, was unsatisfied as a bachelor and longed
for the home which was denied him. And it was probably
true as well that the cultivated women among whom he
might have found a wife failed to arouse in him a completely
normal response. But the unqualified assertion that he was
impotent did him cruel injustice. With certain sorts of women
he was fully potent.

In springing to Brahms' defence, the poet Widmann unfortunately made two tactical blunders. Brahms, he argued,
could not be such a person as Nietzsche had described, because the composer gave the impression of extreme, often
harsh, virility. This was a weak contention, in view of the
well known fact that men wholly impotent often produce—
sometimes in self-defence—an effect of exaggerated masculinity. In the second place, he failed to point out that the works
of Brahms, far from being consistently "melancholy" music
for "the unsatisfied," brim over, more often than not, with
joyous exhilaration.[31]

This exuberant quality reflects singular credit on the composer. For a man of weaker character, suffering from the
same inner conflicts, might easily have let his failures in love
sour his life and his art. Not so the Master. The further he
progressed through his succession of amorous fiascos, the more
vigorously was he able to use the self-defence of quips and
slurs and cynical inveighings against the institution of marriage, and so

> Pluck from the memory a rooted sorrow;
> Raze out the written troubles of the brain;

[31] See p. 454 ff.

And, with some sweet oblivious antidote,
Cleanse the stuffed bosom of that perilous stuff,
Which weighs upon the heart.

At the first informal reading of the F major quintet, the composer turned up and offered an occasional suggestion to the players. Frau von Kaiserfeld, who was present because her husband had been pressed into service at the second viola desk, remembers how "Brahms told them that, in the second movement, the soft passages before the changes to faster tempo 'should sound like sighing.' With an impish glance at me he added: 'The married men here can do that more naturally.'"

The Master's scepticism about wedded bliss showed even in such unlikely places as his own copy of the Koran where, on page 25, I found these words underlined: "Divorce is twice permitted." He annexed, and often used, Daniel Spitzer's winged word: "Unfortunately I never married and am, thank God, still single."

In his fifty-fourth year he once sat at table with a recently wedded couple, a middle-aged man and a beautiful girl. With even more than his customary outspokenness the old bachelor remarked how terrible a moment it must be when the newly made husband brings his wife home and inserts the key—that symbol of the free man—into the lock of his own door, behind which he is to be for ever tied to a strange person. Presently the bridegroom smilingly observed that Brahms kept looking at him as who should say: "So, he has actually risked it!" On which the Master, with an almost reverential glance at the lovely bride, responded: "As for me, I must say I *wouldn't* have risked it!"

Thereupon he asked the company at large when they thought a single man should celebrate his bachelor's silver jubilee. He himself was inclined to choose his fifty-fifth birthday. But that he had some doubt whether he would win the right to this distinction is shown by those words of his to Kalbeck about fearing to commit a folly. To the same friend he remarked with bitter cynicism: "Who can know what he is marrying?"

At breakfast, after the first night he ever spent in his publisher's luxurious guest-room, he said to Frau Simrock: "Last night in my bridal-bed I slept very well—alone." When she asked whether the experience had not made him want to marry, he cried in honest terror: "No, indeed! Why, I'd run away from her the third day!" In this exclamation his deep-seated fear of marriage rose for an instant to the level of consciousness. The words seem to reveal his true state more veraciously than all the sentimentally melancholy utterances that are attributed to him about his lost matrimonial chances.

Yes, it was probably a blessing both for Brahms and for lovers of his music that he successfully ran the marriage gauntlet of the respectable singing girls. This was recognized by even such a happily wedded disciple as Kalbeck:

Would it have been fortunate for him and his art if, in his young years, he had taken upon himself the sometimes none too mild yoke of matrimony and the not always sweet cares of the family? Stilled yearning, satisfied desire, wish-fulfilment are seldom fortunate gifts for the artist, in whose works the eternally unattainable lives and resounds. And the fate which he so terribly denounces deals more kindly with him when it refuses that which, as a usual thing, it graciously accords to the least of mortals.[32]

Despite occasional heart-burnings, Brahms had too much shrewd proletarian common sense to make a continuously tragic grievance of the fact that he could not have his brightly candled cake of artistic independence, and eat it too, in the form of wedding-cake—especially as this common sense must occasionally have flashed him hints of the truth about the psychic bias which would so seriously have imperilled his marriage with any respectable woman.[33]

Shrewdness and advancing years, however, brought small mitigation of the struggle. The more he wrestled with the marriage problem, the stronger grew the hold of his habit and of his need for solitude and freedom. So that, the more determined and aggressive the society women became who were attracted by his celebrity and genius, the more ruthlessly he fought them back and held them off and hurried away from them.

Here again, as in most things, he ran true to both his humble origin and his early taste.

Several quite independent informants have concurred [wrote Florence May] in describing him . . . as being [at eighteen] . . . something less than indifferent to the society of ladies, and especially of young ones.

---

[32] Kalbeck, I, ii, 329.

[33] Indeed, that wise old fellow-bachelor, Wilhelm Busch, the creator of *Max und Moritz*, once implied to Herr Michelmann that Brahms was conscious of the nature of this obstacle. "One must marry young—if one can!" said Busch. "Ah, believe me, Brahms would not have confided to his best friend the real reason why he never married." (*Agathe von Siebold*, p. 304.) Busch had lived near the scene of the Agathe episode, and had known the composer.

When a party was being arranged at Lüneburg in honour of the twenty-year-old musician, he earnestly begged his hosts to invite no ladies. "It is so much nicer without them," he seriously urged.[34] And all his life he usually preferred to talk to men.

The women bombard me with letters [he complained to Kalbeck].[35] After fourteen epistles one must finally answer once in a way. The more furious one is, the sweeter one writes.

Kalbeck's daughter has shown me a curious note in which the Master sought to avoid a tête-à-tête with a young lady of Vienna. One imagines the enterprising girl's crestfallen look on reading:

GREATLY RESPECTED FRÄULEIN,—

I should long ago have thanked you for the delicious sequel to our rendezvous in the Prater [probably a gift and an invitation]. But I would have said in answer that one enjoys this sort of thing more with father and mother along, and a few good friends. And only now am I able to inquire whether Wednesday or Thursday of next week would be agreeable to you?

Yours very truly,
J. BRAHMS

By dint of long practice, he grew as clever in forestalling attempts to cast him for the somewhat ridiculous rôle of Joseph, as he was in foiling the endeavours of yearning lady pianists to play for him.[36] Dr. Max Friedländer tells me that he was once calling on Brahms in Vienna when two very pretty girls of good family were announced. "They had quite

---

[34] May, I, 91 and 98.
[35] IV, II, 491.
[36] See p. 227 f.

evidently come to offer themselves to their idol. I rose to go, but he absolutely forced me to stay, in order to spoil their game."

A number of people who knew Brahms well have assured me that, except the possible one with Clara, he never had a liaison with a lady. And Frau Dr. Truxa recalls that, during her decade as his housekeeper, he had no affairs at home: "Ladies never stayed long in his rooms, and the door always stood ajar so that I might have gone in at any moment."

Let us briefly summarize: Brahms' early environment and life caused a psychopathic condition which probably made him impotent to all but women of a low class. This probably defeated his projects for marriage with one respectable woman after another. He explained these defeats by rationalization, salved his wounded pride with the healing balsam of wit, and grew expert in evading the embarrassing advances of his lady admirers.

All this, however, does not by any means indicate that the vital force pulsed feebly in the Master. The music of Brahms is full of sex appeal; only, it is, at the same time, so full of many other important qualities, that the former is not obtrusive. His work is like a super-vital person, well fused and balanced, splendidly sexed, but also endowed so richly in all sorts of other ways, mentally and emotionally, that the sensuous is forced to keep its appropriate place in the scheme of life.

"Without a mighty erotic impulse," writes the Viennese

critic, Frau Maria Komorn,[37] "there can be no creative power. And Brahms was strongly erotic." "He was highly sexed," Prof. Robert Kahn tells me. And this is confirmed by many of his other living friends.

Such a powerful force was, naturally, compelled to find an outlet somewhere. And Brahms-lovers, while they regret the fatal dike between tenderness and passion that cheated the Master of the married happiness and the children he craved, should realize that any change in his way of life would probably have affected his music for the worse.

They should also recognize that young Johannes' lifelong infatuation for his mother enriched his music more directly by stimulating dreams of greatness; for a boy with such an infatuation invariably regards a father as a rival. And Johannes' ambition to become a better musician than his parent was one of the prime sources of the unflagging industry and merciless self-criticism which helped him to mastery and fame.

On hearing of the Master's sexual limitations, the music-lover's first reaction is indignantly to deny them. "No man," he argues, "who is in the clutches of such a low thing as a prostitute habit could possibly compose such pure and trans-figured pages as abound in the *Requiem*, the clarinet quintet, the C minor symphony, and the *Four Serious Songs*."

On further reflection, however, one comes to apprehend the actual gain for music that resulted from precisely the one-sided, spiritually unsatisfying nature of the only sex-life that Brahms could count on. For his limitation would always have stood in the way of the sort of happy marriage which

---

[37] *Johannes Brahms als Chordirigent in Wien, und seine Nachfolger*, 1928, p. 62.

more fortunate composers have enjoyed. This gain, one sees, sprang from the necessity which made Brahms convert the greater part of his unutilized sexuality into lofty music (his substitute for love and domesticity) created through a sublimation as far-reaching as any recorded in the history of the arts.[38]

So soon as the music-lover realizes this—so soon as he recognizes the benefits which Brahms' limitation conferred on music and on humanity—his unsympathetic attitude will alter; and in return for untold hours of delight in the Master's music, he will refuse to take offence at any happiness, however far short of the sublime, which any woman, however humble, was able to bring him.

[38] See the description, p. 367, of his emotional orgy while composing.

Postscript.—As this volume goes to press I have received a new book, *Die Brahmsfreundin, Ottilie Ebner*, by her daughter Ottilie von Balassa (1933, Franz Bondy, Wien), which adds to the picture of Brahms' relations with respectable women. Ottilie Hauer was one more "singing girl." Brahms met her soon after his first arrival in Vienna. On December 18, 1862 she took part in the first Viennese performance of his *Wechsellied zum Tanze*. On Christmas day, 1863 he came to her lodgings to offer her marriage—only a few hours after she had accepted Dr. Edward Ebner. This may have been a case of unconsciously purposive procrastination akin to the purposive forgetting described by the psychologists.

The case of Ottilie increases to four the number of intervening affairs which Brahms no longer remembered when, in 1864, he remarked about the finished *"Agathe"* sextet: "Here I have emancipated myself from my last love." (See p. 268.)

This narrow escape from Ottilie turned out to be even more fortunate than his many others; for the lady developed into a decided martinet.

Chapter XXI

HEALTH AND LAST DAYS

BRAHMS inherited the rugged endurance and superb vitality of his robust Dithmarsh ancestors. Almost to the end of his life he could outwalk, outtalk, and outwake all his companions. "One had to pull oneself together vigorously," wrote Widmann, "to keep fresh on the plane of his tirelessness." After a strenuous day of mountaineering and music, he liked to sit up until two or three o'clock, talking vivaciously. And after five hours' sleep he would bound from bed as fully rested as if he had slept nine. On climbing excursions his irrepressible energy made him leave his companions plodding far behind while he violently stormed the peaks and plunged into the valleys alone. He was no mean acrobat, and once astonished the Schumann children by using the stair landing-rail as horizontal bar and wooden horse.

One secret of his health was a rare ability to shed disturbing influences and infectious negative moods, much as a canvasback duck sheds rain. Little more than a year before he was killed by a terrible disease, this old Titan could, with apparent impunity, allow himself alarming extravagances. In Menzel's Berlin studio he once breakfasted with the old painter, lingered until nightfall drinking Rhine-wine and champagne, rushed to his room, immersed his venerable head in cold water, stormed to a banquet, played trios until three in the morning, snatched two hours' sleep, and appeared at the breakfast table radiantly fit. Whereupon Frau Simrock, his hostess, exclaimed: "You are not only a God-blessed artist but also a giant of health." "Well," was the reply, "what do you expect? I have never in my life omitted a meal or taken a drop of medicine."

Graph of the composer's pulse, made January 30, 1878, by his friend, the famous physiologist, Dr. Theodor Engelmann of Utrecht, to whom the B flat string quartet was dedicated.

On various occasions he declared that he had never been sick; though Kalbeck shows that he had suffered—and forgotten—more than one attack of influenza. Such a claim must be received with the grain of salt usually accorded to the widow who declares: "My husband never gave me an unkind word."

He was not spared some of humanity's minor ills. His chronic hoarseness he attributed to overmuch singing in the mutation period. Prof. Max Friedländer believes that this condition came from his sleeping out of doors as a lad, after playing the piano late for the Singing Girls of Hamburg. And Dr. Grünberger, as we have seen, thinks it a result of the vocal gymnastics by which, at twenty-four, he highhandedly transposed his girlish treble to the bass clef. All three indiscretions probably helped to ruin his voice.

At fifty-seven he had a temporary aural catarrh accompanied by deafness, and was terrified by visions of Beethoven's fate.

The newspapers report [Grimm wrote him] that you got yourself an ear-trouble in the wet grass. . . . When I think of those nocturnal Düsseldorf walks in 1854 to the Grafenberg . . . and then recall that night in '58 on the Plesse, it worries me, to be sure. You may have counted too much on your endurance.

His truly peasant-like hatred of the dentist condemned him eventually to lose all his upper teeth. His housekeeper tells me that he wore a plate; which is confirmed by the death-mask in the museum of the Friends of Music, with its sunken upper lip.

What was Brahms' attitude towards alcohol? Some writers have given the impression that he drank himself to death. Specht, on the other hand, categorically denies that anybody ever saw Brahms drunk. That this is an overstatement has been shown in Dr. Friedländer's story on page 224 ff. Specht might, however, have truly claimed that Brahms did not habitually take alcohol enough to harm his health. The Master's salvation lay in putting into practice his conviction that temperance begins at home. In his rooms he was Spartanly abstemious. The daughter of the Grubers, in whose house he spent his Ischl summers, told me: "I never saw Brahms intoxicated; and I never would have believed it possible that, when invited out, he drank as much as they say he did."

His Viennese housekeeper assured me that he never indulged in alcohol at home, and that, whatever his libations in dining out, he always returned steady enough to take off his shoes in the vestibule and, with his peasant-like economy, to put out the oil lamp which she had left burning there for him.

For all that, this valiant trencherman could drink as heartily as he could eat.[1] Prof. Paul Fischer of the Rosé Quartet sometimes took the Master home from the convivial sessions of the Tonkünstler Verein. On various occasions when the latter had looked too deep into the tankard, he would sit down on a Karlsplatz bench to pull himself together—as it happened, on the very spot where the white marble monument to himself now gleams. Fortunately for the intactness of the present preposterous muse of music, that lady had not yet been made to sprawl at his feet and, with mawkish squirmings, claw her marble lyre. For if Brahms, who loathed all sentimentality, had ever seen the creature, he would doubtless have made short work of her with the first paving stone handy.

The sound wine of Italy easily tempted him to unusual indulgence. Playing on the Master's partiality for Chianti in a huge, straw-covered *fiasco*, Hanslick once informed his travelling companions that he had an astonishing "scoop" to telegraph the newspapers back home. The dispatch would be headed: "BRAHMS' GREAT FIASCO!"

Frau Gottinger-Wilt told me how, at sunset in the Venetian Piazza San Marco, she once happened upon Brahms walking with Billroth: "There was a great hurrah-boys. They bore me off to dinner, and both of them grew heartily tipsy. Then we strolled on the Riva, where there is no rail between the footway and the water. Brahms sang with much volume,

[1] See the account of the boisterous banquet when Dr. Bauer called him *"Meister in Unfugen,"* p. 112 f.

in his funny, hoarse voice, gesticulated wildly, and seemed to have no idea that he was not in an ordinary street. I noticed that, in his exhilaration, he was about to walk straight into the canal that flows under the Bridge of Sighs. At the last moment I seized him. It was a very hilarious evening!"

So ample were Brahms' physical reserves that up to the final year of his life he continued, with rare success, to flout the ordinary precepts of health. But on his last birthday, May 7th, 1896, he seemed to have vague misgivings, and voiced the opinion, so astonishing from him, that one really should go to a doctor for an annual physical examination. "When one is old," he added, "one can never know what's up." According to Kalbeck,[2] "he said this in a rather uncertain tone, as if he did not entirely trust that health of which he was for ever boasting."

Despite the strain and exposure of his sudden dash to the funeral of Clara Schumann a fortnight later, he did not know that anything was seriously amiss until July. Shortly before his death he told Kalbeck [3] that a vigorous bout of exercise, followed by cooling off in the open, first gave him grounds for alarm:

One very hot day, when I set out to walk from Ischl to Lauffen, I was so deep in thought that I just walked and walked, without looking about me much; and so, to my astonishment, I was all of a sudden in Steg [eight miles from Ischl]. Then, in addition, I walked back a good stretch of the way. That night I was so ill I thought I was going to die, and went from one swoon into another. It seems that I had already been suffering from my jaundice for six weeks.

[2] IV, II, 433.
[3] IV, II, 479–480.

The local doctor diagnosed a slight trouble with the gall duct, and urged a brief cure at Karlsbad. His friends secretly summoned a great Vienna specialist, who recognized a fatal disease, but mercifully gave the Master no inkling of it. When an anxious Brahmin consulted this specialist in private about the advisability of the proposed Karlsbad trip, he shook his head: "Poor fellow, poor fellow! It will not make the slightest difference where he spends his money."

Dr. Grünberger, now a splendid octogenarian, has told me of the terrible experience through which he passed when Brahms appeared in his Karlsbad office. Kalbeck states that this popular physician had already been warned by letter of the Master's true condition.[4] But this Dr. Grünberger denies. All he knew was that Dr. Hertzka of Ischl had diagnosed his illustrious patient as having a catarrh of the gall duct which could easily be cured by three weeks of the Karlsbad régime.

"When Brahms entered my office," says Dr. Grünberger, "I asked him to let me examine him at his home. (You see, I did not want to keep my anteroomful of patients waiting so long.) But, very brusquely, he barked:—'I am here now. Examine me at once!'

"I began at the head. All was well until I reached the abdomen. This was much swollen, and the liver seemed twice its normal size. I feared I knew what that meant! At once I began to sweat in mental agony. 'This is terrible!' I told myself. 'Here is this great genius in my care; and here is something that looks like a malignant growth fit to make him a candidate for the cemetery!'

" 'When did you eat last?' I inquired.

[4] IV, II, 463.

" 'Two hours ago.'

" 'Then I must make another examination in the morning, when your stomach is empty.'

"This I did at his lodgings, and found my worst fears confirmed: cancer of the liver. It was a dreadful situation. If I allowed him to take the Karlsbad cure, which was very bad for his disease, he would be dead in a fortnight. On the other hand, it would not do to alarm him. For two or three minutes I thought quickly, desperately. Then I declared that he was now too weak to take the big cure. I would first prescribe a preparatory one consisting of half a mug of the water, morning and evening. This would stimulate his appetite and strengthen him so that he might come back in a few months to take the real Karlsbad cure, which was as necessary to him as bread to the hungry. But he must give me his solemn word of honour that, after a few months, he would return for this treatment. By saying this very earnestly and impressively I put him completely off the scent, and greatly relieved his mind.

" 'Doctor,' he answered, 'what you say has head and foot [*hat Kopf und Fuss*]. I pledge you my word of honour!' And I was thinking: 'My poor Brahms—where will you be in a few months?' "

The good doctor was kind enough to get out his old record books and look up for me the entry under September 3, 1896. There, following the numerals 1033 (the number of the patient in that year), stood:

Hr. Johannes Brahms—Wien.   hep. hyp. m.

The cabalistic abbreviations signified: "*hepatis hypertrophia maligna,*" malignant swelling of the liver.

When the Master returned to Vienna, and, growing steadily worse, saw how completely the kind physician had deceived him for his own good, he was very angry. His housekeeper tells me that even the name of Karlsbad became anathema to him. And he ordered her to refuse anything sent from there; so that she was forced to turn away many an offering of table delicacies and wine stamped with the hated postmark.

Naturally, the concern of Brahms' circle of friends over his tragic condition was enormous, and they vied with one another in devising thoughtful and ingenious ways of putting him at his ease. Prof. Julius Wachsmann tells me: "About two months before his death, I dined with him at the Conrats'. Our hostess had curtained the windows heavily and put red bulbs in the electric light sockets, so that the Master's dark greenish bronze complexion would not be conspicuous. One noticed his terrifying colour only in the daylight of the anteroom.

"He ate and drank a lot—had several helpings of pepper-carp, and took his Burgundy in a big beer mug. With his coffee he demanded a large amount of rum. Tenderly admonished by the daughter of the house that it would not be good for him, he insisted, exclaiming, '*Ach was,* that will make no difference!'—words which showed his realization that he was doomed."

Almost to death's door the Master's wonderful constitution sustained him. "The last time I saw Brahms alive," Prof. Seligmann recalls, "was three weeks before his death. I was dining at the house of Billroth's widow. On entering the

dark lift, I noticed a strange little man, but paid no attention
to him. Then, as we rose into the light, I saw that it was Brahms.
His complexion was a dark brownish yellow. He was horribly
emaciated, with hollows even in the back of the neck on
either side of the spine. His beard stood out unkempt and
lifeless. Curiously enough, he was in good spirits, eating and
drinking with his usual gusto; though, as old people do, he
nodded off to sleep once or twice during dinner. Afterwards
he started on foot for his home, half an hour away. I went
along to see that he was safe; but he walked with such astonishing vigour as to tire me."

"In my final talk with the Master," says Mr. Abell, "he was
so reminiscent about Reményi, and his mother and the old
days in Hamburg—the tender side of his nature came out so
surprisingly—that I felt the end must be near."

The actual facts about Brahms' last moments have never
before been put on paper, because his housekeeper, who was
alone with him when he died, cherished the old-fashioned
idea of biography, still widely prevalent—that if a genius
does not make an exit from life which seems in keeping with
the sublimity of his work, then a more fitting exit should be
composed for him—something noble and dramatic in the
style of the mythical "More light!" attributed to Goethe.

"I did not tell Kalbeck the details of Brahms' death," Frau
Dr. Truxa confessed to me, "because they seemed unworthy
of a great man. But, as you insist, I will give them to you. At
half-past eight on the morning of April 3, 1897, when I went
to his bedside, he sat up and tried to tell me something. But
his plate of artificial teeth kept falling down and prevented
him from speaking. When he found that these attempts were

useless, great tears came into his eyes and rolled down his wasted cheeks. Gazing wistfully at me, he sank back and drew his last breath."

How much better it is to know the homely truth, even though realistic to the verge of the grotesque, than to be misled by fancy fictions and deathbed will-o'-the-wisps that never were on sea or land!

It is tantalizing that we shall never know those last words that Brahms wished to say. His inability to utter them, however, strikingly completed the long chain of resemblances between his career and that of his predecessor, Beethoven. For the latter's last words, breathed not very far from the Karlsgasse, were an exclamation of regret that he could not enjoy a gift of Rhine-wine: "Pity, pity, too late!" And, strangely enough, the last recognizable words of Brahms were also about a gift of Rhine-wine. They were addressed to a now prominent Viennese physician, the son of the doctor [5] who cared for Brahms after his return from Karlsbad. He has told me the story of the Master's final hours on earth:

"On April second, 1897, my father came to me and said: 'Brahms is nearly finished. Would you go and spend the night watching over him?' Of course I was glad to. When I arrived at Karlsgasse 4, and was presented to the Master, he was very weak, but still kind and thoughtful, and showed hospitable concern about finding the best place for me to rest.

"He slept until half-past one, then grew uneasy. I asked whether he had pain. 'Yes,' he said, 'but it is not unbearable.' Then he slept. Again, about four, I heard him tossing, and

---

[5] This was the Dr. Josef Breuer who gave Freud the germinal idea which led to the invention of psychoanalysis, and who collaborated, 1893 and 1895, in his first two books.

offered to give him a hypodermic. He said: 'Perhaps it would be better.' When this was done, I asked him if he would like some wine, and he nodded.

"So I poured him out a glassful of the fine old Rhine-wine from his friend the Duke of Meiningen's cellars, which had been put out for me by the housekeeper. With scarcely any assistance, Brahms sat up, drank it off in two draughts, and, in his hoarse, North-German voice, exclaimed with satisfaction: '*Ja, das ist schön!* (Yes, that is beautiful!)' Then he slept, and was still asleep at seven, when I was forced to hasten to my clinic. At half-past eight he died. His last words had been: '*Ja, das ist schön!*' "

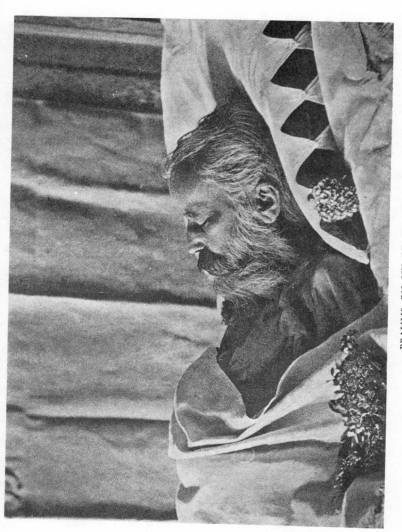

BRAHMS ON HIS DEATH-BED

Courtesy of the photographer, Herr Eugen von Miller zu Aichholz

PART IV

THE MUSIC

Their works do follow them.
REVELATION, XIV, 13.

Chapter XXII

A PROFILE OF BRAHMS' MUSICAL STYLE

SOME people hold that no creative artist can be a genius of the first rank unless he is, at the same time, a mighty innovator. This involves a confusion of ideas. The pioneers in constructing new forms have seldom been great artists like Wagner. A Wright is not expected to produce the ideal airplane. The supreme artists, on the other hand, usually begin where the inventors stop. Brahms' clarinet quintet, C minor symphony, *Feldeinsamkeit,* and *Requiem* are far too finished products to have been pioneer works. They rank among the most perfect of their kind because their composer profited by, and built upon, the labours of older musicians, and carried them forward in the modern spirit.

FORM

Thanks to the early drill of his teacher, Marxsen, Brahms could express himself in the traditional forms as naturally as breathing at a time when these were even more despised by the seeker after originality than they are today. In these forms he had so much to say which was spontaneous, personal, and original, that there was no need to worry about pioneering. But he never set up an architectural scheme *a priori* like a mould for cement, and then poured in the notes to harden. On the contrary, his schemes were determined in each case by the nature of the material; and that is why he made no two of his rondos or fugues or sonata-form movements exactly alike.

His few novelties in form are of no considerable importance. His sets of variations achieved the greater unity and climactic power through a closer resemblance between adjacent variations, by which one seemed to grow out of the preceding, and through a sparing use of violent contrasts.

He introduced a more ample working-out of themes into the expositions of sonata-form movements.[1] Perhaps he was impelled to this by his towering mastery of thematic development, which often yielded even more of charm and interest than the themes themselves.

Indeed [writes Dr. Daniel Gregory Mason, in his delightful and penetrating book, *The Chamber Music of Brahms*], the intellectual and emotional grasp revealed in this unceasing reshaping of the musical thoughts, especially in their rhythmic coördination, is probably his fundamental quality.

In the C minor piano quartet (Op. 60) he happily substituted for the usually developed second subject a series of free variations on a short theme. He successfully wove a Hungarian *puszta* fantasy into the *Adagio* of the clarinet quintet. He invented a more summary and final form of coda. He enlarged the scope of the sonata by eliminating, in his later works, the sacrosanct repetition of the first part; by successfully introducing a *passacaglia finale* into the E minor symphony; and by offering the characteristic Brahmsian *Allegretto* as an alternative to the traditional *scherzo*.

---

[1] See the first movements of Op. 25, 26, 34, and 51, No. 2. This innovation has influenced a number of the more important composers of the twentieth century.

THEMATIC TRANSFORMATION

The importance of his contribution to the development of thematic liaison-work has not even yet been fully recognized. As a young man of twenty-two he copied into his quotation book this maxim of Lessing's:

Without inner cohesion, without the most intimate connexion of each and every part, music is nothing but a sand-heap, incapable of any lasting impression. Inner cohesion alone can make of it the solid marble, on which the hand of the artist may immortalize itself.

This truth he took deeply to heart. Few artists have ever shown a more peasant-like economy of material, or achieved thereby a more unpeasant-like opulence and a more artistic unity. Dr. Mason is right in calling "the two essential powers of Brahms's genius, the power to conceive elements of a simplicity that give them universality, and the power to evoke from them an undreamed richness of meaning."

Very early he seized upon Beethoven's inventions, the germ-motive and source-motive,[2] and carried them even further than his predecessor had. In studying these devices our chief interest lies in seeing how constantly, yet how unobtrusively, the resourceful Master could use the same material, yet each time make it so new that the identity is swallowed up in the variety. "In complex thematic continuity," writes

---

[2] "Not wishing to resort to clumsy foreign expressions, the writer has been driven to coin the term germ-motive, meaning a germinal phrase, cyclically used with more or less disguise, to interlock the parts of a sonata or symphony into a unified whole." Schauffler, *The Mad Musician*, p. 38. "A source-motive is a musical phrase which recurs, more or less identically, in a number of distinct compositions, and produces in the group an effect of thematic unity." *Ib.*, p. 334.

Dr. Guido Adler, in *The Musical Quarterly*, April, 1933, "Brahms is scarcely to be outdone. This . . . is in keeping with his character."

The best known of his germ-motives was a development of his friend Joachim's personal motto F–A–E. This stood for *Frei aber einsam* (Free but lonely), which young Johannes modified for his own use into F–A–F, *Frei aber froh* (Free

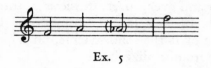

Ex. 5

but glad).[3] The apparent illogicality of this latter motto used to puzzle me. Why free *but* glad? Surely there should be no ifs or buts to the happiness conferred by freedom! Later, however, when I learned of Brahms' peasant streak, the reason for the "but" appeared. According to the Dithmarsh countryman's traditional code, a foot-free person without fixed duties or an official position should go bowed by the guilty feeling that he is no better than a vagabond. Brahms the musician was able to conquer this conventional sense of inferiority, but Brahms the man—never.

His use of Ex. 5 as a source-motive will be discussed on page 311. As a germ-motive he employed it only in the F major symphony, where it is overshadowed by another germ-motive [4] hitherto apparently unnoticed, though the first three of its four notes have long been well known as liaison material

[3] In choosing this motive Brahms may possibly have been somewhat influenced by Schumann's string quartet in F—then a prime favourite with Joachim and his circle. This eminently "free" and "glad" music starts with the notes C–F–A–F.

[4] See p. 429, Ex. 56.

in the D major symphony.[5]

Brahms' germ- and source-motives are shorter and simpler than Beethoven's, just as his melodies usually move within a somewhat narrower compass. He liked such figures terse, ele-mental, and infinitely workable. Even though these qualities meant that the motives could be nothing more than the tritest of musical formulas, he was confident that in the depths of his imagination they must surely

> . . . suffer a sea-change
> Into something rich and strange.

And he was right!

We shall see how surprisingly a small figure locks together the whole C minor string quartet;[6] another, the F major symphony;[7] and how, in the B flat string quartet[8] the composer invented a clever contrapuntal equivalent for a germ-motive. In the main, however, he was faithful to the following single short figure which, under his hand, became as Protean as four notes can well be.

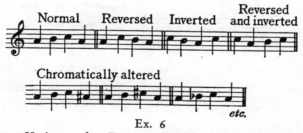

Ex. 6
Some Variants of a Favourite Germ- and Source-Motive

[5] See p. 425, Ex. 52, bracketed notes.
[6] See p. 396, Ex. 39.
[7] See p. 429 f., Ex. 56–62.
[8] See p. 401.

Two or more of these variants are occasionally dovetailed together to make a single figure. Any note may be of any length, and may be repeated; so that the rhythmical variants of the motive are even more numerous than the melodic. Taken together, the possible number of permutations and combinations is large.

This little four-note design constitutes, of course, one of the flattest commonplaces of music. All composers have used it freely. But Brahms seems to have employed it with especial lavishness and unusually telling organic effect. He used this figure, *to the elaborate extent which entitles it to be called a germ-motive,* in the themes of an overwhelming majority of his larger compositions. Considering merely two classes of these, all the orchestral works are unified by it, except these three: the orchestral versions of the *Hungarian Dances* (originally) Nos. 1 and 3, and the D minor concerto. It figures most importantly in the violin concerto (here is a reversed example, marked by a bracket, from the *Adagio*),

Ex. 7

the B flat concerto, the F major symphony, and the *Haydn Variations.*[9] Two most characteristic employments of this motive (both bracketed) commence the *Andante moderato* of the E minor symphony (Ex. 8).

Ex. 6 is also used as a liaison agent in nineteen of the twenty-four works of chamber music. The five exceptions

---

[9] Brahms may possibly have felt drawn to this old theme, if for no other reason, because it was trapeze-like (see p. 308), and contained five variants of the motive (Ex. 6).

Ex. 8

are: B flat sextet, C minor piano quartet, clarinet trio (where it is strong in the *finale,* but weak in the other movements), and the sonatas in G for violin, and in E minor for 'cello. Details of its amazingly profuse employment in the G minor piano quartet and the quintets with piano and with clarinet are given in another chapter.[10] The four notes play an almost equally vital rôle in the two string quintets, the A major piano quartet, the trios in B and C minor, and the F major 'cello sonata; while its part in the three string quartets and in the C major and horn trios is but little less striking.

Thus, in more than three quarters of his orchestral and chamber music (leaving out of count the hundreds of vocal, piano, and organ compositions), Brahms actually employed the same germ-motive. This is oftener than Beethoven used his entire repertory of germ-motives in all his music.[11] And yet the younger master repeated his fixed idea with such infinite discretion and varied resource that the identity of this figure in the works that are most permeated by Ex. 6 has never before been publicly noted. One feels in these compositions no more repetitiousness or melodic monotony than if they were destitute of all interlocking devices.

MELODY

Though sometimes harsh and astringent, Brahms' melody

[10] See pp. 390 (see Ex. 37, bracket), 405–06, 409 (see Ex. 46, first two brackets).
[11] See the author's *Beethoven,* etc., pp. 530–65.

is only by rare exception banal or mawkish. It usually has the diatonic ruggedness and the basic simplicity of people who live close to the soil. "Open my heart," he could have truly declared, "and you will see graved inside of it—the folk-song!" He did not hesitate to borrow occasionally, but nearly always made the alien idea his own.

Often he built his tunes on the degrees of the triad,[12] although not so often as Beethoven. Frequently he used an arpeggio formation which forsakes the triad, progressing continuously by regular steps in the same direction, like the upward fourths and downward thirds in the *finale* of the A major piano quartet.

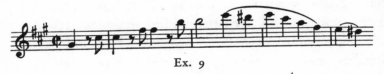

Ex. 9

These look and sound so much like climbing a ladder that we may, for convenience, call this general type of melody the ladder tune. The uniform steps are of any width from thirds to sixths.[13]

Another type of ladder tune is made up of intervals unevenly spaced, as though here and there a rung were missing.[14] The G major sextet (Op. 36) gains a mysterious unity

[12] *E. g.*, opening of D major symphony and D minor concerto; opening and *Adagio* of violin concerto; *Sapphic Ode* and *Feldeinsamkeit*.

[13] "[Brahms] rediscovered the arpeggio and elevated it from the lowly position of an accompanying figure to an integer of the melodic phrase." Huneker: *Mezzotints in Modern Music*, 1899, p. 7.

[14] The theme may have as its main feature an ascent in two fourths and a third (G minor piano quartet, *Gypsy Rondo*, 7 bars after first *Meno Presto*); a third and two fourths (A major violin sonata, *Allegro*, 2nd theme); a third, a fourth, and a third (start of *Tragic* overture, D minor concerto, *Maestoso*, 2nd bar of *Poco più moderato*); a third, a sixth, and a third (C minor symphony, opening *Allegro*, first subject); a third,

by being filled with ladder tunes. The opening theme

Ex. 10

climbs up and down, mainly in thirds, fourths, and fifths. Its start is subtly echoed in diminution at the beginning of the *Poco Adagio,* with an upward fourth, second and fourth. In the last three movements the alternate motion of hand and foot on the ladder seems at times to be traced.[15]

Many of the arpeggio effects just described are so closely concerned with some of his loveliest and most completely Brahmsian inspirations that the Master might well have confessed, with the poet, Hermann Hagedorn,

> I have climbed ladders through the blue!
> For apples some, and some for heaven!
> The rungs of some were six and seven,
> But some no earthly number knew.

a fourth, and a fifth (B flat concerto, start of *scherzo*); a fourth, a third, and a fourth (opening themes of: A major violin sonata [see bracket, Ex. 31, p. 374], G major quintet, and F major 'cello sonata [see bracket, Ex. 34, p. 380]); a fifth, a fourth, a fifth, and a fourth (*Tragic* overture, first subject). Similar combinations are used for descent; but the climber seems to go up more often than down.

[15] This hand-and-foot design is even worked freely into the accompanying parts of the *Adagio*. At letter F the first 'cello has eight consecutive ascending fourths. The first four of these climb down one degree at a time; while nos. 4–7 give the opening of the movement twice in rhythmic augmentation.

The second theme of the *finale* consists almost entirely of nine descending and two ascending fifths, each of which begins, as a rule, one degree from the start of the preceding. The second subject of the C minor symphony's first movement is another good example of the hand-and-foot ladder tune.

As a melodist Brahms is terse and compact, with an almost infallible flair for proportion. In designing his tunes he is usually guided, consciously or unconsciously, by principles akin to those by which artists impart unity to compositions in paint or bronze. His melodic contours, with their planes of repose, their axes, and their convincing unity, yield in beauty to those of no other music-maker.

One form of tune which Brahms made even more peculiarly his own than the ladder pattern rotates on its own axis like an athlete's body about the bar of his trapeze. The B flat sextet is thickly studded with trapeze tunes quite as typical as the one with which it opens.

Ex. 11

This revolves about A, while the axis of the following, from the *Andante* of the E minor symphony, is E.[16]

Ex. 12

The violin concerto is full of the pattern. See how the principal theme of the *Adagio* revolves about F.

Ex. 13

[16] This theme, rhythmically somewhat changed, also occurs at letter G in the *Allegretto* of the C minor string quartet.

It is worthy of note that the measures (marked with brackets in Ex. 14) which Brahms borrowed from the *Hymn to Joy* for the great trapeze melody of the C minor symphony's *finale*

Ex. 14

were the only two trapeze measures in Beethoven's theme—and the only ones upon which Brahms here emphatically insisted.[17]

This melodic pattern is prolific of symmetrical proportions, because it helps to preserve the unities of design by establishing a central point of reference—the bar of the trapeze. It grew so dear to the heart of Brahms, and he came to use it in a way so idiosyncratic, as to identify it very closely with his personal style.

Sometimes he complicated its effect by raising or lowering the bar of the trapeze several times during the course of a single melody, as in *Vergebliches Ständchen,* the horn trio, and throughout the E minor 'cello sonata and the G major quintet. The last, for example, starts

[17] In searching through Beethoven's works for this form of theme I was struck by his sparing use of it. Perhaps the older master's instinctive melodic range was too wide to suit the formula; for a tune turning consistently about an axis must evidently keep within moderate limits.

Ex. 15

with the axis at low G, then raises it to high D, and later, in the course of the long melody, establishes it at A, at E, etc.[18]

Why was Brahms so fond of the trapeze? Let us hazard a theory. There is a certain tune which comes so naturally to the children of most countries, particularly when singing together in mockery of grown-ups, that it deserves to be called *The Junior Internationale*. It has been incorporated by the students of Princeton into their *Faculty Song*:

John - ny, John - ny Daig - nan,   John - ny, John - ny   Daig - nan

Ex. 16

This is a trapeze tune, pure and simple. Perhaps Brahms had the pattern ground into his two-year-old brain in Schlüter's Hof where his young comrades always sang at their play. Perhaps, later on, the little friends for whom he always carried his pockets full of candy and coppers, and whom he loved so fervently, infected him with the elemental formula. At any rate, trapeze tunes occur in each of the 14 *Children's Folk-Songs* which he arranged for the young Schumanns.

18 The Master's attachment to this pattern might explain his love of the turn, which is in itself a tiny trapeze.

Such melodic designs as the ladder and the trapeze are, in essence, substitutes for germ- and source-motives; for if many of the themes of a group of movements or compositions conform to the same general pattern, and are used with the subtle skill of a Brahms, they are bound to lend the group, and the composer's work in general, a mysterious consistency, personality, and unity.

Those who decry any study of germ- and source-motives, fearing that it might prove how easy musical composition is, may set their minds at rest; for such study proves the exact opposite. In doing liaison-work, nothing is harder to avoid than bald monotony and intolerable banality. To escape these requires genius of a very lofty kind. Though Brahms used only short and commonplace germ- and source-motives, and simple design-formulas, his resource incredibly transfigured these musical bromidioms by weaving out of them, under scores of convincing disguises, his more original and individual themes.

The Master had very few source-motives. The F–A–F theme,[19] besides the systematic use of it as germ-motive in the F major symphony, occurs detached, so far as I am aware, in only ten other works.[20] The four-note figure, Ex. 6, is of course such an ordinary incident of musical speech that detached appearances of it have no significance whatever; but its astonishingly frequent use as a germ-motive entitles it to the distinction of an important source-motive.

[19] See Ex. 5, p. 302.
[20] *Viz.* Op.: 10, No. 2 (start); 11 (first movement, 2nd subject); 15 (first movement, bar 31); 26 (*finale,* bar 88 ff., inverted and reversed); 38 (*finale,* bars 5 and 63); 51, No. 1 (*Romanze,* 4 bars before E); 67 (*Andante,* 4 bars before B); 68 (first *Allegro,* bar 5); 75, No. 3 (3rd bar); 84, No. 4 (3 bars before end).

One of Brahms' habits was to commence a piece with the
interval of a rising fourth. It is worth noting that, of the 63
folk-songs for adults and children which he arranged for solo
voice and piano, 36 begin thus. Here the folk-song may be
imitating the inflections of common speech, to which it is so
close; for it is natural to begin many sorts of sentence with
the rise of a fourth. And it is possible that Brahms caught
this habit from the folk-song, on which all his writing was
based. In any case, 60 of his 198 solo songs—or nearly one
third—begin this way. Elsewhere there are 44 different movements with the same start; so that we find Brahms using an
initial rising fourth no fewer than 140 times in his published
work—surely a sufficient number to justify us in calling it
a source-motive of an unimportant kind.

It would be interesting to know how much these source-
and germ-motives and favourite melodic designs have to do
with that intimately personal quality in the Master's music
which appeals to us as most Brahmsian. Years of study would
be needed to solve this problem; for these same motives and
patterns have been used, more or less, by all composers. It is
significant, however, that when, as in Ex. 7 and 8, the composer's favourite source-motive (marked by brackets) and
his favourite trapeze pattern coincide, the Brahmsian flavour
seems somewhat intensified; and that still more is added when
to this combination the initial rising fourth is prefixed, as in
the opening of the piano quintet.[21]

Ex. 17

21 The axis of this trapeze pattern is F; the source-motives are marked by brackets.

HARMONY

The Master's harmonic idiom, based primarily on the three most common triads, is characterized by exuberant invention, a fullness almost too rich to be compressed within four parts, an unexpectedness which keeps the listener on the alert for surprises, a tendency towards harmonic syncopation [22] inherited from Beethoven, and sometimes a flavour of pre-Bachian influence and of the archaic modes.[23] It also has an occasional harshness resulting, as Joachim once pointed out, from a too ruthless clash of voices in polyphonic writing. There is such a profusion of change in his harmony that an unduly rapid pace easily blurs and travesties the music. This is one reason why, with the years, Brahms insisted more and more on moderate tempos in performance. His friend Franz Kneisel assured Mr. Richmond Houston that "when (as rarely in Brahms' music) the designation *Allegro amabile* occurs, the *amabile* means much more than the *Allegro*."

RHYTHM

The personal note is even stronger in his rhythm than in his melody or harmony. Dactylic | ♩ ♪♪| and anapæstic |♪♪♩| motion appealed to him strongly. A sure feeling for gypsy rhythms helped him to create even better Hungarian music than Hungary herself. He had a habit of intensifying

---

[22] See the author's *Beethoven*, etc., p. 441.

[23] As in *Andante moderato* of E minor symphony (Ex. 8); F minor quintet (*Finale*, *Presto non troppo*, bars 15–26); and opening of A major piano quartet.

a tune with triplets, and then dampening its ardour with syncopation.[24] He liked to alter the rhythm of his tunes by lengthening a note here and there in repetitions, as one pulls out a piece of hot taffy.

His passion for disagreeing with the statements of his friends is reflected in the structure of his periods. Only as a rare exception did the elder composers depart from the established two- or four-measure grouping; but Brahms' departures [25] were so frequent as almost to make the exception his rule. No matter how apparently lopsided his rhythmical clusters were, he could produce from them an effect as convincing and satisfying as any four-square hymn-tune.

As Dr. Mason has fascinatingly demonstrated in his book on the chamber music, Brahms had fully as great a genius for rhythmic transformation as for thematic. He liked to puzzle the listener by stating a phrase regularly and conventionally, then suddenly repeating it with wholly different accentuation, as in the first movement of the D major symphony.

Ex. 18

It pleased him to begin his tunes in unexpected parts of the measure. These Puckish habits of rhythmical transposition

[24] E. g., F minor quintet, *Andante, poco f, molto espress.*
[25] E. g., B flat concerto, *scherzo*, second subject.

were most in evidence during his forties.[26]

In his last period he borrowed from his favourite Viotti the custom of slurring unaccented notes over to accented ones.[27] His contrary nature, like Schumann's, revelled in syncopation, in cross-rhythms, and in making music with one time-signature sound as though it had another. Described in words, much of all this reads like anarchy; but tested in actual practice, the most delicate ear can find no imperfections in the Master's time sense. Indeed, the glorious fecundity, originality, and impeccability of his rhythmical imagination and its poetic freedom were probably the qualities which first aroused Schumann's enthusiastic confidence in the future of the twenty-year-old lad.

CHARACTER TRAITS IN HIS MUSIC

Intimate glimpses of the character traits studied in the preceding chapters are constantly afforded by his works. We are reminded of his peasant streak by their terseness, conservatism, and simplicity; by the bleakness and grim realistic quality of such pages as the *Burial Song* (Op. 13) and the Sarabande of Death (*Requiem*, Part II), and by the fact that nearly everything he wrote is essentially out-of-door music, based on the folk-song. There is rough, peasant humour in the *scherzo* of the B flat sextet.[28] The rustic directness, sincerity, and economy of his orchestration suit the personal character

26 See the first three symphonies and the violin concerto.

27 This trait is characteristic of the E minor symphony (movements I and III), the D minor violin sonata (*scherzo*), the Double concerto, a large majority of the last piano pieces (Op. 117–119), and all the clarinet works.

28 Herr Niemann, with curiously little insight into the composer's character, is astonished at such an utterance by the "aristocratic Brahms"! *Brahms*, Amer. ed., p. 297.

of his music far better than would, for example, the opulent and elaborate ornateness of a Richard Strauss.

The fact that he assimilated from the dear, happy-go-lucky Viennese some of their own particular youthful zest in life, their sparkling gaiety and insouciance, is suggested by the *Waltzes*, opus 39, by the *Liebeslieder*, and most happily of all by the G major quintet, opus 111. At times, however, Vienna appears to have had a somewhat cheapening, not to say vulgarizing, effect, as in the two clarinet *Ländler* (trio and F minor sonata), with their unfortunate reminders of second-rate *Heurigen* at Grinzing. On the whole, the popular music of Buda-Pest inspired him to better purpose than that of Vienna.

In the subtle skill with which he veils his musical greetings, tributes, quotations, allusions, anagrams, and thematic liaison-work there is many a hint of his reserve, so painfully shy, his passion for privacy, and his horror of verbal self-revelation.

The wit and humour so abundantly displayed in his letters and life are less obvious in his scores. It is curious that a composer of such keen wit and such infectious humour should have allowed these gifts to peep so seldom from between the lines of the staff. Not that his music is predominantly sombre. Often it makes one smile with joy. But only in rare instances does it cause the sort of smile which is the comparative degree of the superlative, laughter. The *Allegro giocoso* of the C major trio has, in the course of my long and intimate friendship with this work, never developed such mad "giocosity" as to affect the corners of the mouth. And the same may be said of the *Allegro giocoso* of the E minor symphony, of *Ständchen*, and of *Salamander*.

WHAT NINE YEARS, 1866–1875, DID TO BRAHMS

The inscription reads: "*Johannes Brahms zur freundlichen Erinnerung an Klara (und Fritz) Simrock.*"
[in friendly remembrance of Klara (and Fritz) Simrock].

We know that, as a tonal humourist, he started betimes. At fourteen he set the Alphabet for four-part chorus, ending with the date "Winsen 1847," sung *Lento fortissimo*. But this *jeu d'esprit* unfortunately found its way to the furnace.

At twenty-three he composed, and likewise destroyed, another frankly farcical vocal work. "I send you herewith," he wrote Clara, "a fear-inspiring sermon for naughty children (with well known text!). To be sung with much pathos!" One wonders whether its text could have been anything like *Max und Moritz*. Or was it a forerunner of Hilaire Belloc's *Cautionary Tales for Children*? And did Brahms perhaps anticipate Liza Lehmann's deliciously funny musical setting of this masterpiece? In view of the delicate, smiling insight into the child's point of view in his settings of the *Children's Folk-Songs,* we must always regret our inability to judge for ourselves the worth of this *Sermon for Naughty Children.*

His bearish side is suggested by movements like the opening ones of the Symphony, string quartet, and trio, in C minor, and the *Allegro* of the *Schicksalslied*. That he had the heart of a child is attested by the B flat sextet, the *Adagio* of the violin concerto, the *finale* of the B flat concerto, the clarinet quintet's *Andantino,* and the *Allegretto grazioso* of the D major symphony.

A generation or two ago, Brahms was supposed to be the good grey composer, wrapped away from common, warm-blooded humanity in a forbidding mantle of frosty cerebration. The *Adagio* of the Second symphony, the outer movements of the Fourth, and the start of the *"Werther"* piano quartet (Op. 60) were held up as typical of these qualities.

More recently, however, as we shall see in the final chapter, it has been generally realized how little grey there is about the man or the music, and how fervid a pulse of human feeling throbs in them.

The Master's whole life-work is a love-token of one sort or another. One often catches in his music a reflection of his pleasure in the "adorable children" (*allerliebste Kinder*) whose caresses were like a cooling drink to him. This reflection is to be found not only in *Children's Folk-Songs* like *The Little Sandman,* but also in much of the Second symphony and the slow movement of the Third, the fourth section of the *German Requiem,* the openings of the B major trio, B flat sextet, and A major violin sonata, and in such late piano pieces as the *Intermezzo,* Op. 118, No. 2, the start of the *Romanze,* Op. 118, No. 5, and the middle part of the *Intermezzo,* Op. 119, No. 2.

In all these one finds the fresh, dewy simplicity and directness, the naïve charm and exuberant happiness of lovely and unspoiled children at play. One has only to hear them to know what incalculable inspiration came to him from association with those whom he so touchingly called "my little ones." The origins of *Nänie* and the *Requiem* show how he loved his friends and his mother. The first movement of the *"Werther"* piano quartet bears witness what despairing and devastating inner conflicts the love of women could precipitate in him; and its *Andante* shows him as Romeo. On a lower plane, the touch of ribaldry beginning O *liebliche Wangen* suggests how he may have discoursed with the gallant daughters of the people.

Readers of the chapter, "The Singing Girls," will perhaps

wonder how any man of such unsavoury sex habits could show so lofty a character as is revealed in the chapters, "Greatheart" and "Uncle Bahms," and in such music as the *Requiem,* the symphonies, and the chamber music. It is evident, however, that in this latter, more exalted rôle, he was the natural Brahms, the product intended by the chromosomes which formed him. And one can only marvel that the accident of his birth and early environment in Hamburg's red-light district, while necessarily moulding his sex habits, could scarcely harm the tenderness, nobility, singleness of purpose, breadth and essential purity of that generous nature. These qualities, pre-eminent in his music, were what Robert Bridges, the late Poet Laureate, had in mind when, in a sonnet, he admonished Percy Buck to

"Ply the art ever nobly, single-souled,
   Like Brahms."

Chapter XXIII

THE SONGS AND PART-SONGS

BRAHMS AS A SONG-WRITER

THOUGH at heart more of an absolute musician than either Bach or Beethoven, Brahms was, curiously enough, the chief song-writer of the Three B's. The arias and other extracts from Bach's cantatas and oratorios—they may scarcely be called "songs"—are narrowed in emotional range by their almost exclusively sacred character. Beethoven was essentially an unvocal writer. All but a rare handful of his lyrics are perfunctory, and belong with his weaker efforts.

Brahms' songs equal Schumann's in melodic beauty, surpassing them in harmonic and contrapuntal interest, in the symphonic blending of the piano and voice parts, and consequently in wearing power. He had all of Hugo Wolf's merits, except the younger man's correct accentuation, and in addition was able to breathe into his pages a warmer, more full-blooded humanity. Here, it is true, he seldom equalled the naïve, spontaneous outpourings of pure melody which sometimes make Schubert's songs seem like natural phenomena; yet he was so much more consistent and self-critical that quite as many of his 198 original songs are used in modern recitals as of the more than 600 left by Schubert.

As befitted the most absolute musician among the great writers of song, Brahms nearly always avoided those realistic imitations which are the delight of the program musician, and even texts which demanded such treatment. We search in vain through these pages for the whirr of spinning-wheels, the rattle of dice and hail, the croak of frogs, the gallop of horses, the din of battlefields, the roar of lions or locomotives, and the braying of jackasses. He evidently took to heart Beethoven's *Pastoral* symphony motto: "More expression of feeling than tone-painting"—far more conscientiously than Beethoven himself. A distant echo of winds or waves, the patter of rain, a subtle suggestion in *Der Schmied* of hammer on anvil, and in the *Tambourliedchen* of drums, was as far as he deigned to go in the direction of tonal photography.

Brahms' contrarious spirit, and his love of doing the unexpected and startling, often made him torture the word-music of the poems he set, with even more brutality than the average song composer. If a lyric like the *Minnelied* was written in double time, the Puckish Master's first reaction was toward music in triple; or vice versa, as in the case of *Vorüber*. Such high-handed proceedings naturally resulted in a disastrous dislocation of the natural word-accents. One of his supreme love songs, for example, twists into triple time the iambic tetrameter of Daumer's poem,

> *Wie bist du, meine Königin,*
> *Durch sanfte Güte wonnevoll!*

laying grotesque emphasis on *Wie, gin,* and *voll,* while robbing *bist, Kö, sanf,* and *won* of their rightful accents;

Ex. 19

which has about the same literary effect as though Byron should be made to cry:

> Maid óf Athéns, ere wé part,
> Give, Ó give mé back mý heart! [1]

Let us remember, however, that when it comes to mutilating word-music, all composers without exception are desperate sinners. And even Wolf could not prevent his music from slowing up the natural pace of the poems he set, so that alliteration, vowel arpeggios, rhyme, and everything else that goes to make the melody of verse are almost totally obliterated. Whenever word-music encounters music-music they naturally assume the respective rôles of the smiling "young lady of Niger," and her chosen mount, the tiger. And they invariably return

> . . . from the ride
> With the lady inside,
> And the smile on the face of the tiger.

Musically speaking, of course, the tiger's rapacity is fully justified. The melody of Ex. 19 would certainly have suffered if Brahms had allowed his inspiration to be hampered by considering the feelings of poor Daumer and the rights of the art of poetry. Those interludes, in certain other songs, which not only disrupt the play of vowel and consonant, but even obscure the very sense of the words; those violent repetitions of phrases; those arbitrary subtractions from, and additions to, the original texts—all made the music better, no doubt, than

---

[1] One translator of Daumer's lines managed to dislocate the sense more lamentably than Brahms dislocated the accents. "'*Wie bist du, meine Königin*' becomes 'How dost thou fare, my beauteous queen?' a species of health-inquiry which was far from the poet's thoughts." LOUIS C. ELSON, in *The Musical Quarterly*, Apr., 1920, p. 212.

any more sympathetic regard for the rights of poetry could have made it.

To balance these sanguinary ethics, Brahms had certain rare virtues. He possessed a wide knowledge of poetry and an eclectic literary taste, rare in makers of song. Here, as in the rest of his work, his rhythmical schemes, while surprisingly novel and piquant, are always convincing. His treatment of the words is usually more thoughtful than even Schubert's. His accompaniments, of high interest in themselves, and most intensively worked out, often rise above the level of mere accompaniments to that of an equal part in a duet for voice and piano.

In glancing over Brahms' songs, however, one is struck by the narrow range of his subjects. While Schubert's interest coursed wide over the whole expanse of human thought and feeling, his successor's interest seems to have been chiefly focussed on the single theme of love with which most of his *Lieder* are concerned.

SOLO SONGS

In view of the general tendency among biographers to represent the Master as a tragically pessimistic person, it is significant that he left more great songs of happy, than of unhappy, love. There is the impetuous *Botschaft* with its fifteen-measure melody, the sly humour of the twice-repeated *"höchst bedenklich,"* the characteristic Brahmsian two-against-three-note accompaniment after the second *"eile nicht,"* and the climax, whose impressiveness is in direct proportion to the simplicity of the means used. This song was written soon after the *Requiem*, in Beethoven's town, Bonn. There is the charming *Sonntag*, with its folk-quality, and the gaily passionate *O liebliche Wangen*, in which the uncertain alternations of major and minor express the lover's fluctuations of hope and despair. The somewhat *risqué* double meaning in the first stanza is the sort of sally which would have appealed less to the prim Elisabet von Herzogenberg than to the Singing Girls of Hamburg.

Other songs of happy love are: *Der Gang zum Liebchen; Meine Liebe ist grün*, which he set to the words of his godchild Felix, the eighteen-year-old son of Clara Schumann; *Komm bald*, a declaration of love for Hermine Spies, who (fortunately) misunderstood it; *Von ewiger Liebe*, ending in the maiden's memorably heroic declaration of fidelity; *Dein blaues Auge; Liebe und Frühling I; Willst du, dass ich geh?; Magyarisch;* and the tender *Wir wandelten*. The best of all are the most famous. The *Sapphic Ode*,

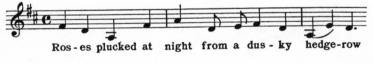

Ros - es plucked at   night   from a dus - ky   hedge-row

Ex. 20

in its handling of the difficult Greek stanza, would alone have stamped the composer a masterly metrist. It comes as near as any of his songs to the characteristic glow of the tenderest passages in his chamber and orchestral music. As regards rhythm and melodic outline Ex. 20 resembles the *Adagio* of the violin concerto (see p. 308, Ex. 13). *Wie bist du, meine Königin* (see Ex. 19) is one of the most supremely passionate acts of worship in all love-music; but the involved and expressive modulations of the middle portion are a treacherous No Man's Land for the unmusical singer. The leit-motif on the word *wonnevoll* at the close of each stanza, though eagerly awaited, is so adroitly varied as to bring an ever renewed surprise. Notice the characteristic design of this cadence, which is identical with the end of the fourth *Serious Song* (Op. 121). Brahms' frequent use, at the end of his lyrics, of a falling sixth or diminished seventh interval, followed by a rising minor second, amounts almost to mannerism. This crowning song of opus 32 has all the exuberant youth of the B flat sextet, opus 18. He wrote it when he was teaching the beautiful sixteen-year-old Elisabet, and falling in love with the future Frau von Herzogenberg.

The great *Lieder* of unhappy love are not so numerous. There is the mighty *Liebestreu* (Op. 3, No. 1) with which Brahms made his notable *début* as a vocal writer, *Klage* (*O Felsen, lieber Felsen*), *Todessehnen*, the touching *Am Sonntag Morgen*, and *Trennung* (*Da unten im Tale*). In *Nicht mehr zu dir zu gehen*, the Master created a new kind of musical lyric, a novel blend of recitative and aria, which has exerted a profound influence upon his successors.

When he used the same theme in a song and in an instrumental piece, the latter was nearly always the more successful; but *Immer leiser wird mein Schlummer*, which he took from the *Andante* of the B flat piano concerto, was an exception and surpassed its original. There is a suggestion of Schumann's *Widmung* in the fiery *Vivace* part of *Unbewegte laue Luft*, set between passages of painful yearning. Supreme in its class, and indeed among all Brahms' songs, is *Die Mainacht*. Herr Ernest has pointed out to me that its melody begins identically with that of Chopin's F sharp Impromptu.

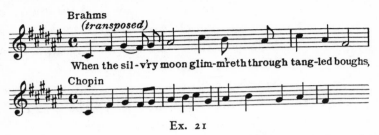

Ex. 21

In spite of this resemblance, Brahms made *Die Mainacht* so entirely his own that it became one of his particular favourites. Here is a silver-grey atmosphere almost as magical as that which suffuses the *Poco Adagio* of the A major piano quartet, and a poignance of misery such as suddenly bursts forth at the *f espressivo* of that memorable movement.

The great songs of wistfulness and sadness were nearly all composed after Brahms had reached middle age. There is the delicate, melancholy of the *Regenlied* (*Walle, Regen*), which inspired the G major violin sonata; and the faint bitter-sweet of *Wie Melodien*, which gave the second violin sonata (A major) one of its most endearing cantilenas; and the delicious, intimate poignancy of *Erinnerung's* simplicity; and the subtler, deeper poignancy of *O wüsst' ich doch den Weg zurück*. All of these might well bear as their motto Dante's lines about the pain of recalling in sadness the felicity of times past:

> . . . *nessun maggior dolore,*
> *che ricordarsi del tempo felice*
> *nella miseria* . . .

Ein Wanderer, Der Tod, das ist die kühle Nacht, the gruesomely lovely *Auf dem Kirchhofe*—that miniature *Alto*

Rhapsody culminating in the echo of O *Haupt voll Blut und Wunden*—and the *Four Serious Songs*, all deal with thoughts of death.

These last constitute a sort of solo-cantata epilogue to the funeral march in the sombre second part of A *German Requiem*. Finished on May 7, 1896, and inspired perhaps by a vague premonition of his own approaching end, they were written, he confessed, "as a birthday present for myself," to words taken by the composer from Ecclesiastes, Ecclesiasticus, and First Corinthians. "Death," the first three songs proclaim, "is universal, but is better than life. Though bitter, it brings peace." Then the clouds of pessimism are swept aside with the heartening words: "Now we see through a glass, darkly; but then face to face. And now abideth faith, hope, love, these three; but the greatest of these is love." Nothing like this stark and powerful music was ever before uttered. In it we hear the very soul of the austere, taciturn peasant who inherited from Bach and Beethoven. And it ends with a revealing glimpse of the same high heart that uttered the chorale in which the C minor symphony culminates.

Brahms wrote but few outstanding songs of Nature. Like those of wistfulness and sadness, these were products of his maturity: *Dämmernd liegt der Sommerabend, O kühler Wald*, and the blithe *Auf dem See* (Op. 59, No. 2), with its rocking accompaniment and its charming setting of the lines:

Also spiegle du in Liedern
Was die Erde Schönstes hat.

(Therefore mirror in your *Lieder*
All the beauty earth can show.)

—an injunction which the composer went far towards fulfilling in that masterpiece, *Feldeinsamkeit.*

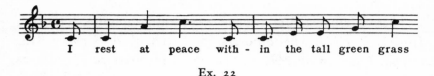

I   rest   at   peace   with - in   the   tall   green   grass

Ex. 22

This song closely parallels the *Sapphic Ode* in popularity, in musical worth, in metrical mastery, in expressive treatment of the words, in achievement of atmosphere, and in various technical details. In both the Master set two short stanzas in 4/4 time. Both begin on the notes of the tonic triad, over an organ-point; both contain equally memorable modulations, and close with much the same cadence as Schubert's *Am Meer,* a song with which the composer had been obsessed ever since, three decades before, he had quoted it in the *Adagio* of the B major trio (Op. 8). The last six measures of the voice part of *Feldeinsamkeit* demand a great singer with superb breath-control. This is one of the most perfectly modelled passages in song literature.

Brahms' humour barely reaches the surface in *Ständchen* (Op. 106, No. 1), with its imitation of a guitar-playing students' serenade, and its appropriate reminiscence of the *Academic Festival* overture (bars 15–13 from the end). Note, in passing, the interesting contrapuntal accompaniment. There is *Salamander,* a waggish descendant of Schubert's *The Trout.* There is *Unüberwindlich,* with its happy quotation from ·Domenico Scarlatti, and its jovial but finely observed delineation of an incorrigible toper. How surprised old Scarlatti would have been to find himself in this galley! The delicate humour of *Therese* appeals strongly to me. Here Brahms' bad habit of displacing the natural literary accent, reinforced by the poet's similar error, becomes a merit in the closing words. Their curious pronunciation, *"dann hörst du etwás"* (instead of *étwas*), only intensifies the atmosphere of playful mystification. *Vergebliches Ständchen* is a perfectly characterized dialogue between the overeager lover and the canny maiden at the window. Even the taciturn Brahms could not contain his satisfaction over this *jeu d'esprit*, and replied to Hanslick's felicitations:

Such as we cannot mark a big N. B. opposite any one of our songs, however much we may think of it, but it is the most charming flattery if someone else does it. This time, however, you have hit the centre of the bull's-eye. For this one song I would sacrifice all the others.[2]

Outside of the five subject-divisions just treated,[3] only three songs seem to me among Brahms' best: *Der Schmied, Meine Lieder,* and the highly popular *Wiegenlied.*

Most writers dissolve themselves into ecstasies and bring all heaven before their eyes in writing of the cycle of fifteen songs which Brahms composed to the more or less disconnected lyrics scattered through Tieck's fairy-tale of *The Beautiful Magelone.* I, for one, cannot follow them. It is true that, in opus 33, Brahms showed himself an influential pioneer. He poured out on these *cliché*-ful verses a wealth of ideas and sought, with his absolute musician's instinct, to overcome the limitations imposed upon music by poetry. But the *Magelonen Lieder* are highly uneven in quality. Where

[2] *I. e.,* of opus 84.
[3] Happy love, unhappy love, wistfulness and sadness, Nature, and humour.

he tried to be dramatic, he often merely became melodramatic and cheap, somewhat after the manner of *Rinaldo,* with a hint of bad Italian operatic influence—which would once more tend to show that he could never have made a success of opera. *Ruhe Süssliebchen* (No. 9), the most famous number of all, suffers from the Master's occasional fault of oversweetness, and a diffuseness exceedingly rare with him. Only one third of the cycle—nos. 1, 2, 12, 13, and 15—rank among his fifty choicest songs. Nos. 4 and 5 are slightly inferior to these. Brahms always protested vigorously against the practice of singing the whole cycle in one program.

Although in everything he wrote, Brahms was strongly influenced by the folk-song, and although his arrangements of the 49 *German Folk-Songs* and of the *Children's Folk-Songs* are pre-eminent of their kind, for some reason only a few of the original *Lieder* that he wrote in this style, like *Sonntag, Der Gang zum Liebchen, Magyarisch, Wiegenlied,* and *Vergebliches Ständchen,* stand among his best.

THE BRAHMSIAN TOUCH

The fact is highly remarkable that fewer of Brahms' 198 original songs and of his vocal duets, quartets, and lesser choral works bear the authentic hall-mark of that quality which music-lovers agree to call essentially "Brahmsian," than any other class of his compositions. Not that other composers could have written these pieces; but they could have come nearer to them than to the absolute music and the larger choral works.

Only fourteen of the solo songs sound to me like full-weight Brahms: the *Sapphic Ode, Wie bist du, meine Königin, Liebe und Frühling I, Immer leiser wird mein Schlummer, Die Mainacht, Wie Melodien, Regenlied* (Op. 59, No. 3), *Erinnerung,* the *Four Serious Songs, Auf dem See* (Op. 59, No. 2), and *Feldeinsamkeit.*

Eleven others fall but very little short of this authentic personal quality: *Botschaft, Komm bald, Von ewiger Liebe, Dein blaues Auge, Magyarisch, O wüsst ich doch den Weg zurück, Sommerabend, Therese, Vergebliches Ständchen,* and *Wiegenlied.*

What is the reason for this? Why should Brahms have breathed the very essence of his personality so consistently into his chamber and orchestral music, and yet have left it out of at least seven-eighths of his songs? Schubert, Schumann, and Wolf were able to pour out their souls as fully in song as in instrumental music; while even in *Feldeinsamkeit* and *Mainacht,* Brahms never attained quite the degree of self-expressive abandon that he did in the outer movements of the C minor symphony, in the *Adagios* of the D major symphony and of the clarinet quintet, in the *"Agathe"* sextet, the piano quartets, the quintets in F minor and G major, and the first and the slow movements of the B major trio.

I think that one cause lay in the Master's shy North German reserve. This was so painfully intense that it doubtless cost him many a struggle to associate himself, as publicly as a song-writer must, with the poets and their passionate, intimate confessions of love, joy, or sadness. We have already seen how impossible it was for this extraordinarily self-contained man to confide his most private thoughts to even his best friends. These lyric struggles must often have made his soul involuntarily shrink back into its shell, in a way which absolute music, with its greater soul-privacy, could never do. The very shamefacedness of his reluctant personal revelations in song, however, sometimes lent his lyrics a peculiar exotic charm of their own, unparalleled in the work of the heart-on-sleeve masters.

Brahms was embarrassed by the fact that song-writing is essentially autobiographic program music—and he was the typical antithesis of the program musician. As such, he was further handicapped by finding so little scope in song for one of those gifts that lend the most permanent interest to his other music—his powerful thematic imagination. Lyrics offered him small opportunity to employ his precious gift of development and indulge in the free contrapuntal play which makes his larger works always new, and causes them to wear so enduringly. Occasionally a touch of these qualities lends a rare distinction to lyrics otherwise of the common run. *Liebe und Frühling I,* for example, without the subtly interweaving counterpoints which parallel the interweaving of the grapevines, would never have attained its Brahmsian flavour and its perennial charm; nor would *Wir wandelten,* without the free canonic imitations which represent the two lovers' oneness in diversity. Such instances are, however, alas! too few.

Brahms evidently needed the larger forms as elbow-room for his soul, and as personal guards for his almost pathological shyness. Considering what he accomplished in this narrower field, despite the handicaps of his anti-lyrical temperament, it is evident that, if he had not been thus handicapped, he would have stood head and shoulders above all other makers of song.

PART-SONGS

The part-songs must be treated as summarily as those for a single voice. In his duets Brahms did not throw off the influence of Mendelssohn until opus 28, where *Vor der Tür* with its roguish canon reveals the hand that was to write *Vergebliches Ständchen*. In sharp contrast is *Die Nonne und der Ritter*, which closes with a line of memorable poignancy. The first two numbers of opus 61: *Die Schwestern*, and *Klosterfräulein*, offer another contrast: the light with the heavy treatment of tragedy. The former, with its subtle suggestiveness and its understatement, lies closer to the composer's own character. In *Phänomen* (No. 3) Brahms makes Goethe's somewhat unmusical verse strangely musical, because, in performance, one understands the composer's message so much more clearly than that of the poet. There is a communicative thrill in the passionate flight of *Die Boten der Liebe* (No. 4).

The best of opus 66 is the pathetic *Klänge II* (No. 2), founded on the same theme as the *Andante* of the F sharp minor sonata; and the *Jägerlied* (No. 4), with its moving transition from gaiety to the depths of despair.

Opus 75 contains two duets of wildly tragic power: *Edward* (No. 1)—a worthy companion to the piano *Ballade,* opus 10—and *Walpurgisnacht* (No. 4), in which the mother chills one's blood as she confesses to her daughter that she is a witch.

The vocal quartets deserve far more popularity than they have as yet received. Of the roguish numbers of opus 31 (*Wechsellied zum Tanze, Neckereien,* and *Der Gang zum Liebchen*) Kalbeck justly notes that "Brahms later scarcely sang anything so sweet, so purely lovable and naïve."

In the *Liebeslieder* (Op. 52), a set of waltzes for piano four hands, with charming parts *ad libitum* for vocal quartet, we feel the strong instinct of the true absolute musician, for whom notes must always take precedence of words. Brahms caught here the gay, teasing, exhilarated, and often voluptuous spirit of popular Viennese music even more fully than in the instrumental *Waltzes,* opus 39. The colouring is laid on with an unerring brush; and the impersonal, subordinate use of the voice lends this experiment a unique quality. Of all the pieces, perhaps the most infectious in their humour are: *Ein kleiner hübscher Vogel* (No. 6), *Am Donaustrande* (No. 9), and the half-frowning *Nein, es ist nicht auszukommen* (No. 11), with its Brahmsian contrariety and Puckishness. Despite the relief of rhythmical ingenuity and of certain more serious and passionate numbers like *Am Gesteine rauscht die Flut* (No. 2), and *Ein dunkler Schacht ist Liebe* (No. 16), the constant waltz rhythm grows somewhat tiring before the end.

A second series, *Neue Liebeslieder,* was published as opus 65. In this collection the voices assume more importance; the players, less. Effervescence and spontaneity yield ground to sombre drama and harsh passion. But the peroration, *Nun, ihr Musen, genug,* in the lovely serenity of its apostrophe to woman ("but from you, the good, alone does comfort come"), provides a notably satisfying close, as it transmutes the dance rhythm into a broadly flowing 9/8 movement.

Of the remaining miscellaneous quartets, the most memorable are *An die Heimat* and *Der Abend* (Op. 64, Nos. 1 and 2); *O schöne Nacht* (Op. 92, No. 1) with its erotic ecstasy; two more magical nocturnes: *Abendlied* (Op. 92, No. 3), and *Nächtens* (Op. 112, No. 2); and the tender elegy, *Sehnsucht* (Op. 112, No. 1).

The *Gypsy Songs* (Op. 103 and 112, Nos. 3–6), like the *Liebeslieder*, treat of love, possess their own natural colouring, and adhere consistently to one time-signature (2/4). But within this double time they provide a far richer rhythmical variety than the waltzes. One hears at once that the Master had plunged heart and soul into the composition of these delectable pages. They possess as vivid a local colour as the *Hungarian Rhapsodies*, and as pure music surpass them immeasurably. "Brahms' gypsies," declares Hugo Riemann, "are better trained musicians than Liszt's, but without having sacrificed any of their fiery verve."

My favourites among these songs are the passionately sombre *Hochgetürmte Rimaflut* (No. 2), the merry *Lieber Gott, du weisst* (No. 4), the resilient dance of *Brauner Bursche* (No. 5), and the daintiness and sparkle of *Röslein dreie in der Reihe* (No. 6). Then there are: *Mond verhüllt* (No. 10), with its imitation of the cembalo in the accompaniment, and *Rote Abendwolken* (No. 11), the lusciously satisfying conclusion of the first collection. Among the supplementary gypsy songs from opus 112 I prefer the piercing loveliness of *Rote Rosenknospen* (No. 4) and the *presto* swallow-flight of *Liebe Schwalbe* (No. 6). Of all the pieces written by Brahms for more than one solo voice, these *Gypsy Songs* are the most Brahmsian, even though they are, at the same time, as completely suffused with Magyar feeling as the *Rondo alla Zingarese* of the G minor piano quartet, and the *Adagio* of the clarinet quintet.

Chapter XXIV

THE SMALLER CHORAL WORKS

FEW of the lesser choral compositions can be considered much more than studies for the impressive group of choral works with orchestra which began with *A German Requiem* (Op. 45) and ended with the *Gesang der Parzen* (Op. 89). Some of them are examples of how a great composer may at times mislay his own personality, while treading in the footsteps of Bach. Here, more often than in the songs, the Master lost his Brahmsian touch. Far more easily than almost any of his orchestral, piano, or chamber music, we can imagine that most of these compositions might have been written by others. Eight of the lesser opuses have secular, and ten, sacred, words.

SECULAR WORKS

Among the secular, the most memorable pieces for women's voices are: the *Song from Ossian's Fingal,* with obbligato horns and harp (Op. 17), *Barcarole* and *Märznacht* (both Op. 44). In the latter, by a master touch, the harsh chromatic imitations which represent the storm brighten and grow aware of spring's approach. And there is the six-part *tour de force, Einförmig ist der Liebe Gram,* from the *13 Canons for Women's Voices* (Op. 113).

The Master's single work for men's chorus (Op. 41) consists of a hunting song in the old style, *Ich schwing mein Horn,* archaically harmonized, and four virile soldier pieces, full of folk quality. Of these, *Marschieren*, with its boister-ous barrack-room humour, and the alert *Gebt Acht!* deserve more than their present popularity.

Among the secular pieces for mixed chorus, the mellifluous *Vineta* (Op. 42, No. 2) stands out on account of its 5-bar periods, its *Sunken Bell* atmosphere, and its melodic tribute to the *Larghetto* of Beethoven's Second symphony. *Es geht ein Wehen* (Op. 62, No. 6) employs another sort of carillon. From the basses, according to Kalbeck, "there comes a long-drawn-out tolling, as of the bells of darkness. Above it, through the swaying tree-tops, billows the song of the wind's bride."

In the six short and simple choruses of opus 93a, *The Hunchbacked Fiddler* attracts by its lively Rhenish humour and the realistic touches suggestive of Walpurgis Night and of tuning the fiddle. The honeyed melancholy of *Fahr wohl* is captivating; but the climax of this collection comes in the splendidly male setting of Goethe's *Beherzigung,* whose mas-terly double canon gives forth no smell of the lamp.

The finest of all the secular choruses are in opus 104. *Verlorene Jugend* and *Herbst* glow with a rich and tender sadness. These, however, are surpassed by two pieces called *Night Watch,* which, in a small way, are as perfect as their namesake, the miscalled canvas by Rembrandt. The second *Night Watch* was appropriately sung at Brahms' own funeral. It must have been an overpowering moment when the solemn question, "Rest they?" was answered with its own inversion, passed from one watchman's voice to another: "They rest!" —followed by the magnificent closing injunction:

Confident, put out the lamp;
Wrap thy spirit in peace.

SACRED WORKS

Turning to the lesser choral works with sacred words, we find three of them written for Brahms' beloved ladies' choir in Hamburg. The *Ave Maria* with small orchestra (Op. 12) is somewhat stiffly conventional and bears too evident traces of Italian influence. The terse, austere *Psalm XIII* with organ (Op. 27) contains, before the imposing culmination, distinct premonitions of the delicious fourth part of the *Requiem*. Here, however, the young composer's inexperience in handling voices led him to score so awkwardly high for the first sopranos that he became as cruel a "tyrant over all the vocal organs" as the singers of Beethoven's day had declared the composer of the Ninth symphony and the *Missa* to be. The *Three Sacred Choruses a capella* (Op. 37) are difficult Palestrinesque studies in canon form.

There is more quality in the smaller pieces for mixed chorus. The *Burial Song* with wind instruments (Op. 13) is founded upon a bleak melody that Bach had in his *Erhalt' uns, Herr, bei deinem Wort*. Brahms used something very like it again, nearly four decades after, at the beginning of the *Four Serious Songs*. This sombre *Burial Song* was also the forerunner of the dead march that was sketched soon after as a part of the D minor concerto (Op. 15), and afterwards transferred to the *Requiem*. One feels in opus 13 the crude, heavy folk-character of the North Sea peasant, and his harsh, realistic attitude toward such primal things as death and burial.

The *Marienlieder* (Op. 22) are interesting specimens of the German music of the sixteenth century, reflected by a genius of the nineteenth. They treat with delicate tenderness seven legends about the Virgin. The best are the expressive *Ruf zur Maria*, the *Magdalena* where Brahms allows us to catch a faint breath of his own authentic personal note, and *Marias Kirchgang* in which, after the young boatman, rowing Mary to church, vainly implores her to be his bride, "all the little bells begin to ring."

The *Geistliches Lied* (Op. 30) is an archaic study whose profound learning is so cunningly concealed that few hearers, in enjoying its smoothness, warmth, and agreeable tone-quality, realize they are in the presence of a formidable portent: a double canon at the ninth below. The Babel-like unintelligibility with which the composer invests Paul Flemming's simple stanzas reminds one how much more cruel is the customary fate of a poem when set for a chorus than for a single voice. In solo song merely the music of vowel and consonant is brutalized out of existence; but choral writing often carries the process on from that point to the extreme of absurdity, by turning even the sense of the poem into mere nonsense. In opus 30 Brahms only followed tradition in making the soprano, alto, tenor, and bass simultaneously pronounce different words. Within a single measure, for example, the four voices, insisting on four different parts of the lines:

> *Was willst du heute sorgen*
> *Auf morgen—*

produce the following madhouse farrago:

Sop.	sor	—	gen	auf
Alt.	heu-	—	—	te
Ten.	willst	du	heu-	te
Bass	—	Was	willst	du

All of the sacred works I have named were by-products of Brahms' contrapuntal studies with Joachim, and of his least richly productive period. They represent an important part of his preliminary training. This is true as well of the two motets, opus 29: *Es ist das Heil,* and *Schaffe in mir, Gott, ein rein Herz,* the latter taken from the 51st Psalm. On paper both of these look magnificent. One admires, for example, the masterly counterpoint of the fugue in No. 1, and, at the opening of No. 2, the clever augmentation whereby bass and soprano start with the same theme,[1] but the former takes nine measures to sing what the latter compasses in four and a half. Curiously, the third movement of No. 2 begins (second measure) with a reminiscence of the very song, *Nimm sie hin denn, diese Lieder,* from Beethoven's opus 98, which Brahms, as a lad, had smuggled into his B major trio, only to excise it when he reached maturity.

Of the pair of motets, opus 74, *Warum ist das Licht gegeben* (No. 1) is the more popular; but *O Heiland, reiss die Himmel auf* (No. 2) is, in my opinion, the most successful of Brahms' efforts in this form; and the *Amen,* a double canon in inversion, rises to the level of authentic inspiration.

[1] Identical with the first two measures of the chaconne's ground-bass in the *finale* of the *Haydn Variations.*

The three highly mature, sombre, rugged, and difficult motets of opus 110 are perhaps nearer to Bach, but so much the farther from the true Brahms. In general one may say of these seven motets, as of the organ preludes and fugues, that they are marvellous eye and brain music, and able imitations of Bach, but that heart-throb, spontaneity, and the personality of their composer are strangely absent from all but a few pages.

The *Fest- und Gedenksprüche* (Op. 109), like Nos. 1 and 3 of opus 110, are set for eight-part choir *a capella*, but—unlike those motets—are full of the divine fire and the authentic Brahmsian quality. Opus 109 was dedicated to the burgomaster of Hamburg when the composer received the freedom of his native city. It is a companion piece to the *Triumphlied*, but without the latter's jingo spirit. The three movements commemorate the battles of Leipzig and Sedan, and the year 1888, which was marked by two imperial deaths and coronations. The text, chosen by Brahms from the Bible, is one of his happiest ventures in this field of compilation. As here used, it constitutes an impassioned plea to Germany to shun internal dissension and live worthy of her glorious past. In the light of recent history, this plea suggests that Brahms was endowed with a political vision unparalleled among musicians. The *Fest- und Gedenksprüche* is a broad, simple, powerful, deeply convincing work, full of thrilling excitement and quiet beauty. In view of its profundity, its magnificence, and its highly modern quality, one wonders why it is almost never given.

Chapter XXV

THE LARGER CHORAL WORKS

MORE of the real Brahms is to be found in his larger choral works than in his other vocal pieces. The wider the form, the more easily could he be himself. Cantata and oratorio offered more commensurate scope for his characteristic specialties—contrapuntal imagination and thematic development—than the limits of the short chorus or *Lied*. And the less personal texts of these larger works did not abash his shy soul by suggesting intimate revelations in public.

A German Requiem (Op. 45) was inspired by his sorrow and need for comfort after the tragic death of that benefactor and friend, Robert Schumann. Part V was added later, in memory of his idolized mother, soon after her passing.

Among all oratorios since Beethoven, this work stands supreme. The *Missa Solemnis*, indeed, though it contains greater pages, also contains many far inferior to any in the *Requiem*. The first half of Beethoven's Mass is so far below the level of the rest as to make Brahms' oratorio the most consistently sustained choral work since Bach's B minor Mass and Handel's *Messiah*, though in universality, power, and grandeur it falls far short of those predecessors.

The *Requiem* has its faults. A too rigid adherence to the simple architectural scheme A–B–A in each part except the third makes for structural monotony. The similar alternations of slow-sad with fast-joyful in Parts II, III,[1] and VI

---

[1] The fugue ending Part III bears no faster tempo mark, but, to the ear, the shorter notes increase the pace.

results in a too strict parallelism of effect, which is heightened by the culmination of each in a fugue or fugato.

This parallelism is emphasized by the sudden and insufficiently motivated change from the happy optimism and reassurance which prevail from the middle of Part III, until suddenly contradicted by the pessimistic note on which Part VI opens. It is almost as though this pessimism had been dragged in expressly to furnish a foil for the blazing climax, "Worthy art Thou" (Ex. 24), thus repeating once too often the effective arrangement of II and III. The blemish would be less apparent if Brahms had scattered a few more sombre pages through the middle of the work. These defects, however, are comparatively unimportant. Neither they, nor any others, can justify Herr Niemann in his monstrous comparison of the *Requiem* to the art of Thorwaldsen.[2]

Specht was equally wide of the mark when he called the last splendid fugue (Ex. 24) "chilling" and "hypertrophied," and called Ex. 23 "overloaded," and "eye-music," declaring that they represent the Brahms whom we "respect" but do not "love." [3] He actually concluded that the *Requiem* would have been better without its fugues! Such a glaringly false estimate can be pardoned only when one recalls that Specht lived in Vienna, where the first partial performance of the *Requiem* was so ridiculously bad as to raise a storm of hisses, and that this Protestant oratorio has never enjoyed enough sympathy in the Catholic metropolis to win it a fully adequate reading or hearing. Particularly since the Great War disrupted their musical life, the Viennese have been unable to

---

[2] Amer. ed., p. 419.
[3] German ed., pp. 222–23.

appreciate the quality of the work, or comprehend how vitally necessary are its admirable climactic fugues. Each time I hear the latter I give thanks that they are not, like most of those in the motets and organ works, merely watered Bach, but true Brahms.

The text, compiled by the composer with consummate skill from the German Bible, treats of the transience of earthly things, the bliss of heaven, comfort in sorrow, the sad lot of mortals, resurrection, and the blessedness of those who die in the Lord.

The first of the seven parts, "Blessed are they that mourn, for they shall be comforted," is unique for the limpid simplicity, clarity, and nobility with which the serene voices detach themselves from the dusky background of the lower strings. It is a perfect opening.

Parts I and II could have been created only by a genius who possessed a strain of the peasant and a passion for Nature. One feels this in the spontaneous comeliness of the passages: "They that sow in tears shall reap in joy. . . . Who goeth forth and weepeth and beareth precious seed, shall doubtless return with rejoicing, and bring his sheaves with him." And in Part II, how grimly close to the soil, like the typical Dithmarsh husbandman, is the spirit of "Behold all flesh is as the grass"! The music has the grisly, grotesque, forbidding tone of a Dürer woodcut of a Dance of Death. There is something horribly uncanny about the monotonous counterpoint of the hopeless, macabre voices, set against the funereal sarabande of the orchestra.

And then, how deeply, comprehendingly patient, tender, and comforting is the middle section: "See how the husbandman waiteth for the precious fruit of the earth, and hath long patience for it, until he receive the early rain and the latter rain." The suave beauty of this sudden change from minor ghastliness to major sunshine at the *più animato* is memorably reassuring.[4] After this interlude, the Dance of Death returns with a menace all the more oppressive.

Then suddenly its pagan measures are arrested by a shout: "But the word of the Lord endureth forevermore." And, in a fugato riot of joy, which sounds for a few notes curiously like the *Russian National Hymn,* "The redeemed of the Lord . . . return again, and come rejoicing unto Zion."

In the midst of this jubilee, nobody seems to have noticed one of those subtle personal references so dear to the heart of Brahms. At the words, "and tears and sighing shall flee," he introduces into the bass instruments, as a secret allusion, the oscillating motto [5] of the first movement of the *"Agathe"* sextet (Op. 36), that work in which, but a short time before, he had "said good-bye" to the girl whom he had passionately loved, thus ridding himself, by creative catharsis, of the tears and sighing incident to that lamentable affair.

Although Part II of the *Requiem* is one of the most splendidly stirring movements in all oratorio literature, Part III is by no means a let-down. There are dark questionings by the solo baritone, echoed from time to time by the chorus, which finally cries out, in the agitated *stretto* of a short fugato, "Now Lord, O what do I wait for?" The answer, "My hope is in Thee," ushers in a notable fugue,

---

[4] Notice how in the fifth measure Brahms again alludes to that Beethoven song, *Nimm sie hin denn, diese Lieder,* which he had already used in the *finale* of the B major trio and in the motet opus 29, No. 2. See pp. 341 and 383.

[5] See p. 415, Ex. 48, first measure.

But the right-eous souls are   in   the hand of God, nor pain nor

fear can   touch them

Ex. 23

which rejoices above a mighty organ-point D, like the souls
of the righteous exultingly confident that underneath them
"are the everlasting arms."

It would be difficult to find a page of more pure and
serene felicity than Part IV, "How lovely is Thy dwelling
place, O Lord of Hosts!", where the hearer rests from the
violent emotions of the last two movements. For counterparts of this music we must go back to the *Andante con moto*
of Beethoven's *"Archduke"* trio (Op. 97), and to the *Larghetto* of Bach's concerto for two violins. It starts with
a subtle touch, a flute phrase that seems less like the opening of a movement than some question of irresistibly beatific promise; yet it turns out to be only the inversion
of the following choral melody. Here the polyphonic
style of the preceding choruses is simplified toward ho-
mophony.

Part V continues the hearer's opportunity for rest and
recuperation. This movement was a fortunate afterthought
inspired by a great loss. There are infinite tenderness and
yearning in the soprano solo: "Ye now are sorrowful. . . .
Yea, I will comfort you as one whom his own mother comforteth." This music welled up from the depths of a man
whose fundamental adoration of his mother had a profound

influence over the whole course of his own love-life,[6] and chiefly caused the extreme sublimations which begot these celestial pages.

Here we find the Master's favourite device of accompanying a tune by a differently paced version of itself. Three bars after letter E, the tenors support the sopranos' eighth-notes by imitating them in quarters.

The first portion of the climactic and most impressive movement, Part VI, is the Protestant counterpart of the Roman Church's *Dies Irae*. With dull hopelessness the choir laments: "Here on earth have we no continuing city." "Lo," strikes in the solo baritone, "I unfold unto you a mystery." Then follows the representation of the change that shall come "in a moment, in the twinkling of an eye, at the sound of the last trump." After one of the most exciting and overpowering passages in all oratorio literature, death is swallowed up in victory, and the exultant chorus bursts into the Master's greatest fugue,

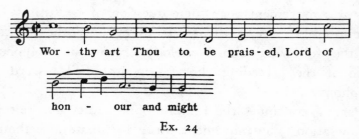

Wor - thy art Thou to be prais - ed, Lord of

hon - our and might

Ex. 24

culminating in a tremendous *stretto*, the voices crowding eagerly upon one another and catching the hearers up in a whirlwind of enthusiasm.

Then Brahms does the impossible. After this supreme cli-

[6] See p. 252 ff.

SKETCHES FOR *A GERMAN REQUIEM*

This sheet begins with Part VII at the words *dass sie ruhen von ihrer Arbeit; denn ihre Werke folgen ihnen nach* (that they rest from their labours; and that their works follow after them). Held upside down, the sheet begins with part of the fugue which ends Part VI.

max, he adds a final movement in which he not alone escapes
the imminent danger of anticlimax, but, in a long emotional
decrescendo like the epilogue to a Greek tragedy, unerringly
conducts the hearer back to a world in which it is practicable
to live.

Part VII seals the unity of the composition in various ways:
by beginning with something like a free inversion of the
first melody in Part V; [7] by using words similar to those of
Part I; and, near the close, by repeating the very music of
that inspired exordium, with a magic that recalls the wonder
of the similar echoing at the close of the clarinet quintet.

"Blessed are the dead. . . . They . . . rest from their
labours; and their works do follow after them." We leave the
concert with these last words ringing in our ears, and reflect
how truly they apply to the genius who set them to im-
perishable music.

This work is not so much a song of dissolution as one of
comfort and blessed reassurance. In considering the problem whether Brahms was a happy or a miserable man, it
should be borne in mind that the music of his oratorio of
death, if dissociated from the words, leaves a predominant
impression of zest in beauty and exhilarated joy in life.

Rinaldo, a cantata with words by Goethe, for tenor solo,
men's chorus, and orchestra (Op. 50), was far from a successful venture. A strange phenomenon, surely, to follow
hard on the footsteps of the *Requiem!* Here the undramatic
Brahms vainly strove to be dramatic, but only revealed how
fortunate it was that he never wasted his force in trying to

---

[7] A subtly appropriate touch; for Part VII's accompanying words, "Blessed are the
dead," complement those of V, "Ye now are sorrowful."

compose opera. Throughout *Rinaldo* the part-writing and orchestration are admirable. One is constantly coming upon tantalizing bits of the real Brahms, and reminiscences of his other works. The best pages are the chorus, *Nein, nicht länger ist zu säumen* (No, we may delay no longer); the *Andante con moto* where, curiously enough, two bars before the solo *Zum zweitenmale* (Again appearest), we find the memorable third measure of the clarinet quintet anticipated; and the beginning and end of the final chorus, where the relieved composer abandons all pretence of being dramatic.

Gold-en days a-gain oh win me,

Days of Pa-ra-dise a-gain,

By a no-ble pal-ace bound-ed,

Gay par-terres like jew-els gleam,

Ex. 25

At its worst, as in Ex. 25, *Rinaldo* stoops to rival the strains of Gounod. It is painful to find such a virile and consistent foe of the sentimental and the banal as Brahms descending, even in his weakest moment, to such sorry depths.[8] Music like

---

[8] Herr Niemann, Amer. ed., p. 439, incredibly estimates Ex. 25 as one of "Rinaldo's three great love-songs, full of deep, tender passion . . . the most important and valuable part of the work."

Ex. 25 gives true Brahmins somewhat the same feeling that
Noah's sons must have had when the patriarch took a drop
too much, and they beheld his nakedness.

The *Rhapsody* (Op. 53) is also for men's chorus, but with
the solo part taken by an alto, ensuring the shadowy colour-
scheme which the composer loved. The text is a fragment of
Goethe's *Harzreise im Winter*. Brahms set it while under the
illusion of being cut off from his kind, in one of those periods
of dejection to which all creative artists are occasionally
subject. This was, as we have seen,[9] brought on by his love
for Julie Schumann, and the lady's sudden engagement to
Count Marmorito.

The text describes Goethe's encounter with a young man
named Plessing, who had become morbid while reading
Werther. In this richly eloquent night-piece Brahms makes
us feel the wintry gloom of the mountains and of the young
man's heart—at first objectively, then changing in the *Poco
Andante* to sympathy for his plight. With soft harmonies
on the horns, and the entry of the choir, the mode turns to
major, and the alto raises her memorable chant of comfort
and reassurance—

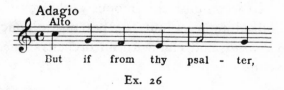

Ex. 26

—one of the composer's most genuine inspirations.[10] Despite

---

[9] See p. 273.

[10] Ex. 26 was long afterwards used by Humperdinck in a popular number of *Hänsel
und Gretel*.

the difficulty of comprehending this profound work in a few hearings, its pregnant expressiveness, its power of emotional delineation, and the benignant loveliness of the closing section ensure it a wider appreciation than it has yet received.

The *Schicksalslied,* for chorus and orchestra (Op. 54), contrasts the eternal with the temporal almost as masterfully and convincingly as the *Requiem.* Both works confront the lot of those children of light

> Whose blessed eyes
> Gaze into quiet
> Eternal radiance,

with that of mortals—wretched beings who have "no continuing city," but

> Who blindly are hurled
> From hour to hour
> Like water from cliff
> To cliff, yearlong
> Down into the deep unknown.

And in both works Brahms concludes with this mortal triumphantly putting on immortality and death being engulfed in victory. To accomplish this in opus 54, however, the composer is obliged to piece out the pessimistic conclusion of Hölderlin's poem, and end with an orchestral piece of the purest loveliness,

Ex. 27

which by implication assigns to humans a destiny as serenely happy as was the life of the blessed gods on Olympus in his almost identical opening musical vignette.

It is impossible to agree with Herr Niemann when he relegates the Master to an inferior position among composers on the evidence of this modern reading of a classical subject. It shows, he argues,[11] that Brahms "lacks that universality of feeling which is the heritage of none but very great artists and is inseparable from real greatness." Here Herr Niemann sweepingly condemns a musician on literary, rather than musical, grounds. For my part, I cannot imagine how any lover of music could sincerely deny universality of feeling to the composer of the C minor symphony; nor can I understand how any but a very great artist could have written the *Schicksalslied*.

The *Triumphlied*, for eight-part chorus, baritone solo, and orchestra (Op. 55), is a highly chauvinistic work. It was inspired by enthusiasm over the Prussian victory of 1870, and dedicated to Emperor Wilhelm I, who returned coldly grudging thanks through official channels. This *Te Deum* of conquest, filled with noisy but infectious enthusiasm, smacks less of Brahms than of Handel in his weaker moments. The leading idea of the first movement is the tune known to us as *God Save the King*, but made almost unrecognizable because the contrary Master violently alters its rhythm to common time. With mischievous, adolescent glee Brahms vents his hatred of the French in a coarse but subtle musical witticism. After the choir sings "For true and righteous are his judgments," the composer makes the orchestra intone, in

11 Amer. ed., p. 427.

strongly accented and significant unison, eleven notes which all but pronounce the words that follow in the Bible: "*Dass er die grosse Hure verurteilt hat*" (For he hath judged the great harlot)—meaning France. Brahms had the reference to Revelation XIX printed on the score, on the piano arrangement, and even on each vocal part, so that the point should escape nobody. This insult was launched at France immediately after the stormy days of 1870, and should now be condoned as war hysteria, aggravated by the dense conservatism of the composer's Dithmarsh blood.

Musically speaking, the high point of the *Triumphlied*, and its most Brahmsian page, is Part II, which works up to the fine old chorale, "Nun danket alle Gott" (Now thank we all our God), given out by the wind against the choir's soft antiphon, "Lasset uns freuen" (Let us rejoice). A baritone solo, "And I saw the heavens opened," leads up to the brilliant *finale*, "King of Kings and Lord of Lords, Hallelujah! Amen!"

With Germany's defeat and humiliation in the Great War, the *Triumphlied* naturally fell into neglect. Since it smacks too much of the occasional piece, and too little of those qualities which we prize in the chamber and orchestral music, its eventual rehabilitation is doubtful.

In *Nänie* (Op. 82) we have Schiller's admirable lament over the perishability of beauty, set to still more admirable music for chorus and orchestra. It was inspired by the death of Brahms' close friend, the painter Anselm Feuerbach. It is steeped in the same mood of soft, sweet, tender melancholy which informs the *Intermezzo* of the G minor piano quartet and the clarinet quintet. At the close, as in the *Schick-*

salslied, the composer shows himself more optimistic than his poet.

This he does once more in his third and last choral work on a classical subject—the *Gesang der Parzen,* for six-part chorus and orchestra (Op. 89). The argument of Goethe's poem is related to that of the *Schicksalslied* by the idea of the happy gods taking their ease in relentless indifference to the miseries of mankind. When Brahms reached the penultimate stanza, he could not help showing how much of a Christian he was, and how little of a pagan, by creating music whose warmth of hope is curiously inconsistent with the grim, Olympian cruelty of the text.

When all is sung and played, the impression persists that Brahms was more essentially an instrumental than a vocal composer. In writing for voice he had many apocalyptic moments which enriched us with *Die Mainacht, Feldeinsamkeit,* the *Serious Songs,* the *Gypsy Songs,* the culmination of the *Alto Rhapsody,* the *Schicksalslied,* and Part VI of the *Requiem.* But, even in his best choral works, one is never fully satisfied by that sense of untrammelled creativeness, of convincing progression, of perfect homogeneity which fills one on hearing the Master's supreme orchestral and chamber music.

Chapter XXVI

THE PIANO MUSIC [1]

(SONATAS, VARIATIONS, AND SMALL PIECES)

IN COMPOSING for his own instrument, the contrarious and original Master took pains to avoid well worn pianistic effects, and invented a new finger-language which all must, with labour and travail, acquire who would even pretend to be Brahms players. This technic bristles with formidable difficulties: crowded chords with doubled thirds and octaves, richly rapid harmonic changes, frequent tenths and twelfths, fantastically tortured fingerings, and so on. It is further complicated by treacherous rhythms and cross-accents. At the very outset of his career he sometimes overcrowded the staff as if, under a compulsion to use all parts of the keyboard at once, he had resolved to annul physiology, and compose for a three-handed player. Rubinstein once assured Mr. Arthur M. Abell that he hated Brahms because the man wrote "such a terrible piano idiom."

SONATAS

Though the defiantly boisterous exuberance which fills the first two sonatas lends them an adolescent likableness, it is tantalizing to feel how much the music would have been im-

---

[1] Space permits no discussion of the piano arrangements; nor of the organ works, which are of deep contrapuntal interest but contain little of the true Brahms.

proved by a little more discipline. In a letter to Joachim about another composition of his, Brahms well described this boisterousness:

Especially in the *finale* it is nothing but a bad boy raising an uproar; and I should like to be a good journeyman and create something, instead of raving, as I sometimes did in the sonatas.

In the first two of these we feel a very young man's zest in exhibiting his precocious learning. They are conscientiously fastened together by germ-motive work of a rather coolly mechanical sort, degrees below the fusing point of the inspiration that really unifies. Though full of palatable tidbits, these compositions interest us chiefly as preliminary studies for the riper work to come, and as showing command of a classical technic unparalleled since Beethoven.

The sonata in C major (Op. 1) was written after that in F sharp minor (Op. 2) and the E flat minor *Scherzo* (Op. 4), but was published before them because, as Johannes explained to Louise Japha, "when you first show yourself, people should see your forehead, not your—foot." He was right. The C major is better adapted for the instrument than opus 2, which frequently sounds more like an arrangement than an original composition, and recalls Schumann's remark that Johannes wished to turn the piano into an orchestra.

The lad started opus 1 with a youthfully defiant allusion to Beethoven's *Hammerklavier* sonata, for "every donkey" to recognize and bray about in preparation for the more stentorian brayings, nearly a quarter of a century later, which announced the slight connexion between the *finale* of his C minor symphony and the *Hymn to Joy*.

The *Andante* is a set of variations labelled: "After an old German *Minnelied*." This was, in point of fact, a bogus folksong by Zuccalmaglio, the notorious folk-song imitator, who had no trouble in deceiving the guileless Johannes.

The third movement is one of the most elaborately developed *scherzos* in sonata literature. Its Trio recalls the corresponding portion of Schumann's D minor masterpiece for violin, 'cello, and piano. Some rather artificial germ-motive work begins the *finale;* but the second theme, and especially the third, which is akin to the folk-song, *Mein Herz ist im Hochland*, offer faint premonitions of the Brahms to come.

Though the young composer did the F sharp minor sonata (Op. 2) some injustice in calling it a "foot" as contrasted with opus 1, the "forehead," it undeniably lags behind its younger brother in originality, force, and beauty. Despite moments of grandeur and romantic warmth in the opening movement; despite the charm of the variations—founded, this time, upon a genuine *Minnelied*—and of the ingenious *scherzo's* singing Trio, the work holds for us little more than historical interest.

Both opus 1 and 2 reveal a command of counterpoint previously unheard of in a beginner. When Johannes first played them in Düsseldorf, the wonder was that they did not fill the contrapuntally feeble Schumann with jealousy rather than with frank admiration. Lovers of the elder Master may well be proud to think how triumphantly his character emerged from such an acid test.

The third, and last, piano sonata (F minor, Op. 5) is the first instrumental composition of Brahms to sound the authentic note of greatness. Here is his gift just bursting into bloom. Today this is the most widely played of all piano sonatas written since Beethoven. Without a single concession to popularity, Johannes reduced the mechanical difficulties and suited the technic better to the instrument; so that a talented amateur who despairs of the first two might hope to conquer the third.

The heroic *Allegro maestoso* wears like reinforced adamant, with its grimly virile first subject, the delicate romance of the second, the maturity of the uncanny development, and the crushing might of the coda.

The *Andante* embodies the very essence of youthful romanticism, in holding true to its poetic motto from Sternau:

> The twilight glimmers, by moonbeams lighted,
> Two hearts are here, in love united,
> And locked in a blest embrace.

No wonder that, in places, it draws perilously near the saccharine. From this excess of sensibility, however, it is saved by the splendid final outburst in D flat, which Wagner, who happened to hear it while working on the *Meistersinger*, did not disdain to draw upon for Hans Sachs' first monologue.

The spell is abruptly marred by a much more crude and literal loan, negotiated this time by Brahms himself. The *scherzo* begins by appropriating the first tune of Mendelssohn's C minor trio *finale*. One is soon reconciled, however, by the contagious vitality of the music, by the prophetic modernism of the nine measures of bizarre dissonances beginning at bar 52,[2] and still more by the D flat section, with its

---

[2] "In this passage," remarks my friend Mr. Philip Barr, "we have something very characteristic of Brahms' first pieces. There are touches of it in Op. 2, 4, and 10, No. 3. Here he hinted at a special queer thing which he lost the trick of later."

calm chant of profound comfort.

The brief *Rückblick,* or *Retrospect,* is an extra movement. It casts one lingering, longing look behind, and translates the *Andante's* palpitating lunar bliss to the plane of tragedy. This is a new note in the sonata, a felicitous enrichment of its form.

The *finale* suffers somewhat from a lack of inner unity, from the unhappy experiment of indulging in two elaborate codas, and from a contrapuntal parade closely bordering on ostentation. These faults, however, are more than redeemed by the distinctively Brahmsian appeal of the whole—especially the dreamy second theme, and the deeply inspired

Ex. 28

third, which surely is one of the bravest, most reassuring melodies in the whole realm of music.

VARIATIONS

As a maker of variations, Brahms was excelled only by Bach and Beethoven. Those he composed for piano, however, are curiously uneven in quality.

The *Variations on a Hungarian Song* (Op. 21, No. 2) were written well before the set he first published, which came out as opus 9. Allowing for some crispness, piquancy, and an occasional flash of force, as in variations one and five, and the B flat portion of the *finale,* one feels that in this Hungarian set, young Johannes was chiefly concerned in showing off his technic. His choice of a theme mechanically alternating 3/4 with 4/4 time was in itself enough to drag down the most eager inspiration. The quality of the final *Allegro* as a whole, indeed, falls below that of the average Liszt rhapsody.

An amazing advance over this unfortunate work is registered by opus 9. The *Variations on a Theme of Schumann* were based on the first *Albumblatt* from the elder master's opus 99, and were started in collaboration with Clara, to cheer up Schumann in his illness. Brahms' variations, however, would not mix with those of the woman he loved, any better than oil and water; so two sets instead of one went to rejoice the sick man of Endenich.

In opus 9 Johannes makes poetic charm, nimbleness of imagination, and lightness of touch effectually conceal some astonishingly learned *tours de force.* For the ninth variation he reconstructs all the arpeggio work from Schumann's second *Albumblatt.* The tenth is almost imperceptibly alive with imitations, inversions, diminutions, and all manner of contrapuntal sleight-of-hand. Nos. 1 and 3 he adorns with a melody in counterpoint. Nos. 14 and 15 he treats canonically. One becomes aware of all these things, however, only after long familiarity with the music.

The *Variations on an Original Theme* (Op. 21, No. 1) are on a somewhat higher plane than the Hungarian variations which share the opus number; but, except for the charming fourth variation, the exquisitely modelled theme is the high point. Opus 21 represents a low ebb in Brahms' inspiration. The fact that he consented to publish it at all would suggest that his judgment, usually so austerely self-critical, must have been under a momentary cloud.

The four-hand *Variations on a Theme of Robert Schumann* (Op. 23) are based on a melody which had been given to Schumann—as he imagined—by the spirits of Schubert and Mendelssohn, who had bidden him vary it. In the midst of the fourth variation, the insane composer had cast away his pen and rushed forth to hurl himself into the Rhine.

This theme, with all its tragic connotations, was actually the one which the tactless Johannes innocently chose as the basis for music which should bring joy and consolation to the dead master's dear ones. The labour of love was carried out in a spirit of reverential piety. In these elegiac pages we find none of Brahms' bearish, contrary, caustic, or defiant side. One hears a tenderness akin to Schumann's, and a gentle sweetness as of Mendelssohn; but the heavy-hearted canon of the fourth variation and the free dead-march of the close are moving tributes to tragedy, worthy of Schumann's protégé.

Johannes dedicated the piece to Julie Schumann, whom he was beginning to love. He wrote Joachim that he felt as if Clara "had something against the work." The truth is, of course, that it aroused in the poor lady memories too poignant for tears.

The *Variations and Fugue on a Theme of Handel* (Op. 24) is the greatest detached set of variations for piano solo since Bach's *Goldberg* set; for neither Beethoven's in F nor in E flat (Op. 34 and 35) nor that on Diabelli's waltz (Op. 120) can compare with the younger work, which earned the praise of even the usually hostile Wagner. This is so far from being a salon piece that it is safe in the hands of none but the supreme virtuoso.

Brahms found Handel's tune in an old book called *Lessons for the Harpsichord*. One reason for his choice may have been that—as in the subject of the later *Haydn Variations*—he recognized in Handel's melody an excellent example of the trapeze pattern. Kalbeck [3] called the theme

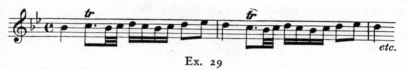

Ex. 29

"massive, as if carved from marble," and many critics have echoed him. For my part, however, I can feel nothing "massive" about these rippling notes. They produce more the effect of a blonde beauty shaking out her ringlets. If they must be carved, let the material be light curly maple!

The first variation has a healthy sparkle and twinkle which recalls Huneker's happier characterization of the theme as "a ruddy-cheeked tune." Among the following numbers my favourites are: 6, a broken-hearted canon in the true Handelian spirit; 10, with its dramatic series of staccato chords, *decrescendo;* the engaging oboe ditty of 11; 13, a fragment of some gorgeously sombre Hungarian rhapsody; 19, a daintily animated *Siciliano,* yielding in charm only to that in the *Haydn Variations;* and 23–25, which gradually increase the emotional pressure because they lead up to the stresses of the tremendous four-part fugal peroration.

[3] I, i, 461.

"STUDIES FOR PIANOFORTE." In very large letters Brahms thus labelled his two books of *Variations on a Theme of Paganini* (Op. 35). It is a commentary on his genius that, though the approach here is from the coolly scientific side, and though he heaps up technical difficulties almost beyond mortal endurance, yet, when the variations are interpreted by a born field-marshal of the keyboard, we find Brahms' inspiration foaming, roaring, and smashing like an elemental force through all the laboriously erected dikes of technic, and carrying us away in its irresistible flood.

SMALL PIECES

The E flat minor *Scherzo* (Op. 4) is the oldest of Johannes' published works for piano. It is probably the sole survivor of one of his frequent sonata-massacres. His defiant energy seethes here, his youthful, northern romanticism, and his capacity for the unconscious assimilation of other men's music. Beethoven's influence is strongly evident. The piece starts curiously like Chopin's B flat minor *Scherzo*. When this fact was pointed out by Raff on the historic occasion when Liszt read the piece from manuscript, Brahms indignantly declared that he had never seen or heard a note of Chopin. Herr Ernest, however, feels that his memory must have deceived him, and makes out a plausible case in proof.[4] The remarkable note-for-note resemblance between the second theme and the *Larghetto* of Marschner's *Hans Heiling* was noticed by Kalbeck.[5] This opera was a favourite with the

---

[4] *Johannes Brahms,* 1930, p. 45.
[5] I, 1, 83.

young composer, who had recently attended performances
of it. Opus 4, to offset its fiery *élan*, has an occasional smirch
of vulgarity, extremely rare in Brahms.

Taken together, the four *Ballades* (Op. 10), unified as
they are by their northern, runic atmosphere, might be considered as an unconventional sonata of sorts, if they possessed
any thematic unity, and if the pace of the fourth were not too
deliberate for a *finale*. The first number, founded on the gory
old Scotch ballad *Edward,* is one of the most widely appreciated of all the piano pieces. Its popularity is actually due less
to any story interest than to the vivid, harrowing quality of
the music itself. With its sinister Gaelic note, and its terrific
concentration, it provides a valid example of how the best
narrative music summarizes, instead of losing itself in details. Here we can see how triumphantly the Master might
have excelled as a programmatist if he had thought it worth
while. Even more vividly than the memorable poem, these
measures make us hear the bloodstained parricide casting off
his wife and bairns, and cursing his mother. The notes, moreover, so far transcend the words that they could characterize
as appropriately almost any other horrible situation of tragic
balladry.

For those who, stimulated by the literary title, *Ballades,*
insist on attaching programs to these pieces at any cost, No. 2
might illustrate the romance of Perseus and Andromeda, after
the sea-monster had been dispatched and the love-making
had begun. One notices that the *doppio movimento* com-
mences with the same progression as the theme of the B flat
sextet variations (Op. 18), which emphasizes the latter's
ballad-like quality. In the *molto staccato e leggiero* portion of

No. 2 one might easily imagine spirits of water and air mistily hovering above the hero and his bride.

No. 3, a *scherzo*-like *Intermezzo,* starts with a reminder of the E flat minor *Scherzo* (Op. 4). Huneker feels that this ballade might be taken as "a sarcastic, ironic commentary upon the earlier composition." [6] Its second tune suggests the *Mein Herz ist im Hochland* theme from the first sonata.

The melodiously insinuating No. 4 has less ballad quality than the others. There is a welcome Brahmsian touch after the Tempo I—a far variant, in full chords, of the opening theme, with the four-bar period stretched to five.

The *Waltzes* (Op. 39), originally written for piano four hands, are more usually heard in the composer's own arrangement for a single performer. They represent his first essay in handling the most popular musical idiom of Vienna. With hidden irony Brahms dedicated the little pieces to Eduard Hanslick, as a subtle indication of what he considered the basic frivolity of that Grand Panjandrum's musical taste.[7] Nothing could have pleased the critic more; and he began his review with a cry of joyful surprise: "The serious, taciturn Brahms, the true disciple of Schumann [*sic!*], North-German, Protestant, and unworldly as he is, writes waltzes!" Thanks to the recent activities of the radio, this set of engaging tunes, which have no organic connexion with one another, has become almost as popular as the *Hungarian Dances.* Let us hope that the missionaries of the air will soon perform a like service for the *Liebeslieder* and the *Gypsy Songs!*

In 1879, after a dozen years of vacation from music for

---

[6] *Mezzotints in Modern Music,* 1899, p. 34.

[7] We have already heard the Master remark that Hanslick preferred his Bach in compound form—as Offenbach.

piano solo, Brahms brought out the eight *Capriccios* and *Intermezzi* (Op. 76). Except the popular and obvious B minor *Capriccio* (No. 2), with its pert staccato beginning and its Schubertian second section, these compositions strike one as having been created less for the piano and the ordinary listener than in defiance of them. If one is supplied, however, with the instinct and the equipment of the miner, they offer an enticing lode. In this subtle, difficult, and sometimes crabbèd collection, almost as truly as in the wealth of subsequent more approachable pieces, Brahms is found tête-à-tête with his innermost self. The music shows him to us as he cowers above the keyboard, uttering fantastic noises, with the world well lost; or as he rages, driven by his dæmon, over the wet upland pastures at dawn. To pierce the outer and inner defences of these last piano compositions is to feel something of what Max Kalbeck, the praiseworthily indiscreet, must have felt on that memorable morning when the workroom door stood ajar and he overheard the Master at the piano, weeping and groaning in a veritable orgy of creative emotion; or when he encountered him, very early, composing by the edge of the Ischl forest:

Bare-headed and in shirt-sleeves, without waistcoat or tie, he swung his hat with one hand, dragged his coat behind him in the grass with the other, and hurried as if to escape some invisible pursuer. Even at a distance I heard sounds of laboured breath and moaning. As I approached I saw his hair hanging down into his face and the sweat running from it over his hot cheeks. His eyes stared straight forward into emptiness, and gleamed like those of a beast of prey. He seemed like one possessed. Before I had recovered from my fright he had shot by me, so close that we almost brushed elbows. I understood at once that it would have been a mistake to address him; for he glowed with the fires of creation. Never shall I forget that sight, and the terrifying impression it made upon me of elemental force! [8]

The two *Rhapsodies* (Op. 79) show Brahms at the height of his originality and vigour. "There is more of the young, heaven-storming Johannes in both these pieces," exclaimed Billroth, "than in the last works of the mature man." The famous doctor was right. Excepting the outer movements of the C minor symphony (Op. 68), nothing so "heaven-storming" had been heard from him since Part VI of the *Requiem*. The technic of opus 79, though so unhackneyed and so characteristic of the composer, is better adapted to the piano than almost any of his other compositions. "Here," writes Herr Ernest, "Brahms won from the instrument new colours: the ghostly, dæmonic place in the middle part of the G minor Rhapsody, swathed as it were in mist, has no equal in the entire literature." [9]

These virile works justify their titles by the truly rhapsodic way their melodies have of suddenly breaking off and turning back on themselves. Both are relentlessly logical masterpieces of development. Both are novel in structure: the G minor, a sort of fiercely condensed sonata-form; the B minor combining this innovation with a *scherzo*-like Trio of a poignant, unearthly loveliness.

With opus 79, the twenty pieces, opus 116–119, constitute the cream of Brahms' smaller piano compositions. One reason why the last twenty are so extraordinarily moving—when

[8] Kalbeck, III, 1, 247–248.
[9] *Johannes Brahms*, 1930, p. 243.

BRAHMS' SUMMER LODGINGS AT ISCHL, AND AT THUN

BRAHMS AT THE MILLER ZU AICHHOLZ VILLA AT GMUNDEN

(Left) He plays the affected old maid and holds out his hand to see if it is still raining. (Right) In the parlour with a score of *Siegfried*.

By courtesy of Herr Eugen von Miller zu Aichholz

we can persuade an adequate performer to take up his cross and play them—is that they are music first, and piano-music second. We shall cherish them as an invaluable part of our spiritual possessions, long after pages primarily designed for pianistic effect are quite forgotten.

In most of the *Fantasien* (Op. 116) we find a sombreness unusual in Brahms. Hanslick called this collection "a breviary of pessimism." It consists of seven *capriccios* and *intermezzi*. The latter appeal more to me than the former, especially the simple, tranquil mysticism of No. 2 in A minor, the delicate faith of No. 6 in E, and, notably, the dreamy spirituality of No. 4, in E. This last affected Huneker to such an extent that he wrote:

In the entire range of piano literature I cannot recall a more individual and more beautiful piece of music, and I am fully conscious that I am writing these words and all they implicate.[10]

The popular piece which begins opus 117, and which is based on a Scotch lullaby, needs no recommendation. "Uncle Bahms" could write such good cradle songs, with or without words, because he adored children. In the thick and somewhat abstrusely adult middle section, the understanding hearer smiles to discover him still conscientiously rocking the cradle with his coarse boot, but immersed, for the moment, in grey-bearded philosophical speculations which seem slightly odd for the nursery.

The second of these three *Intermezzi*, with its will-o'-the-wisp arpeggios, is one of Brahms' daintiest and most deftly pianistic pieces. No. 3 has the rough-hewn quality of some

[10] *Mezzotints in Modern Music*, p. 69.

ancient, tragic ballad, and is a worthy companion for the primitive *Edward* (Op. 10, No. 1).

My favourites in opus 118 are: No. 2, every note an ecstasy of sheer loveliness; No. 3, the passionate, brave ballade in G minor; the delicate and tranquil romanza, No. 5; and above all, the E flat minor *Intermezzo*, No. 6. With its unspeakably dolorous opening wail,

Ex. 30

and its other-worldly triple-time march, this piece holds for me a deeper wealth of fantastic poetry than any of the other pieces. It is supposed to have originally been conceived as the slow movement of an unwritten fifth symphony.

Not a note can be spared of opus 119, the last group to be written for piano. There are three *Intermezzi* and a rhapsody. Brahms filled No. 1 subtly full of Schumann's style and spirit; but Clara, for whom it was composed, disappointed him by failing to grasp his recondite and delicate musical allusions. The E minor *Andantino* (No. 2), a thing of tremulous and sensitive melancholy, turns its minor plaint, at *grazioso,* into one of the most convincing love songs ever entrusted to the piano. The C major *Intermezzo* (No. 3) is blithe as a school of dolphins, using the sunlit surface of a choppy, mid-ocean sea as their flying trapeze.

The E flat *Rhapsody* (No. 4), like No. 1, contains hints of Schumann. The resemblance of its sonorous opening to the march of the Davidsbündler may have been a genial tribute to

Johannes' discoverer, who did such stout battle for him against the Philistines. Though not so relentlessly logical and powerful in its development as either number of opus 79, Brahms' third venture in this form is worthy of its two great forerunners.

When we savour these final groups of pieces, we are often inclined to feel, like the guests at Cana, that our host has kept the best wine until the last.

Chapter XXVII

THE CHAMBER MUSIC

(DUET SONATAS, TRIOS, QUARTETS, QUINTETS, AND SEXTETS)

THIS is the longest chapter in the book, because Brahms'
most important contribution was made to the literature of
chamber music, especially to that for three or more instruments. His other music is important, but deprived of it we
can still imagine the soloist, the vocal quartet, the orchestra,
and the chorus struggling along. Where, though, would
chamber music be to-day without the trios and piano quartets, and most of all without the quintets and sextets?

DUET SONATAS

In my opinion, most violin-and-piano sonatas by most
composers labour under handicaps not suffered by other
forms of chamber music, or by music for piano alone. *Unless
the performers are of the first rank,* this combination is in
danger of sounding dry and monotonous. The accompaniments falling to the violinist are commonly thrust into irritating and meaningless prominence. Owing to the shortness
of the violin strings, the *pizzicati* are usually unpleasant, and
the high range of the small instrument often results in relentless shrillness. For some unexplained reason, the slow
movements are apt to sound sententious. In this combination

the incomplete blending of a stringed instrument with the piano seems more evident than in trios, quartets, etc., or even than in 'cello sonatas. And, three times out of four, the fiddle is overwhelmed, because most operators of the piano-forte leave the *piano* out of account, and specialize on the *forte*. For this, of course, the vehicle—not the composer —is responsible.

From such handicaps the Brahms sonatas for violin and piano enjoy no immunity. That in G (Op. 78) seems to suffer more, indeed, at the interpreter's hands than almost any other piece of the Master's chamber music. The score has always looked to me tantalizingly better than it sounds. During most of my life one unsatisfactory performance of it after another has put me so far out of sympathy that eventually I almost decided the fault was not with the players but with the music itself.

Recently, however, Toscha Seidel's and Arthur Loesser's phonograph record of it has made me more enthusiastic; though I still find the *Adagio* too long-drawn-out and sententious, while the insistence on the jerky, dotted rhythm inherited from this sonata's parents, the *Rain Song* and *Nachklang* (Op. 59), so agreeable in the opening movement, becomes a bit wearing when repeated with equal pertinacity in the *finale*. And when, in that movement, there also comes a quotation from the already quite sufficiently heard *Adagio*, one feels that the Master has for once somewhat relaxed his cardinal principles of terseness, reticence, and understatement.

This *"Rain"* sonata, as it is appropriately called, is a highly personal and intimate composition. Those who either do not know it, or do not like it, would be well advised to spend some hours, score in hand, with the phonograph recording, in the privacy of their own homes, before deciding that it is not for them. Though scarcely a supreme reading, this phonograph interpretation is better than any likely to be heard, except by some happy chance. And it gives the listener a cardinal advantage: he can choose his own time and place.

While the sonata was still in manuscript, Billroth declared that it was so intimate as to make a concert-hall performance a desecration. And Brahms agreed with him. The ideal place to hear it is in one's home; the ideal time, when a gush of friendly rain, such as probably inspired opus 59, is drumming dotted tunes on the thirsty leaves outside.

Hearing the liquid music of opus 78, one likes to remember that Brahms had as deep a passion for water as his predecessor Beethoven,[1] and that many of his best ideas came to him while bathing, or strolling through the rain.

The second composition for violin and piano (A major, Op. 100) is usually called the *"Prize Song"* sonata because its first measure

Ex. 31

quotes that of Walther's well known *Preislied* in *Die Meistersinger*. But as Beethoven (in the *"Geister"* trio) and scores of other composers had used a downward fourth and an upward second before Wagner, the A major's nickname might

[1] See the author's *Beethoven*, etc., p. 283.

be more appropriately curtailed into the "*Song*" sonata. At
the outset, besides briefly suggesting Wagner, it alludes with
characteristic Brahmsian subtlety to its maker's song *Komm
bald!* (Op. 97, No. 5). On his own admission the second
theme is taken bodily from *Wie Melodien zieht es* (Op.
105, No. 1); while the *finale* contributes echoes, more or less
veiled, of the songs: *Auf dem Kirchhofe* (Op. 105, No. 4),
Meine Lieder (Op. 106, No. 4), and *Meine Liebe ist grün*
(Op. 63, No. 5)—all of which had been recently finished or
were still in the making.

The first two movements of the A major are so clear and
approachable, so infectious in their joy, so thrilling in their
communicative excitement, and so easy to comprehend, that
they are popular with many who appreciate little else of
Brahms except the *Hungarian Dances*. But they are perhaps
a little too sweet to wear as well as most of his chamber music,
because, like the *Vivace* of Beethoven's Seventh symphony,
they are apt to cloy after many repetitions. And the middle
part of the *Allegro amabile* is among his weaker essays in
development. The long main theme of the *finale,* however, a
typical air for G string, is one of the noblest, best modelled,
and most fundamentally Brahmsian tunes that the Master
ever wrote.

It is interesting to watch how unobtrusively the sonata
is unified by the use of ladder patterns in each part. The first
theme of the first movement has a rising fourth followed by
a third and a fourth (see bracket, Ex. 31); the second theme
has a rising third and two fourths. The second movement
has ladder devices in its middle section before the second
Vivace; while the *finale's* chief melody has a third and a

fourth upwards, and a third and a sixth in both directions.

The third violin sonata (D minor, Op. 108) was dedicated
to Hans von Bülow. In its broadly conceived, almost symphonic scale, its brilliant effectiveness for the concert-stage,
its eccentricities, the nervous irritability [2] of many of its
melodies, and the mastery with which the tarantelle-like *finale*
carries all before it, the work suggests a tone-portrait of
the impetuous conductor and virtuoso who did so much to
make the world accept Brahms.

The high points of the *Allegro* are organ-points. The first
enlivens the exposition; the second, with surprising transformations of motive and kaleidoscopic modulation, constitutes the whole 46 measures of the development. In a
subdued way this development is magical. What might have
been its most exciting part was characteristically put by
Brahms into the exposition. Yet none the less the whole movement turned out to be a marvel of inspired construction.

The *Adagio* begins with a spacious sweep of melody, 24
measures long—as true a violin tune as that of the A major's
finale. To my mind this is the supreme movement of the
three sonatas.

The *scherzo*, like the little *Presto non assai* in the clarinet
quintet's *Andantino*, tries to perform again such a little
miracle of opulent economy and childlike simplicity as Beethoven performed in the *Presto* of his great B flat quartet.
But this attempt, though more successful than that in opus
115, does not quite avoid monotony in its constant repetition
of the tiny figure

[2] Notice for instance the surprising *sforzando* on the second note of the F major second
subject of the *Allegro,* and the equally eccentric accents on notes eight and ten of the
first theme.

Ex. 32

out of which, with deft sleight-of-hand, almost the entire movement is conjured.

The *Presto agitato finale* is an exciting, rugged, masculine movement with a piano part demanding virtuosity. The second subject, first given out by the piano alone, is a welcome reminiscence of that splendid tune from the middle of the F minor sonata's *finale* [3] which is there treated canonically to become one of the high-lights of that masterpiece. It has the same characteristic full dusky chords, and is as well adapted for a violin sonata as is the other for a piano sonata. This tarantellish close is Brahms' counterpart to the ending of Beethoven's "*Kreutzer.*" I, for one, like it even better.

It is worthy of note that the piano parts of these three duet sonatas contain much of Brahms' most "pianistic" piano music.

Though the two 'cello sonatas are, on the whole, not quite so approachable, so magnetic, or so spontaneously inspired as the last two for violin, they came as a far more needed and more welcome boon to chamber music; for the literature of the violin was already opulent, while that of its baritone brother was so poverty-stricken that these contributions were hailed as the two most important 'cello sonatas since Beethoven's A major. And this they remain today.

The E minor (Op. 38) starts, as a 'cello piece should start, with a long, noble, highly masculine, slightly elegiac melody

[3] See p. 360, Ex. 28.

which well covers the most effective range of the instrument and ushers in the most successful of the movements. One feels that in the *Allegretto quasi Menuetto*, with its faint suggestion of Schubert, and its Schumannesque Trio carved out of the start of the main portion, Brahms just failed to realize his dream. It sounds as though a genuine inspiration had met with a trifling mishap—been devitalized, perhaps, by some intervening fit of anger. But one cannot sufficiently admire the mastery of thematic and rhythmic transformation shown here, especially the way in which the starting motto, hitherto a mere prelude, is just before the Trio suddenly invested with independent importance.

The closing movement is an impetuous fugue on three themes, the first of which, though seemingly suggested by the *più animato* variation of the G major sextet, was in reality taken, as Wilhelm Altmann has discovered, from the duet for two pianos in J. S. Bach's *The Art of Fugue*. While more inspired than the scholarly end of the F major quintet, this *finale* cannot approach in spontaneity the fugues in the *Requiem*. And, even when played by consummate artists, it usually leaves an impression, less of ensemble music, than of a spirited steeplechase, with slight odds on the pianist. One reason for this may be that, as Dr. Donald F. Tovey asserts, "the look of the page is exciting enough to tempt the pianist to far too quick a tempo." [4]

As already stated, there is reason to believe that the slow movement which constitutes the crowning glory of the 'cello sonata in F (Op. 99) was originally written for the E minor, and then taken out because Brahms felt that the piece was

[4] In Cobbett's *Cyclopedic Survey of Chamber Music*, Vol. I, p. 172.

"stuffed too full of music." In support of this idea, there
are several additional reasons that have not yet been brought
forward. The four measures before the first change of key,
one of the most ineffably tender and exalted passages in all
the Master's works, recall in their intimately comforting
quality, and somewhat in melodic outline, the music that he
set to the words, "Yea, I will comfort you, as one whom his
own mother comforteth," in Part V of the *Requiem,*

Ex. 33

composed early in 1868, two years and a half after cutting
the slow movement out of the first 'cello sonata. What more
natural than that Brahms should, in the *Requiem,* have made
use of suggestions from a recently discarded movement which
might never see the light? [5]

Furthermore, the principal theme of the F major's *Adagio*
is unrelated to anything else in that sonata, but is a sister
of the second half of the E minor sonata's opening subject.
Then, too, for Brahms' day the present key-sequence seems
strikingly awkward: the F sharp major *Adagio* bluntly follows the F major *Allegro vivace,* whereas, if this slow movement had originally been intended to come after the E major
close of the first sonata's *Allegro non troppo,* the change
would have been less abrupt. Note that without the *Adagio*

---

[5] We know that he used other elided material in the *Requiem;* for the triple-time
dead march in Part II of the choral work was originally a "slow *scherzo*" discarded from
the D minor concerto.

the key-sequence of the second sonata would have been: F major, F minor, F major.

Lastly, as a slight piece of possibly contributory evidence, the *Adagio's* themes, like a heavy majority of those in the E minor sonata, are of the trapeze type; while those of the F major's other three movements are predominantly of the ladder type.

These ladder tunes are especially pronounced in the first movement. In the transition from first subject to second there is an upward progression: a fourth, a third, and a fourth (marked by a bracket),

Ex. 34

whose well concealed identity with that in the opening subject of the following opus, the *"Song"* sonata for violin,[6] reveals itself more to eye than to ear.

Both 'cello sonatas were written for Hausmann, the 'cellist of the Joachim quartet. And that virtuoso's long-demonstrated ability to make almost anything sound well may have unconsciously lessened Brahms' care to make the second sonata technically 'cello-*mässig.* The first movement, at least, with its awkward shrill jumps and its rapid tremolos on the heavier strings is apt to become slightly uncouth when performed by any but a master. Casals indeed takes the liberty of playing the tremolos as solid double-stops, with happy effect.

This opening movement is energetic, excited, impassioned.

[6] See Ex. 31, p. 374, bracketed notes.

The declamatory start, with its abrupt leaps, is curiously akin in rhythm to the corresponding page of Schumann's piano sonata in F sharp minor. Observe the highly original way in which the broken line of the principal theme is later developed into sustained figures. The *scherzo* starts like a paraphrase of the F major symphony's *finale,* to heighten the energy, the excitement, and the passion. Its Trio is one of those wholly delicious cantilenas with which this worthy descendant of Schubert so consummately embellished the *scherzos* of his trios in B, C, and E flat. At this point all 'cellists rise up and call him blessed.

With the *finale* we pass from intensity into an atmosphere of blithe cheer, like a sunny and youthful old age after a life of *Sturm und Drang* and exalted passion; one hears at the outset a plain reminder of the old student song *Wir hatten gebauet ein stattliches Haus,*[7] with its jocund reminiscence of the *Academic Festival* overture.

Despite the popular prejudice against this sonata, due perhaps to its initial inaccessibility and the difficulty of hearing a worthy performance, it seems to me the better unified, the more spontaneous, and I prefer it to the E minor by as much as I prefer the third violin sonata to the first.

The high average quality of Brahms' work would have been still higher if he had ceased writing chamber music after finishing the clarinet quintet (Op. 115); for in the two sonatas for clarinet and piano (in F minor and E flat, Op. 120), one finds little of the Master's best and most characteristic music. True, the *Andante* of the F minor sonata and the *Sostenuto* in the second movement of the E flat—

[7] Mahler's Third symphony contains an evident parody of this theme.

with its echo of the Trio of the *scherzo* of the B major trio—
are genuine Brahms. So are the glowing, autumnal variations
of the latter sonata. And it goes without saying that both are
constructed with inimitable technic. But on the other hand,
the *Allegretto grazioso* of the F minor and the opening theme
of the E flat [8] are of an oversweet triviality suggesting that
of the unfortunate *Ländler* movement in the clarinet trio,
and of the Gounodish tunes in *Rinaldo*. The aged composer
was patently a tired man. One must realize, however, that the
vehicle is here a distinct liability. When heard alone with a
piano, the clarinet seldom sounds at its best. In the orchestra
or in chamber music with strings it is far more magical.

TRIOS

About the first four trios I often feel as Mr. Alexander
Smallens, the conductor, tells me he feels about the Brahms
symphonies: "The one I happen to be doing seems the best
of the lot." When one realizes that none of Haydn's or
Mozart's piano trios, and only two of Beethoven's, measure
up to their respective composers' average level of quality;
that Schubert left only two; and that Brahms' first four
surpass all but those in B flat by Beethoven and Schubert,
it is evident how epoch-making in the world of chamber
music was the advent of the Brahms trios.

Those who blame the Master for rewriting the B major trio
in 1891, thirty-seven years after its composition, thus robbing
it of a certain amount of youthful freshness, forget three

---

[8] Which starts almost exactly like the *Internationale*.

things: (1) that part of this "freshness" consisted of borrowings from the classics; (2) that the second version merely supplemented the first instead of supplanting it—so that chamber music, far from being impoverished, was actually enriched by one more masterpiece; and (3) that by this operation the Master afforded us a glimpse into the secret laboratory of creative genius, unparalleled in the history of music.

The only melodies whose absence one really regrets in the revision are: the little *poco scherzando* tune in the first movement, which revives the atmosphere of the Rondo of Mozart's G minor piano quartet (last half of first subsidiary subject); the somewhat too literal quotation of Schubert's *Am Meer* in the *Adagio;* and the equally literal restatement, as the *finale's* second subject, of the last song from Beethoven's cycle, *To the Distant Beloved.* In place of these gems of purest ray serene, Brahms in 1891 gave us music slightly less inspired, doubtless growling to himself as he did so: "Poorer things, but mine own!" Note, however, that though he put an entirely different melody in place of the Schubert tune, his obstinacy and fine subtlety lightly sketched *Am Meer* in the *Adagio's* syncopated piano accompaniment. So what he took away with the right hand he insinuated back with the left.

A comparative study of the two versions reveals that, along with the reminiscences, Brahms got rid of not a little dullness, such as the crabbèd *fugato* digression, and various other passages in which, as lads of twenty will, he had exhibitionistically revelled in learning for learning's sake, at the expense of unity and well knit, logical form. Moreover, in giving new second subjects to the *Allegro con brio* and *finale* he breathed into them a far more dramatic and sonata-like sense of movement; and introduced that necessary element of rhythmic contrast which is so woefully lacking in the original composition.

In the opinion of Dr. Hans Gál, co-editor of the complete edition of Brahms, the new version of opus 8, the ripe product of a master at the height of his career, is heavens above the original. "Before one has edited this work," exclaimed Dr. Gál to me, "one has no idea how many subtle and marvellous changes the Master made in it! It was absolutely miraculous that he could have approached it with so objective a detachment; for this particular piece was, in 1891, perhaps the best-known and most popular of all his chamber music."

Who knows to what we owe the exhilarating outburst of the joy of youth embodied in opus 8? Certainly not, as Herr Niemann believes, to Brahms' passion for Clara, for that passion had scarcely begun when the trio was completed. Perhaps it was the ecstasy of escape from the slums of Hamburg into the hitherto unsuspected great world, which thrilled to his genius and brought him such inspiring young kindred spirits as Grimm and Joachim, and such soul-renewing adventures as knapsack tours along the Rhine.

The later version offers that almost unique combination: the exuberance of a mighty youth, kept within the bounds of superb form by the experience of maturity. Certainly there are for the chamber musician few more enlivening pleasures than to take part in the young, radiant opening of the B major—

Ex. 35

a tune which was to be a lifelong favourite of the composer's
—or in the quintessential coda, or in the spiralling Beethovenian fervours of the *scherzo's* Trio,[9] or in the celestial intensities of the *Adagio*.

Pioneer America may well be proud that, in giving opus 8
a world première, it was actually the pioneer in publicly performing Brahms' chamber music. For the B major trio had its
first concert hearing in New York City on November 27,
1855, at the hands of William Mason, pianist, Karl Berg-
mann, 'cellist, and, as violinist, no less a personage than Theodore Thomas, the father of American music.[10]

In memory of his adored mother, his first great love,
Brahms wrote the E flat trio (Op. 40) for instruments which
he himself had learned as a boy at home: French horn, violin,
and piano. It was the first notable work ever written for this
strange combination; and is not even yet appreciated at its
full value because of the difficulty of finding a hornist with
enough command of himself and his instrument not to tyr-
annize over the violin. When adequately given, this piece
endears itself in various ways: by the strangely romantic atmosphere of its first melody, the nobly infectious grief of the
superb *Adagio*, the meltingly mellifluous second subject and

[9] There is a large symphonic breeze blowing here, which seems to call aloud for eight
horns supported by a vast orchestra. This Trio suggests a cantabilized inversion of the
scherzo's main theme; the resemblance becoming clearer when the latter is frankly inverted, twenty-four bars after the first second ending of the movement.
[10] Florence May, *The Life of Johannes Brahms*, 1905, Vol. I, pp. 162–163.

Trio of the *scherzo,* and the *élan* of the *finale.* The opening theme of the last, it is true, leans rather too obviously on the closing movement of Beethoven's youthful quintet for piano and wind instruments, opus 16, while the first movement, a dreamy *Andante,* borrows its odd sectional scheme from Beethoven's sonata in F, opus 54—a scheme admirably suited to the peculiar character of the horn. The authorized arrangement of this trio, for piano, violin, and 'cello, is surprisingly satisfactory and, in the absence of a first-rate hornist, should always be preferred.

It is as hard to explain why the C major trio (Op. 87) was for many decades despised and rejected, as why, since the Great War, it has so suddenly come into its own, and even perhaps into a little more than its own. For in concert halls and over the air it has recently been more heard than any other work written by Brahms for this combination.

Here is music stripped to running garments and encumbered by no unnecessary ounce of flesh. Hard-trained, it advances straight and dynamic as a sprinter. It is frugal, clear, logical. The composer, it is plain, has now definitely put away the discursiveness of his youthful romanticism.

What maximum significance in what a minimum of notes! How resourcefully the sinewy first motive is varied throughout the opening movement, and what superb contrasts result as its varied implications unfold! Even by the twenty-first measure, as Dr. Mason points out,

Brahms has made more of his theme than he was able to make even of a motive so interesting as that of the G minor quartet in the whole exposition.[11]

[11] *The Chamber Music of Brahms,* 1933, p. 140.

The theme of the variations—one of his most successful pieces in this form—has a slightly Hungarian gypsy flavour, recalling his young days of vagabondia with Reményi. And the delicate pensiveness of all the variations but the fourth might well serve to mirror the bitter-sweet renunciation of the great artist who can never found a home, but still has the never-failing refuge of his art.

The sotto voce *scherzo* is one of his best. It might—among an infinite number of interpretations—represent the troubled dreams of one who, tantalized by hopeless longing, has sought distraction in Grimm's *German Mythology,* and nodding asleep, is attacked by imps, trolls, nixies, and all the minute genii who infest fire, air, earth, and water. The Trio, with its delicious interweaving counterpoint, brings a beatific vision of the happiness that might have been. It gleams for a moment, then is effaced by the returning rush of the malignant Little People.

In the *giocoso finale* it seems as though the awakened Master were bitterly jesting at his own plight, but with the obscure point of the joke guarded as subtly from profane comprehension as the points of so many of his other musical and verbal witticisms. The often heard refrain of this movement

Ex. 36

is a strange jest indeed! One catches here the poignant smile of "The Man Who Laughs."

Enlivening as is the *Allegro,* with its memorable first subject and the compelling augmentation of it in the two
animato passages; charming as are the highly Brahmsian variations; one remembers the shadowy *scherzo*—so wholly foreign to any suggestion of *Scherz* [12]—as the banner page of
the C major. Here Brahms turns pioneer and creates a new
type of movement. To this day it stands without a rival in
its own uncanny class.

The exciting trio in C minor (Op. 101) is, if possible, even
more concise and relentlessly logical than that in C major.
Emotionally it is better unified. Note how economically the
first movement is built almost wholly out of the rising triplet
in the bass of the opening measure; and how the *scherzo* is
deftly made of Brahms' favourite source-motive.[13]

Whenever I am launched down the majestic rapids at the
head of this torrent of music, I am sure that this is the most
satisfying trio experience of all. Nor is the feeling dissipated
by the little phantom *Presto non assai* [14] whose muted elves
are benignant counterparts of the evil genii which make the
scherzo of the C major a thing of terror; nor by the love
dialogue of the *Andante grazioso* which causes the insistent
alternation of one bar in triple with two in double time to
seem an inevitable rhythm for whispers of passionate tenderness; nor by the fiery 6/8 swing of the *finale* which has a Hungarian tinge,[15] though fainter than that in the variations of
the C major trio.

---

[12] In particular it is no joke to the pianist, who finds it almost impossible to perform
with a sufficiently delicate touch.

[13] See Ex. 6, p. 303.

[14] See p. 234.

[15] Note the resemblance of the *finale's* first six notes, read backwards, to the beginning of the *scherzo.*

Even the unpopular work for clarinet, 'cello, and piano
(A minor, Op. 114) has enough breadth and wearing power
in the romantic first movement, and enough resplendent colouring in the second, to make me feel that its first half
reaches the standard of quality set by the other trios. But
then, alas! there comes the banality of the *Ländler* movement,
and the somewhat less than fully spontaneous *finale*.

Besides certain similarities of theme and phrasing between
this trio and the Double concerto (in the same key), the two
works have this in common: that they were both made of
abandoned symphonic material.[16] And indeed the first two
movements of the trio, designed as corresponding portions of
the Fifth that was never to be, impress one with their symphonic amplitude and richness of theme.

In the opening *Allegro* the ageing Brahms ventures on a
bit of pioneering in the field of form, through the daring
freedom of the reprise. He makes it not so much a recapitulation of his story as a radical revision and improvement.

PIANO QUARTETS

In their own special sphere, the piano quartets enriched
music even more momentously than did the trios in theirs.
Before the appearance of these exciting works, the classical
literature for piano, violin, viola, and 'cello consisted of two
compositions by Mozart and one by Schumann. So that
Brahms' three actually doubled the list.

To my taste, the first two of these exuberant quartets (G
minor, Op. 25, and A, Op. 26) are more delightful to play,

[16] According to Kalbeck, IV, I, 64 and 241.

hear, and carry in memory than any other whole work by Brahms for piano and strings, except the F minor quintet. Here we find him in the full glow of youthful passion and unchastened enthusiasm, emitting music at a rate that reminds one of Cæsar crossing the Alps while dictating letters to a dozen secretaries at once. But the miracle of spontaneous fecundity which created the many and infinitely varied melodies of these quartets is almost equalled by the self-control that constrained such tropical luxuriance within the limits of appropriate and logical form, and welded four movements into an interdependent whole through a subtle interplay of germ-motives.

There is an amusing misprint in the Encyclopædia Britannica [17] which states that the sections of Schumann's D minor symphony are "thermatically" connected. The typographical error might well apply to Brahms' G minor piano quartet, whose various movements seem fused together even more by the thermal intensity of the composer's youth, than by the four notes of his favourite liaison-device (Ex. 6, p. 303), here bracketed in the first subject of the opening *Allegro*.[18]

Ex. 37

This germ-motive recurs in the second measure of the *Intermezzo*, the thirteenth of the *Andante con moto*, and the first two of the *Rondo alla Zingarese*.

---

[17] 12th ed., Vol. 25, p. 398.
[18] This subject is related to some small figures in the first slow movement of Mozart's G minor string quintet. Brahms changed them just enough to make them his own.

The *Allegro* seems resolved, at first, to be sad; but in spite of himself young Brahms cannot resist the exhilaration of all the melody that is bubbling out of him. The second subject begins with a duskily passionate 'cello solo in D minor, but soon slides into major, and from there on to the sorrowful ending, the music secretly rejoices as a strong man to run a race. Note that the D minor solo falls away entirely in the reprise, which, like that of the clarinet trio, is rather a revision than a recapitulation. The superb coda turns out to be the one truly tragic page in the work.

The *Intermezzo,* with its soft, dreamy, luxurious melancholy, is a progenitor of that slower, softer type of movement which Brahms usually labelled *Allegretto* and substituted for the traditional *scherzo.* In this form he made some enriching contributions to his art.

The strong, courageous *Andante con moto* begins with a tune which might well have served as the ideal Crusaders' hymn, for it constantly discovers new sonorities and excitements. It is marred, however, by certain of those cheap operatic *clichés* which Brahms was curiously long in outgrowing —especially by the shabbily vulgar cadence of the first theme (bars 36–40). Here we have a strange souvenir of young Johannes, the concocter of *pot-pourris* from popular operas, who had once signed himself "G. W. Marks." [19] In the *Animato* the willing ear may catch echoes of "the drums and tramplings of three conquests." One cannot imagine a more virile slow movement than this, or a more exciting *finale* than the *Rondo alla Zingarese,* which brings to the naïve folk-music of the Hungarian gypsy the refined artistic skill that

[19] See p. 39.

this music had always lacked. One might naturally suppose that this Rondo, and the scarcely less Hungarian *finale* of the sister quartet, were the first fruits of Brahms' contact with Vienna and its gypsy-bands. They were finished, however, the year before his first visit to Austria-Hungary. Genius requires little outer stimulus. Johannes' short association with Reményi and one or two other Hungarians in north Germany had been sufficient to inspire the best Hungarian music ever written up to that time. But there was even better to come.

When these two quartets were first heard in Vienna, they had no instantaneous success. Hanslick, the famous critic whose literary skill almost perfectly concealed a questionable musical taste, pronounced the themes of the A major "dry and prosy"; and successive generations of critics down to our own time have, after the way of critics, inherited this stupid opinion like a disease. They have persisted in calling the A major less spontaneous than the G minor, though claiming for it more concentration and skill in workmanship. Having played and heard and carried the quartets in memory nearly all my life, I cannot follow these gentlemen. Few things in music strike me as more spontaneous than the rich, shadowy triplet opening of the A major; or the soaring, ecstatic second subject; or the movement's close where the musical snake bites its tail with all the verve of the corresponding page in the *Choral* symphony; or the opulent simplicity, the veiled exaltations and sudden passionate outbursts of the slow movement; or the rustic blitheness of the adorable *scherzo,* of whose lilting second theme Mozart might well have been proud; or the thrilling Romany tumult of the *finale,* relieved

by the vibrating stillness of the *espressivo*—a passage worthy
to have come bodily out of that C major quintet of Schubert's to which many choice parts of these two quartets are
indebted for their inspiration. Specht and Dr. Mason found
this *finale* too long; but I, for my part, could not spare a note.
In my opinion, if anything in the A major suffers from a
slight diffuseness it is the slow movement, which Brahms
himself, at the time when he revised the B major trio, wished
to cut down. The Master stayed his hand, as he explained,
only because opus 26 was too firmly established in the concert
repertory. But he never seems to have thought the *finale*
needed similar cutting. As for Hanslick's charge of prosiness,
the only page that comes near it is the somewhat stiff canon
which begins the Trio of the *scherzo*.

This A major quartet does not offer its heart so readily to
the public, nor set bodies to swaying and feet to stamping
with quite such abandon. It takes more knowing. But when
known, it is as a full co-equal of the G minor.

The opening movement of the C minor piano quartet (Op.
60) contains music (first subject) which Brahms later confessed he had written in a suicidal mood brought on by his
relations with Clara. It also contains, in the theme that does
duty as second subject,[20] a bit of calm, confident loveliness

Ex. 38

which might well be used as a successful antidote against
despair. Despite a touch or two of pomposity, the develop-

[20] The novelty of its treatment has already been mentioned on page 300.

ment section, with the mystery of its poetic opening and the might of its two terrific climaxes, is one of the most electrifying pages in chamber music.

The *Andante*, a favourite with the composer,[21] though faintly cloying in spots, is one of the freshest, most naïvely moving love songs he ever wrote, particularly in the syncopated second theme and in the incomparable summary of the last page. No one seems to have noticed the likeness in mood between this *romanza* and another E major *Andante*, the slow movement of the C minor symphony (Op. 68), on which the composer was working simultaneously. The melodic resemblance is most striking throughout the second part of the principal themes (in the symphony, the first oboe solo), which both begin with the same five notes: B–D sharp– E–F sharp–D sharp.

The second movement is one of Brahms' more successful essays in traditional *scherzo* form. Kalbeck makes the unqualified assertion that it was originally written for an unpublished composite sonata, concocted by Johannes at twenty with Schumann and Albert Dietrich, as a surprise for Joachim, who correctly guessed the authorship of the various movements. Each of these was based on Joachim's own personal theme F–A–E.[22] But so drastically did the mature Brahms revise the movement before using it in opus 60, that no trace of the original F–A–E motive remains. If this astonishing story is true, it offers an accidental peep into Brahms'

---

[21] See p. 175 f.

[22] According to Kalbeck, I, i, 129. Tovey asserts, in Cobbett, without citing his authority, that the theme was based, not on F–A–E but on Gis–E–La, as a tribute to Gisela von Arnim; and that, after Brahms' death, Joachim gave up his conviction that the *scherzo* of opus 60 came from the composite sonata.

workshop, and sheds light on his amazing industry; for even Beethoven, with all the agonizing pains he took, and the resultant chronic dissatisfaction, never—so far as I know— rewrote any piece to the point of wholly revising away its principal theme.

The *finale* of the C minor is the one comparatively weak movement in this trinity of quartets. Inspiration apparently running thin, Brahms became somewhat too reminiscent of the *finale* of Beethoven's *Appassionata,* of the so-called "Fate" motive rhythm of the Fifth,[23] of the opening of Mendelssohn's C minor trio, and of the way the latter, in the same work, used a chorale for contrast in the closing movement.

STRING QUARTETS

It will be recalled that, before publishing his first string quartet (C minor, Op. 51, No. 1), Brahms had painfully elevated himself from the exuberant flamboyance of youth to the necessary austere economy and lucid simplicity of his prime, by writing, and burning, a score of essays in this most difficult medium. The C minor is as truly a *"Serioso"* quartet as Beethoven's F minor. Indeed, there is a veiled greeting to that master in the breathless, tortured middle part of the *Romanze,* which should have been labelled *"beklemmt"* in allusion to its ancestral passages in the *Cavatina* of Beethoven's B flat quartet, opus 130, and to the broken music in Scene IV of *Fidelio.* There are greetings to Wagner, as well, in the first two movements, for they start respectively with echoes of the *Erda* and the *Walhalla* motifs.

[23] Particularly as employed by Mendelssohn in the *finale* of his D minor trio.

This is essentially a dour, masculine work, a thing of as stern struggle and courageous endurance as the first movement of the C minor symphony. Even the deep consolations of the *Romanze* are twice interrupted by those grievous *"beklemmt"* passages. The dark-brown *Allegretto* is a thousand removes from the gay and sparkling *scherzo* of convention. And the *finale* is, if possible, grimmer and sterner than the opening movement. Let me confess that this *finale*, despite a lifetime of intimacy, never seemed to me fully successful until a few months ago, when I was fortunate enough to hear a really superb performance of it by the Roth Quartet of Buda-Pest. Which merely goes to show that before blaming Brahms for a failure, one should first make sure whether the fault may not lie in those traditional concert readings which most interpreters inherit from their masters, just as certain music-lovers inherit their parrot-like but sacrosanct dicta.

During three movements we may have noticed none of that thematic liaison-work in which Brahms so often excels. Then, in one amazing flash of revelation, the start of the *finale* ties the whole work together. It is an astounding *tour de force;* for the first five notes

Ex. 39

give not only an echo of the *Romanze's* opening, but also an inverted paraphrase of the start of the *Allegretto*. The first six notes of the *finale* form a terse telescoped summary of the first *Allegro's* principal theme. And the *finale's* second subject actually starts at *poco tranquillo* with the very F, two G's and two A flats that begin the first subject. That Brahms deliberately planned these thematic transformations is avowed, as clearly as notes can talk, by the *agitato* passage after this *poco tranquillo*.

Readers of Part III will recognize that the subtle, laconic wile of such cyclism is highly characteristic of the man who loathed the obvious and ostentatious, was a master of economy, and delighted in recondite allusions, secretiveness, and long-delayed surprises—often sprung in terms so obscure as to baffle his acutest friends. Many of the latter, for example, were years in discovering that *Auf dem Kirchhofe* and the *Triumphlied* alluded respectively to *O Haupt voll Blut und Wunden* and *God Save the King;* or that the G major sextet contained the Agathe anagram.

San Galli announced—and Specht echoed him—that while the themes of the C minor quartet are chiefly vertical, those of its twin, the A minor (Op. 51, No. 2), are chiefly horizontal. A glance at the music explodes this idea. There are no more mountain or plain tunes in the one than in the other. Perhaps sex would furnish a truer distinction between these twin works; since, except for the vigorous gypsy masculinity of its *finale,* the A minor is evidently female to the C minor's male.

The C minor [as Dr. Mason well observes] is far the more profoundly conceived, is more tragic in its feeling, more contrapuntal in its striving melodies, more severe in its search for musical unity.

In perfection of design, harmony of content, euphony of part-writing, magic of soft half-melancholy atmosphere, and sheer comeliness of melody, harmony, and counterpoint, string quartet literature has seldom surpassed the first movement of the A minor. It lingers as my most delightful memory of the first complete public cycle of Brahms' chamber music that I ever heard.

The magnificently modelled first subject, 20 measures long, might easily be taken as a character-sketch in tones of Joachim, from whom Brahms was temporarily estranged but who was to give this piece a worthy introduction to the world of music. Indeed, Joachim's personal motto F–A–E is cited in the second, third, and fourth notes.

Ex. 40

Notice how, toward the end of the development section (3 bars after letter H), the lower strings thrice give out an echo of the twin quartet—that opening of the *finale* (Ex. 39) which we have seen unifying the whole C minor at a stroke. And almost at once the upper strings transform this into a premonition of the way the slow movement of the A minor begins.

This *Andante moderato,* the most approachable and popular movement in the three string quartets, has a wistful sweetness rare in Brahms—a sweetness almost cloying. Nobody seems to have remarked the covert gesture of loyalty to Beethoven just after the little storm-flurry of the second subject, where, with a slight rhythmical disguise, he quotes the memorable start of the first Rasoumowsky quartet.

Ex. 41

Except for the lively little *vivace* episodes which diversify the *Quasi Menuetto, moderato,* like intrusions of sparkling mica in a ledge of sandstone, and for the Slavic suggestion of its bits of drone bass, the third movement has much the same atmosphere as the minuet of the E minor 'cello sonata. Eight measures before the first *vivace,* Brahms' Beethovenian love of practical joking gains the upper hand. He causes all four fiddles to lag behind, then scurry frantically, and give a *sforzando* of relief when they have caught up. This illusion is produced by making the instruments start the first part of the passage sooner and perform it slower than its original statement, then play the rest faster. It is as good a joke as Beethoven's in the E minor quartet where he made the 'cello appear to lag behind his comrades. This humour is excellent realism because it reproduces the sort of involuntary effect one hears too often at all amateur, and most professional, rehearsals.

In the *finale* Brahms again Puckishly trifles with the performer's dignity. After the second subject he makes the 'cello, playing on the beat, appear to have fallen behind his syncopated companions. And in the following unison passage, that unfortunate player is demoralized for four measures into complete silence, and seems to summon enough assurance to join the unison of the others only on receiving the emphatic cue of the highest note. Behind such pranks as these one recognizes the gleeful owner of the trick rocking-chair and the forger of the Beethoven sketch wrapped around Nottebohm's cheese.[24] Perhaps it was to get square with him for such treatment that Robert Hausmann pretended, in the group photograph,[25] to use the Master's venerable head as a 'cello.

The *finale* is conspicuous among these three quartets for its fire, its infectious *élan,* and the variety of transformations in which the headlong first subject is presented. These range from a gypsy dance which seeems determined to abjure its triple rhythm and break into a *csárdás,* through a cantabile, a weird page where the tune is accompanied by its own speeded-up inversion, a series of long, slow, pianissimo chords, and three other disguises, to a brilliantly effective coda, *più vivace.*

The third string quartet (B flat, Op. 67) is less known and appreciated than the other two, perhaps because—on account of its manifold difficulties—it is almost never superbly played. And anything less than an inspired reading bears far more cruelly on it than on the comparatively foolproof A minor.

At one time I was indignant at Richard Specht for his caustic aspersions on this piece.[26] I could not fathom how he could bring himself to ridicule the fresh and delightful sub-

---

24 See pp. 141 and 139 f.
25 See p. 135 and plate opposite p. 134.
26 *Johannes Brahms,* German ed., p. 345.

ject matter of the *Vivace;* call the *Andante* "an aged beauty
with a little cosmetic assistance"; and discover wrinkles
about the eyes of the *Agitato.* But after living for two years
in Specht's ruined, post-war Vienna, I understood. There—
and then—a superb performance of anything was an almost
unheard-of rarity. I found masterpieces usually given in such
a way as to kill one's pleasure in them for weeks or months
to come. So I could pardon Specht, because I realized that he
must have heard the B flat habitually maltreated before he
wrote that regrettably unfair page.

Almost every theme in the B flat quartet is in trapeze shape,
which lends the work a certain unity. Some tunes, like the
first three of the *Vivace,* and the theme of the variations, are
perfect examples of this form of melody.

In addition, Brahms evidently tried out here a highly difficult method of unification. On the last page of the *Vivace,*
the first and third themes, though with different time-signatures, are simultaneously yoked in double harness. The coda
of the *Agitato* combines suggestions of both the *Agitato* and
the Trio themes. While the *Doppio Movimento* of the *finale,*
after making subtle play with the first two tunes of the
Vivace, ends with the former in playful counterpoint against
the theme of the variations. This method of liaison, though
effective, is like the bow of Ulysses—fit only for Ulysses. Its
thematic material must be selected with the utmost rigour,
and handled by a contrapuntist as experienced and inspired
as Brahms.

While the *Andante,* from the critic's standpoint, has just a
suggestion of the derivative and the stereotyped, from the
standpoints of the first violinist and the 'cellist it is one of

the most delightful of movements. The dignified opening
subject has something of what we are conventionally accustomed to regard as a *religioso* atmosphere. It could be played
in church more appropriately than most of Brahms' music.
But the middle portion smells ever so faintly of the "lamp at
midnight hour."

The Master once assured Henschel that the *Agitato* of opus
67 was "the tenderest and most impassioned movement"
that he had ever written. The reader of Part III has seen how
small faith should be placed in remarks of this kind. Here it
is likely that Brahms either was having his little fun or was
actuated by his ever ready spirit of contradiction. None the
less, this *Agitato*, a broad expressive viola solo with muted accompaniment, though it takes much knowing, grows
mightily on long acquaintance. And one remembers that, fifteen years after its composition, Brahms informed Joachim,
with every appearance of good faith, that of all his string
quartets he preferred the B flat.

The *finale's* variations are full of the spirit of Haydn, with
a little Mozart, and still less early-Beethoven, thrown in for
good measure, though emotionally they are a somewhat laboured reminder of the *"Harp"* quartet's *finale*. The witty
ending of the theme surprises one by almost literally turning
the two measures of the really initial opening into a convincingly final close. The ear formally recognizes that the notes
are the same; yet they sound surprisingly different at the end,
with a fine suggestion of terseness and economy.

Brahms took delight not only in confusing the listeners'
ears, but also in horsing—and unhorsing—the players as well.
Nineteen bars from the end of the *Vivace* there is a ticklish

place where the upper and lower strings jostle each other, equipped with two different time-signatures and three different rhythms. This is a famous hazard in the Brahms steeplechase, warranted to spill amateur and professional alike, or at least to convince the audience that all four riders are simultaneously off the course.

QUINTETS

"It is never useless to take pains," the Master once wrote Kalbeck.[27] "The advantage need not necessarily appear at the place you intend."

Brahms took infinite pains with a string quintet in F minor. It turned into a sonata for two pianos and, at almost the same time, into the form we know—the quintet for piano and strings (Op. 34). Perhaps the very intensity of his struggle with the earlier versions lent the latest much of its magic quality.

Next to the "*Song*" sonata, this work is today the most popular example of Brahms' chamber music. This speaks well for the public taste; because the Master never invented lovelier melodies, or wrote with a more exuberantly creative fecundity, and nowhere else worked out his material with the passionate verve of youth so perfectly balanced by the profound mastery and inner creativeness of a recently attained maturity.

It is curious to find how often the critics—true to their habit of exaggerating the gloomier side of the Master's character—describe the F minor quintet as a tragedy. Specht, for

[27] II, II, 159 ff.

instance, calls it a thing of melancholy, "painted black on black," "created by a clenched fist." [28]

This dictum sounds as though it had been unquestioningly inherited by one who had never paused, without prepossessions, to hear the quintet with his own ears; for when we approach the work unbiased, we find that all this extreme verbal agony is appropriate merely to the start of the opening movement.

Ex. 42

Thence, from theme to theme, the rich melodic material of the exposition grows less and less stern, progressively anticipating the consoling serenities of the *Andante's* happy flow of thirds and sixths [29] and the flashing ardours and confident enthusiasms of the greatest *scherzo* Brahms ever conceived. How much genuine tragedy, pray, could an unprejudiced scribe squeeze out of this *scherzo's* grotesquely galumphing second theme, or its rhythmic variant, the electrifying third?

Ex. 43

One has but to compare these with the pair of Schubert melodies which, I think, inspired them,[30] to see how far they

[28] *Johannes Brahms,* German ed., p. 236.

[29] The thirty-second measure of the *Allegro non troppo's* development, indeed, begins a passage which anticipates part of the main theme of the *Andante*.

[30] The two chief themes of the *finale* of Schubert's D minor string quartet.

surpass their exemplars in joy of life. The Trio is no less than
Utopian in its glowing contentment. As for the *finale*, between the half-smiles, chuckles, and gurgles of defiantly
suppressed laughter, the somewhat laboured triplet-chain
passages, and the magnificently exciting whirlwind coda, one
finds sombre spots; but even these are far brighter than the
quintet's opening. No! The critics who describe this work
as "black on black" have not been able to see the house for
the door—the whole quintet for its start. It is as though they
had made a sweeping emotional analogy of the convention
that labels a work of several movements by the key of its
first few measures.

Brahms toiled tremendously not only to prepare for his
new themes and recapitulations with an art which conceals
art, but also to unify the work thematically. As in the B flat
string quartet, almost every tune is in trapeze form, down to
such inner parts as the accompanying 'cello counterpoint at
un pochettino più animato in the *finale*. And there is even
more inter-movement liaison-work than in the G minor piano
quartet. Indeed, on looking closer one finds that the germ-
motive of the quintet (bracketed in Ex. 42) is nothing but
that of the G minor quartet turned end for end (bracketed
in Ex. 37). In some form—inverted, reversed, transposed,
chromatically narrowed, lengthened out, or speeded up—
Brahms actually used this figure in all the subject matter of
the whole quintet, except the first intermediate theme of the
loose Rondo which serves as *finale*. To mention one clever
effect out of a score—in its first full measure the main subject of the Rondo gives the germ-motive upside down. And
when, in the thirteenth measure, this subject is inverted, it is

amusing to see our motive appear in its original shape, right-side up. In all music I know no other instance of a germ-motive being so intensively used as in the F minor quintet, yet with no suggestion of monotony.

It took Brahms two decades, after his failure with strings alone as a vehicle for the F minor, before he succeeded in writing a string quintet to his own satisfaction. The new venture was scored, not—like the former attempt—with two 'cellos, but for the somewhat easier combination of two violins, two violas, and 'cello. In spite of this cautious delay, however, the F major quintet (Op. 88) turned out to be an uneven piece.

At its *début* Brahms jested that it had been written by his friend Ignaz Brüll. And indeed, the un-Brahmsian harmless-ness and naïveté of the first movement suggest a core of seri-ousness in the fiercely self-critical Master's quip. Its suave and somewhat shallow first subject might almost have occurred to Brüll or Bargiel or Raff in one of their moments of su-preme inspiration. And the second subject, despite the satisfy-ing contrast of its characteristic rhythmical scheme, appears —unlike the true poet—to have been made, not born.

The splendid *Grave ed appassionato,* which starts with the same progression as the corresponding movement of the clar-inet quintet,[31] is Brahms at his best; but the idea of sand-wiching-in little fast movements to form a *mélange* of *Adagio* and *scherzo* was not carried out so successfully as in the A major violin sonata, and the effect is somewhat patchy.

[31] In both, the first 3 notes of the first two measures have the same intervals; the general contours of the melodies are very similar; and the resemblance continues even to the unexpected natural in the fourth measure of each. No wonder that the two are often confused in memory!

As for the well unified triple-fugue *finale* with sonata-form leanings, which Herr Niemann unbelievably calls "the crown of this work" and "a magnificent masterpiece," [32] its *élan* and its able handling of a most difficult intellectual problem cannot fully overcome a touch of pedantry and a lack of spontaneous inspiration.

The themes of the F major are almost consistently in trapeze form. The piece is somewhat better to play than to hear; and somewhat better to hear the third time than the twentieth. It has never won wide affection.

The sister string quintet in G (Op. 111) with two violas is, on the contrary, a continuous joy. A friend once confided to the composer that its opening movement reminded him of the Prater, the great park beloved by the light-hearted Viennese. "You've guessed it!" was the smiling response. "And all the delightful girls there, what?" That was why he unleashed a wild gypsy band in the tabloid sonata-form *finale*, and made the dusky voice of the first viola announce, as the second subject of the *Allegro non troppo*, a more luscious Viennese waltz than his friend Johann Strauss ever invented. Its first

Ex. 44

part, Ex. 44, might be taken as a question, and its continuation as a most satisfactory answer.

The short, tender, wistful *Adagio* has an *innig* quality of which I can never get enough. One wonders at the curious

[32] *Brahms*, Am. ed., p. 285.

touch of Grieg, which grows more pronounced towards the end. The simply effective *Un poco Allegretto*, with its hidden wealth of polyphonic detail, is a slightly scherzified edition of the *Adagio*. But the best of all is the first movement, with its magnificently genial opening 'cello solo.[33]

Ex. 45

The whole work—which might well be called the *"Prater"* quintet—has the grace, the charm, the magnetic momentum, the sparkling spontaneity, the absence of pedantry which have made Vienna the darling of the world. And these Southern traits have never been more eloquently set forth in tones than here by a thorough, conscientious, orderly, industrious, painstaking, typically Northern musician from Hamburg!

In the B minor quintet (Op. 115) for clarinet and strings, we have the ageing composer's halcyon days: "the last"—and, we sometimes feel, the best—"of life for which the first was made." It breathes an amazingly sweet, fragrant melancholy, a pain that is more than half joy, for it is spiced with the pleasant disappointment of an old man who had resigned himself to renouncing composition, then suddenly had found, with rapture, that he could write better than ever.

[33] See pp. 146 f. and 309 f.

BRAHMS IN HIS WORK-ROOM AT KARLSGASSE, 4

The Karlskirche, a church that he greatly admired, is seen through the window.

Etching by Prof. Ludwig Michalek, by whose courtesy it is reproduced

The *Allegro* begins unconventionally with a four-measure condensation of the first subject:

Ex. 46

two turns and two pairs of appoggiaturas—each obviously a little trapeze tune on a different level.

Specht [34] follows Kalbeck [35] in talking of "the derivation of the whole work from a single phrase"—the bracketed 3rd measure of Ex. 46; calling it "a leit-motif which pervades the whole work" [36]—a sort of Goethean *Urpflanze*. This seems rather too broad a claim. I can find no trace of it in the two middle movements. And in the *finale*—unless an imaginative effort should call the first six notes an expansion of it —the motive does not apparently figure until the artfully prepared coda, with its quotation from the *Allegro*.

The real *Urpflanze*, however, is present—not in the third, but in the first and second measures (bracketed), where it turns out to be an old friend, Ex. 6, the source-motive that more than any other pervades Brahms' music. In this quintet it occurs in the thematic material of each movement.

Let me confess that opus 115—especially the first half—

[34] Engl. ed., p. 325.

[35] IV, 1, 248.

[36] This four-note figure had already done yeoman service under Beethoven in the *scherzo* of the A minor, and the first *Allegro* of the C sharp minor, quartet.

is one of my particular favourites. Elsewhere the clarinet never sings with such transcendent sorcery; the strings never blend with such mellowness. What incredible miracles the man performs with those apparently commonplace turns and appoggiaturas of Ex. 46 which start the first movement! The resolutely contrasting staccato chords that follow—what rare feelings they produce in the marrow of one's spine! And modulations such as those at the ninth measure of the tender D major second subject and the ninth of the *Quasi sostenuto* make my heart leap up higher than any rainbow in the sky can do.

The *Adagio* with its serene cantilena so reminiscent of the *Grave* in the F major quintet, alternating with a wildly impassioned *puszta* fantasy for that virtuoso, the clarinet, is a record of one of the Master's most supremely inspired hours. As Hungarian music it surpasses even the *Gypsy Songs* and the *finales* of the first two piano quartets and of the *"Prater"* quintet.

The last two movements, though delightful enough to be the making of almost any other work, give one here a slight feeling of anticlimax, but only because they follow such a supreme *Allegro* and *Adagio*. The simplicity and slightly quaint archaic flavour of the *Andantino,* however, offer a grateful moment of recuperation after the recent half-delirious rhapsodies. Suddenly it is transformed into a *scherzo, Presto non assai, ma con sentimento,* based largely on a little theme built out of the *Andantino's* first three notes. This, like the *scherzo* of the C minor trio, is a child of the humorous little *scherzo* in Beethoven's B flat quartet (Op. 130), and makes as full organic use of its tiny motive as these do.

Unlike them, however, it does not fully succeed in keeping its *idée fixe* from the peril of monotony. Interpreters of this *Presto non assai* usually take it too briskly. Mr. Richmond Houston was told by his teacher Franz Kneisel: "When I first played it for Brahms he said: 'Would you please do me the favour of not taking that so fast?' He should have printed the *non assai* in capital letters!"

The idea of risking monotony again in the *Con moto* by making it a set of variations on a theme derived from the *Andantino* would seem even more foolhardy than his procedure long before in the F minor quintet, of deriving the Trio of the *scherzo* from that movement's third theme. But here, more than there, the Master was in such a conquering mood that he simply could not go wrong. We accept the *Con moto* with eager gratitude and are only sorry that it is not longer.

Though the two themes are not at all alike, these variations are an *édition de luxe* of the youthful ones in the B flat sextet (Op. 18). The first variation of each is a 'cello solo handled in an archaic style quite new in modern chamber music. It reminds one now of old Christopher Simpson's "Divisions" for the viola da gamba, now of Jean Louis Duport's *Exercises*, and now of J. S. Bach's 'cello suites. And towards the end is an ethereal major variation, the gem of each movement.[37] The *un poco meno mosso* coda of the clarinet quintet, with its yearning echo of the chief subject of the *Allegro*, is one of the few almost unbearably beautiful and poignant pages in all music.

[37] Mrs. Elizabeth C. Moore has discovered that in the clarinet quintet this major variation conjures up memories of the *Prometheus* theme in the *finale* of Beethoven's *Eroica* symphony.

SEXTETS

The true chamber musician is seldom so happy as when
he can bring together a pair each of violins, of violas, and of
'cellos and plunge into the two Brahms sextets, rounding out
the evening—because any other piece for this combination
would be an anticlimax—with the Schubert C major quintet.

The B flat sextet (Op. 18) begins with a typical trapeze
tune.

etc.

Ex. 47

It revels in those rich dusky colours of the lower strings in
which Brahms had recently overindulged in the Second Serenade (Op. 16), and which, in hue, recall the divided 'cellos
ushering in the *William Tell* overture. The second subject
anticipates the idyllic mood of the D major symphony's corresponding theme. Climbing its ladders of thirds and sixths,
the final part of this subject is glowing enough to warm even
the chill of age. This music is all ardent youth just beginning
to feel its own full strength and its coming mastery of form,
still full of delicious illusions—and allusions—sure that nothing is impossible, that youth is as eternal as love. And as it
frolics and flames along, the whole exuberant piece—except
parts of the slightly sombre variations—sparkles with this
same spirit. No wonder that it is called the *"Spring"* sextet!

Note how the composer of opus 18 has already outgrown

the fragmentary quality of opus 8, and has learned how to cache in his score subtle anticipations of each new coming rhythm, thereby unifying his material and preparing the ear for quicker appreciation.

The *Andante* variations found such favour with Brahms himself that he arranged them as a piano solo which he often played for friends. As far as intervals go, the theme begins with an obeisance to the *Eroica* Funeral March; but it contains nothing funereal—only a touch of the heroic and the ballad-like. One appropriate text for these variations might well be: "Rejoice, O young man, in thy youth." The highlights are: the third, with the tremendous bass billows rolling up and down in thirty-second notes; the beatitude of the fourth; and the sixth where the first 'cello softly rocks the beloved theme to rest.

The *scherzo* is a headlong carouse of boyish high jinks in the most "unbuttoned" Beethovenian manner, bordering on the uncontrollable in the *animato* middle-part. Here Brahms continued the practice, already begun in opus 8, of borrowing material from his *scherzos* in order to fashion Trios for them. This he accomplished subtly and successfully in the B major and C minor trios, the G minor piano quartet, and the G major sextet; [38] but more obviously and with less success in the F minor quintet and the B flat string quartet.

The *Rondo* with its dainty Mozart-like principal theme and its thrilling interludes is a high favourite with all 'cellists; for here the Master has showered upon them a bewildering profusion of his choicest tunes. It culminates, *animato*, in a

[38] In Op. 36 notes 1–6 of the *Presto giocoso* correspond to notes 6–11 of the *scherzo* proper.

truly original and amusing coda, *pizzicato* for all but the wildly struggling and apparently indignant first viola.

In harmonic interest, contrapuntal and instrumental skill, unusual rhythmical structure, economy of material, simplicity, profundity, and general craftsmanship, the lightly scored G major sextet (Op. 36) far surpasses the more sonorous, regular, naïve and obvious B flat with its ready-made eight-bar periods and its heart in evidence on its sleeve. A perfectionist would lament in the G major the comparative lack of dewy freshness and mad exuberance. But it is unreasonable and ungrateful to demand such opus-eighteen qualities in an opus thirty-six. The sober truth is that of the two, the latter, with its subtle depths and ever new revelations, wears better.

This is called the *"Agathe"* sextet because in writing it Brahms bade farewell, as he confessed, to his sweetheart, Agathe von Siebold; and because he smuggled into it anagrams of her name. True, the musical scale, seldom strong on orthography, could not quite manage to spell A–G–A–T–H–E. But, considering that the composer was handicapped by the absence of any note called T, and by his ideal of beauty *über Alles*—anagrams or no anagrams—he did well, without forcing or compromise, to hail his lost love twice in the first movement.[39] One finds A–G–D in the principal theme, and A–G–A–D–E in a subsidiary tune. In the latter, however, his artistic conscience uttered the D, not in the melodic instrument, but so markedly accented in the accompaniment as to stand out above the H [40] of the melody.

From the oscillating first measure, which serves as a motto

---

[39] Bars 12–13, and twenty-eight bars after letter C.
[40] H is German for B natural.

for the opening movement, with its long, original ladder
theme,

Ex. 48

the whole sextet has a veiled mysterious quality, a silvery
shimmer, pierced now and then by such glorious high-lights
as the second subject of the *Allegro non troppo*, the *Presto
giocoso* Trio of the *scherzo*, the touching final variation of
the *Poco Adagio*, and the last pages of the *finale's* [41] coda.

[41] This *finale* was finished in 1864. Its opening melody (*tranquillo*) apparently started
Goldmark, a few months after, on the main theme (bars 25–26) of the famous *Sakuntala*
overture.

Chapter XXVIII

THE ORCHESTRAL WORKS

(SERENADES, VARIATIONS, SYMPHONIES, CONCERTOS, AND OVERTURES)

SERENADES

THE two Serenades [1] were written in Detmold, 1857–1859, and served their purpose as exercises for the future symphonist. Both are now definitely dated.

VARIATIONS

The *Variations on a Theme of Joseph Haydn* (Op. 56a), however, except for the unhappy mixture of horn with oboe in the fourth variation, bear no sign of an apprentice hand. This engaging work was composed fourteen years after the Second Serenade and five years after the completion of the *Requiem*. C. F. Pohl, the biographer of Haydn, had unearthed some unpublished music supposed to have been written by his hero. Among this Brahms found a *divertimento* in in B flat for wind instruments. Its second movement, labelled *Chorale St. Antoni*,[2] pleased him so much that he copied it out and used it as the theme of eight variations and *finale* for large orchestra. He also set it identically for two pianos (Op. 56b). Its charmingly irregular rhythmical plan, beginning with two five-measure periods, continuing with four

---

[1] In D, Op. 11, and in A, Op. 16.
[2] A misspelling of *Antonii*.

fours, and ending with a three, might have been conceived by such a master of exotic rhythms as Brahms himself.

For all its wide variety and wealth of contrast, the majority of its movements have one feature in common besides their often thoroughly hidden theme. Variations II and III are in the mood of those *Allegrettos*—like that of the C minor symphony—which Brahms developed as substitutes for the traditional light and rapid middle movements of his larger works; while Nos. V, VI, and VIII are true *scherzos*. We know that the Master liked to indulge in subtle and purely musical greetings to the shades of his mighty predecessors. Did he give the Variations their marked *scherzoso* character as a tribute to Haydn for his pioneer deed in first popularizing the term *scherzo?*

Next to the *finale*, No. VII, a delicate idyll for the innocent flute, in *Siciliano* rhythm, is the most effective variation. It is marked *grazioso*. Kalbeck,[3] whose weakest point was his desire to embellish absolute music with far-fetched literary programs, seriously contended that this work represents the temptations of St. Anthony the Great in the Egyptian desert; and that, of these temptations, "the most terrible because the sweetest," "a Leda awaiting her swan," a super-houri who embodies "the quintessence of human voluptuousness," is none other than—the blameless *Siciliano!* Programmatists have seldom fallen to lower depths of absurdity than this.

The *finale* is a chaconne built upon this *idée fixe*,

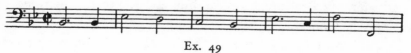

Ex. 49

[3] II, ii, 467 f.

which is repeated seventeen times as a ground-bass and several times more in the upper voices. The instrumentation is that of a past master, the colours clear and glowing, the single, double, and triple counterpoint so cleverly concealed as always to leave something more to discover next time. And the tremendous culmination, with the sonority of the brass and the wild runs in wood-wind and strings, is a more than worthy son of Weber's *Jubilee* Overture, and a true father of the *Academic Festival* which followed eight years after. Such a preliminary study for the *passacaglia* which was to end his symphonic pageant could have been written by none but a very great master.

These variations may not have shown forth St. Anthony's triumph over the powers of darkness, but they did unmistakably proclaim Johannes' triumph over the difficulties of orchestral technic.

SYMPHONIES

The Serenades, the D minor concerto, the *Haydn Variations,* and the early choral works were not Brahms' only preparation for his career as a symphonic writer. Before publishing, at 44, his First, in C minor (Op. 68), he had already composed and destroyed many a symphony. At the time, Bülow was widely ridiculed for calling this "The Tenth." But the years have justified him by stamping it, not as an advance on Beethoven's nine, but as the greatest symphony since the *Choral.*

And indeed some parts of the C minor: the opening pages and the introduction and coda of the *finale,* are worthy to stand on equal terms with anything in the immortal nine. The work begins *Un poco sostenuto,* with the violins soaring in one theme while the wood-winds descend in another, over the relentlessly throbbing ground-bass of the tympani.

Ex. 50

"It comes in like God Almighty!" exclaimed the composer Carl Ruggles to me after one memorable performance.

In the *Allegro* we are plunged into the cross-currents of grim spiritual conflict. Such movements are rare in the work of Brahms. Beethoven first created this sort of music; and without the inspiration of the opening movements of his Fifth and Ninth, the opening *Allegro* of Brahms' C minor symphony [4] would probably have remained for ever unachieved.

The main subject of the *Allegro* seems, at a first hearing, almost as bald and uncompromising as the *"Fate"* motive that starts Beethoven's Fifth. And the wistful second subject seems a little too reminiscent of its composer's A flat minor organ fugue, which was written at about the same time. But soon one is completely swept away by the rhythmical *élan* of the music and by the development which, casually snapping up unconsidered trifles of subject matter, reveals their abysmal potentialities and conducts them through two mysterious organ-points on G, in the Master's inimitable

[4] And of his C minor string quartet.

manner, to the surprise-beginning of the reprise. For me a high point in this development begins just before letter G, where the angrily sputtering groups of three descending eighth-notes (*marcato*) change to big confident legato chords that point secretly forward to the main theme of the *Un poco Allegretto.*

In this movement, as so often elsewhere, Brahms persistently makes his music sound rhythmically different from the way it looks on the page. Often he repeats the same figure in rapid sequence, but in different parts of the measure—a trick yet more consummately played in the staccato theme (*quasi ritenuto*) of the D major symphony's corresponding movement.[5] Thus he not only lends his score added interest, subtlety, and wearing power; but also epitomizes the function of the poet—whether of word or of tone—to reveal the significance underlying the apparently insignificant surface appearance of common things.

This terrific movement closes perfectly with 17 slower measures, marvellously prepared, which, in theme and throbbing ground-bass, recall the Introduction, but which appropriately seem to look backward at the mighty experience just finished. Too late for revision Brahms wished to change the *Poco sostenuto* time direction of this epilogue to *Meno allegro,* in order to avoid duplicating the designation of the Introduction.

After the dourest struggle in all Brahms' music follows a serene page of comfort. The *Andante sostenuto,* which at first acquaintance seems to have no room in its thoughts for anything but a pure and exalted tenderness, proves on further

[5] See Ex. 18, p. 314.

acquaintance to possess a fascinating hidden intellectual life
of its own. Notice how it recognizes, in measures 5–6, the
symphony's opening notes; and how, in measures 14–15, the
start of its own principal theme appears inverted, in a
rhythmical disguise; and how the *dolce legato* oboe melody
is accompanied by a stammering, gasping minor version of
this same principal theme. Observe the perfect modelling of
each tune, the celestial effect of the violin obbligato near the
end, and the mysterious way in which, by means austerely
simple, the Master seems to turn these pages into a revelation
of souls which

> . . . stand up erect and strong,
> Face to face, silent, drawing nigh and nigher,
> Until the lengthening wings break into fire.

Almost any other composer who attempted this with such
materials would have sunk into a slough of banality or sentimentality. It is the strong intellectual element which, in the
last analysis, saves the music. Its blonde, feminine beauty is
rescued from insipidity by a brilliant mind. And it commands
the additional advantage that no man need shun association
with it for fear of having his mental deficiencies exposed.

Then follows one of the most winning of the characteristic short Brahmsian *Allegrettos*. It is often criticized as a
drop from the sublime altitudes of the other movements;
but that is precisely its reason for existence. After these intensities of struggle and bliss, and before the even whiter
intensities of the vast *finale,* frail human flesh absolutely
needs a breathing space for recuperation. Hence the short
Un poco Allegretto e grazioso. For me the high spot occurs
just before the Trio when the main theme re-enters above a

running string accompaniment characteristically fashioned out of four notes of this theme at double speed.

The *finale* is built on imposing lines. With its spacious *Adagio-Andante* introduction, it requires almost as many pages as the other three movements combined. These all prepare for it in a truer sense than the first three movements of the *Choral* prepare for that afterthought, the *Hymn to Joy,* which Beethoven wished to cancel and replace.

In the *Adagio,* with its ominous *pizzicato stringendos,* there are sombre distortions of the rejoicings to come, mingled with Doré-esque memories of the *Allegro's* battlefield. Stern confidence comes with the *Più Andante,* and a noble horn solo like the sound of bells from a venerable ivy-clad Cambridge tower,[6] heard against a shimmering background of string tremolos. This is interrupted by a faint adumbration of the trombone chorale which is to lift the heart and still the breath in the incredible final peroration. Again the horn solo. Then comes the main body of the *finale,* and one of the most satisfying, most heartening, most fundamentally joyful melodies that Brahms or anyone else ever conceived.

Ex. 51

[6] The C minor was finished a few months after Cambridge University had offered Brahms a doctor's degree. In the New York *Times* for Nov. 30, 1930, Mr. Olin Downes, discussing the resemblance of this horn call to the Cambridge chimes, suggests that Brahms may have brought it in deliberately as his subtle "Thank-you." But it should be remembered that, on Sept. 12th, 1868, Brahms sent this very tune to Clara on a birthday postcard from Switzerland, and labelled it: "To-day the Alpenhorn blew thus."

The prize commonplace, in talking of Brahms' music, is to point out the resemblance of the bracketed notes in Ex. 51 to two bars of Beethoven's Joy theme, and to cite the composer's famously impolite remark: "Every donkey hears that!" But, when one considers that, except for a general similarity in rhythm and tempo, all Beethovenship ceases, in the *finale*, with these two measures and their variants, one marvels that so much should be made of such a slight resemblance, and yet, on the other hand, that so little should be made of Brahms' rashness in bodily appropriating the opening tune of Mendelssohn's C minor trio *finale* for the *scherzo* of his F minor piano sonata (Op. 5).

In all music it would be hard to find a more sustained and infectious outburst of joy and triumph than this *finale*. And when, in the coda, after what might well be the exultant hoof-beats of the horses of the Apocalypse, that culminating choral shout of wild ecstasy is intoned by the brasses, the spacious firmament on high seems to open more sublimely than it did to John on Patmos. "Even pedestrian and earthbound imaginations," as Mr. Lawrence Gilman comments, will feel that some such event is taking place;

though this overwhelming peroration may remind them rather of the magnificent affirmation of Jean Paul: "There will come a time when it shall be light; and when man shall awaken from his lofty dreams, and find his dreams still there, and that nothing has gone save his sleep."

Hard upon these sublimities followed a sister symphony of a quite different order. The D major (Op. 73) is full of the sunshine, the sparkling air and water, and the spicy woods-smell of Pörtschach, where it was composed. And these friendly, tonic qualities come out all the more invigoratingly as set against the splendidly sombre background of the finest *Adagio* in the four sonatas for orchestra.

It has recently been the fashion for orchestral leaders to try to make the cheerful parts of the Second symphony tragic, and the tragic parts of the First, cheerful. In order to be different, some conductors would not hesitate to turn the *Invitation to the Dance* into an *Invitation to the Tomb*. But they can not for long enfeeble the bracing quality of the D major.

Its first movement is my chief specific against all sorts of harmful emotions. The moment I am aware of fear, anger, anxiety, sadness, or similar plagues, I know what to do.

THE MUSIC CURE

Often within my mind's front parlour door
I find a most unwelcome visitor.
It is Dame Worry in her best black mitts;
Her rakish bonnet, heaving pinafore,
And hunted eyes tell me the ancient bore
Is working up one of her famous fits.

I used to think I must, at any cost,
Smooth her hot brow and cut her creaking stays;
But if I ever did that I was lost!
A herd of buffalo stampeding fleetly,
Or prisoned panthers with the house ablaze,
Would not have wrecked my parlour more completely.

Now, when the dame appears, I coldly laugh,
And start, upon my mental phonograph,
Brahms Symphony D Major, Movement One.
When that begins she knows that she is done.
No longer, by effrontery or stealth,
Within my house will she enjoy poor health!

The horns and fiddles cause the dame to squirm.
The 'cellos make her wriggle like a worm.
When pearly light from flute and oboe pours
Over my mind, she scuttles out of doors.
There is not room enough within the same
Four walls for music, me, and that old dame.

Indeed, this blithe opening movement is splendidly adapted for such service on account of its simplicity, clarity of theme, transparence of orchestration, good cheer, infectious charm, and the ease with which its richness of detail can fill the mind and automatically expel unwelcome intruders.

The symphony is organically knit together by the simplest means. In going through Brahms' personal library in the Gesellschaft der Musikfreunde, and opening his well worn set of Haydn scores, I noticed that the first three notes of Haydn's First symphony were what the Master had chosen as a motto prefixed to the first subject of the D major,

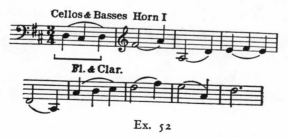

Ex. 52

and often recurring to bind the four movements thematically together.

Except for the famous F–A–F motto, these three notes constitute the sole Brahmsian germ-motive familiar to the musical public at large. We shall, however, find the same three, with one note added, playing a similar rôle as germ-motive of the following symphony.[7]

This *Allegro non troppo* owes much to the corresponding part of Beethoven's *Eroica* symphony. Their first subjects, as Sir George Grove long ago pointed out, move up and down on the notes of the tonic chord, in almost identical rhythms. But no one seems to have noticed that, in the D major, the skipping staccato clusters of an eighth with two sixteenths, ten bars after the *quasi ritenuto,* were plainly fathered by the Beethoven passage at measure 65, which connects the first and second subjects; or that the contour of Brahms' singing second subject

Ex. 53

bears a superficial resemblance to that of the *Episode* at measure 284 of the *Eroica,* which becomes closer the more it is studied.

Curiously enough, Ex. 53 also sounds like an expansion, with rhythmical alterations, of an orchestral phrase in *Siegfried,* Act I, Scene II, where Mime begins to question the Wanderer (Ex. 54).

[7] There the motto starts the *finale,* as here it starts the first movement. See p. 429, Ex. 56.

Ex. 54

Siegfried had made its *début* in 1876, the year before the D major was written. And Wagner, in turn, had derived his inspiration for the Mime motive from the start of the *scherzo* in Schubert's D minor string quartet.

The *Adagio non troppo* is the most profoundly brooding page in Brahms' work for orchestra. But it is also for us what the Master's capacious pocket was for the eager children who trooped behind him on his walks: each time we approach, it yields us, though brusquely and with apparent reluctance, some new surprise and pleasure. The opening 12-bar 'cello cantilena is one of the richest presents which the Master ever made to that instrument of his boyhood. It is miraculous how he contrived to keep the third measure, for example, from sounding like a finger-exercise, and to invest it, through a simple quarter-note figure in the trombones, with a profound glamour. Such feats are among the most positive evidences of genius.

In the *Allegretto grazioso* we might seem to have a young shepherd—so young that the piece overflows with the naïve wonder and crisp high spirits of childhood—piping the ideal pastoral melody on the oaten stop "that never was on sea or land," and twice whirling his dainty theme into dances that skip swiftly as a ball of spume in a gust, over a sparkling ocean floor. "This number has its encore in its pocket!" said one of Brahms' friends when he first saw the manuscript. And he was right. Note the debt owed by the dotted part of the first *Presto ma non assai* to the similarly dotted passage in the first movement of Beethoven's jolly Eighth symphony.

The opening of the brilliant *finale* seems slightly intellectualized; but in the second subject we have a true Brahms melody, magnetic and glowing with genial warmth. The coda provides this symphony of youth with a properly thrilling close.

Hans Richter once named the Third symphony (F major, Op. 90) "Brahms' *Eroica*," and numerous writers have echoed him. This name seems overdrawn. The opening melody and the *finale* are the only pages that could begin to justify such a thought. But even in them there is no warrant for dreams of dragon-spearing, of Horatian exploits at the bridge or Leonidan at Thermopylæ, of Gorgon slayings, Hundred Days, or chargings with the Light Brigade. Even the very instrumentation tells against such an idea. There is no brilliant "heroic" work for the brasses; and *bravura* passages are pointedly absent.

If this symphony must at all costs have a label, one of a thousand equally pertinent would be—"Portrait." The work might be taken as a portrait in tones of a healthy, strong, turbulent, tender, indomitable, kindly, aggressive, ironic, tempestuous, self-distrustful, incisive, concentrated, modest, fiery, rude, genial man—a person, in fact, just like the one who created it. Such a label would, of course, have the advantage of rhyming with the commentators' insistence that Brahms' personal motto F–A–F

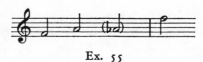

Ex. 55

is the one keystone that binds this symphonic structure together. Unfortunately for the theory, however, this motto,
while it plays a large rôle in the first movement, is touched
upon but incidentally by the *Andante;* is relegated to an obscure accompanying figure in the *Poco Allegretto;* and is
merely quoted by the coda of the *finale* in its reminiscence
of the first movement, in counterpoint, *nota bene,* with another figure, which seems to have escaped comment but
which plays somewhat more consistently the part of germ-
motive throughout the four movements.

To illustrate Brahms' incredibly unobtrusive command of
variety-in-unity, the chief subject matter of the symphony
will be given, with the germ-motive indicated by brackets.
This motive,[8] which is most emphatically used (in diminution) as the first three notes of the *finale,*

Ex. 56

is also to be found, with the variants common to such liaison
material: [9] in the first movement's opening theme, here reversed, and disguised by the abrupt change of octave between
B natural and C;

---

[8] Brahms also employed it as the basis for the *scherzo* of the F major 'cello sonata.
[9] For various examples of such disguises in the case of another germ-motive, see Ex. 6,
p. 303.

Ex. 57

at the end of the first subject, reversed;

Ex. 58

in the second subject, both reversed and normal;

Ex. 59

in the first and second themes of the *Andante,* inverted, normal, and again inverted;

Ex. 60

in the first three of the *Poco Allegretto;*

Ex. 61

and—most strikingly of all—in the second theme of the *finale* and, in the coda, functioning as bass to the F–A–F motto.

Ex. 62

This four-note figure is, of course, almost as universal a commonplace of all music as is the D major symphony's even simpler three-note motto, of which it is a slight prolongation. But in my opinion the four notes are no more accidental here than the three notes there. Each motto is used in its own symphony with much the same lavishness and with much the same unifying effect. Such short, simple germ-motives as these were characteristic of Brahms' style.[10]

[10] In *The Musical Quarterly* for April, 1933, the eminent music historian Dr. Guido Adler announces that the "motto" of the First symphony is C–C sharp–D; and that "in the Fourth symphony the second theme of the first movement may be regarded as the quasi-motto of the second and third movements." But, in my opinion, these patterns are not used sufficiently often to warrant calling them germ-motives.

This symphony does not stand, like the Second, under Beethoven's influence, but under Schumann's. Rhythmically its dashing, impetuous opening is a kinsman of the gallant melody which begins Schumann's *"Rhenish"* symphony (E flat), while melodically it comes straight from the *Larghetto* of that same master's B flat symphony (bar 70), Brahms' own copy of which bore the dedication from "Robert and Clara." Curiously enough, the start of the *Poco Allegretto* (Ex. 61) of Brahms' Third derives almost equally from the beginnings of the slow movements of Schumann's symphonies in B flat and D minor; while the *Frei aber Froh* germ-motive is to be found, as we have seen,[11] at the start of the older master's F major quartet.

The first movement did some bold pioneering in the domain of form. Its development section was pared down to the quick and much of the working out of themes transferred to the exposition. Note the witty frugality and ingenuity with which he made the long, lovely, and apparently well varied melody of the second subject (Ex. 59) out of a single measure's-worth presented time after time in slightly different ways. At each reappearance its identity is concealed by some adroit change in accent, time-value, or harmony. This is the king of all scissors-and-paste tunes. It is a neat exemplification of the two most fundamental principles in all art: economy of material, and variety in unity. The movement is brimfull of virility and the joy of life.

Charming, simple, and delicious though it is, the *Andante*, which opens like a hymn, in Brahms' favourite reedy colour —clarinets and bassoons—means less to me than any of his

11 See p. 302, n. 3.

other symphonic *Adagios.*

In its own class, I should assign a similar place to the *Poco Allegretto* which, despite the lavish use of the four-note germ-motive, seems to have but little in common spiritually with the rest of the symphony. Indeed, this very lavishness of thematic work was responsible for one of the chief defects of the little salon-piece—the lack of contrast between the opening theme and the middle portions (all shown in Ex. 61), due to an insufficient disguise of the germ-motive. The movement is scarcely worthy of its companions. Seven years later Brahms was to say the same thing better in the *Un poco Allegretto* of the *"Prater"* quintet (Op. 111).

The crown of the symphony—and one of the high-lights in all the Master's production—is the *finale,* which reminded Joachim of Leander swimming the Hellespont; to which Brahms noncommittally replied: "That lets itself be heard." The indomitable drive of its heroic first theme (Ex. 56) is thrown into vigorous relief by the soft chorale of the trombones (Ex. 62), and by the sweeping second subject where the horn brings back a reminiscence of the chimes that rang in the introduction to the C minor symphony's *finale.* The ethereal coda, where the chorale and the two germ-motives reach their apotheosis, is one of the supreme pages in all music. "Consider the end of the last movement," writes that poet among music-critics, Mr. Lawrence Gilman,

with its heart-easing, sunset peace and its murmuring quietude: where in all symphonic literature is there a nobler dying of sunset fires, a lovelier evocation of the peace of evening, than in that brooding, irradiated descent of the tremulous strings through the F major hush of the sustaining horns and

wood and trumpets that brings the great work to a close?
. . . Nowhere else in his symphonies has he spoken quite as he
has [here]. That slow subsidence at the end into a golden twilight peacefulness, mystically contemplative and serene, is the
achievement of a mood that he never quite recaptured, and it
is among the indescribable things of music.

The Fourth symphony, in E minor (Op. 98), is Brahms'
most virile work for orchestra. Its themes have little of the
colour or the ingratiating lusciousness found so often in the
other three. At a first or second hearing they may seem a bit
noncommittal. But, in the long run, how they unbend! Then
their very initial reticence becomes an added allurement.
Except possibly in the *scherzo,* one finds here none of that
dangerous tendency toward the oversweet which, if anything
can, may prematurely threaten the lives of the first three.

A generation ago the E minor used to be generally considered drearily philosophical and murkily elegiac. Today,
although the myth of Brahms' tragically sad heart has been
fostered by most of his biographers, the accustomed modern
ear, with the best will in the world, can find in this symphony
little or nothing of such stuff as tears are made on. The more
we hear it the better it wears; and the better it wears the
more cheerful and heartening it sounds. The first movement
is music fit for the musings of a strong man who, "afoot and
light-hearted," takes to the open road with a salt breeze in
his nostrils, and several four-pound trout waiting at the end
of the woods-trail. To my ear, the second subject, introduced
by its flourish of horns, often has a positively jubilant sound.
And how that marvellous development, with its inexhaustible

FRONT VIEW OF THE HOUSE IN MÜRZZUSCHLAG WHERE BRAHMS WROTE THE FOURTH SYMPHONY

Taken specially for this book

treasures for mind and spirit, fills one with increasing wonder and exhilaration at each new hearing!

One of the most fanatical anti-Brahmins and adorers of Bruckner, whom I met in Vienna, admitted to me that Brahms had one strong point: the characteristic use he made in his harmony of the old Greek and ecclesiastical modes. Here in the *Andante moderato* he secured a mysteriously romantic and exotic flavour by resorting to the Phrygian mode.[12] This is one of the Master's great slow movements.

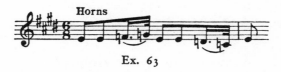

Ex. 63

The second subject, a sustained and particularly grateful 'cello melody, for which every true 'cellist must offer thanks, is wittily ushered in by a staccato abridgement of itself at thrice the speed, shuttlecocked back and forth between strings and wind.

The *Allegro giocoso,* the only movement of its kind in the four symphonies, is, next to those in the piano quintet and in the B flat concerto, the most successful of Brahms' true *scherzos.* The peasant side of the Master is here in full force, with its hearty naïveté, rustic roughness, and rude vitality. Mark how (just before C in the score) the middle voices keep suggesting the opening subject of the first movement.

The *finale* is a loose *passacaglia* on a theme borrowed from J. S. Bach's *Cantata No. 150:*

[12] Whose scale is: E–F–G–A–B–C–D–E.

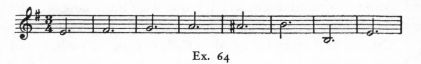

Ex. 64

On this, with the most masterful ingenuity of his brain and all the resources of his great heart, Brahms built up thirty-two eight-measure variations unique in all symphonic literature for their form and their appeal, with a coda not so strict in form, consisting of six more variations.

The privileged Elisabet von Herzogenberg, who was the first to see any part of this symphony, wrote to the Master:

As for the last movement, shall you mind if I proclaim it my favourite—at least, for the time being? I am fascinated by the theme itself, and the fascination grows as I follow it through its different phases, first in the bass, then in the top part or skilfully hidden somewhere in the middle, and—most impressive of all, surely, for susceptible listeners—in its trombone effort in the golden key of E major! How splendid it must sound—lucky trombone players! You asked, the other day, whether I should have the "patience to sit through" the last movement. I can only say I should not mind if it were three times as long. Surely it must go down with an audience, too, even if they neither understand nor are able to follow the *passacaglia* form; for there is no laborious weaving of threads, but a succession of novel combinations, all imbued with a vigour that must have an arresting, overpowering effect. And one need not be a musician, thank Heaven! to come under its spell.

I agree with Frau Elisabet that the most impressive part of all is the golden double variation (16 and 17) for trombones.[13] But this is without prejudice to the wistful flute solo (No. 14), and the Gothic sweep and noble intensity of the coda. Such a *finale* is an achievement which the father of music himself might well have been proud to sign.

Near the end of his life Brahms stated the belief that no modern composer could give the best he had to his symphonies and write more than four. And undeniably he threw more subtle artistry, intricate craftsmanship, wealth of original ideas, and emotional force into each of these works than a light-hearted early symphonist, like Dittersdorf or Boccherini, did into his entire output.

CONCERTOS

Brahms wrote four concertos: two for piano, one for violin, and a double one for violin and 'cello.

The First piano concerto (D minor, Op. 15) took six years to finish, gave him a more anguished struggle than even the F minor quintet, and underwent a somewhat similar metamorphosis. He had already sketched it as a symphony when, in March, 1854, he was so overcome by a first hearing of Beethoven's Ninth (in the same key of D minor) that he recast the composition as a sonata for two pianos. Finally, realizing that it was essentially orchestral, he combined these two versions into a piano concerto. A slow *scherzo* written for this work was discarded, to appear later in the second

---

[13] Note its curious rhythmic and melodic resemblance to the popular Italian song, *Santa Lucia*. For example, the fifth and sixth measures of both become identical in tune and rhythm when those of *Santa Lucia* are transposed a fourth higher. This likeness is possibly an unconscious souvenir of Brahms' frequent trips to Italy.

section of the *Requiem*.

The rugged and militant first movement was finished under the dire impression produced on him by Schumann's attempted suicide and subsequent confinement in an insane asylum. The passionate first subject was made ineffective by the young composer's lack of experience in orchestration and his too austere endeavours to keep the piano to a modest rôle and allow no virtuoso foolishness. But even the anti-Brahmins must admit the magic of the *Poco più moderato* theme

Ex. 65

which, in its rich, dusky hue and its emotional appeal, reminds one of the third *finale* theme [14] in the F minor piano sonata.

Throughout this concerto there is a striking disparity between Brahms' skilful writing for his own specialty, the piano, and his clumsy treatment of the other instruments; although this clumsiness grows progressively less noticeable, as if, measure by measure, the youngster were gaining valuable experience.

The serene opening of the simply constructed *Adagio*, a grateful relief to these agonizing struggles, bears a distant resemblance to the *Larghetto* from Bach's concerto for two violins. Brahms admitted that in these pages he had tried to paint a portrait of Clara. And indeed, the motto prefixed to it in the manuscript score, *"Benedictus qui venit in nomine Domini"* (Blessed, who cometh in the name of the Lord),

[14] Ex. 28, p. 360.

was a plainer hint of his state of mind when composing than Brahms usually accorded the world; for did not Clara Schumann bear his name whom Johannes adoringly called *"Domine"*? The youth worked on this movement during the height of his passion for her.

The Rondo begins with a slight suggestion of Hungary— a bounding D minor *arpeggio* theme over a lively bass. The movement is easier to grasp and more popular than the others; but one feels that its genesis was rather the necessity for producing a *finale* than a true inner urge. It has various passages of lagging interest which make the First concerto— though actually thirty-two pages shorter than the Second— seem longer. In his maturity, Brahms should have taken his blue pencil and done for this youthful work what he did so successfully for the B major trio, opus 8.

The piano concerto in B flat (Op. 83) was begun in 1878, immediately after his first Italian journey, and shares the sunlit mellowness that spread itself over one of the happiest creative periods of the Master's life—the three summers he spent at Pörtschach, where he wrote such radiant companion works as the violin concerto and the D major symphony.

In spite of the somewhat too sweet quality of its *Andante*, which now and again threatens to cloy even sympathetic ears, the B flat is my favourite among all piano concertos. The exhibitionistic feature of music in this form is usually a liability. But this concerto is at heart a symphony. Its piano obbligato is discreet. There is almost nothing in it to mar one's pleasure.

The first movement is the finest. It opens with an unforgettable horn theme,

Ex. 66

each phrase canorously echoed by triplets which seem spontaneously evoked from a living piano. In these pages the solo instrument, despite its limitations, has no need to apologize for its intrusion into the orchestra. It sounds almost better than it knows how. One is constantly surprised by its colour, its wealth of tone, and its happy power of combination with different instruments. To secure these surprising results Brahms had to invent a piano technic so novel that it seems to have descended, not from Mozart, Beethoven, Schumann, Chopin and Liszt, but out of the blue.

The second subject, which finds trouble in settling down to any particular key, has just the mysterious quality to offset Ex. 66 most effectively. And the coda, by a stroke of genius, treats the familiar end of the first subject in such a way that we there seem to appreciate it for the first time.

Brahms told Billroth that he had introduced the *scherzo* (which Kalbeck surmises to have been a discard from the violin concerto) "because the first movement is too simple." This is a commentary on the Master's inability to put his ear to the ground. For, to the man in the musical street, the *Allegro non troppo* is a thing of the subtlest complication, while the *scherzo* is comparatively simple. The hearer revels in the fiery opening section, the winsome *tranquillo e dolce;*

and the infectious rustic dance of the Trio, through which he seems to catch the gay clamour of festival chimes.

Out of the long 'cello obbligato on which the *Andante* is almost entirely founded, Brahms afterwards made a more successful composition—the favourite song *Immer leiser wird mein Schlummer*. But the *Più Adagio* portion has a citation from a song already composed, *Todessehnen* (Op. 86, No. 6). Rhythmically this obbligato is an apt example of the mischievous Master's fondness for appealing differently to the ear and to the eye; for though written in 6/4 time, it is made to sound like 3/2. The best part of the movement lies between the piano's first entrance and the solo 'cello's reappearance.

The *Allegretto grazioso*, like the *finale* of the D minor concerto, is in loose rondo form, but its naïve, piquant, and joyous dances, with their faint gypsy flavour, are far more comprehensible and attractive, both to layman and to connoisseur.[15]

The violin concerto (D major, Op. 77) stands with Beethoven's in the same key, at the head of its class. It is clear, simple, cut on a large pattern, filled with warm human emotion and other qualities that make for greatness. Brahms dedicated it to Joachim and asked for his criticism. But in taking this, his spirit of contrariety was his guide. It was remarkable, as Andreas Moser, the biographer of Joachim, observed, "how easily accessible Brahms was to Joachim's counsels about composition, and what a deaf ear he turned to the other's hints on technic." The result was a mass of

[15] Here Mr. Philip Barr noted on the margin of my manuscript: "I consider this *finale* Brahms' most perfectly constructed movement, in the sense of the marvellous appropriateness with which each bit is followed by what comes next."

novel difficulties, which daunted the ablest violinists of the day. Even Joachim, the king of these, at first declared the concerto unplayable. And it took many years to win its present place high in the repertory of every virtuoso. An added stumbling-block to interpretation lies in the fact that the heroic technical difficulties find no answering heroic atmosphere in the music, which is in the main happily idyllic; so that these difficulties must, in performance, be made to sound as easy as child's play. Here any smell of the practice lamp is a double abomination.

The opening theme of the first movement is own brother to the start of the D major symphony (see Ex. 52, p. 425); and both are the pacifist children of the *Eroica's* opening. This melody, the entire *Adagio,* and the second subsidiary theme of the rollicking rondo *finale,* are all true products of the Pörtschach sunshine. So is the second subject of the first *Allegro.*

Ex. 67

Brahms' economy in omitting this gracefully modelled tune from the orchestral introduction, and letting the solo violin first introduce it near the middle of the movement, secured one of his happiest effects.

Max Bruch once told my friend, Mr. Arthur M. Abell,

that the first theme of the *Adagio* is based on a forgotten Bohemian folk-song.

Ex. 68

This tender, childlike melody is appropriately announced by the oboe, with a wood-wind accompaniment so delicious in tone-quality that it escapes oversweetness only by a miracle. Remarkably enough, the solo violin never plays more than the first three notes of this tune, but accompanies it in descending octaves or opposes it with florid counterpoint.

The difficult rondo is full of a somewhat rough, impetuous jocosity and—perhaps in greeting to Joachim—has a distinct Hungarian quality. Its three simple themes are exploited with an erudition whose depth is equalled only by its light-fingered concealment of erudition. See, for example, how the second theme is accompanied by its own inversion.

This concerto, so highly unified, so intensely Brahmsian, is very slightly marred by the incongruity of two brief passages which suddenly remind one of Italian opera, and of the fact that the composer had but recently returned from that dream of a lifetime—his first trip to Italy. One of these, in the first subject of the *Allegro non troppo,*

Ex. 69

calls up echoes of the popular baritone aria, *Il balen del suo sorriso,* from Act II of *Il Trovatore.* The other, in the *Allegro giocoso,* eight bars before letter C, reminds one of the sort of choral *stretti* to be found *passim* in the lower forms of Italian opera; and this resemblance is underlined by the cheaply dramatic tremolo accompaniment. In view of the movement's *giocoso* label it is not unlikely that the witty Master was deliberately indulging here in a bit of burlesque; for he was not at all blind to the more ridiculous aspects of the Italian musical stage; and once, on returning north, told with glee of having heard an opera "which wholly consisted of final cadences." Perhaps he was thinking back with a rueful smile to that sin of his own youth, the atrocious operatic cadence in the *Andante* of the G minor piano quartet.

The Double concerto for violin, 'cello, and orchestra (A minor, Op. 102) has, until our own day, been usually shunned with discretion by fiddlers who, even if they could manage to surmount its grisly difficulties, would reap but little reward in the way of personal acclaim. None but the supreme virtuoso is fit to interpret it. But to have heard Casals' and Kreisler's reading is a memorable experience.

This work represents the most successful modern development of the ancient *concerto grosso,* in which groups of soloists were opposed to the orchestra. It strikes the modern listener with a novel, but not at first with a wholly pleasing, effect. The ear must accustom itself by degrees to the exotic blend of chamber with orchestral music. Considering the organic incorporation of the soloists in the whole, the suppression of *bravura* in their parts, and—particularly in the *finale*—the truly symphonic wealth of thematic material, one might call this work, even more fittingly than the B flat concerto, a symphony with (double) obbligato.

Both the first and the second subjects of the opening *Allegro* contain allusions, by way of subtle tribute, to the A minor violin concerto of Viotti, the father of modern violin-playing, whom, as we have seen,[16] Brahms pedestalled absurdly high above himself. In 1867 Joachim had written him in connexion with plans for their concert at Vienna: "I will commence with *your* Viotti concerto."

One is struck at a first hearing by the almost complete absence of those luscious, tender purple passages of cantilena which are the most immediately popular features of Brahms' music. But on long and intimate acquaintance, the listener is recompensed for this lack by the unexpected way in which he grows progressively enamoured of such unobtrusive themes as the *Allegro's* second subject, the happy leading idea of the *Andante,* and the both ladder-like and hymn-like second theme of the *Vivace non troppo,* with its faint resemblance to the Trio of the F minor quintet's great *scherzo.*[17] The unsuccessfully repressed high spirits of this rich movement, which seems vivacious in spite of its moodiest resolutions, is highly characteristic of the Master—so shyly reserved, so suspicious and caustic, yet so bursting with the exuberance of rude health, and so exhilarated by his own rare mental and spiritual resources.

The more I hear the Double concerto the more I delight in it. Like the E minor symphony and the *Four Serious Songs,*

---

[16] See p. 241.

[17] The resemblance, both in its melody and in its characteristic treatment of the thirds, fourths, and sixths, is closer to the first of Jean Louis Duport's epoch-making 21 *Exercises* for 'cello, which Johannes may have practised as a boy.

it needs generous amounts of hearing. One of the radio's best services to music has recently been to multiply performances of this rarely heard composition. It increases one's pleasure in these durable pages to recall that, by writing them, Brahms won back the estranged Joachim, the inestimable friend of his youth.

OVERTURES

With two overtures: the *Academic Festival* (Op. 80), and the *Tragic* (Op. 81), the tale of the orchestral works is complete. They are complementary: the centre of levity and the centre of gravity; the Janus with one laughing and one weeping face.

The *Tragic* overture might well be named *"Prologue to Any Tragedy."* Kalbeck [18] thought that it was composed in consequence of an invitation from Dingelstedt, impresario of the Viennese Burgtheater, to write incidental music for Goethe's *Faust*. The complete plan eventually miscarried because Dingelstedt offended the composer by treating him too cavalierly. Opus 81 is an unobtrusive work that creates a sombre suspense and refrains from attracting any attention vivid enough to betray its attendant drama into anticlimax. When he composed it, Brahms must already have learned that lesson in dramatic proportion which Beethoven had mastered only through writing *Leonore Nos. 2* and *3*—and then realizing that these were too overpowering to serve as proper overtures for *Fidelio*. Though merely an unpretentious and self-effacing bridge to tragic illusion, this overture

[18] III, 1, 256 ff.

sounds better and means more to me at each successive hearing. It has a decorous reserve which would qualify it for the title *"Academic"* more appropriately than its uproarious twin.

We have already seen [19] how the *Academic Festival* overture was bred of Brahms' contrarious and Puckish spirit. It must have profoundly shocked the good dignitaries of Breslau University when he, whom their diploma had named *"princeps artis musicæ severioris"* (foremost exponent of musical art in the severer style), presented as his learned doctor's dissertation this bubbling *mélange* of student songs, including even the unworthy *Fuchslied*, burschikosly set for two staccato bassoons. But the overture is far more than the "Suppé *pot-pourri*" which he once modestly called it. Much of the material is original, invented with consummate skill to blend, and blend with, the student songs. This masterpiece of instrumentation calls for a larger, more sumptuous orchestra than Brahms employed elsewhere. The tone colours are clear and brilliant, the inspiration gaily spontaneous; and the closing version of *Gaudeamus igitur,* for the full might of wind and percussion, supported by a lively contrapuntal bass, and raked fore and aft by mad fiddle scales, furnishes one of the most vigorous electric spinal massages in the orchestral repertory.

[19] On p. 147 f.

BRAHMS TO-DAY

BRAHMS TO-DAY

As LATE as Brahms' death, in 1897, advanced musical thinkers were still trying to persuade a cautious public that this composer belonged among the immortals.

The demand for his music, slow in starting, had not yet grown brisk. Simrock the publisher confessed that he had "made Bohm pay for Brahms." The latter's position at the turn of the century was graphically shown by the new building of the Carnegie Institute in Pittsburgh. High on its walls the names of the world's composers were carved; but Meyerbeer jostled Brahms in an obscure corner.

Those were the days when Boston, then the most musical city in America, approvingly echoed Philip Hale's *mauvais mot*: "Exit in case of Brahms!" And the concert management actually announced that a pause would occur before the Brahms number in order to allow hostile listeners to leave; thus anticipating Mr. Stokowski who to-day warns the conservatives to escape from the hall before some especially modern composition is played.

Finck in New York, Runciman in London, and Romain Rolland in Paris saw eye to eye with Boston's anti-Brahmin, and were fully as influential as he. The old-fashioned partisan feeling still ran high. It was felt that one must swear allegiance to either Wagner or Brahms, but could not care for both. It was not done!

The public looked upon the latter as a simon-pure classicist, and concluded that he must therefore be cold and formal.

People felt that he had "no melody," that he was dry, abstruse, philosophical, and that if the music was occasionally tinged with emotion, it was sorrowful, bitter, pessimistic emotion: in a word, that Brahms was the sad grey singer of an empty day.

Since then, in only a third of a century, this attitude has undergone a radical change. Though Brahms has now fewer imitators among composers than at his death, he has swiftly multiplied his passionate adherents among interpreters and music-lovers.

To-day such witticisms as Mr. Hale's fall flat. Political partisanship has almost wholly gone out of fashion, and the ordinary music-lover's heart has widened until it can give equal and catholic welcome to Bayreuth, Vienna, and any other source of the best music. Symphonic audiences demand Brahms with almost exactly the same eagerness which they show for those perennial headliners, Wagner and Beethoven; and in chamber music Johannes and Ludwig lead the van together.

Perhaps owing to the fact that the human ear is generally attuned to the melody of the preceding generation, the world has awakened to the striking fact that Brahms—once the supposedly "tuneless" composer—is brimfull of the most delicious melody.

With equal surprise it has discovered in the works of this supposedly dry-as-dust classicist, as it has in those of Bach, strongly romantic pages of emotional power elemental enough to stand comparison with the climaxes of *Tristan*. The vivid romanticism in this sturdy classicist is daily coming to be more and more fully savoured. Indeed, the most dangerous threat against the longevity of Brahms' music seems now to be, not that we consider it grey, dry, and pedantic, but that we fear the perishability of certain pages here and there which we have come to regard as erring on the side of oversweetness. It is the Twentieth Century's achievement to discover in Brahms that potent combination of classicist with romanticist—that fine balance between shaping intellect and enriching emotion—which is characteristic of the highest in art. And such a critic as Dr. Mason can today declare that "in all the elements of music he shows himself a *central* person."

Brahms' progress, though it has suffered various temporary setbacks, like the present one in central Europe, has on the whole been brilliantly victorious. Of course the victory has not been complete. No composer's ever is. But the large number of young Brahmins today is highly significant of contemporary trends.

Not long ago, Mr. Ernest Newman wrote in the London *Times:*

There is a queer sort of latter-day mind about that affects to believe that none but old fogies like Brahms. . . . If they would just look around them, they would see that the world is not divided neatly into old fools who swear, say, by Brahms, and young Solons who swear, say, by Milhaud. There are any number of young people who think Brahms a composer of genius and Milhaud only a cross between a talent and a *gamin.*

This latter class is rapidly growing—though more rapidly in English-speaking lands than elsewhere. It is a curious fact that Vienna, for example, the supposed headquarters of the Brahms cult, has never heard all twenty-four of his chamber music works in a single series; whereas New York has twice recently heard them thus, and Philadelphia once.

To-day Brahms sits secure in the seats of the mighty, recognized as one of the pre-eminent masters of form and of rhythm since Bach—if not the most pre-eminent. But the tremendous popularity of his symphonies (alas, too few!), which are already being overplayed by phonograph, radio, and concert, suggests that at this rate there may soon be a possible danger of their Tschaikowskian descent into the too familiar "Pop"-concert division of the repertory. Now, it may or may not be true that every man has his price; but it is certain that every musical composition has its point of diminishing returns. Heard beyond a certain frequency, even the best Bach begins to pall. If anything can avert this fate from the Brahms symphonies, I think it will be the inexhaustible richness of their intellectual resources—rhythmic, harmonic, architectural, and contrapuntal—and the profound interest of their thematic development.

Some of the chamber music, as well, is now being heard almost too often for its own good; while lighter pieces like certain of the *Hungarian Dances,* the *Waltzes,* opus 39, and the *Wiegenlied* have received the mass accolade of the accordion and the hurdy-gurdy, and have even suffered on the distorting racks of jazzdom.

Brahms is no longer hooted as a "high-brow." He has come to be one of the most beloved of all the classic masters. Even the hostility of French music-lovers, so long irreconcilable, has gradually begun to relent.

With the growing appreciation and understanding of Brahms' music has come a change of feeling about its general emotional quality. At the turn of the century it was considered by the large majority to be inherently mournful stuff,

sicklied o'er with the pale cast of thought.

This idea arose partly through the accidentally wide dissemination of Nietzsche's venomous catchwords about "the musician of the unsatisfied," who was supposedly bowed down by "the melancholy of impotence"; [1] partly because music which people are slow to understand seldom sounds cheerful until it is fully grasped; and partly because profundity of feeling in art is often superficially mistaken for sadness.

The earlier critics labelled Brahms' work in the main "sorrowful," and most of the later critics automatically echoed the dictum. Thus Herr Niemann—the writer whom we have already found singling out precisely the most vulgar passages of *Rinaldo* for special praise, and who, conversely, speaks of the "conscious pathos" and "unconvincing tragedy" of the C minor symphony—defines Brahms as the "melancholy exponent of . . . sorrow and *Weltschmerz*," and categorically insists that his music "contains no gospel of joy." [2]

Recently, however, music-lovers have begun to suspect that the supposed sombreness of the Brahmsian canvas was due largely to the dust of inherited prejudice. They have begun to wipe that dust away, and find underneath it an unsuspectedly brilliant and cheerful gamut of colours.

The E minor symphony, for instance,[3] though no longer felt to be forbiddingly metaphysical, has until recently been

[1] See p. 277.
[2] See Am. edition, pp. 212, 263, 439, and 442.
[3] As has already been pointed out on p. 434.

used as a stock exemplar of Brahms' "sorrow and *Welt-schmerz*." But Mr. Lawrence Gilman now points out [4] that a good deal too much has been made of its presumably tragic content.

Its autumnal hue is not pervasive. . . . There is small warrant for distorting the frequent gravity and soberly compassionate melancholy of Brahms the tone-poet into a fundamental depression; and to exhibit the Fourth symphony as an exercise in pessimism is to show it in a misleading light. Dejection is hardly its fundamental note. Much of the first movement sounds (in Reimann's phrase) "ballad-like"—in the bardic, old-world sense. Those "cries of pain" which Reimann heard in it are not very piercing to modern ears. In the beautiful *Andante,* with its haunting coda, there seems to be no emotion more tragic than a dark-hued romantic melancholy. The *scherzo,* with its boisterous vigour and its contrasting vein of delicately sportive humour and lyric tenderness, is of course anything but sombre; and the Gothic sweep and amplitude and soaring splendour of the great *finale* seems, despite its passionate earnestness and its occasional solemnity, infinitely remote from the mood of Sophoclean tragedy.

Such an utterance by one of the leading critics of our day is significant. We are beginning to dare to judge Brahms in all his aspects with our own eyes and ears, and not solely with those of tradition. And as we do so we discover that his music is filled with a refreshing abundance of sheer happiness. Many passages, like the *Allegretto* of the F major symphony and the *Intermezzo* of the G minor piano quartet, which used to seem downright sorrowful, are now considered more like sweetly pensive vignettes of some momentarily sighing

[4] In his program notes for the New York Philharmonic-Symphony Orchestra.

Ariel or regretful Undine.

Ridding ourselves of prepossessions, and approaching Brahms' more important works unbiased, we are surprised to find how essentially happy most of them are. In the symphonies there is almost no tragedy, or even authentic sorrow; for Mr. Gilman is right in feeling that the *Andante* of the Fourth does not overstep "a dark-hued, romantic melancholy." We find that pain has well-nigh vanished from the superb *Adagio* of the Second; and the opening movement of the First—like those of the D minor concerto, and of the string quartet and trio in C minor—is cast in a nobly profound mood of struggle rather than of grief. Likewise one can now find no sorrow in the four concertos. And even the *Tragic* overture does not forestall the pain and trouble of the imaginary drama to which it might serve as prelude.

There is relatively little darkness in the large body of the chamber music. I find melancholy in the first movement of the D minor sonata for violin; a little in the sonata in G, and in the variations and *scherzo* of the C major trio. There is sorrow in the *Adagio mesto* of the horn trio, at *f espressivo* in the *Poco Adagio* of the A major piano quartet, in the coda of the G minor piano quartet's *Allegro,* in the slow movements of the viola quintets and the first of the clarinet trio, and in the openings of the C minor piano quartet and F minor quintet. There is much, too, in the C minor string quartet, but little in the clarinet quintet, where resignation was silvered by the consciousness of how sweetly an old man could still sing. And there is less in the G major sextet, even though in writing it the composer was bidding farewell to his sweetheart, Agathe.

In the piano music pain is felt principally in the *Rück-blick* of the F minor sonata, the *Edward* ballade, parts of the four-hand *Schumann Variations* (Op. 23), the *Handel Variations* Nos. 6, 9, 13, and 20, the first two rhapsodies, and the truly tragic E flat minor *Intermezzo,* opus 118, No. 6.

In the vocal works there is more of dark emotion than in the instrumental, perhaps because *Il Penseroso* moods are apt to offer musicians more attractive texts for setting than those of *L'Allegro.* But even so, we have seen in a previous chapter that the great *Lieder* of happy love outnumber those of unhappy love. Among the Brahms songs which appeal to me as supreme, joy speaks more often than sadness. It is highly significant that even the Master's final message in the *Four Serious Songs* culminates in a thrilling outburst of faith and hope.

We have also noted that the larger choral works are remarkable for the optimistic endings which he imposed on such classically tragic texts as the *Schicksalslied, Nänie,* and the *Gesang der Parzen.* The *Rhapsody* for alto, the most tragically poignant of these works, ends in a strain of major consolation still more compelling. Even *A German Requiem,* whose subject is death and dissolution, leaves with us a predominant impression, not so much of grief, as of zest in beauty and the joy of life.

If we examine all of Brahms' music we shall find that the darker pieces, which range from melancholy through sorrow to tragic despair, are decidedly outnumbered by those which range from neutral moods, through such gaiety as that of the *Liebeslieder* and the *Gypsy Songs,* to happiness and triumphant joy.

These brighter pages are so numerous that one can scarcely do more than name a few typical movements. In the symphonies there are notably the *finale* of the First, all but the *Adagio* of the Second, the first of the Third, and the second of the Fourth. The violin and B flat concertos are brimfull of sunshine. The *Academic Festival* overture lives up to its festive name with gusto.

In the chamber music, consider the radiant opening of the B major trio, nearly the whole of the B flat sextet, the jolly *finale* of the horn trio, the *Andante* and *Rondo alla Zingarese* of the G minor piano quartet, and the fast movements of its twin in A. Think of most of the B flat string quartet, all of the A major violin sonata, the middle movements of the piano quintet, and the outside ones of the *"Prater"* quintet. And with these we have merely begun to mention the wealth of happiness to be found in this composer's pages. All told, what other man's music sparkles more exhilaratingly than his with the joy of physical, mental, and spiritual exuberance?

Taking into account the positive quality of his compositions as a whole, the reader of the recent literature on Brahms will naturally ask himself how so much exultant music could have been written by one whom his biographers have depicted as a profoundly sorrowful creature. But the fact is that in correcting the traditional estimate of the emotional balance of the music, we must do likewise for the composer. The current, widespread idea that Brahms was a predominantly sad person is as far from the mark as the notion that his music is predominantly sad.

It is true that Kalbeck, who knew him longer and was in

closer contact with him than any others who have written his life, drew him as a person rather more cheerful than melancholy. But most of the later biographers have deleted the sunlight and laid on the shadow, "black on black," with heavy hands. Some of these writers may—all unconsciously— have been influenced by the fact that tragedy makes a far more effective story than happiness; and the best way to make your hero interesting is to make him sad.

In citing certain impulsive remarks of the Master's they fail to recognize that these were merely ephemeral expressions of swiftly passing moods and thus provide no fit basis for general characterization. One such was Brahms' remark to Rudolph von der Leyen that he never "laughed internally"; for the composer could feel with such concentrated intensity and sensitivity that the illusion of permanence and universality which he received from some swiftly transient emotional crisis of his often temporarily deceived him into rash generalization of the particular.

Another such remark was his quotation to Joachim from that ancient pessimist who declared that the best which can happen to a man "is never to be born."

A striking instance of the swift passing of such black moods is given by Ophüls.[5] After attending the funeral of Clara Schumann, Brahms spent the night at a large estate on the Rhine. That evening he was visibly overcome by grief. He tried to take part in playing his C minor trio but had to stop after a score of measures. As the circle of friends sat about endeavouring to give the forced conversation a natural turn, Brahms got abruptly to his feet, exclaimed in trem-

---

[5] *Erinnerungen an Johannes Brahms,* 1921, p. 11 ff.

bling tones: "Ah, well, all is vanity in this world! . . . Good-night, *meine Herrschaften!*"—and went to his room. The party broke up with gloomy fears for the emotional atmosphere of the morrow.

"But," wrote Ophüls, "we had not reckoned with Brahms' robust nature." Early the next morning Barth and Ophüls found the Master walking in the park.

He was no longer the innerly torn, *Weltschmerz*-bowed person of the previous evening, but a strong man well-nigh overflowing with the joy of life. He simply could not express the full extent of his delight in the sunny morning, the wonderful park, and the hospitality which he was permitted to enjoy. . . . So we saw that he had overcome his sorrow and pain, and clearly was again in the very best of moods.

Instances like this might be multiplied. They show how little reliance, in trying to prove that he was a man of sorrows, should be placed on the significance of Brahms' impulsive utterances.

Herr Ernest's contention that the Master's whole life was tragically darkened by his supposed longing to possess Clara Schumann as a wife is scarcely borne out by the impatient expressions about her which are scattered through his correspondence with other friends, or by Johannes' disloyal words to Agathe von Siebold in 1858, about Clara's jealousy,[6] or by the entry in Laura von Beckerath's *Journal* for Sept. 10, 1883: "After telling about all sorts of difficulties which he had with Frau Clara Schumann, Brahms ended: 'So I thought to myself, you must give up associating with women.' "

Other biographers have argued that his life was made

6 See p. 266.

wretched, not by his longing for any wife in particular, but
simply by bachelorhood. But their assumption of his deeply
tragic attitude towards the single state is difficult to reconcile
with his emphatic declaration to Frau Simrock that, even if
he should ever take a wife, he would run away from her on
the third day,[7] and with his many other caustic remarks about
matrimony.

In depicting the Master's supposed unhappiness, a great
deal is made by Specht of the fact that he died weeping. But
surely there could be no more appropriate place for anyone's
tears than his own deathbed—particularly the deathbed of a
man who had so long been head over heels in love with life
as Brahms.

Indeed, life was good to him. He enjoyed such robust
health and endurance as almost everybody might well covet.
After his adventurous youth he had few money troubles. His
beloved parents both lived to old age. He possessed a large,
stimulating, appreciative, and utterly devoted circle of true
friends. He took enormous zest in eating, drinking, reading,
walking, in travelling, in the love of Nature and of children,
and in making poor people happy with his open purse. He
revelled in his manuscripts and prints. He austerely enjoyed
his fame. As for his work—the reader will remember his
modestly admitting to Henschel what "a great joy" it was to
him when he really succeeded in the shaping of some movement.[8] Indeed, in his creative life alone, the composer of the
D major symphony must have tasted more concentrated happiness than falls to the average man from all sources during

[7] See p. 280.
[8] See p. 175 f.

This cheerful unpublished picture of Brahms in the 90's has a curiously
Slavonic look. It was discovered by a house-wrecker in 1930, hanging in
the Havemeyer mansion at 65th Street and 5th Avenue, New York City.
On the back was written: "Portrait of Johann Brahms. Unique copy.
Taken for me and given me by William von Sachs in Brahms' summer
home in the garden.

I prize it very highly. Do not destroy— Give it to some Musical Society.
Louise W. Havemeyer"

The wrecker, Mr. Albert A. Volk, passed it on to the University Settlement, with the following comment: "The only picture abandoned in the
entire place was this one upon which she had made this special personal
request, something which she had probably done with no other possession.
It might be that her spirit, hovering over the ruins of her beloved home
and observing the neglect of her cherished wish, acted through the medium
of a humble house-wrecker to carry out her design."

Soon after receiving it, the University Settlement kindly offered it for
reproduction in this book.

his whole life. Though he had abundant grounds for being sorrowful, Brahms had far more for being glad. And he was. Florence May bears witness that he "had learned from early youth to find happiness in the realities of life. . . . The cultivation of happiness he viewed not only as a part of wisdom, but as a duty." [9]

Joachim depicted Johannes at twenty-one as "a radiant, blissfully happy young man." [10] And Frau Bertha Flegmann, who knew him for many years at the other end of his career, told me most emphatically: *"Brahms was the happiest man I ever knew in all my life!"* She said this in Ischl at the table of the Otto Julius Bauers; and both our host and hostess expressed their concurrence. Many of the Master's other friends have given me similar testimony.

The Miller-Aichholz diary bears witness that Brahms, in most of his numerous meetings with this family, was cheerful and happy. *"Brahms war lieb und lustig* [Brahms was amiable and jolly]" is a very frequent entry.

It seems to me that, even with far less to be thankful for than he had, Brahms' credit would have exceeded his debit in that ledger entitled Satisfaction in Life. His independence of the material machinery of existence, his signal talent for keeping his wants few and simple, were gifts in which he gloried. "So long as I have healthy legs and a good book," he once asserted, "I can snap my fingers at the universe." The reader will note how drastically this revises and cuts down Fitzgerald-Omar's famous list of the half-dozen essential desiderata for "Paradise enow": a book, a bough, a jug, a loaf,

[9] *The Life of Johannes Brahms,* 1905, Vol. II, p. 28.
[10] A. Moser: *Joseph Joachim,* 1910, Vol. II, p. 18.

a girl, and a song. How many professional optimists can honestly say as much?

After studying his music and his letters, and weighing all the biographical evidence available, I am convinced that the preponderance of joy over sorrow in Brahms' music came from that very preponderance in the man himself.

Perhaps, however, we need extraordinary words to describe adequately the emotional conditions of such an extraordinary man. When I asked Dr. Gerhart Hauptmann whether Brahms had personally given him the impression of being happy or unhappy, he answered that happiness and unhappiness are scarcely terms which can properly be applied to men like Brahms. He quoted Goethe to the effect that men of genius work under such exacting conditions that they are debarred from the sort of happiness which ordinary men enjoy. But, in compensation, they know very great rapture.

He spoke of how Beethoven agonized over his work, but agreed that when he finally managed to struggle through to the ultimate form of some deathless melody or movement, his joy must have been all the more intense on account of what preceded it. "The fact is," concluded Dr. Hauptmann, "that we need a new vocabulary to describe what a great genius gets out of life."

Many critics look upon Brahms as the end of an historical movement, the last of the mighty masters of strict form. This short-sighted view disregards the cyclical element in art, the eternal alternation of classicism and romanticism. The great musical forms are like those cognate literary forms, the sonnet and the drama: they so fully answer a fundamental human need that, if they were to be blotted by some cataclysm from the consciousness of the race, they would, in the course of time, inevitably be re-created.

Instead of closing the line, I cannot doubt that Brahms stands near the beginning of a long succession of masters of strict form, extending onward through ages to come. Nor can I doubt that the adamantine wearing quality of his music assures it a span of life many times longer than that "score of years" which Brahms once so modestly declared to be "immortality" for a person like himself.

THE END

APPENDICES

Appendix I

SOURCES

In order to bring the footnotes within a reasonable compass, many references and other sources of information are given here.

ABBREVIATIONS

cf.	see
Cor.	*Brahms Correspondence* (16 vols.)
Diet.	Albert Dietrich, *Erinnerungen an Johannes Brahms*
E.	Gustav Ernest, *Johannes Brahms*
Ehr.	Alfred von Ehrmann, *Johannes Brahms, Weg, Werk und Welt*
ff	and following pages
i.	informant
ib.	same reference as preceding
i.e.	that is
K.	Max Kalbeck, *Johannes Brahms*
Kom.	Maria Komorn, *Johannes Brahms als Chordirigent*
Ley.	Rudolph von der Leyen, *Johannes Brahms als Mensch und Freund*
Ma.	Daniel Gregory Mason, *The Chamber Music of Brahms*
May	Florence May, *The Life of Johannes Brahms*
Mich.	Emil Michelmann, *Agathe von Siebold*
Mil.	Viktor von Miller zu Aichholz, *Ein Brahms Bilderbuch*
n.	footnote
qu.	quotation

Rei.   Heinrich Reimann, *Johannes Brahms*

Sch.   *Clara Schumann–Johannes Brahms. Correspondence, 1853–1896*

Wid.   Josef Viktor Widmann, *Johannes Brahms in Erinnerungen*

PAGE

81 "first appearance in . . . Detmold," Mich. 142–3.

82 "Kalbeck describes," K. IV, 1, 197–8.

83 "Widmann tells," Wid. 141 ff.

84 "squeeze . . . double-bass up . . . stairs," Ehr.
    6, and n. 1.
    "He wrote to Clara," Sch. I, 24.
    "to Clara," Sch. I, 24.
    "room could not be heated," Cor. III, 44.
    "to Clara," Sch. II, 614.

85 "never look at my watch," i. Frau Ribarz-Hemala.
    "to visit the Herzogenbergs," K. III, 1, 132.
    "five lines," Cor. II, 114.

86 "hated to be called Meister," i. Dr. Otto Julius
    Bauer.

87 Rindspilaw, Ehr. 305, n.

88 "incident in . . . Alt-Aussee," i. Baroness An-
    tonie von Kaiserfeld.

89 "he wrote Clara," Sch. II, 231.

90 "reluctance to put enough stamps on his letters,"
    i. Herr Johann Spring.
    "He was always asking," K. III, 1, 244 n.

91 "Perger . . . bore witness," Kom. 59.
    "Joachim described him," Mich. 181–82.

92 "turned fireman," K. III, 11, 444.

95 "admired a sidewalk artist," Wid. 147.

96 "dragged out Fräulein Witzl," K. IV, 1, 95.
    "the Master had his facts wrong," Ehr. 387, quot-
    ing Frau Conrat.
    "he wrote Simrock," Cor. X, 42.

99 "solo audience," K. III, 1, 228.
    Kindness "to his young colleagues," K. III, 1,
    151–57, and E. 339–40.
    "he wrote Simrock," Cor. IX, 208.

PAGE

108   "A Viennese lady," i. Frau Prof. Alfred Finger.
For the ladder episode, cf. Kom. 59–60.

112   "Widmann described," Cor. VIII, 10.

113   "for a musical gathering," at the Wittgensteins',
i. Prof. Finger.

115   "he wittily replied," Wid. 27.
"a dribble of kreutzers," i. Frau Anna Brauneis.

116   "the eldest daughter," i. Frau Weinberger.
"he wrote to Clara," Sch. II, 419.

117   "a friend once sent him," Frau Maria Fellinger,
Cor. VII, 267. Passage explained by her son,
i. Dr. Richard Fellinger.

118   "he wrote wistfully to Simrock," in 1873, Cor.
IX, 136.
"The present owner," i. Herr Johann Spring.

119   "Best greetings," 1873, Cor. IX, 141.

120   "a regrettable incident," i. Frau Ribarz-Hemala.

121   "Baroness Rinaldini," daughter of Dr. Otto
Julius Bauer.
"Kalbeck's daughter," i. Frau Prof. Luithlen.
"wrote Kalbeck," K. III, ɪɪ, 320 n.

122   "tease the Scholz children," ib.

125   "Yule Fire in a Slum," written, Vienna, 1930, as the
author's Christmas card.

127   Chapter motto, Cor. VII, 242.
"a child among children," E. 341–42.
"Even as a man," Diet. 34.
"captivated and thrilled him." K. IV, ɪɪ, 377 n.
"At twenty-three," Cor. V, 149.

128   "began a letter to Clara," Sch. II, 491.
"a kneeling grasshopper," Sch. II, 551.
"as pleased as a cockchafer," Sch. II, 568.

129   "decorated with a lady-bird," Sch. II, 547 and n.

PAGE

141   "Widmann recalls," Wid. 109–10.
143   Bela Haas' story, i. Herr Max Breitenfeld.
145   "wrote Hanslick," Cor. XI, 183; and "d'Albert,"
         K. IV, II, 497.
146   "he wrote Joachim," Cor. VI, 255.
147   "he once declared," K. IV, II, 483.
         "confided to a friend," i. e. Mandyczewski; K. IV,
         I, 247.
148   "informed the scandalized Kalbeck," K. III, I,
         252 and n.
         "defended a passage in . . . 'Emperor' concerto,"
         K. IV, II, 397.
149   Interest in the banjo, K. IV, II, 383–84.
150   "Kalbeck relates," K. IV, II, 342.
151   "he wrote Widmann," Cor. VIII, 83.
         "I had much grief," K. II, I, 98.
153   "answer kindness with insults," K. III, II, 373.
157   "he confessed to Clara," Sch. II, 422.
158   "He wrote Elisabet," Cor. I, 32.
         "he wrote Simrock," Cor. X, 56–57.
159   "refused to be painted, . . . had . . . restaurant
         cleared," K. III, II, 438–39.
         Contributed anonymously, Cor. X, 131.
         "he wrote his stepmother," K. IV, II, 511.
160   "A Viennese doctor," K. IV, II, 378.
161   "a Delphic sentence," Cor. VI, 98.
         "What Spitta wrote," K. IV, II, 305.
162   "to . . . Hermine Spies," K. IV, I, 39.
         "to Miller zu Aichholz," Mil. 53.
         "trip by a certain pianist," i. e. Emma Engelmann.
         Cor. XIII, 160.
         "When Franz Wüllner," Cor. XV, 74.
163   Emma Engelmann's loss, Cor. I, 83.

PAGE

182   "he wrote Clara in 1860," Sch. I, 323.

183   "wrote Oscar Wilde," *Intentions*, Tauchnitz ed., 165.

    Of Liszt's *Christus, Cor.* III, 45.

184   "writes to Clara of *Die Meistersinger*," K. III, 1, 84 n.

185   "Major Desjoyaux relates," i. Major Desjoyaux.

186   Cosima to Richter, E. 149.

189   "the Master interrupted," K. III, 1, 72.

    "wrote to Clara," Sch. I, 35.

190   Wahliss story, K. III, 1, 149 n.

    "Wrap it daily," K. III, 11, 417.

    "He admonished Simrock," *Cor.* XI, 119.

    "Sending the same friend," K. IV, 11, 306.

191   "he wrote in 1879," *Cor.* X, 124.

    "To the same," *Cor.* XII, 39.

    "most flatteringly unlike," K. IV, 11, 263.

    "*O liebliche Wangen*," K. IV, 11, 426.

192   "Brahms reported," *Cor.* 42–44.

194   "*The Death of Titian*," i. Frau Flegmann.

195   "He ironically advised," K. III, 1, 262 n.

    "*Cradle Song* in a minor key," *Cor.* X, 38–39.

    "*Sapphic Ode*," *Cor.* XI, 196.

    "Brahms playfully contended," *Cor.* XI, 39.

    "Offering him the F major quintet," *Cor.* X, 224.

196   "a Beethoven-like pun," *Cor.* X, 109.

    "Notes already on page 6!" *Cor.* XII, 8.

    "You can get along," *Cor.* XII, 18–19.

    "How were the stairs in Leipzig," *Cor.* XI, 190.

197   "With the highly Bohemian name," *Cor.* X, 71.

    "postcard to . . . Fritsch," *Cor.* XIV, 417.

PAGE

207   "to scare and tease Simrock," *Cor.* X, 14–15.
208   "He had a weakness," K. II, II, 328.
        "to Bertha Faber," K. II, II, 327.
        "to Maria Fellinger," *Cor.* VII, 251.
209   "to Simrock this card," *Cor.* X, 10.
        "to the Fellinger boys," *Cor.* VII, 263.
        "An excuse he sent Simrock," *Cor.* IX, 149.
        "You see, the local eels," *Cor.* IX, 208.
        "Few publishers," *Cor.* XI, 153.
210   "One more surprise," *Cor.* XIII, 74.
        "he wrote his late host," Wid. 76.
        "No less Biblical," *Cor.* VI, 77.
211   "wrote Simrock from Rügen," *Cor.* X, 10.
        "Even in his last illness," K. IV, II, 502.
        "Have you beflagged," K. IV, I, 11.
212   "Overwhelming success!" K. II, II, 301.
        "for second violin alone," K. III, II, 54.
213   "he begged Clara," Sch. I, 71.
214   "When Simrock greedily wrote," *Cor.* X, 101.
216   "*Certainly* I received your picture," *Cor.* I, 87.
        "In his letters," Sch. I, 46.
        "an unexpected turn," *Cor.* VI, 206.
        "small nuggets of wisdom": Sch. I, 222; K. IV, II,
            336; *Cor.* V, 321; Sch. I, 159.
217   "Thanking Simrock," *Cor.* XII, 31.
        "In declining an invitation," K. IV, II, 348.
        "Wonder-children," *Cor.* II, 112–13.
218   "he wrote to Schubring," *Cor.* VIII, 201.
        Advice to Marschner, i. Prof. Franz Marschner.
        "productive only until fifty," K. IV, II, 391.
        "wrote Clara," Sch. I, 208.
219   "he wrote Simrock from Vienna," *Cor.* XI, 17.
        "as if I were telegraphing," *Cor.* XIV, XXXI.

PAGE

231   "An old Swiss lady," i. e., i. Frau Marie-Louise Röthlisberger, through her nephew, Herr Berthoud.

232   "Here comes Reuss!" i. Frau Müller-Campbell.

233   *"Aber warum denn?"* i. Frau Olga von Miller zu Aichholz.

      "the following ironical lines," *Cor.* I, 42.

234   "first Viennese rehearsal of the C minor trio," K. IV, 1, 29 n.

      "he wrote . . . Simrock," *Cor.* XI, 67.

235   "Another playful sally," i. a Viennese lady who wishes to be nameless.

      "Bruch is terribly angry," *Cor.* X, 51.

237   "When he asked Simrock," *Cor.* X, 104.

238   "alarmed at the 'trials,' " *Cor.* XIV, 224.

      "wrote to Clara," Sch. II, 363.

      "if the songlets are too vulgar," *Cor.* X, 204.

239   "wrote to Elisabet," K. III, 11, 446.

240   "Taking it all in all," *Cor.* XI, 103–04.

      "Once he consented to play," i. Herr Emil Hess.

      "Almost as meek," *Cor.* VI, 256.

      "he wrote Joachim," *Cor.* V, 233–34.

241   "For his own publications," Sch. II, 552.

      "these songs to Simrock," K. IV, 11, 351.

      "In Krefeld," K. III, 11, 375.

      "Ah yes," (*Ach ja, davon leben wir!*) i. Prof. Julius Winkler.

242   "he exclaimed to Frau Brüll," i. Frau Brüll.

      "he showed Barth," K. IV, 11, 380.

243   "he wrote to Clara," Sch. II, 445.

      "I am not vain enough," *Cor.* XI, 17.

      "He informed . . . Widmann," K. IV, 1, 73–74.

PAGE

244 "to have a son of genius," *ib.*

"When Simrock wanted to buy," *Cor.* XI, 181–82.

245 "he confessed to Billroth," K. III, i, 121.

To Elisabet, *Cor.* II, 67.

"The praises that . . . Bülow," K. III, ii, 497–98 n.

"how fruitful the two-spots are!" K. III, ii, 347.

246 "Such a person!" Sch. I, 175 n.

"written myself out," Sch. I, 131.

"assured Simrock," *Cor.* XI, 20 n.

"tricks," *Cor.* IV, 123.

247 "a friend of mine," i. Frau Hermine Waschmann.

"My studio!" Sch. II, 419.

"Widmann tells," Wid. 21.

248 Ex. 4, K. III, i, 227.

249 "the place that Cherubini once had," K. IV, ii, 348.

"he wrote to Bülow," K. III, ii, 455-56.

"When Clara," Sch. II, 524.

"in response to a lady," i. e., Frau Ellen Vetter, *Cor.* VIII, 153.

250 "Happily impossible," K. IV, ii, 422.

"a horrible example," K. IV, i, 11.

251 "too boring for my taste!" (*Dass ist mir zu langweilig!*) i. Sigmund von Sonnenthal, through Frau Brüll.

"to Mandyczewski in 1891," *Briefwechsel,* 1933, p. 351.

252 Ellis qu. *An Open Letter to Biographers,* 1896, in *Views and Reviews.*

Adler qu. *Johannes Brahms, Musical Quarterly,* Apr. 1933.

255 "Herr Ernest's words," E. 34.

PAGE

255   "I shall be a fool," *Cor.* V, 334.

"I must marry!" K. II, 1, 172.

"assured Prof. . . . Kahn," i. Prof. Kahn.

256   "writes Dr. Hitschmann," *Brahms und die Frauen, Psychoanalytische Bewegung,* March, 1933, 114.

258   "Adulterers' Walk," Ehr. 7.

"his old friends," Dr. Friedländer, Mr. Ullmann, and many others.

259   "he would give them two gulden," i. Dr. Friedländer.

"A now celebrated musician," who prefers to remain incognito.

260   "always had plenty of time," K. III, 1, 197.

"dissolute way of life," K. III, 1, 224.

261   "informed Frau Flegmann," i. Frau Flegmann.

"often patronized," told me by many of his friends.

"confided to her diary," May I, 136.

"Brahms once attributed," May II, 163.

262   "Schmidt . . . remembers," May I, 215.

263   "*Frau Mama,*" Sch. I, 40.

"he confided to Grimm," ff., E. 85.

265   "a bachelor was . . . a 'vagabond,'" May II, 173.

"missing . . . the best things," K. I, 11, 329.

266   "I must walk with her," Mich. 155–56.

267   "Grimm wrote . . . admonition," Mich. 171.

268   "Clara . . . reproached Johannes," Sch. I, 297.

"I have played the scoundrel," Mich. 206.

"told Gänsbacher," K. II, 1, 154 n.

270   "He wrote to Joachim," *Cor.* V, 299.

"his note to Joachim," *Cor.* V, 326.

"She married a Herr Faber," K. I, 11, 366–68.

Appendix II

ACKNOWLEDGMENT

For new material, the use of unpublished pictures, suggestion, criticism, and other generous assistance, the author is grateful to:

Mr. Arthur M. Abell	Hastings-on-Hudson
Prof. Guido Adler	Vienna
Mevrouw Jo van Ammers-Küller	Amsterdam
Mr. Philip Barr	New York
Mr. Harold Bauer	New York
Miss Marion Bauer	New York
Dr. and Frau (†) Otto Julius Bauer	Vienna
Mr. Ernest Blyth	Vienna
Mr. Artur Bodanzky	New York
Frau Anna Brauneis	Vienna
Frau Dora Breisach	Vienna
Herr Max Breitenfeld	Vienna
Mrs. Anne Reed Brenner	New York
Miss Mildred BruBaker	New York
Frau Marie Brüll	Vienna
Miss Lily Bugbird	Vienna
Prof. Friedrich Buxbaum	Vienna
Mr. Fitz Roy Carrington	New York
Frau Ida Conrat	Vienna
Miss Julie Cottet	Alhambra, Cal.
Miss Fanny Davies	London
Major Noël Desjoyaux	Paris
Mrs. Allen Dulles	New York
Herr Alfred von Ehrmann	Baden, Vienna

Mr. Carl Engel	New York
Frau Prof. Theodor Engelmann	Berlin
Prof. J. Lawrence Erb	New London, Conn.
Herr Gustav Ernest	Berlin
Dr. Dorian Feigenbaum	New York
Dr. Richard Fellinger	Berlin
Dr. Robert Fellinger	Berlin
Prof. and Frau Alfred Finger	Vienna
Prof. Jakob Fischer	Vienna
Frau Bertha Flegmann	Vienna
Herr Gustav Frenssen	Barlt, Holstein
Geheimrat and Frau Max Friedländer	Berlin
Frau Rose Fuchs-Fayer (†)	Vienna
Dr. Hans Gál	Mayence
Mr. Paolo Gallico	New York
Frau Bertha Gasteiger	Graz
Frau Dr. Wilhelm Gericke	Vienna
Mr. Lawrence Gilman	New York
Frau Gottinger-Wilt (†)	Vienna
Sektionschef Dr. Otto Gottlieb	Vienna
Dr. Alfred Grünberger	Vienna
Dr. and Frau Gerhart Hauptmann	Agnetendorf
Sir George Henschel	London
Prof. Emil Hess	Gmunden
Mr. Gustav Hinrichs	Mountain Lakes, N. Y.
Dr. Eduard Hitschmann	Vienna
Dr. and Frau Rudolph Stefan Hoffmann	Vienna
Mr. Richmond Houston	Charleston, W. Va.
Mr. George C. Jell	New York
Prof. Robert Kahn	Berlin
Baroness Antonie von Kaiserfeld	Vienna
Dr. Alfred Kalmus	Vienna
Dr. Stefan Kantor	Vienna
Dr. Paul Kaufmann	Berlin

Dr. Paul U. Kellogg	New York
Mr. and Mrs. Albert J. Kennedy, and the University Settlement	New York
Prof. Wilhelm Kienzl	Vienna
Dr. Otto Kinkeldey	New York
Frau Maria Komorn	Vienna
Dr. Hedwig Kraus	Vienna
Frau Else Kurzbauer	Vienna
Prof. Ivan Langstroth	Vienna
Miss Dorothy Lawton	New York
Herr Leo Liepmannssohn	Berlin
Frau Dr. Luithlen	Vienna
Dr. Viktor Luithlen	Vienna
Prof. Franz Marschner	Vienna
Frau Erna Martin	Vienna
Miss Rela van Messel	New York
Frau Rudolph Meyszner	Vienna
Prof. Ludwig Michalek	Vienna
Dr. Emil Michelmann	Berlin
Herr Eugen von Miller zu Aichholz	Vienna
Frau Olga von Miller zu Aichholz (†)	Vienna
Mrs. Elizabeth C. Moore	New York
Mrs. Ira Nelson Morris	New York
Frau Lucy Müller-Campbell	Vienna
Dr. Sigmund Münz	Vienna
Mr. Charles Muller	New York
Mr. Morris Nathan	New York
Mr. C. B. Oldman	London
Dr. Alfred Orel	Vienna
Mrs. Frederick Partington	New York
Frau Henriette Ribarz-Hemala	Vienna
Baroness Rinaldini	Vienna
Dr. Julius Roentgen (†)	Bilthoven, Holland
Frau Marie-Louise Röthlisberger	Neuchâtel

Prof. Arnold Rosé	Vienna
Frau Emilia Rutschka	Vienna
Mr. Pitts Sanborn	New York
Mrs. Anne Putnam Sanford	New York
Mr. Frederick N. Sard	New York
Prof. Heinrich Schenker	Vienna
Frau Helene Scheu-Riesz	Vienna
Herr Ferdinand Schumann	Berlin
Frau Alexander Schwarz	Vienna
Fräulein Dorrit Schwarz	Vienna
Frau Hermine Schwarz	Vienna
Frau Helene Seeauer	Ischl
Prof. Alfred Seligmann	Vienna
Mrs. Sidney Sherwood	Cornwall, N. Y.
Mrs. Vieva Dawley Smith	New York
Frau Marie Soldat-Röger	Vienna
Dr. Carleton Sprague-Smith	New York
Herr Johann Spring	Thun
Mr. George Stevens	New York
Mr. Percy Such	New York
Miss Muriel Tankard	New York
Mr. Stephen Townsend	Boston
Frau Dr. Celestina Truxa	Vienna
Mr. Oscar Ullmann	New York
Mr. Joseph Vieland	New York
Frau Carmen von Villiers	Vienna
Frau Hermine Waschmann	Vienna
Dr. Karl Weigl	Vienna
Frau Weinberger	Ischl
Fräulein Grete Winkler	Vienna
Prof. Julius Winkler	Vienna
Fräulein Klara Wittgenstein	Vienna
Herr Zerbs	Ischl

The Beethoven Association	New York
The British Museum	London
The Brunswick Radio Corporation	New York
The Columbia Phonograph Co.	New York
The Congressional Library	Washington
The Deutsche Brahms-Gesellschaft	Berlin
Dodd, Mead & Co.	New York
(my intelligent and generously resourceful publishers)	
The Gesellschaft der Musikfreunde	Vienna
Heck & Co.	Vienna
The Preussische Stadt Bibliothek	Berlin
The Public Library	Boston
The Public Library	New York
Simrock & Co. (†)	Berlin
The Stadt Bibliothek	Vienna

† Deceased.

Appendix III

A CATALOGUE OF BRAHMS' MUSIC

I. WORKS WITH OPUS NUMBERS

Abbreviations: (arr.) arranged; (c.) year of composition; (f.) year finished; (p.) year published; (pr.) probably.

Opus 1. (First) Sonata in C for pianoforte, dedicated to Joseph Joachim (c. 1852–3, p. 1853).

Opus 2. (Second) Sonata in F sharp minor for pianoforte, dedicated to Frau Clara Schumann (c. 1852, p. 1853).

Opus 3. Six Songs (*Gesänge*) for tenor or soprano solo with pianoforte accompaniment, dedicated to Bettina von Arnim (c. 1852–3, p. 1854). (1) Liebestreu. (2) Liebe und Frühling, I. (3) Liebe und Frühling, II. (4) Song from Bodenstedt's *Ivan*. (5) In der Fremde. (6) Lied.

Opus 4. Scherzo in E flat minor for pianoforte, dedicated to Ernst Ferdinand Wenzel (c. 1851, p. 1854).

Opus 5. (Third) Sonata in F minor for pianoforte, dedicated to the Countess Ida von Hohenthal, née Countess Scherr-Thoss (c. 1853, p. 1854).

Opus 6. Six Songs (*Gesänge*) for soprano or tenor solo with pianoforte accompaniment, dedicated to Fräulein Luise and Minna Japha (c. 1852–3, p. 1853). (1) Spanisches Lied. (2) Der Frühling. (3) Nachwirkung. (4) Juchhe! (5) Wie die Wolke nach der Sonne. (6) Nachtigallen schwingen.

Opus 7. Six Songs (*Gesänge*) for solo voice with pianoforte accompaniment, dedicated to Albert Dietrich (c. 1851–3, p. 1854). (1) Treue Liebe. (2) Parole. (3) Anklänge. (4) Volkslied. (5) Die Trauernde.

(6) Heimkehr.

Opus 8. (First) Trio in B for pianoforte, violin, and violoncello (c. 1853–4, p. 1854; new version by the composer, 1891).

Opus 9. Variations in F sharp minor for pianoforte on a theme by Robert Schumann, dedicated to Frau Clara Schumann (c. and p. 1854).

Opus 10. Four Ballades in D minor, D, B minor, B, for pianoforte, dedicated to Julius O. Grimm (c. 1854, p. 1856).

Opus 11. (First) Serenade in D for full orchestra (c. 1857–8, p. 1860).

Opus 12. Ave Maria for female choir, with orchestral or organ accompaniment (c. 1858, p. 1861).

Opus 13. Begräbnisgesang for choir and wind instruments (c. 1858, p. 1861).

Opus 14. Eight Songs and Romances (*Lieder und Romanzen*) for solo voice with pianoforte accompaniment (c. 1858, p. 1861). (1) Vor dem Fenster. (2) Vom verwundeten Knaben. (3) Murrays Ermordung. (4) Ein Sonett. (5) Trennung. (6) Gang zur Liebsten. (7) Ständchen. (8) Sehnsucht.

Opus 15. (First) Concerto in D minor for pianoforte with orchestra (c. 1854, p. 1861).

Opus 16. (Second) Serenade in A for small orchestra (c. 1857–60, p. 1860; new and revised version, 1875).

Opus 17. Songs (*Gesänge*) for female choir with accompaniment of two horns and harp (c. 1860, p. 1862). (1) Es tönt ein voller Harfenklang. (2) Lied von Shakespeare. (3) Der Gärtner. (4) Gesang aus Fingal.

Opus 18. (First) Sextet in B flat for two violins, two violas, and two violoncellos (c. 1860, p. 1862).

Opus 19. Five Poems (*Fünf Gedichte*) for solo voice with pianoforte accompaniment (c. 1858–9, p. 1862). (1) Der Kuss. (2) Scheiden und Meiden. (3) In der

Ferne. (4) Der Schmied. (5) An eine Äolsharfe.

Opus 20. Three Duets for soprano and alto with pianoforte accompaniment (c. 1858–60, p. 1861). (1) Weg der Liebe, I. (2) Weg der Liebe, II. (3) Die Meere.

Opus 21. Variations in D for pianoforte (early work, f. 1857, p. 1861). (No. 1) On an original theme. (No. 2) On a Hungarian song.

Opus 22. Marienlieder for mixed choir (c. 1859, p. 1862). (1) Der englische Gruss. (2) Marias Kirchgang. (3) Marias Wallfahrt. (4) Der Jäger. (5) Ruf zur Maria. (6) Magdalena. (7) Marias Lob.

Opus 23. Variations in E flat on a theme by Robert Schumann, for pianoforte duet, dedicated to Fräulein Julie Schumann (c. 1861, p. 1863).

Opus 24. Variations and Fugue in B flat on a theme by Handel, for pianoforte (c. 1861, p. 1862).

Opus 25. (First) Quartet in G minor for pianoforte, violin, viola, and violoncello, dedicated to Baron Reinhard von Dalwigk (c. 1861, p. 1863).

Opus 26. (Second) Quartet in A for pianoforte, violin, viola, and violoncello, dedicated to Frau Dr. Elisabeth Rösing (c. 1861, p. 1863).

Opus 27. Psalm XIII for three-part female choir with organ or pianoforte accompaniment (c. 1859, p. 1864).

Opus 28. Four Duets for alto and baritone with pianoforte accompaniment, dedicated to Frau Amalie Joachim (c. 1860–2, p. 1864). (1) Die Nonne und der Ritter. (2) Vor der Tür. (3) Es rauschet das Wasser. (4) Der Jäger und sein Liebchen.

Opus 29. Two Motets for five-part mixed choir unaccompanied (c. 1860, p. 1864). (1) Es ist das Heil uns kommen her. (2) Schaffe in mir, Gott, ein rein' Herz (from Psalm LI).

Opus 30. Sacred Song (*Geistliches Lied*) by Paul Flemming,

for four-part mixed choir, org. or pf. (c. 1856, p. 1864).

Opus 31. Three Quartets for four solo voices with pianoforte (c. 1859–63, p. 1864). (1) Wechsellied zum Tanze. (2) Neckereien. (3) Der Gang zum Liebchen.

Opus 32. Nine Songs (*Lieder und Gesänge*) by A. v. Platen and G. F. Daumer, set to music for solo voice with pianoforte accompaniment. Two books (c. and p. 1864). Book I: (1) Wie rafft' ich mich auf in der Nacht. (2) Nicht mehr zu dir zu gehen. (3) Ich schleich' umher. (4) Der Strom, der neben mir verrauschte. Book II: (5) Wehe, so willst du mich wieder. (6) Du sprichst, dass ich mich täuschte. (7) Bitteres zu sagen, denkst du. (8) So stehn wir, ich und meine Weide. (9) Wie bist du, meine Königin.

Opus 33. Fifteen Songs (*Romanzen*) from L. Tieck's *Liebesgeschichte der schönen Magelone und Grafen Peter von Provence* for solo voice with pianoforte accompaniment, dedicated to Julius Stockhausen. Five books (c. 1861–8, p. 1865 and 1868). Book I: (1) Keinen hat es noch gereut, der das Ross bestiegen. (2) Traun! Bogen und Pfeil sind gut für den Feind. (3) Sind es Schmerzen, sind es Freuden, die durch meinen Busen ziehn? Book II: (4) Liebe kam aus fernen Landen. (5) So willst du des Armen dich gnädig erbarmen? (6) Wie soll ich die Freude, die Wonne denn tragen? Book III: (7) War es dir, dem diese Lippen bebten? (8) Wir müssen uns trennen, geliebtes Saitenspiel. (9) Ruhe, Süssliebchen, im Schatten der grünen, dämmernden Nacht. Book IV: (10) Verzweiflung ("So tönet denn, schäumende Wellen"). (11) Wie schnell verschwindet so Licht als Glanz. (12) Muss es eine Trennung geben, die das treue Herz zerbricht. Book V: (13) Sulima ("Geliebter, wo zaudert dein irrender Fuss?"). (14) Wie froh und frisch mein Sinn sich hebt.

(15) Treue Liebe dauert lange.

Opus 34a. Quintet in F minor for pianoforte, two violins, viola, and violoncello, dedicated to H. R. H. Princess Anna of Hesse (First version as a string quintet, c. 1861–2; second version as sonata for two pianos, see below, Op. 34b; third version as piano quintet, c. 1864; p. 1865).

Opus 34b. Sonata for two pianofortes (arranged from the quintet Op. 34) (arr. 1864, p. 1872).

Opus 35. Studies for the pianoforte: Variations on a theme by Paganini. Two books (c. 1862–3, p. 1866).

Opus 36. (Second) Sextet in G for two violins, two violas, and two violoncellos (c. 1864–5, p. 1866).

Opus 37. Three Sacred Choruses for female voices unaccompanied (c. 1859–63, p. 1866).

Opus 38. (First) Sonata in E minor for pianoforte and violoncello, dedicated to Herr Dr. Joseph Gänsbacher (c. 1862–5, p. 1866).

Opus 39. Sixteen Waltzes in B, E, G sharp minor, E minor, E, C sharp, C sharp minor, B flat, D minor, G, B minor, E, B, G sharp minor, A flat, C sharp minor, for pianoforte duet, dedicated to Dr. Eduard Hanslick (c. 1865, p. 1867).

Opus 40. Trio in E flat for pianoforte, violin, and horn (or viola or violoncello) (c. 1865, p. 1868).

Opus 41. Five Songs (*Lieder*) for four-part male choir (c. 1861–2, p. 1867). (1) Ich schwing' mein Horn. (2) Freiwillige her! (3) Geleit. (4) Marschieren. (5) Gebt Acht!

Opus 42. Three Songs (*Gesänge*) for six-part choir unaccompanied (c. 1859–61, p. 1868). (1) Abendständchen. (2) Vineta. (3) Darthulas Grabesgesang.

Opus 43. Four Songs (*Gesänge*) for solo voice with pianoforte accompaniment (c. 1857–68, p. 1868). (1) Von ewiger Liebe. (2) Die Mainacht. (3) Ich schell' mein Horn. (4) Das Lied vom Herrn von Falkenstein.

Opus 44. Twelve Songs (*Lieder und Romanzen*) for female choir unaccompanied, or with pianoforte ad libitum (c. 1859–63, p. 1866). Book I: (1) Minnelied. (2) Der Bräutigam. (3) Barcarole. (4) Fragen. (5) Die Müllerin. (6) Die Nonne. Book II: (1–4) Four Songs from *Der Jungbrunnen*. (5) Die Braut. (6) Märznacht.

Opus 45. A German Requiem (*Ein deutsches Requiem*) to words from the Bible, for solo voices, chorus, and orchestra (organ ad libitum) (c. 1857–68, p. 1868).

Opus 46. Four Songs (*Gesänge*) for solo voice with pianoforte accompaniment (c. 1864, p. 1868). (1) Die Kränze. (2) Magyarisch. (3) Die Schale der Vergessenheit. (4) An die Nachtigall.

Opus 47. Five Songs (*Lieder*) for solo voice with pianoforte accompaniment (c. 1858–68, p. 1868). (1) Botschaft. (2) Liebesglut. (3) Sonntag. (4) O liebliche Wangen. (5) Die Liebende schreibt.

Opus 48. Seven Songs (*Lieder*) for solo voice with pianoforte accompaniment (c. 1855–68, p. 1868). (1) Der Gang zum Liebchen. (2) Der Überläufer. (3) Liebesklage des Mädchens. (4) Gold überwiegt die Liebe. (5) Trost in Tränen. (6) Vergangen ist mir Glück und Heil. (7) Herbstgefühl.

Opus 49. Five Songs (*Lieder*) for solo voice with pianoforte accompaniment (c. 1864–8, p. 1868). (1) Am Sonntag Morgen. (2) An ein Veilchen. (3) Sehnsucht. (4) Wiegenlied. (5) Abenddämmerung.

Opus 50. Rinaldo. A cantata by Goethe, for tenor solo, male choir, and orchestra (c. 1863–8, p. 1869).

Opus 51. Two Quartets in C minor, A minor, for two violins, viola, and violoncello, dedicated to "his friend Dr. Theodor Billroth in Vienna" (c. 1859–73, p. 1873).

Opus 52. Love-songs (*Liebeslieder*), words from Daumer's *Polydora*. Eighteen waltzes for pianoforte duet and vocal parts (four solo voices) ad libitum (c. 1868–9, p. 1869).

Opus 52a. Waltzes for pianoforte duet, after the Liebeslieder Op. 52 (arr. 1874, p. 1874).

Opus 53. Rhapsody from Goethe's *Harzreise im Winter* for alto solo, male choir, and orchestra (c. 1869, p. 1870).

Opus 54. Song of Destiny (*Schicksalslied*) by Friedrich Hölderlin for chorus and orchestra (c. and p. 1871).

Opus 55. Triumphlied for eight-part chorus and orchestra (organ ad libitum), dedicated to H. M. the German Emperor William I (c. 1870–1, p. 1872).

Opus 56a. Variations on a theme by Joseph Haydn in B flat for orchestra (c. 1873, p. 1874).

Opus 56b. Same for two pianofortes (c. and p. 1873).

Opus 57. Eight Songs (*Lieder und Gesänge*) by G. F. Daumer, for solo voice with pianoforte accompaniment. Two books (c. and p. 1871). Book I: (1) Von waldbekränzter Höhe. (2) Wenn du nur zuweilen lächelst. (3) Es träumte mir, ich sei dir teuer. (4) Ach, wende diesen Blick. Book II: (5) In meiner Nächte Sehnen. (6) Strahlt zuweilen auch ein mildes Licht. (7) Die Schnur, die Perl' an Perle. (8) Unbewegte laue Luft.

Opus 58. Eight Songs (*Lieder und Gesänge*) for solo voice with pianoforte accompaniment. Two books (c. and p. 1871). Book I: (1) Blinde Kuh. (2) Während des Regens. (3) Die Spröde. (4) O komme, holde Sommernacht! Book II: (5) Schwermut. (6) In der Gasse. (7) Vorüber. (8) Serenade.

Opus 59. Eight Songs (*Lieder und Gesänge*) for solo voice with pianoforte accompaniment. Two books (c. 1871–3, p. 1873). Book I: (1) Dämmrung senkte sich von oben. (2) Auf dem See. (3) Regenlied. (4) Nachklang. Book

II: (5) Agnes. (6) Eine gute, gute Nacht. (7) Mein wundes Herz. (8) Dein blaues Auge.

Opus 60. (Third) Quartet in C minor for pianoforte, violin, viola, and violoncello (c. 1855–75, p. 1875).

Opus 61. Four Duets for soprano and alto with pianoforte accompaniment (c. and p. 1874). (1) Die Schwestern. (2) Klosterfräulein. (3) Phänomen. (4) Die Boten der Liebe.

Opus 62. Seven Songs (*Lieder*) for mixed choir unaccompanied (c. and p. 1874). (1) Rosmarin. (2) Von alten Liebesliedern. (3) Waldesnacht. (4) Dein Herzlein mild. (5) All' meine Herzgedanken. (6) Es geht ein Wehen. (7) Vergangen ist mir Glück und Heil.

Opus 63. Nine Songs (*Lieder und Gesänge*) for solo voice with pianoforte accompaniment. Two books (c. 1873–4, p. 1874). Book I: (1) Frühlingstrost. (2) Erinnerung. (3) An ein Bild. (4) An die Tauben. Book II: (5) Junge Lieder, I. (6) Junge Lieder, II. (7) Heimweh, I. (8) Heimweh, II. (9) Heimweh, III.

Opus 64. Three Quartets for four solo voices with pianoforte (c. 1862–74, p. 1874). (1) An die Heimat. (2) Der Abend. (3) Fragen.

Opus 65. Neue Liebeslieder. Fifteen waltzes for four solo voices and pianoforte duet (c. 1874, p. 1875).

Opus 65a. Waltzes for pianoforte duet, after the Neue Liebeslieder-Walzer, Op. 65 (c. and p. 1877).

Opus 66. Five Duets for soprano and alto with pianoforte accompaniment (c. and p. 1875). (1) Klänge, I. (2) Klänge, II. (3) Am Strande. (4) Jägerlied. (5) Hüt' du dich!

Opus 67. (Third) Quartet in B flat for two violins, viola, and violoncello, dedicated to "his friend Professor Th. W. Engelmann of Utrecht" (c. 1875, p. 1876).

Opus 68. First Symphony in C minor for full orchestra

(c. 1855–76, p. 1877).

Opus 69. Nine Songs (*Gesänge*) for solo voice with piano-forte accompaniment. Two books (c. and p. 1877). Book I: (1) Klage, I. (2) Klage, II. (3) Abschied. (4) Des Liebsten Schwur. (5) Tambourliedchen. Book II: (6) Vom Strande. (7) Über die See. (8) Salome. (9) Mädchenfluch.

Opus 70. Four Songs (*Gesänge*) for solo voice with pianoforte accompaniment (c. 1875–7, p. 1877). (1) Im Garten am Seegestade. (2) Lerchengesang. (3) Serenade. (4) Abendregen.

Opus 71. Five Songs (*Gesänge*) for solo voice with piano-forte accompaniment (c. and p. 1877). (1) Es liebt sich so lieblich im Lenze! (2) An den Mond. (3) Geheimnis. (4) Willst du, dass ich geh? (5) Minnelied.

Opus 72. Five Songs (*Gesänge*) for solo voice with piano-forte accompaniment (c. 1876–7, p. 1877). (1) Alte Liebe. (2) Sommerfäden. (3) O kühler Wald. (4) Ver-zagen. (5) Unüberwindlich.

Opus 73. Second Symphony in D for full orchestra (c. 1877, p. 1878).

Opus 74. Two Motets for mixed choir unaccompanied (c. 1863–77, p. 1879). (No. 1) Warum ist das Licht gegeben dem Mühseligen? (No. 2) O Heiland, reiss' die Himmel auf.

Opus 75. Four Ballads and Songs (*Balladen und Romanzen*) for two voices with pianoforte accompaniment, dedi-cated to "his friend Julius Allgeyer" (c. 1877–8, p. 1878). (1) Edward. (2) Guter Rat. (3) So lass uns wandern. (4) Walpurgisnacht.

Opus 76. Piano Pieces (*Klavierstücke*) in F sharp minor, B minor, A flat, B flat, C sharp minor, A, A minor, C. Two books (c. 1871–8, p. 1879).

Opus 77. Concerto in D for violin with orchestral accompaniment, dedicated to Joseph Joachim (c. 1878, p. 1879).

Opus 78. (First) Sonata in G for pianoforte and violin (c. 1878–9, p. 1880).

Opus 79. Two Rhapsodies in B minor, G minor, for the pianoforte, dedicated to Frau Elisabet von Herzogenberg (c. 1879, p. 1880).

Opus 80. Academic Festival Overture (*Akademische Festouvertüre*) in C minor for orchestra (c. 1880, p. 1881).

Opus 81. Tragic Overture (*Tragische Ouvertüre*) in D minor for orchestra (c. 1880–1, p. 1881).

Opus 82. Nänie by Friedrich von Schiller, for chorus and orchestra (harp ad libitum), dedicated to Frau Hofrat Henriette Feuerbach (c. 1880–81, p. 1881).

Opus 83. (Second) Concerto in B flat for pianoforte with orchestral accompaniment, dedicated to "his dear friend and teacher Eduard Marxsen" (c. 1878–81, p. 1882).

Opus 84. Five Songs (*Romanzen und Lieder*) for one or two voices with pianoforte accompaniment (c. 1878–81, p. 1882). (1) Sommerabend. (2) Der Kranz. (3) In den Beeren. (4) Vergebliches Ständchen. (5) Spannung.

Opus 85. Six Songs (*Lieder*) for solo voice with pianoforte accompaniment (c. 1877–9, p. 1882). (1) Sommerabend. (2) Mondenschein. (3) Mädchenlied. (4) Ade! (5) Frühlingslied. (6) In Waldeseinsamkeit.

Opus 86. Six Songs (*Lieder*) for low voice with pianoforte accompaniment (c. 1877–8, p. 1882). (1) Therese. (2) Feldeinsamkeit. (3) Nachtwandler. (4) Über die Heide. (5) Versunken. (6) Todessehnen.

Opus 87. (Second) Trio in C for pianoforte, violin, and violoncello (c. 1880–2, p. 1883).

Opus 88. (First) Quintet in F for two violins, two violas, and violoncello (c. 1882, p. 1883).

Opus 89. Song of the Fates (*Gesang der Parzen*) by W. von Goethe, for six-part chorus and orchestra, "most respectfully dedicated to H. H. Duke George of Saxe-Meiningen" (c. 1882, p. 1883).

Opus 90. Third Symphony in F for full orchestra (c. 1883, p. 1884).

Opus 91. Two Songs (*Gesänge*) for alto solo with viola and pianoforte (c. 1863–84, p. 1884). (1) Gestillte Sehnsucht. (2) Geistliches Wiegenlied.

Opus 92. Four Quartets for soprano, alto, tenor, and bass with pianoforte (c. 1877–84, p. 1884). (1) O schöne Nacht. (2) Spätherbst. (3) Abendlied. (4) Warum?

Opus 93a. Six Songs (*Lieder und Romanzen*) for four-part mixed choir unaccompanied (c. 1883–4, p. 1884). (1) Der bucklichte Fiedler. (2) Das Mädchen. (3) O süsser Mai. (4) Fahr wohl! (5) Der Falke. (6) Beherzigung.

Opus 93b. Tafellied for six-part mixed choir and pianoforte, dedicated to "his friends at Krefeld for January 28, 1885" (c. 1884, p. 1885).

Opus 94. Five Songs (*Lieder*) for deep voice with pianoforte accompaniment (c. chiefly in 1884, p. 1884). (1) Mit vierzig Jahren. (2) Steig auf, geliebter Schatten. (3) Mein Herz ist schwer. (4) Sapphische Ode. (5) Kein Haus, keine Heimat.

Opus 95. Seven Songs (*Lieder*) for solo voice with pianoforte accompaniment (c. chiefly in 1884, p. 1884). (1) Das Mädchen. (2) Bei dir sind meine Gedanken. (3) Beim Abschied. (4) Der Jäger. (5) Vorschneller Schwur. (6) Mädchenlied. (7) Schön war, das ich dir weihte.

Opus 96. Four Songs (*Lieder*) for solo voice with pianoforte accompaniment (c. 1884, p. 1886). (1) Der Tod, das ist die kühle Nacht. (2) Wir wandelten. (3) Es schauen die Blumen. (4) Meerfahrt.

Opus 97. Six Songs (*Lieder*) for solo voice with pianoforte accompaniment (c. 1884, p. 1886). (1) Nachtigall. (2) Auf dem Schiffe. (3) Entführung. (4) Dort in den Weiden steht ein Haus. (5) Komm' bald. (6) Trennung.

Opus 98. Fourth Symphony in E minor for full orchestra (c. 1884–5, p. 1886).

Opus 99. (Second) Sonata in F for violoncello and pianoforte (c. 1886, p. 1887).

Opus 100. (Second) Sonata in A for violin and pianoforte (c. 1886, p. 1887).

Opus 101. (Third) Trio in C minor for pianoforte, violin, and violoncello (c. 1886, p. 1887).

Opus 102. Concerto in A minor for violin and violoncello (known as the Double Concerto), with orchestral accompaniment (c. 1887, p. 1888).

Opus 103. Gipsy Songs (*Zigeunerlieder*) for four voices with pianoforte accompaniment. (Eight of them are arranged for various solo voices.) (c. 1887, p. 1888.) (1) He, Zigeuner, greife in die Saiten ein. (2) Hochgetürmte Rimaflut. (3) Wisst ihr, wann mein Kindchen am allerschönsten ist? (4) Lieber Gott, du weisst. (5) Brauner Bursche führt zum Tanze. (6) Röslein dreie in der Reihe. (7) Kommt dir manchmal in den Sinn. (8) Horch, der Wind klagt in den Zweigen. (9) Weit und breit schaut niemand mich an. (10) Mond verhüllt sein Angesicht. (11) Rote Abendwolken.

Opus 104. Five Songs (*Gesänge*) for mixed choir unaccompanied (c. 1888, Nos. 4 and 5 pr. 2 years earlier, p. 1889). (1) Nachtwache, I. (2) Nachtwache, II. (3) Letztes Glück. (4) Verlorene Jugend. (5) Im Herbst.

Opus 105. Five Songs (*Lieder*) for low voice with pianoforte accompaniment (c. 1886, p. 1889). (1) Wie Melodien zieht es. (2) Immer leiser wird mein Schlummer. (3) Klage. (4) Auf dem Kirchhofe. (5) Verrat.

Opus 106. Five Songs (*Lieder*) for solo voice with pianoforte accompaniment (c. 1886, p. 1889). (1) Ständchen. (2) Auf dem See. (3) Es hing der Reif im Lindenbaum. (4) Meine Lieder. (5) Ein Wanderer.

Opus 107. Five Songs (*Lieder*) for solo voice with pianoforte accompaniment (c. 1886, p. 1889). (1) An die Stolze. (2) Salamander. (3) Das Mädchen spricht. (4) Maienkätzchen. (5) Mädchenlied.

Opus 108. (Third) Sonata in D minor for violin and pianoforte, dedicated to "his friend Hans von Bülow" (c. 1886–8, p. 1889).

Opus 109. Festival and Commemoration pieces (*Fest- und Gedenksprüche*) for eight-part mixed choir unaccompanied, "respectfully dedicated to His Magnificence Dr. Carl Petersen, Burgomaster of Hamburg" (c. 1886–8, p. 1890).

Opus 110. Three Motets for four- and eight-part choir unaccompanied (c. 1889, p. 1890). (1) Ich aber bin elend, und mir ist wehe. (2) Ach, arme Welt, du trügest mich. (3) Wenn wir in höchsten Nöten sein.

Opus 111. (Second) Quintet in G for two violins, two violas, and violoncello (c. 1890, p. 1891).

Opus 112. Six Quartets for soprano, alto, tenor, and bass with pianoforte (c. 1888–91, p. 1891). (1) Sehnsucht. (2) Nächtens. (3–6) Four Gipsy Songs (*Zigeunerlieder*): (3) Himmel strahlt so helle und klar. (4) Rote Rosenknospen künden schon des Lenzes Triebe. (5) Brennessel steht am Wegesrand. (6) Liebe Schwalbe.

Opus 113. Thirteen Canons for female voices (c. 1863–90, p. 1891). (1) Göttlicher Morpheus. (2) Grausam erweiset sich Amor an mir! (3) Die Nachtigall. (4) Wiegenlied. (5) Der Mann. (6) So lange Schönheit wird besteh'n. (7) Wenn die Klänge nah'n und fliehen. (8) Ein Gems auf dem Stein. (9) An's Auge des Liebsten. (10) Nachtwache, I. (11) Ich weiss nicht, was im Hain die Taube girret. (12) Wenn Kummer hätte zu töten Macht. (13) Einförmig ist der Liebe Gram.

Opus 114. Trio in A minor for pianoforte, clarinet (or viola), and violoncello (c. 1891, p. 1892).

Opus 115. Quintet in B minor for clarinet (or viola), two violins, viola, and violoncello (c. 1891, p. 1892).

Opus 116. Fantasias in D minor, A minor, G minor, E, E minor, E, D minor for pianoforte (*Fantasien*). Two books (f. and p. 1892).

Opus 117. Three Intermezzi in E flat, B flat minor, C sharp minor, for pianoforte (f. and p. 1892).

Opus 118. Six piano pieces (*Klavierstücke*) in A minor, A, G minor, F minor, F, E flat minor (c. 1892, p. 1893).

Opus 119. Four piano pieces (*Klavierstücke*) in B minor, E minor, C, E flat (c. 1892, p. 1893).

Opus 120. Two Sonatas in F minor, and E flat for clarinet (or viola) and pianoforte (c. 1894, p. 1895).

Opus 121. Four Serious Songs (*Vier ernste Gesänge*) for solo bass voice with pianoforte accompaniment, dedicated to Max Klinger (c. and p. 1896). (1) Denn es gehet dem Menschen wie dem Vieh. (2) Ich wandte mich und sahe. (3) O Tod, wie bitter bist du. (4) Wenn ich mit Menschen- und mit Engelzungen redete.

Opus 122. Eleven Chorale-Preludes for organ. Two books. Sole posthumous work with opus number (c. 1896, p. 1902). Book I: (1) Mein Jesu, der du mich. (2) Herzliebster Jesu. (3) O Welt, ich muss dich lassen, I. (4) Herzlich tut mich erfreuen. Book II: (5) Schmücke dich, o liebe Seele. (6) O wie selig seid ihr doch, ihr Frommen. (7) O Gott, du frommer Gott. (8) Es ist ein Ros' entsprungen. (9) Herzlich tut mich verlangen, I.

(10) Herzlich tut mich verlangen, II. (11) O Welt, ich muss dich lassen, II.

II. WORKS WITHOUT OPUS NUMBERS

Fourteen Children's Folk-songs (*Volks-Kinderlieder*), with the addition of a pianoforte accompaniment, dedicated to the children of Robert and Clara Schumann (p. 1858). (1) Dornröschen. (2) Die Nachtigall. (3) Die Henne. (4) Sandmännchen. (5) Der Mann. (6) Heidenröslein. (7) Das Schlaraffenland. (8a, b) Beim Ritt auf dem Knie. (9) Der Jäger in dem Walde. (10) Das Mädchen und die Hasel. (11) Wiegenlied. (12) Weihnachten. (13) Marien-würmchen. (14) Dem Schutzengel.

Fourteen German Folk-songs (*Deutsche Volkslieder*), ar-ranged for four-part choir, dedicated to the Vienna Sing-akademie (arr. and p. 1864). (1) Von edler Art. (2) Mit Lust tät ich ausreiten. (3) Bei nächtlicher Weil. (4) Vom heiligen Märtyrer Emmerano, Bischoffen zu Regenspurg. (5) Täublein weiss. (6) Ach, lieber Herre Jesu Christ'. (7) Sankt Raphael. (8) In stiller Nacht. (9) Abschiedslied. (10) Der tote Knabe. (11) Die Wollust in den Maien. (12) Morgengesang. (13) Schnitter Tod. (14) Der englische Jäger.

Fugue in A flat minor for organ (c. 1856, p. 1864).

Mondnacht, by Eichendorff, for solo voice with pianoforte accompaniment (p. 1854).

Hungarian Dances (*Ungarische Tänze*) in G minor, D minor, F, F minor, F sharp minor, D flat, A, A minor, E minor, E, A minor, D minor, D, D minor, B flat, F minor, F sharp minor, D, B minor, E minor, E minor, arranged for pianoforte duet. Four bks. (arr. 1852–69. Books I and II, p. 1869; III and IV, p. 1880). Also arranged for orchestra.

Chorale-Prelude and Fugue on O *Traurigkeit, o Herzeleid* for organ (c. 1856, p. 1882).

Fifty-one Exercises (*Einundfünfzig Übungen*) for pianoforte. Two books (f. 1890, p. 1893).

German Folk-songs (*Deutsche Volkslieder*) with piano accompaniment. Seven books (Books I–VI for solo voice, Book VII for soloists and small chorus) (arr. 1854–8, p. 1894). Book I: (1) Sagt mir, o schönste Schäf'rin mein. (2) Erlaube mir, fein's Mädchen. (3) Gar lieblich hat sich gesellet. (4) Guten Abend. (5) Die Sonne scheint nicht mehr. (6) Da unten im Tale. (7) Gunhilde. Book II: (8) Ach, englische Schäferin. (9) Es war eine schöne Jüdin. (10) Es ritt ein Ritter. (11) Jungfräulein, soll ich mit euch geh'n. (12) Feinsliebchen, du sollst. (13) Wach' auf, mein Hort. (14) Maria ging aus wandern. Book III: (15) Schwesterlein. (16) Wach' auf, mein' Herzensschöne. (17) Ach Gott, wie weh tut Scheiden. (18) So wünsch' ich ihr ein' gute Nacht. (19) Nur ein Gesicht auf Erden lebt. (20) Schönster Schatz, mein Engel. (21) Es ging ein Maidlein zarte. Book IV: (22) Wo gehst du hin, du Stolze? (23) Der Reiter. (24) Mir ist ein schön's braun's Maidelein. (25) Mein Mädel hat einen Rosenmund. (26) Ach, könnt' ich diesen Abend. (27) Ich stand auf hohem Berge. (28) Es reit' ein Herr und auch sein Knecht. Book V: (29) Es war ein Markgraf über'm Rhein. (30) All' mein' Gedanken. (31) Dort in den Weiden. (32) So will ich frisch und fröhlich sein. (33) Och Mod'r, ich well en Ding han! (34) Wie komm ich denn zur Tür herein? (35) Soll sich der Mond. Book VI: (36) Es wohnet ein Fiedler. (37) Du mein einzig Licht. (38) Des Abends kann ich nicht schlafen gehn. (39) Schöner Augen, schöne Strahlen. (40) Ich weiss mir'n Maidlein. (41) Es steht ein' Lind. (42) In stiller Nacht. Book VII: (43) Es stunden drei Rosen. (44) Dem Himmel will ich klagen. (45) Es sass ein schneeweiss' Vögelein. (46) Es war einmal ein Zimmer-gesell. (47) Es ging sich uns're Fraue. (48) Nachtigall, sag'. (49) Verstohlen geht der Mond auf.

Three "Puzzle Canons" (*Rätselkanons*). (1) Töne, lin-dernder Klang (for soprano, alto, tenor, and bass). (2) Mir lächelt kein Frühling (for four female voices). (3) Wann? (Uhland) (for soprano and alto).

III. POSTHUMOUS WORKS

Scherzo (movement of a sonata) in C minor for violin and pianoforte. From the sonata composed for Joseph Joachim with Schumann and Dietrich in 1853 (p. 1906).

Regenlied by Claus Groth, second version; for the first, see Op. 59, No. 3 (arr. 1862 or 1866, p. 1908).

Two Canons for four female voices unaccompanied (Studies for Op. 113, Nos. 2 and 1). (1) Grausam erweiset sich Amor an mir. (2) Göttlicher Morpheus!

Canon for soprano, alto, tenor, and bass ("Zu Rauch muss werden der Erde Schmelz und des Himmels Azur") (Rückert).

Small Marriage-Cantata for soprano, alto, tenor, and bass, with pianoforte accompaniment (Gottfried Keller) (c. 1874, p. 1927).

German Folk-songs (*Deutsche Volkslieder*) Nos. 15–26 ar-ranged for four-part choir (c. 1854–73, p. 1927). (15) Scheiden. (16) Wach auf! I. (17) Erlaube mir. (18) Der Fiedler. (19) Da unten im Tale. (20) Des Abends. (21) Wach auf! II. (22) Dort in den Weiden. (23) Altes Volks-lied. (24) Der Ritter und die Feine. (25) Der Zimmergesell. (26) Altdeutsches Kampflied.

"Dem dunkeln Schoss der Heilgen Erde" from Schiller's *Lied von der Glocke*, for mixed choir (p. 1927).

"O wie sanft!" (Daumer). Canon for female voices (p. 1908).

Spruch (Fallersleben). Canon for voices and viola (c. 1856–8, p. 1927).

Twenty-eight German Folk-songs (*Deutsche Volkslieder*) for voice with pianoforte accompaniment (f. 1858, p. 1926). (1) Die Schnürbrust. (2) Der Jäger. (3) Drei Vögelein. (4) Auf, gebet uns das Pfingstei. (5) Des Markgrafen Töchterlein. (6) Der Reiter. (7) Die heilige Elisabeth. (8) Der englische Gruss. (9) Ich stund an einem Morgen. (10) Gunhilde. (11) Der tote Gast. (12) Tageweis von einer schönen Frauen. (13) Schifferlied. (14) Nachtgesang. (15) Die beiden Königskinder. (16) Scheiden. (17) Altes Minnelied. (18a) Der getreue Eckart. (18b) Der getreue Eckart. (19) Die Versuchung. (20) Der Tochter Wunsch. (21) Schnitter Tod. (22) Marias Wallfahrt. (23) Das Mädchen und der Tod. (24) Es ritt ein Ritter. (25) Liebeslied. (26) Guten Abend. (27) Die Wollust in den Maien. (28) Es *rett ein Herr und auch sein Knecht*.

Two Preludes and Fugues in C and B flat for the organ (c. 1856–7, p. 1927).

Two Gigues in A minor and B minor for the pianoforte (c. 1855, p. 1927).

Two Sarabandes in A minor and B minor for the pianoforte (c. 1855, p. 1917).

Theme with variations in D minor, from the B flat Sextet, Op. 18, arr. for pianoforte (c. 1860, p. 1927).

Seven Cadenzas. For Bach's piano concerto in D minor (p. 1927); two for Mozart's piano concerto in G (p. 1927); for Mozart's piano concerto in D minor (c. 1855 or 1856, p. 1927); for Mozart's piano concerto in C minor (p. 1927); two for Beethoven's piano concerto in G, Op. 58 (c. 1855, p. 1907); for Beethoven's piano concerto in C minor, Op. 37 (p. 1927).

IV. ARRANGEMENTS

Studies for the Pianoforte. Five books (Books I and II, p. 1869; Books III–V, p. 1879). (I) Étude after Fr. Chopin. (II) Rondo after C. M. von Weber. (III, IV) Presto after J. S. Bach, in two arrangements. (V) Chaconne by J. S. Bach, for the left hand alone.

Gavotte in A major from Gluck's *Paris and Helen,* arr. for pianoforte and dedicated to Frau Clara Schumann (p. 1871).

Schumann's Piano Quartet, Op. 47, arr. for piano duet (c. 1855, p. 1887).

Schumann's Piano Quintet, Op. 44, arr. for piano duet.

Demetrius Overture by Joseph Joachim, arr. for two pianos.

Overture to Shakspere's *Henry IV* by Joseph Joachim, arr. for two pianos (posthumous).

Ellen's Second Song from Scott's *Lady of the Lake* (Schubert, Op. 52, No. 2), arr. for soprano solo, female choir, and wind instruments (posthumous).

Arrangements of Schubert's *Gruppe aus dem Tartarus* and *An Schwager Kronos,* for one-part male choir with orchestra.

Six Duets for soprano and alto from Handel, with pianoforte accompaniment (c. 1874, p. 1881).

Arrangement of Schubert's songs for orchestra (c. 1862, p. 1933).

Piano transcription of Schubert's Mass in E flat (c. and p. 1865).

Appendix IV

BIBLIOGRAPHY

THE LARGER BIOGRAPHIES

Alfred von Ehrmann: *Johannes Brahms: Weg, Werk und Welt.* With additional volume, *Thematisches Verzeichnis* (see p. 527). Leipzig, Breitkopf & Härtel, 1933.

Gustav Ernest: *Johannes Brahms: Persönlichkeit, Leben und Schaffen.* Berlin, Deutsche Brahms-Gesellschaft, 1930.

John Alexander Fuller-Maitland: *Brahms.* London, Methuen, 1911.

―――― *J. Brahms.* Authorized German translation by A. W. Sturm. Berlin and Leipzig, Schuster & Loeffler, 1912.

Hugues Imbert: *Johannes Brahms: sa vie et son œuvre.* Paris, Fischbacher, 1906.

Max Kalbeck: *Johannes Brahms.* 8 vols. Berlin, Deutsche Brahms-Gesellschaft, 1904–14.

Florence May: *The Life of Johannes Brahms.* 2 vols. London, E. Arnold, 1905.

―――― *Johannes Brahms.* German translation by L. Kirschbaum. Leipzig, Breitkopf & Härtel, 1911 (2d ed. 1925).

Walter Niemann: *Brahms.* Berlin, Schuster & Loeffler, 1918.

―――― *Brahms.* Translated from the German by Catherine Alison Phillips. New York, Alfred A. Knopf, 1929.

Jeffrey Pulver: *Johannes Brahms.* London, Kegan Paul, Trench, Trübner & Co.; New York, Harper, 1926.

Heinrich Reimann: *Johannes Brahms.* In the series *Berühmte Musiker.* Berlin, Harmonie-Verlag, 1897; now Breslau, Schlesische Verlagsanstalt.

Richard Specht: *Johannes Brahms.* Hellerau, Avalun-Verlag, 1928.

——— *Johannes Brahms*. Translated by Eric Blom. London, Dent; New York, Dutton, 1930.

Sir Charles Villiers Stanford: *Brahms*. New York, Frederick A. Stokes, 1912.

W. A. Thomas-San Galli: *Johannes Brahms*. Munich, R. Piper, 1912.

OTHER BOOKS, STUDIES, AND ARTICLES ON THE
LIFE OF BRAHMS

Guido Adler: *Handbuch der Musikgeschichte*. 2 vols. Berlin, Heinrich Keller, 2d ed. 1930.

Wilhelm Altmann: *Brahmssche Urteile über Tonsetzer*. In *Die Musik*, XII, Vol. I.

Herbert Antcliffe: *Brahms*. In Bell's Miniature Series of Musicians. London, George Bell & Sons, 1905.

——— *Liszt and Brahms*. Same series. London, George Bell & Sons, 1909.

Ottilie von Balassa: *Die Brahmsfreundin Ottilie Ebner und ihr Kreis*. Vienna, Kommissionsverlag Franz Bondy, 1933.

Eduard Behm: *Aus meinem Leben*. In *Deutsche Tonkünstler-Zeitung*, IX, 223–31.

Camille Bellaigue: *Un grand musicien conservateur*. In *Revue des Deux Mondes*, Paris, 1907.

H. A. Berlepsch: *Basel und seine Umgebung*. Basel, Schweighauersche Sort-Buchhandlung, 1867.

Marie von Bülow: *Hans von Bülow: Briefe und Schriften*. 8 vols. Leipzig, Breitkopf & Härtel, 1895–1908.

——— *Hans von Bülow: ausgewählte Schriften. 1850–1892*. Leipzig, Breitkopf & Härtel, 2d ed. 1911.

A. Cametti: *L'accademia filarmonica romana dal 1821 al 1860*. 1924.

Max Chop: *Johannes Brahms*. In *Zeitgenössische Tondichter*,

Vol. I. Leipzig, Rossberg, 1888–90.

Walter Damrosch: *My Musical Life*. New York, Scribner, 2d ed. 1930.

D A S (Dr. A. Schubring): *Schumanniana*. In *Neue Zeitschrift für Musik*, Nos. 12–16, 1862.

—— *Fortsetzung der "Schumanniana."* In *Allgemeine Musikalische Zeitung*, Nos. 6–7, 1868, and Nos. 2–3, 1869.

—— *Von Beethoven bis Brahms*. In *Musikalisches Wochenblatt*, Nos. 25, 27, 44, 1878.

Hermann Deiters: *Johannes Brahms*. In *Sammlung Musikalischer Vorträge*. Leipzig, Breitkopf & Härtel, 1880 and 1898.

Deutsche Brahms-Gesellschaft: *Brahms' Briefwechsel*. 16 vols. Berlin, 1907, etc.

1, 2, Correspondence with Heinrich and Elisabet von Herzogenberg (Max Kalbeck, ed.); 3, with Reinthaler, Bruch, Rudorff, Deiters, Heimsoeth, Reinecke, Bernhard and Luise Scholz (Wilhelm Altmann, ed.); 4, with J. O. Grimm (Heinrich Barth, ed.); 5, 6, with Joachim (Andreas Moser, ed.); 7, with Levi, Gernsheim, and the Hecht and Fellinger families (Leopold Schmidt, ed.); 8, with Widmann, Vetter, Schubring (Max Kalbeck, ed.); 9–12, with P. J. and Fritz Simrock (Max Kalbeck, ed.); 13, with T. W. Engelmann (Julius Roentgen, ed.); 14, with his publishers: Breitkopf & Härtel, Senff, Rieter-Biedermann, Peters, Fritzsch, Lienau (Wilhelm Altmann, ed.); 15, with Franz Wüllner (Ernst Wolff, ed.); 16, with Spitta and Dessoff (Karl Krebs, ed.).

Clara Schumann–Johannes Brahms. Briefe aus den Jahren 1853–1896. Edited under the direction of Marie Schumann. Leipzig, Breitkopf & Härtel, 1927.

Dr. Karl Geiringer, *ed.: Brahms im Briefwechsel mit Eusebius Mandyczewski*. Vienna, Gesellschaft der Musikfreunde, 1933.

Albert Dietrich: *Erinnerungen an Johannes Brahms in*

Briefen, besonders aus seiner Jugendzeit. Leipzig, Otto Wigand, 1899.

Albert Dietrich and J. V. Widmann: *Recollections of Johannes Brahms.* Translated by D. E. Hecht. London, Seeley & Co., 1899.

Anton Door: *Persönliche Erinnerungen an Brahms.* In *Die Musik,* II, 15.

Richard Graf Du Moulin Eckart: *Cosima Wagner: ein Lebens- und Charakterbild.* Munich and Berlin, Drei-Masken-Verlag, 1929.

Arthur Egidi: *Meister Johannes' Scheidegruss.* In *Die Musik,* II, 15.

Louis Ehlert: *Brahms.* In essays, *Aus der Tonwelt.* Berlin, 1877.

———— *Brahms.* In *Deutsche Rundschau.* 1880.

Heinrich Ehrlich: *Johannes Brahms.* In *Aus allen Tonarten.* Berlin, 1888.

———— *Dreissig Jahre Künstlerleben.* 1893.

———— *Modernes Musikleben.* 1895.

———— *Johannes Brahms.* In *Nord und Süd.* Breslau, May, 1882.

Dr. Georg Fischer: *Briefe von Theodor Billroth.* Hanover, Hahnsche Buchhandlung, 9th ed. 1922.

G. Franchi-Verney della Valletta: *L'academie de France à Rome, 1666–1903.* 1903.

John Alexander Fuller-Maitland: *Masters of German Music.* London, Osgood, McIlvaine & Co.; New York, Scribner, 1894.

———— Article *Brahms,* in *Grove's Dictionary of Music and Musicians,* Vol. I.

———— Article *Brahms,* in the *Encyclopædia Britannica,* 14th ed.

Dr. Karl Geiringer, *ed.: Brahms im Briefwechsel mit Eusebius Mandyczewski.* Vienna, Gesellschaft der Musikfreunde,

1933.

Karl Goldmark: *Erinnerungen aus meinem Leben*. Vienna, Rikola-Verlag, 1922.

Max Graf: *Wagner-Probleme und andere Studien: Brahms-studie*. Vienna, 1901.

Klaus Groth: *Erinnerungen*. In *Die Gegenwart*, 1897, Nos. 45–47.

Albert Gutmann: *Aus dem Wiener Musikleben*. Vol. I, Künstlererinnerungen 1873 bis 1908. Vienna, Albert J. Gutmann, 1914.

Oskar von Hase: *Breitkopf und Härtel—Gedenkschrift und Arbeitsbericht*. Vol. I. Leipzig, Breitkopf & Härtel, 4th ed. 1917.

Freifrau von Heldburg (Ellen Franz), Gemahlin des Herzogs Georg II von Sachsen-Meiningen: *Fünfzig Jahre Glück und Leid. Ein Leben in Briefen aus den Jahren 1873–1923*. Edited by Else von Hase-Koehler. Leipzig, Koehler & Amelang, 5th ed. 1926.

Theodor Helm: *Johannes Brahms*. A commemorative address at the celebration of the Master's 50th birthday. 1883.

Sir George Henschel: *Personal Recollections of Johannes Brahms*. Boston, Gorham Press, 1907.

———— *Musings and Memories of a Musician*. London, Macmillan, 1918.

Richard Heuberger: *Johannes Brahms, Lebensskizze*. In *Biographisches Jahrbuch und deutscher Nekrolog*, 1898.

———— *Musikalische Skizzen*. Leipzig, H. Seeman, 1901.

———— *Aus der Zeit meiner ersten Bekanntschaft mit Brahms*. In *Die Musik*, II, 5.

———— *Brahms als Vereinsmitglied*. In *Der Merker*, III, 2.

———— *Zum Gedächtnis an Johannes Brahms*. In *Der Kunstwart*, XX, 13.

Ralph Hill: *Brahms: a Study in Musical Biography*. London, Archer, 1933.

Adolf Hillmann: *Brahms.* Stockholm, Wahlstrom & Widstrand, 1918.

Dr. Eduard Hitschmann: *Brahms und die Frauen.* In *Psychoanalytische Bewegung,* April, 1933.

Hoplit (Richard Pohl): *Johannes Brahms.* In *Neue Zeitschrift für Musik,* 1855, Vol. 43, No. 2, 24/25.

Ilka Horowitz-Barnay: *Berühmte Musiker, Erinnerungen.* Berlin, Concordia Deutsche Verlags-Anstalt, 1900.

Elbert Hubbard: *Little Journeys to the Homes of Great Musicians* (Brahms). New York and London, 1903.

Walter Hübbe: *Brahms in Hamburg.* Hamburg, Lütcke & Wulff, 1902.

Monika Hunnius: *Mein Weg zur Kunst.* Heilbronn, Eugen Salzer, 1925.

Hugues Imbert: *Brahms.* In *Profils de Musiciens.* Paris, Fischbacher, 1888.

——— *Étude sur Johannes Brahms.* Paris, 1894.

——— *Le Guide Musical.* 1896–9.

——— *Johannes Brahms.* In *Revue Bleue,* 1903.

Gustav Jenner: *Johannes Brahms als Mensch, Lehrer und Künstler. Studien und Erlebnisse.* Marburg, N. G. Elwert, 1905.

——— *War Marxsen der rechte Lehrer für Brahms?* In *Die Musik,* XII, 2.

Josef Joachim: *Festrede zur Enthüllung des Brahms-Denkmals in Meiningen.* 1899.

Adolphe Jullien: *Musiciens d'aujourd'hui.* Paris, 1892.

——— *Johannes Brahms, 1833–1897.* In *Revue Internationale de Musique,* Paris, March, 1898.

——— *Johannes Brahms.* In *Le Courier Musical,* VIII, No. 11.

Max Kalbeck: *Schumann und Brahms.* In *Deutsche Rundschau,* Feb., 1903.

——— *Iamben, gesprochen bei Enthüllung des Brahms-*

Denkmals, May 7, 1903.

———— *Aus Brahms' Jugendzeit.* In *Deutsche Rundschau.*

———— *Das Brahms-Museum in Gmunden.* In *Mitteilungen der Brahms-Gesellschaft in Wien.* June, 1907.

———— *Brahms-Häuser. Ib.*

———— *Brahms in Wien.* Festschrift zur Enthüllung des Wiener Brahms-Denkmals. 1908.

———— *Brahms in München.* Programmbuch zum 1. Deutschen Brahms-Fest. 1909.

———— *Brahms in Wiesbaden.* Programmbuch zum 2. Deutschen Brahms-Fest. 1912.

———— *Brahms als Lyriker.* In *Musikalische Seltenheiten*, III. Vienna, Universal-Edition, 1921.

Ludwig Karpath: *Lachende Musiker.* Munich, Knorr & Hirth, 1929.

———— *Vom kranken Brahms.* In *Die Musik*, II, 15.

Louis Kellerborn: *Johannes Brahms.* In *Famous Composers and Their Works.* Boston, J. P. Millet & Co.

Otto Kitzler: *Musikalische Erinnerungen, mit Briefen von Wagner, Brahms, Bruckner und Rich. Pohl.* Brünn, 1904.

Louis Köhler: *Johannes Brahms und seine Stellung in der Musikgeschichte.* Hanover, A. Simon, 1880.

Maria Komorn: *Johannes Brahms als Chordirigent in Wien und seine Nachfolger bis zum Schubertjahr 1928.* Vienna, Universal-Edition, 1928.

Julius Korngold: *Der "Wiener" Brahms: Glossen zum neuen Wiener Brahms-Denkmal.* Programmbuch zum 1. Deutschen Brahms-Fest. 1909.

A. Köstlin: *Johannes Brahms und Heinrich von Herzogenberg.* Korrespondenzblatt des Evangelischen Kirchengesangvereines. XXI, No. 6.

Karl Krebs: *Johannes Brahms und Philipp Spitta.* In *Deutsche Rundschau*, 1909, VII.

Paul Kunz and Ernst Isler: *Johannes Brahms in Thun.* Paper written for the 16th general meeting of the Schweiz. Tonkünstler Verein at Thun. Zürich, Hug, 1915.

E. Kurth: *Bruckner.* 2 vols. Leipzig, M. Hesse, 1925.

Henry C. Lahne: *Annals of Music in America.* 1922.

La Mara (Marie Lipsius) : *Johannes Brahms.* In *Musikalische Studienköpfe,* III. Leipzig, Breitkopf & Härtel, 1878.

———— *Johannes Brahms.* In *Westermanns Illustrierte deutsche Monatshefte,* Dec., 1874.

———— *Johannes Brahms.* Neuarbeiteter Einzeldruck aus den *Musikalischen Studienköpfen.* Leipzig, Breitkopf & Härtel, 10th and 11th eds. 1921.

———— *Marie von Mouchanoff-Kalergis geb. Gräfin Nesselrode in Briefen an ihre Tochter.* Leipzig, Breitkopf & Härtel, 1911.

Ernest Markham Lee: *Brahms: the Man and His Music.* New York, Scribner, 1916.

Franziska Lentz: *Brahms-Erinnerungen.* Jahrbuch der Gesellschaft Hamburgischer Kunstfreunde. 1902.

Rudolf von der Leyen: *Johannes Brahms als Mensch und Freund.* Düsseldorf and Leipzig, Langewische, 1905.

Berthold Litzmann: *Clara Schumann: ein Künstlerleben.* 3 vols. Leipzig, Breitkopf & Härtel, 1925 and 1923.

———— *Clara Schumann–Johannes Brahms. Briefe aus den Jahren 1853–1896.* Edited under the direction of Marie Schumann. Leipzig, Breitkopf & Härtel, 1927.

Franz Ludwig: *Julius Otto Grimm: ein Beitrag zur Geschichte der musikalischen Spätromantik.* Bielefeld and Leipzig, Velhagen & Klasing, 1925.

Eusebius Mandyczewski: *Johannes Brahms.* In *Allgemeine deutsche Biographie,* 1898.

———— *Die Bibliothek Brahms'.* In *Musikbuch aus Oesterreich,* I, 1904.

———— *Zusatzband zur Geschichte der k. k. Gesellschaft der*

Musikfreunde in Wien. Vienna, 1912.

William Mason: *Memories of a Musical Life*. In the *Century Magazine*, 1902.

Léonce Mesnard: *Johannes Brahms*. In *Essais de critique musicale*. Paris, Fischbacher, 1892.

Wilhelm Meyer: *Johannes Brahms*. In *Charakterbilder grosser Tonmeister*. Bielefeld, Velhagen & Klasing, 1920.

Emil Michelmann: *Agathe von Siebold*. Stuttgart and Berlin, J. G. Cotta Nachf., 2d ed. 1930.

———— *Agathe von Siebold, Johannes Brahms' Jugendliebe*. Göttingen, Häntzschel & Co., 1930.

Ludwig Misch: *Johannes Brahms*. In Velhagen & Klasing's *Volksbücher der Musik*, No. 79. Bielefeld and Leipzig, Velhagen & Klasing, 1922.

Andreas Moser: *Joseph Joachim: ein Lebensbild*. New and revised ed. in 2 vols. Berlin, Deutsche Brahms-Gesellschaft, 1908 and 1910.

———— *Geschichte des Violinspiels*. Berlin, Hesse, 1923.

Andreas Moser and Joseph Joachim: *Briefe von und an Joseph Joachim*. 3 vols. Berlin, Julius Bard, 1911–13.

Christian Mühlfeld: *Die herzogliche Hofkapelle in Meiningen. Biographical and statistical*. Meiningen, 1910.

Sigmund Münz: *Römische Reminiszenzen und Profile*. Berlin, Allg. Verein für deutsche Literatur, 1900.

Musikfreunde in Wien, Gesellschaft der: Geschichte. Part I, 1870–1912, by Dr. Robert Hirschfeld. Vienna, 1912.

Willibald Nagel: *Johannes Brahms*. Stuttgart, J. Engelhorn, 1923.

———— *Johannes Brahms als Nachfolger Beethovens*. Leipzig and Zürich, Gebr. Hug.

G. Ophüls: *Erinnerungen an Johannes Brahms*. Berlin, Verlag der Deutschen Brahms-Gesellschaft, 1921.

A. Orel: *Joh. Brahms und Julius Allgeyer. Simrock Jahrbuch* I. 1928.

———— *Anton Bruckner: Das Werk—Der Künstler—Die Zeit.* Vienna, Hartleben, 1925.

Walter Pauli: *Brahms.* In *Moderne Geister,* ed. by Dr. H. Landsberg. Berlin, Pan-Verlag, 1907.

Richard von Perger: *Johannes Brahms.* Leipzig, Reclam, 1908.

Alexander Pilcz: *Brahms über Wagner, Wagner über Brahms.* In *Die Kultur,* III, 1910.

P. A. Pisk: *Johannes Brahms und Anton Bruckner.* In *Almanach für Arbeitersänger.* Vienna, 1930.

Emanuel Probst: *Friedrich Riggenbach-Stehlin.* (Sept. 11, 1821 to March 3, 1904.) *Basler Jahrbuch,* 1905.

Karl Reinecke: *Und manche lieben Schatten steigen auf. (Gedenkblätter an berühmte Musiker.)* Leipzig, Verlag von Gebr. Reinecke, 1910.

Leopold Schmidt: *Johannes Brahms.* In *Meister der Tonkunst im 19. Jahrhundert.* Berlin, Julius Bard, 1908.

Willi Schramm: *Johannes Brahms in Detmold.* Leipzig, Kistner & Siegel, 1933.

Hans Schulz: *Johannes Brahms an Max Klinger.* Druck.

Eugenie Schumann: *Erinnerungen.* In the series *Musikalische Volksbücher.* Stuttgart, J. Engelhorns Nachf., 2d ed. 1927.

———— *Memoirs of Eugenie Schumann.* Translated by Marie Busch. London, W. Heinemann, 1927.

Hermine Schwarz: *Erinnerungen an meinen Bruder Ignaz Brüll, Brahms und Goldmark.* In *Deutsche Revue,* 1918.

———— *Ignaz Brüll und sein Freundeskreis.* Reminiscences of Brüll, Goldmark, and Brahms. Vienna, Rikola-Verlag, 1922.

Otakar Šourek: *Život a dilo Antonina Dvořáka (Life and Works of Anton Dvořák).* 3 vols. Prague, 1928.

Richard Specht: *Zur Enthüllung des Wiener Brahms-Denkmals.* In *Die Musik,* VII, 18.

Julius Spengel: *Johannes Brahms: Charakterstudie.* Hamburg, Lütcke & Wulff, 1898.

Minna Spies: *Hermine Spies. Ein Gedenkbuch für ihre Freunde.* Leipzig, Goschen, 1905.

Friedrich Spitta: *Brahms und Herzogenberg in ihrem Verhältnis zur Kirchenmusik.* In *Monatsschrift für Gottesdienst und kirchliche Kunst,* XII, 2.

Philipp Spitta: *Johannes Brahms.* In *Sechzehn Aufsätze zur Musik.* Berlin, Gebr. Paetel, 1892.

A. Steiner: *Johannes Brahms.* Allgemeine Musikgesellschaft, Zürich, *Neujahrsblatt* Nos. 86 and 87. Zürich, Zürcher & Furrer, 1898 and 1899.

Rose Fay Thomas: *Memoirs of Theodore Thomas.* New York, Scribner, 1911.

Theodore Thomas: *A Musical Autobiography.* Ed. by George P. Upton. 2 vols. New York, Scribner, 1905.

W. A. Thomas–San Galli: *Johannes Brahms. Eine musikpsychologische Studie in 5 Variationen.* Strassburg, Heitz, 1905. Munich, R. Piper, 1922.

Richard Tronnier: *Johannes Brahms.* In *Vom Schaffen grosser Komponisten.* Stuttgart, C. Grüninger, 1927.

Hermann Uhde-Bernays: *Henriette Feuerbach. Ihr Leben in ihren Briefen.* Berlin and Vienna, Meyer & Jessen, 1912.

Helene von Vesque: *Eine Glückliche. Hedwig von Holstein in ihren Briefen und Tagebuchblättern.* Leipzig, H. Haessel Verlag, 3d ed. revised and enlarged, 1907.

Bernhard Vogel: *Johannes Brahms: sein Lebensgang und eine Würdigung seiner Werke.* In the series *Musikheroen der Neuzeit,* IV. Leipzig (now Berlin), Max Hesse, 1888.

Hans Volkmann: *Johannes Brahms' Beziehungen zu Robert Volkmann.* In *Die Musik,* XI, 13.

Wilhelm Joseph von Wasielewski: *Robert Schumann.* Leipzig, Breitkopf & Härtel, 4th ed. 1906.

————— *Aus siebzig Jahren, Lebenserinnerungen.* Stuttgart, Deutsche Verlagsanstalt, 1897.

Fritz Widmann: *Erinnerungen an Ferdinand Hodler.* Zürich, Rascher & Co., 1918.

Josef Viktor Widmann: *Johannes Brahms in Erinnerungen.* Berlin, Gebr. Paetel, 1898.

———— *Sizilien und andere Gegenden Italiens.* Travels with Johannes Brahms. Frauenfeld, Huber & Co., 1912.

Felix Wolff: *Auf dem Berliner Bahnhof. Das Leben einer Hamburger Familie um 1860.* Hamburg, G. Westermann, 1925.

F. Wüllner: *Zu Johann Brahms' Gedächtnis.* An address delivered on May 2, 1897, at the Conservatory of Music in Cologne.

BOOKS, ARTICLES, ETC.
ON THE MUSIC OF BRAHMS

Wilhelm Altmann: *Bach-Zitate in der Violoncello-Sonate op. 38 von Brahms.* In *Die Musik*, XII, 2.

Herbert Antcliffe: *The Symphonies of Brahms.* In *The Monthly Musical Record*, No. 400, 1904.

Richard Barth: *Johannes Brahms und seine Musik.* Hamburg, D. Meissner, 1904.

Gustav Beckmann: *Joh. Brahms' Schwanengesang.* In *Monatsschrift für Gottesdienst und kirchliche Kunst.* IX, 2.

Camille Bellaigue: *Le Requiem allemand.* In *Revue des Deux Mondes*, Oct. 15, 1898, Paris.

Max Burkhardt: *Johannes Brahms. Ein Führer durch seine Werke.* Berlin, Globus-Verlag.

Max Chop: *Brahms' Symphonien.* Reclam's Universal-Bibliothek, No. 6309. Leipzig, 1921.

Henry Cope Colles: *On Brahms.* In *The Music of the Masters.* London, John Lane; New York, Brentano's, 1908.

———— *Johannes Brahms' Werke.* Authorized version by

A. W. Sturm, Leipzig, Breitkopf & Härtel (1913), 1915.

Henry Sandwith Drinker: *The Chamber Music of Johannes Brahms*. Philadelphia, Alkan, 1933.

J. Lawrence Erb: *Brahms*. In *The Master Musicians Series*. London, Dent; New York, Dutton, 1905.

Edwin Evans: *Handbook to the Vocal Works of Brahms*. Historical, descriptive, and analytical. New York, Scribner, 1912.

Max Friedländer: *Brahms' Volkslieder. Yearbook of the Musikbibliothek Peters*. Leipzig, 1902.

———— *Das deutsche Lied im 18. Jahrhundert*. 1902.

———— *Brahms' Lieder. Einführung in seine Gesänge für eine und zwei Stimmen*. Berlin and Leipzig, Simrock, 1922.

———— *Neue Volkslieder von Brahms*. Berlin, Deutsche Brahms-Gesellschaft, 1926.

J. A. Fuller-Maitland: *Charakteristisches in Brahms Kunstschaffen*. In *Die Musik*, XII, 2.

———— Article, *Brahms*. In *Encyclopædia Britannica*, 14th ed.

von Graevenitz: *Brahms und das Volkslied*. In *Deutsche Rundschau*, XXXIII, 2.

William Henry Hadow: *Brahms*. In *Studies in Modern Music*, second series. London, Seeley, 1895.

Walter Hammermann: *Johannes Brahms als Liedkomponist*. Leipzig, Spamersche Buchdruckerei, 1912.

Eduard Hanslick: *Concerte, Componisten und Virtuosen*. Berlin, Allg. Verein für deutsche Literatur, 1886.

———— *Musikalisches und Literarisches. Ib.*, 1889.

———— *Aus dem Tagebuch eines Musikers. Ib.*, 1892.

———— *Aus meinem Leben*. I, II. *Ib.*, 1894.

———— *Fünf Jahre Musik. Ib.*, 1896.

———— *Aus dem Konzertsaal. Ib.*, 1870 and 1897.

———— *Am Ende des Jahrhunderts. Ib.*, 1899.

Richard Hohenemser: *Welche Einflüsse hatte die Wiederbele-*

bung der älteren Musik im 19. Jahrhundert auf die deutschen Komponisten? I, II. Breitkopf & Härtel, 1900.

—————— *Brahms und die Volksmusik.* In *Die Musik*, II, 15 and 18.

James Gibbons Huneker: *Brahms* (a study of the piano music). In *Mezzotints in Modern Music.* New York, Scribner, 1899, 1905.

Gustav Jenner: *Zur Entstehung des d-moll-Klavier-Konzertes* op. 15 *von Johannes Brahms.* In *Die Musik*, XII, 1.

Emil Krause: *Johannes Brahms in seinen Werken.* Hamburg, Gräfe & Sillem, 1892.

Hermann Kretzschmar: *Johannes Brahms.* In *Gesammelte Aufsätze* (articles reprinted from the *Grenzboten*). Leipzig, Breitkopf & Härtel, 1910.

—————— *Das deutsche Lied seit Robert Schumann.* From the same.

—————— *Das deutsche Lied seit dem Tode Richard Wagners.* In *Gesammelte Aufsätze II* (articles reprinted from Peters' *Jahrbuch*). Leipzig, Peters, 1911.

—————— *Führer durch den Konzertsaal*, Leipzig, Breitkopf & Härtel, 1886 f.

—————— *Das deutsche Requiem.* Leipzig, Breitkopf & Härtel.

—————— *Die vier Symphonien von Brahms.* Leipzig, Breitkopf & Härtel.

Paul Landormy: *Brahms.* Paris, Felix Alcan, 1921.

Victor Luithlen: *Studie zu Johannes Brahms' Werken in Variationenform.* In *Studien zur Musikwissenschaft.* Beihefte der *Denkmäler der Tonkunst in Oesterreich.* Vol. 14. Vienna, Universal-Edition, 1927.

Ervin Major: *Brahms és a magyar zene (Brahms and Hungarian Music).* Budapest, Arany János Nyomda, 1933.

Daniel Gregory Mason: *The Chamber Music of Brahms.* New York, Macmillan, 1933.

———— *From Grieg to Brahms.* New York, Macmillan, new and enlarged ed., 1927.

Paul Mies: *Aus Brahms' Werkstatt. Simrock Yearbook I,* 1928.

———— *Der kritische Rat der Freunde und die Veröffentlichung der Werke bei Brahms. Simrock Yearbook II,* 1929.

———— *Stilmomente und Ausdrucksstilformen im Brahmsschen Lied.* Leipzig, Breitkopf & Härtel, 1923.

A. Morin: *Johannes Brahms, Erläuterung seiner bedeutensten Werke* von C. Beyer, R. Heuberger, Prof. J. Knorr, Dr. H. Riemann, Prof. J. Sittard, K. Söhle, und Musikdirektor G. H. Witte. Including an account of his career by A. Morin. Frankfurt, H. Bechold.

William Murdoch: *Brahms.* London, Rich & Cowan, 1933.

Willibald Nagel: *Die Klaviersonaten von Joh. Brahms. Technischästhetische Analysen.* Stuttgart, C. Grüninger, 1915.

Walter Niemann: *Johannes Brahms als Klavierkomponist.* In *Die Musik,* III, 18.

———— *Johannes Brahms und die neuere Klaviermusik.* In *Die Musik,* XII, 1.

———— *Die Musik der Gegenwart und der letzten Vergangenheit.* Berlin, Schuster & Loeffler, 1918.

A. Orel: *Skizzen zu Joh. Brahms' Haydn-Variationen.* In *Zeitschrift für Musikwissenschaft,* March, 1923.

Max Reger: *Ueber seine Bearbeitungen Brahmsscher Werke. Simrock Yearbook I,* 1928.

Hugo Riemann: *Johannes Brahms und die Theorie der Musik.* In *Programmbuch zum* 1. *Deutschen Brahms-Fest.* 1909.

———— *Die Taktfreiheiten in Brahmsschen Liedern.* In *Die Musik,* XII, 1.

———— *Symphonien,* etc., in Bechtold's *Der Musikführer.*

Berlin, Schlesinger.

Heinrich Rietsch: *Die Tonkunst in der zweiten Hälfte des 19. Jahrhunderts.* Leipzig, Breitkopf & Härtel, 2d ed. revised and enlarged, 1906.

William Ritter: *Johannes Brahms, notes d'art.* In *La Revue Générale,* XXIX, 58.

J. G. Shedlock: *The Pianoforte Sonata: Schumann, Chopin, Brahms.* London, 1895.

F. Simrock: *Zur Abwehr. Johannes Brahms und die Ungarischen Tänze.* Berlin, N. Simrock, 1897.

Josef Sittard: *Johannes Brahms als Symphoniker und Eduard Marxsen.* In *Studien und Charakteristiken.* Hamburg, L. Voss, 1889.

Richard Specht: *Zur Brahmsschen Symphonik.* In *Die Musik,* XII, 1.

Donald Francis Tovey: *Brahms' Chamber Music.* In Cobbett's *Cyclopedic Survey of Chamber Music,* 2 vols., London, 1929.

Felix Weingartner: *Akkorde.* Collected essays. Leipzig, Breitkopf & Härtel, 1912.

——— *Die Symphonie nach Beethoven.* Leipzig, Breitkopf & Härtel, 1909.

Hermann Wetzel: *Zur Harmonik bei Brahms.* In *Die Musik,* XII, 1.

Hugo Wolf: *Hugo Wolfs musikalische Kritiken.* Edited by R. Batka and H. Werner. Leipzig, Breitkopf & Härtel, 1911.

ALBUMS, CALENDARS, BIBLIOGRAPHIES,
AND THEMATIC INDEXES

Brahms-Kalender. Berlin, Schuster & Loeffler, 1909.

Brahms-Kalender. In *Die Musik,* 1909.

Alfred von Ehrmann: *Johannes Brahms: Thematisches Ver-*

zeichnis seiner Werke. (Additional volume accompanying Life.) Leipzig, Breitkopf & Härtel, 1933.

Maria Fellinger: *Brahms-Bilder.* Leipzig, Breitkopf & Härtel, 1911.

Otto Keller: *Johannes Brahms-Literatur.* In *Die Musik,* XII, 2.

Karl Krebs, *ed.:* *Des jungen Kreislers Schatzkästlein* (sayings of poets, philosophers, and artists, collected by Brahms). Berlin, Deutsche Brahms-Gesellschaft, 1909.

Viktor von Miller zu Aichholz: *Ein Brahms Bilderbuch.* With explanatory text by Max Kalbeck. Vienna, R. Lechner, 1905.

Theodor Müller-Reuter: *Lexikon der deutschen Konzertliteratur.* Leipzig, E. F. Kahnt, 1909 and 1921.

Gustav Ophüls: *Brahms-Texte.* Complete text of all poems for which Brahms composed music. Berlin, Deutsche Brahms-Gesellschaft, 1897.

Thematisches Verzeichnis. A thematic catalogue of all the published works, with indices, etc. Berlin, Simrock, 1897. New, enlarged ed., 1904.

Werkverzeichnis. Leipzig, Breitkopf & Härtel, 1928.

GENERAL INDEX

GENERAL INDEX

Abell, Arthur M., 42 n., 169, 171, 176, 237, 294, 356
Adler, Dr. Guido, 252, 301-2, 431 n.
d'Albert, Eugen, 134-5, 145, 201, 235
Altmann, Wilhelm, 378
America, Brahms' dislike of, 74
anagrams, musical, 164
—F-A-E, 394, 398
—F-A-F, 3, 302, 311, 426, 428, 432
—Agathe, 55, 268, 414
—B-A-C-H, 164
Anna of Hesse, Princess, 56
Anthony, St., the broom blossom his favourite, 115
Anthony the Great, St., 417
Arnim, Gisela von, 91
Artaria, 26
artists, their inability to judge other artists' work, 183

B-A-C-H anagram in a Brahms cadenza to Beethoven's G major concerto, 164
Bach, Johann Sebastian, 38, 54, 60, 67, 68, 131, 164, 167, 169, 182, 201, 214, 215, 216, 260, 320, 327, 337, 342
—*Goldberg Variations*, 55, 362
—cantata, *Ich hatte viel Bekümmerniss*, 151
—cantata, *Dearest Lord, When Shall I Die*, 193
—F major organ *Toccata*, 216
—G major violin Sonata, 240
—string concerto, 243
—*O Haupt voll Blut und Wunden*, 327, 353, 397
—*Erhalt uns, Herr, bei deinem Wort*, 339
—B minor Mass, 343
—concerto for two violins, *Larghetto*, 347, 438
—*The Art of Fugue*, 378
—'cello suites, 411
—*Cantata No. 150*, 435-6

Bachrich, 199
Baenitz's *Lehrbuch der Geographie*, 84
Balassa, von, *Die Brahms Freundin, Ottilie Ebner*, 285 n.
Barbi, Alice, 274, 275
Bargheer, Concert-master, 81, 137
Bargiel, 406
Barr, Philip, 181, 359 n., 441 n.
Barth, violinist, 202, 461
Bauer, Harold, 184
Bauer, Marion, 171
Bauer, Dr. Otto Julius, 26; poem on Brahms' dress, 75-6; 76, 88; toasts Brahms as *"Schimpfoniker,"* 112; rebukes Brahms, 112-13; 132 n., 289 n., 463
Bayreuth, 184, 185
Becker, Fritz, 34, 45, 67
—"Aus Joh. Brahms Jugendzeit," 34 n.
Beckerath, Laura von, 461
Beethoven, Ludwig von, 5, 7, 14, 21, 26, 45, 52, 55, 62, 67, 68, 79, 98, 101, 108, 136, 140, 145, 154, 167, 169, 176, 178; Brahms on, 179, 183 n.; 189, 193, 211, 216, 218, 223, 243, 295, 301, 313, 320, 321, 324, 327, 339, 357, 364, 374, 419
—use of germ-motive, 305
—melody on degrees of the triad, 306
—sparing use of trapeze melody, 309 n.
—violin concerto, 39, 441
—Ninth symphony, 68, 142, 176, 216, 392, 418, 419, 422, 437
  Hymn to Joy, 309, 339, 357, 422, 423
—*"Emperor"* concerto, 148
—*Eroica* symphony, 164, 413, 426, 442
—G major concerto, 164
—*Fidelio*, 217, 271, 395, 446
—*The Ruins of Athens*, 240
—*Leonore* overture No. 3, 241, 446; No. 2, 446

allusions); quick to see musical jests, 166
strong critical sense, 65, 167-73; many
string quartets burned before publishing
Op. 51, 167, 395; symphonies also
burned before publishing C minor, No. 1,
418; his concentration, 169; contempt
for mere cleverness—"Is it good music?",
169-70; hard on his own works, 171;
painstaking, 171-2; admires sculptors'
minute work, 172; uprightness, 172-3;
calls himself "the Outsider," 174; cuts
out adverbs in referring to *Handel Variations,* 174; sometimes pleased with his
work, 175; mental processes while composing, 176-8; on genius, 178-9; on
Beethoven, 179; attitude toward program
music, 42, 180 (see also Music Index:
program music); his tempi, 181; on taking pains, 403

as a judge of other composers, 182-7;
Dvořák, Grieg, Tschaikowsky, Massenet,
Liszt, 183; Bruch, Bruckner, 184, 188-9;
Wagner, 184-7

as a humorist, his sportsmanship, 189;
tendency to dismal music when gay,
193-4; imagination in his humour, 211;
humour in his letters—see below, methods of correspondence

gift for words, 213-22; shown in
Biblical settings, 214; in his letters—
see methods of correspondence

methods of correspondence, 13, 15;
picture-writing, 127-9; economy of
statement, 161-2, 219; use of postcards,
85-6; in pairs, 209; surprise endings, 209-
10; Biblical style parodied, 210-11; gift
for words shown in his letters, 214; on
immortality, 215; various aphorisms in
letters, 216-22; on Bach, 217; on action
and imagination, 217; on infant prodi-
gies, 217; harmony defined, 217; no
"end" to genius, 218-19; on national affairs, 219, 342; telegraphic style, 219-20;
fanciful, 220; "I hate to give concerts,"
221; on friends' deaths, 221; on moving,
221; on getting time, 222; *"wir gefallen
mir,"* 222; his letters to Clara Schumann,
264; postcard to her with horn-call in
Sym. No. 1, *finale,* 422 n.

manners, 88-9; prejudicial to the cause
of his music, 152; in eating, 88; bearishness—see below under *Anecdotes*

modesty, 176, 237-51; depreciation of
his music—see below: *His music,* allusions to; sometimes humorous, 237; unjust to his own works, 239; tributes to
other composers, 240-2; appreciative of
praise, 244-5, 247; "not yet a real musician" (at 23) and "written out" (at
22), 246; on a composer's productive
period, 218; on his own, 246; opposed to
publishing thematic catalogue, and to all-
Brahms programs, 246; to himself, not a
great man, 247; estimates low his own
future fame, 249-50; poor publicity man
for himself, 250; his horror of artists'
self-worship, e. g., composer who played
his own symphony, 250; "bored" by
hearing his own music, 251; cavalier
treatment of floral tributes, 251

sex life, 252-85; mother-adoration,
129, 254 ff., 263, 343, 347; a mother-
complex?, 255; his own words about her,
255-6; psych. effect of this relation on
his sexual constitution—the "fatal dike"
—, 256, 275, 284; response only to prostitutes, 256; not responsible for persistent
prostitute habit, 257; inclination springing from Hamburg childhood, 258; its
emotional effect, 38, 225-6, 275; kindness to prostitutes, 227, 259; proud of
never having seduced respectable girls,
259; more freedom for work, 260; scandal caused, 260; his defense—a "good
thing for a youth," 261; habit strengthened by physical peculiarities, 261-2 (see
also below: appearance and physique);
physical and psych. handicaps, their effect, 145

his love for Clara Schumann, 129, 262;
more son than lover, 263; his letters to
her, 264; their knapsack tour, 264; their
true relations doubtful, 264-5; 393, 461

marriage—not for him, 73; desirable,
in order to have a musical son, 244; his
own references to, 245, 255; possibility
of, as affected by mother-fixation, 255;
by his sexual limitations, 257; psych. of

muffling his piano, 98; as guest, 98; in duet-playing, 98-9; to one-man audience, 99; of lesser musicians, 99; of oboist in playing Schumann concerto, 99-100; of orchestra playing Symphony No. 3, 100

helps Dvořák and other composers, 99; "more human being than musician," 99; kindness to Marxsen, 100; to Keller, arranger of his piano works, 100; to clarinettist in Op. 115, 101; to Kupfer, copyist, 101; to Gmunden orchestra, 101; to sick persons, 101; to birds and dogs, 102; sympathy for Custer's Indian enemies, 102

generosity to intimates, 104-7; the Clara Schumann cadenzas, 103; sad letters about their quarrel, 103-4; gifts to her, 104; supports friends' dependents, 104; gifts to Spitzer, 104; to Nottebohm, 104-5; to others, 94, 98

legacies, 105; money to his father, 105; to stepmother, 105-6; forgives Simrock's error and bad judgment, 106; offers to take no pay for future music, 106; pretends to be spendthrift, 107; offer about girl's horse, 107; when watch was stolen, 107

temper—the young man and the ladder, 108, 156; Karlsbad physician and the autograph, 108-10; dislike of autograph-hunters, 109, 188; skating-rink snowbank (and canal), 11, 110, 289-90; helps a girl at her sewing, 110-11; recommends student to Nottebohm, 111; girl who called his symphonies "worthless trash," 14-15, 111-12, 114; Bruch's retort, 112; rebuked by Bauer as "Master in *Unfugen*," 113; quarrel with Finger about clothes, 113-14; sends Kiel's music to Winkler and pretends anger, 114

gives toys and candy "stones" to children, 116-17; takes care of Truxa children, 117; on the Simrock children's Christmas, 118; a tree for the Truxas, 118; on Schelling as a boy, 118; teaching music to children, 118-19; plays duets wrong, 118; children at his concerts, 119; called "Onkel Bahms," 119; amused by child's "Mr. Master" mistake, 121; refuses to give to rich children, 122; teases, 122; his story about the Christ Child, 122-3

his lead soldiers, 28, 35-6, 127; picture-writing in his letters, 127-9; drawings of insects, 128; of a sigh, 129; of a gulden note, 129; his toy trumpet, 130; plays with long i's in a note, 130; climbs a tree to conduct, 49, 120; at jolly parties, 131; catching frogs (Henschel) and fishing (Scharwenka), 131-2; "pirates' brawl" with Joachim, 132; delight in fires, 132-3; in fireworks, 133; fond of bowling, 133; hitting bottles in the water, 133; mountain-climbing, 27-8, 134; used as 'cello by Hausmann, 135; enjoyment of roguish gifts, 135-6; "presentation copy" of music, 135; "lady's toilet fittings," 135-6; waste-basket, 136; relish for practical jokes, 114, 136, 141; knocking at doors, 136; on Cologne cathedral, 137; use of false names and identities, 137-8, 162; jests in piano-playing, 93-4, 119, 137, 139; ms. hoaxes on Grimm and Agathe, 138-9; on Nottebohm, 139-40; on Kalbeck, 140-1; his trick rocking-chair, 141; himself fooled—man in clothes-hamper, 142; "you recommend yourself," 142-3; and "memorial to him," 143

contrariety shown in dynamics directions for G major string quintet, 145-6; won't follow Joachim's advice, 145, 441; paradoxical phrases, 146; *"gründlich flüchtig,"* 75, 146-7; on quality of his own work, 147; on getting a fresh start at composition, 147; his Breslau Doctor's thesis a *pot-pourri* of student songs, 147-8; defense of music-boxes, 148-9; of banjo, brass bands, etc., 149, 176; choice of "heathenish" Bible texts, 149-50; about church-going, 150; on smoking at funerals, 150; makes Singakademie do Bach cantata, 151; quarrel about Gluck and Wagner, 152; ignores Duke of Cumberland, 154; getting his clothes mended, 154; the opened waste-basket, 154-5

"I write only half-sentences," 157; anonymous donation, 159; conceals final illness from stepmother, 159; his piano "out of tune," 159; "never invited to dinner," 159-60; code-language, 160; doctor's "beautiful compositions," 160; liked "noisy lodgings," 160-1; his subtle letters, 161-2; dislike of personal questions, 162-3; "economy" in words costs a friend a dedication, 163; about sister, 163; Door-Groag postcard, 164-5; messages in melody, 165-6; *Don Juan* air used three times, 166; appreciates jest about *"Jupiter"* symphony, 166. (See also in Music Index: allusions.)

uprightness the foundation of genius, 172-3; on his methods of composing, 176-9; on ragtime, 176-7; on metronome, 180; on absolute pitch, 181; on Simrock's besieging him for work, 181-2; on difficulty of composing, 182

as a humorist—gibes at Bruckner, 188-9; at a prince's compositions, 189; enjoyment of jokes on himself, 189; on an oratorio, *The Sinner,* 189; on Brehm's *Natural History,* 190; on proof-correction of songs, 191; on sitting to etcher and sculptor, 192; on "a bottle of Bach," 192; on the "Death of Titian-Hoffmannsthal," 194; on Simrock's publishing foibles, 190, 194-6; "God bless Peters," 195; mock complaints of destitution, 195, 206-7; fewer movements, smaller pay, 195; "hono-rare-ium" asked, 196; on high prices, 196; on Simrock's failure to buy the *German Requiem,* 196; burlesque bill to Simrock for B flat string quartet, 207, 260; for repairs on a Nocturne, 208; in Italy, heard an opera "which wholly consisted of final cadences," 444

names for Fräulein Hemala, 197; "the female piano-beast," 197 (see also Frau Ronchetti); extra accents on Dvořák, 197; Desjoyaux, *"Opern Fabrikant,"* 197; on his tormentors, 197; on Viennese tardiness, 198; and lack of musical enterprise, 198; his *Schadenfreude,* 198; "I malicious?", 198; on the Friedländers' friendship, 198; on writing *ab und zu,* 198-9; on Fuchs' imitative works, 199; "very little talent," 199; on the viola's tempo, 199; on Hiller, 199, 201; on

Roentgen's compositions, 200; on Goldmark's violin concerto (*"Sie Glückliche!"*), 200; on Hanslick and Offenbach, 201, 366 n.; on d'Albert's marriages, 145, 201; on Oser's removing spots, 201-2; episode of portraits concealed from Cosima Wagner, 202-3; "I didn't *compose* it [motet] as beautiful as that!", 203; on Hermine Spies and *Vergebliches Ständchen,* 203; pun on *berückenden Zauber,* 203; on civil-marriage between voices, 204; on singing of North German choirs, 204; on faking in the *Triumphlied,* 204; the "octave business" in Paganini "a pure swindle," 204; his Biblical texts and allusions, 149-50, 210-11, 214; on his architectural style, 211; on the wash hanging out, 211-12; on composing for the 2d violin, 212

bearishness—his coarse tirade against women, 6, 224-5, 259; on his own childhood environment, 225-6; woman who fished for compliments, 227; women who wanted to play for him, 13, 227; anger at attack on Bismarck, 229-30; the philosopher's stone for Frau Hanslick, 26, 230; on the Gesellschaft women singers "under Haydn," 230-1; objection to flower gifts, 231; rudeness to strange girl singer, 231-2; cigars and the Prince of Reuss, 232; anger at the rehearsals of the C minor trio, 234; on Simrock's "reputation," 234; on "bringing music into the family" of a conductor, 235; rudeness to Hugo Wolf (?), 235; "How that man *does* play!" regretted, 235-6

modesty—hopes dedication of Op. 38 will not annoy, 239; Clara Schumann asked to criticize *Gesänge,* 239; contrasts his G major violin sonata with Bach's, 240; his works with *Leonore* No. 3 and with Haydn and Viotti, 241, 249; on his accompaniments to *German Folk-Songs,* 241; on Schubert, Mendelssohn, Johann Strauss, 242-3; his product not up to his intention, 243; on de luxe binding of his works, 243; on uniform edition, 244; on works' interpretation and tempo, 244; urges fewer of his "tricks" on programs,

MUSIC INDEX

MUSIC INDEX

Abend, Der, 335
Abendlied, 335
absolute musician, Brahms as, 320-1, 331-2
Academic Festival overture, Op. 80, 3, 43, 147-8, 195, 220, 328, 381, 418, 446, 447, 459
Accentuation, 314, 315; in songs, 321-2, 328; in violin sonata, Op. 108, 376 n.
Agathe anagram, 55, 268, 414
"Agathe" sextet—see sextet in G, Op. 36
Allegretto substituted for *scherzo*, 300, 391, 417
Allegro amabile designation, meaning more *amabile* than *Allegro*, 313
allusions and greetings in his music, 316. (See also Anagrams)
alphabet set for four-part chorus, 317
Am Donaustrande, 334
Am Gesteine rauscht die Flut, 334
Am Sonntag Morgen, 325
Amen of Op. 74, No. 2, 341
An die Heimat, 335
anagrams, musical:
—F-A-E, 394, 398
—F-A-F, 3, 302, 311
—Agathe, 55, 268
—B-A-C-H, 164
anapæstic rhythm, 313
archaic style, 337, 340, 411
arpeggio, Brahms' use of in ladder tunes, 306 and n.
Auf dem Kirchhofe, 326-7, 375; its allusion to O *Haupt voll Blut und Wunden*, 327, 397
Auf dem See, 327, 331
Ave Maria, 49, 339

Ballades, Op. 10, 46, 365-6
—No. 1, *Edward*, 246, 333, 365, 370, 458
—No. 2, 311 n., 365-6
—No. 3, 359 n., 366
Barcarole, 337

Begräbnisgesang—see *Burial Song*
Beherzigung, 338
Beim Abschied, 182
Biblical texts, his choice of, 149-50, 345; from Revelation xix for *Triumphlied*, 354
Boten der Liebe, Die, 333
Botschaft, 323, 331
"Brahmsian" quality, 330, 337, 342, 366
Brauner Bursche, 335
Buda-Pest, popular music of, 316
Burial Song, 315, 339-40

canon-writing, 333
canons, 338, 361, 362, 393
—double at 9th below, 340
—double in inversion, 341
Canons for Women's Voices, 337
Capriccios, Op. 76, 367-8
—No. 2, 163, 367. (For Capriccios, Op. 116, see *Fantasien*.)
carillon effect, 338
character traits in his music, 315-19; peasant, 315, 339-40; out-of-door character, 315; gaiety, 316; little wit, 316; his bearish side, 317; heart of a child, 317; his life-work a love token, 318; his love of children shown in his music, 318, 369; love of his mother, 318; ribald touch, 318; contrariety, 321; hatred of French, 353-4; tenderness and reverence, 362; 364; humour, 399; various traits, in *Vivace* of Double concerto, 445
chauvinism in the *Triumphlied*, 353-4
children, his love of, shown in his works, 318, 369
Children's Folk-Songs (*Volks-Kinderlieder*), 249, 317, 318, 330
chimes, Cambridge (?), in *final* minor symphony, 422 n.
choral works, smaller: